Commentary on
1 & 2 Timothy
& Titus

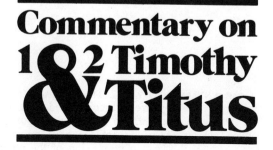

Commentary on 1 & 2 Timothy & Titus

Ronald A. Ward

Word Books, Publisher
Waco, Texas

COMMENTARY ON 1 AND 2 TIMOTHY AND TITUS
Copyright © 1974 by Word Incorporated, Waco, Texas
76703. All rights reserved. No part of this book may be
reproduced in any form, except for brief quotations in
reviews, without the written permission of the publisher.

ISBN# 0-87680-355-9

Library of Congress catalog card number: 74-82661
Printed in the United States of America

First Printing, December 1974
Second Printing, March 1976
Third Printing, October 1976
Fourth Printing, February 1977
Fifth Printing, August 1977
Sixth Printing, May 1978
Seventh Printing, April 1979
Eighth Printing, December 1980
Ninth Printing, November 1981
Tenth Printing, November 1982

Scripture quotations, unless otherwise noted, are from the
Revised Standard Version of the Bible, copyright 1946
(renewed 1973), 1956 and © 1971 by the Division of
Christian Education of the National Council of the
Churches of Christ in the USA, and are used by permis-
sion.

CONTENTS

ABBREVATIONS USED IN THIS WORK

RSV   Revised Standard Version
KJV   Authorized or King James Version (1611)
RV   Revised Version (English)
NEB   *New English Bible*
LXX   The Septuagint or Greek Old Testament
TDNT   *Theological Dictionary of the New Testament,* Kittel and Friedrich, eds.

1 Timothy

INTRODUCTION

I Timothy

AUTHENTICITY AND AUTHORSHIP OF THE PASTORALS

The three epistles, the First and Second Epistles to Timothy and the Epistle to Titus, have been known as the Pastoral Epistles since the early eighteenth century. They form a distinct group in the New Testament, for they are homogeneous and belong to one another, just as Romans "belongs" to Galatians and Ephesians to Colossians. They are both personal and official, for they have wider interests than those of a purely private letter. On a first reading they have sometimes given the impression of being prosaic and flat in style. The apostle's earlier fires have dimmed. It has even been said that in places they are orthodox rather than inspired, with an emphasis on doctrine and the ecclesiastical institution rather than the dynamic energies of a living and experiential faith.

Early Evidence

We may admit the difference of spirit or of atmosphere though reserve judgment on the epistles as a whole. Letters which have enriched the church throughout the centuries and which were not seriously questioned until the nineteenth century at least merit close examination. They profess to be written by the apostle Paul as the name and title appear in the opening greeting of each one. They have an early attestation. C. Spicq (*Les Épîtres Pastorales,*[1] pp. xcv–xcix) lists parallels between the Pastorals and Clement of Rome (c. A.D. 96), Ignatius of Antioch (c. A.D. 110) and Polycarp of Smyrna (c. A.D. 120). The use made by Polycarp is very convincing. Spicq even suggests that 2 Peter 3:15 is the first citation of the Pastorals (1 Tim. 1:15 f.).

The position of the epistles was established by A.D. 150. They were regarded as Pauline by Irenaeus (c. A.D. 130–200), Tertullian (c. A.D. 160–220), the Muratorian Canon (the oldest list of New Testament writings in existence), and Clement of Alexandria (c. A.D. 150–215). Their absence from Marcion's Canon is not surprising: a man who had no time for the Old Testament would not relish a view that "the law is good" (1 Tim. 1:8). It is disappointing that they are not contained in the Chester Beatty Papyrus P46, found in Egypt and passing into the possession of Mr. A. Chester

---

1. Complete information about works of scholarship cited in the text is given in the bibliography at the end of this volume. For works not in the bibliography, full information will be given in a footnote.

Beatty in 1931. This early third-century codex has some leaves missing and room might have been made for the Pastorals. Even if they were left out of the original, complete volume, it does not prove that the Pastorals were not known in Egypt. Clement of Alexandria knew them, and knew them as Pauline.

Their authenticity was thus accepted, and this state continued until the early nineteenth century. From then until the present day a number of scholars have disputed the Pauline authorship, though there have not been lacking distinguished advocates of the traditional view.

Historical Argument

The epistles have been assailed on historical grounds: they cannot be fitted into the narrative of the Acts of the Apostles. The answer is that they come after the events of the Acts and therefore obviously cannot be fitted into them. The ending of Acts (28:30 f.) leaves Paul's future open; Acts 20:25, 38 gives Paul's expectation that he would not return to the East, not the historian's verdict that he did not do so. Paul had his eye on Spain (Rom. 15:24), though the evidence that he actually went there is not certain. Clement of Rome said that he "came to the limit of the West" (1 Clement 5:7) and the Muratorian Canon (lines 38 f.) speaks of his setting out for Spain. Even if he went there he could still have returned to the East in accordance with the testimony of the Pastorals (cf. 1 Tim. 1:3; 3:14).

Ecclesiastical Argument

Further objection has been raised because of Paul's ecclesiastical arrangements. His detailed instructions with regard to bishops, presbyters or elders, and deacons come strangely from the flaming evangelist portrayed in the Acts who speaks so eloquently in the earlier epistles. Organization left him cold. The charge means well but is unjust. Some evangelists of modern times have been accused of gaining many converts and then leaving them high and dry. The lesson has been learned by many, and great efforts are now made to "integrate converts in the life of the church." Paul did not have to learn the lesson. He preached as an evangelist and exercised the care of the pastor. In earlier days he did not leave the new Christians untended; elders were appointed in every church (Acts 14:23; cf. 20:17, 28; Phil. 1:1). In the evening of his life he was not blind to future needs; hence the "organization."

Some have thought that the elders in the Pastorals were no more, or little more, than tradition-bearers, and it is asked how they could be such at a time when the tradition was not fixed. It may be admitted that then, as now, the church had still to learn more of the unexplored riches of Christ (cf. Eph. 3:8). This does not mean, however, that the beliefs of the church were in a permanent state of flux. There was an irreducible minimum, a certain pattern of belief, which was valid for all time. Paul had himself received the tradition and had passed it on to the Corinthians (1 Cor. 15:1–8; cf. 2 Thess. 2:15; 3:6).

It has been said that the church is so established in the picture of it in the Pastorals that it must be later than Paul. In an expanding missionary setting would not all officers have to be recent converts? (Cf. 1 Tim. 3:6.) This forgets that the church at Ephesus could have been in existence for up to a decade. This is long enough for it to have been "established." In any case, if the organization and establishment reflect that of the second century, would not the needs and the qualifications be well enough known to obviate the need of further instruction?

The bishop of the Pastorals (1 Tim. 3:2; Titus 1:7) looks to some like the second-century monarchical bishop, more like a bishop in the modern sense. But no official in the Pastorals has authority concentrated in him. The term "bishop" is generic. We can say "the bishop must be a believer" and "the church member must be a believer" without imposing any restriction of number. Bishops and elders are hardly to be distinguished from one another (". . . appoint elders . . . For a bishop . . ." Titus 1:5–7). Timothy and Titus are themselves not monarchical bishops but apostolic delegates or vicars-apostolic. The ecclesiastical structure, especially the identity of bishops and elders, is primitive and does not have to be later than Paul.

Doctrinal Argument

Another objection to Pauline authorship concerns doctrine. God is remote and there is little emphasis on his fatherhood. The mystical union of the believer with Christ can hardly be found and there is scant reference to the Holy Spirit. Traces of Pauline doctrine are but phrases. The power has gone and we are left with parts of a skeleton. The use of Hellenistic terms in theology would turn the real Paul into a syncretist. At this stage it is enough to say that the Holy Spirit appears as rarely in Colossians and Second Thessalonians. We must reserve judgment until we have considered the theology more fully.

Language Argument

The main attack has been in the field of language. The vocabulary and the style differ profoundly from what is to be observed in Paul's other epistles. For example, there are 175 hapaxes in the Pastorals—*hapax* is Greek for "once," and the term is used for words occurring in these epistles but not elsewhere in the New Testament. In addition there are 130 words which are not found in the rest of the Pauline literature but do appear in other New Testament books. Over 100 particles and other indications of style present in the other Pauline epistles do not appear in the Pastorals. By statistical methods it is suggested that the language of these letters has no affinity with that of Paul's genuine letters but rather belongs to the second century.

This is an impressive array of force. The facts may be there but can they win a battle? In other words, do the facts justify the inferences? The connection with second-century language goes beyond what is warranted by the evidence. Most of the hapaxes were being used by Greek writers before A.D. 50, and about half of them may be found in the Septuagint—a Greek book which Paul knew if he knew nothing else in Greek. We are not forced to assign the Pastorals to the second century. It has been claimed that in any case they are too short for the statistical method to be trustworthy, though modern techniques certainly carry great weight.

We may admit that in point of language the Pastorals are a distinct, homogeneous group. But this need not imply that the apostle Paul did not write them. The situation and circumstances were new and the resultant subject matter was new. When the subject is church organization, we cannot expect the lyrical utterances which extol the love of Christ. The time spent in the West, the possible impact of the Latin language, and his own advancing years could well have affected the style and vocabulary of the apostle. The use of an amanuensis or secretary also (cf. 2 Thess. 3:17) would nullify much stylistic comparison. It is difficult to see how Paul could have avoided having such assistance. The laborious business of writing might be very difficult for a man in chains (2 Tim. 1:16). Some freedom of language would be given to the amanuensis, but it was a controlled and not an absolute freedom. Paul would amend anything which he did not like and in any case he would be responsible for the final result.

Other Theories of Authorship

If Paul did not write the Pastorals, they are either pure fiction, though in the style of a historical novel in which the author exercises his imagination on characters already known, or they are the product of a writer who incorporated some genuine Pauline elements. This "fragment theory" has commended itself to many who have accepted the linguistic arguments, though there is not unanimity on which sections are Pauline and which not. An approximation would be Titus 3:12–15; 2 Timothy 4:9–15, 20–22; and 2 Timothy 1:16–18 with some parts of chapters 3 and 4 as Pauline. The theory raises more problems than it solves. What is the origin and history of the fragments? On what principle were they put where they are in the epistles? Was it expected that they would be recognized? J. N. D. Kelly,[1] a leading patristic scholar, not unnaturally regards the theory as a tissue of improbabilities.

The fragment theory raises the whole question of pseudonymity. It is claimed that there was an established literary convention whereby literary products were published under assumed names. In the case of Jewish writings this device may have been used because the law was fixed and final, and prophecy had ceased—or was suppressed. Any man with a message had to publish in the name of some illustrious personage of the past. This may be admitted. But does it apply to epistolary pseudonymity? It is hard to find exact parallels to the Pastorals. A doctrinal treatise giving apostolic teaching and published in the name of an apostle might be one thing; but a letter containing vivid personal details is another, especially if the author's aim was to deceive. On at least one occasion the church expressed its views. The so-called Third Epistle to the Corinthians, published in the name of Paul, was the work of an elder of the province of Asia and he was con-

---

1. J. N. D. Kelly, *A Commentary on the Pastoral Epistles.*

demned and deposed for his pains. The spirit of the Pastoral Epistles, their deep religious feeling for faith and love, conscience and good works, have about them a ring of truth. Could a deceiver have that touch of reality? Could a believer bring himself to invent? These moral problems have to be faced and answered by more than a reference to an alleged literary convention.

On a comprehensive view we can say that the Pastoral Epistles do not compel the belief that they arose in the second century. Even the alleged Gnosticism is incipient and not developed. The traditional view which accepts their authenticity has not been proved to be wrong, and until other theories have been shown to be superior in their explanation of all the facts we can regard Paul as the ultimate author.

DATE

The First Epistle to Timothy was written to Timothy from Macedonia (1:3). It is impossible to state a definite date at which this was done. It was obviously after Paul's release from prison at the end of the two-year period mentioned in Acts 28:30. Time must be allowed for travel to the West, if indeed he did go to Spain; and then for a return to the East. The date is earlier than the Second Epistle which must have been penned just before the apostle's death. After allowing for the travel, the most we can say is that the First Epistle was written toward the end of his life and that an interval followed in which he came to a prison in Rome (2 Tim. 1:17).

THEOLOGY

We must now try to summarize the theology of the epistle. Paul was opposed to the false teaching and he recognized that there was a "deposit" (6:20), but he did not set out a formal system. It is our task to gather together the evidence scattered throughout the epistle and present it in order. We shall consider the doctrine of God, of Christ, and of the Holy Spirit; then the way of salvation and the duties of salvation; and finally the church, the company of believers.

God

God is the living God (4:10). This is explicitly stated here and it is implied when Paul charged Timothy "in the presence of God . . ." (5:21). As a Jew, Paul was a convinced monotheist and for him there could be one God and one only. He spoke of "the only God" (1:17) and said that "there is one God" (2:5). God is unseen, invisible, and inaccessible. He alone is immortal and eternal. He is blessed and is to be worshiped and is not to be blasphemed (1:17, 20; 6:1, 15 f.).

God is the Creator (4:3 f.) and what he has created is good. It is he who gave life to created beings (6:13). Man is thus dependent on God and should give him thanksgiving. God has not abandoned his creation and it is not out of hand. He is still its Sovereign and dominion is eternally his (6:15 f.). Providence is therefore in his hands and the course of history is in his control. There are men who, from the human point of view, divert the stream of history, rulers who, from their strong position (seized, inherited or obtained by election), impose their will on their weaker and subordinate fellows. Even they are under control because God is the King of those who are actually ruling as kings and Lord of those who are actually exercising their lordship. The invisible and unapproachable God is not entirely un-known for he has revealed himself. This is implied by the reference to the Scripture (5:18 f.; cf. 4:13) in the background of which lies the thought of the election of Israel.

God the Sovereign is Lord of the moral as well as of the physical universe. This must be so because the apostle spoke of sin, which is moral evil con-sidered in relation to God (1:9, 15; 5:20, 22, 24; cf. 6:4 f., 10). The law reveals what is God's will, and the sins described indicate what is contrary to his will. The mention of judgment shows that the moral ruler is indeed the ruler: he does not ignore sin, even though due to ignorance or unbelief (1:13). The characterization of Eve as a transgressor (2:14) recalls Paul's earlier teaching about transgression. The will of God is given precision when it is set forth before men as law; and sin is given precision when it is seen as transgression of a known law. Eve broke a direct commandment (Gen. 3:2 f.) and "the law brings wrath." Adam was a transgressor also. Trans-gression implies a law and a broken law implies wrath. Many have sinned, though not in precisely the same way as Adam, though the consequence is analogous. Adam and Eve were driven out of Eden (Gen. 3:23 f.); and sinners may not approach God. He is unapproachable. Hence sinners are "far off" and can only be brought "near" in one way (1 Tim. 6:16; Eph. 2:13), and Paul could speak of "access" as a privilege which does not belong to man merely as man (Rom. 5:2). (Cf. Rom. 4:15; 5:14; Gal. 3:19.) This of course is not given in detail in the epistle sent to Timothy; but the thought is beneath the surface. It can hardly be an accident that in the same epistle God is described as unapproachable and Eve is called a trans-gressor—who, as Paul knew, was expelled from Eden.

But sin is not the last word. God is Savior (1:1; 2:3) and through his desire for all men to be saved (2:4) is called the Savior of all men (4:10). It is in accordance with this desire that God has a gospel (1:11; cf. 6:19) and that he is the source (1:2) of grace (6:21), mercy and peace. It is because of the gospel that we understand the term "Father" (1:2). The gospel is not self-evident but has to be made known to men. God accord-ingly commanded the apostleship of Paul (1:1) and actively follows the work of evangelism. When the gospel is preached he calls men (cf. 6:12 and discussion). God is the object of the hope of the widow and should be the object of the hope of the rich. The widow continues in supplications and prayers (5:5; 6:17). The implication is that the living God hears and is responsive and is a firm foundation for believers' hope.

In view of all this it is difficult to see how some can say that the author's conception of God is remote. God is indeed remote—to the sinner; even the spirit of sonship is nothing to the unbeliever who has not met with God the Father in Christ (Rom. 8:15). But the epistle throbs with authentic Christian life, and it is because the author has known the Father that he wrote as he did. And those who have so known the Father have the first qualification for meeting him in the epistle.

Christ

When we turn from God the Father to Christ, we notice at once that he is mentioned in the same breath. Grace, mercy and peace are from God the Father and from Christ Jesus our Lord (1:2). What comes from God comes also from Christ: grace (1:14), mercy (1:13, 16) and peace. Christ is the Lord (1:2, 12; 6:3, 14). The cross is thus implied because it was in virtue of the cross that the name of Lord was given to Jesus (Phil. 2:9–11); and because Paul spoke of Pontius Pilate (6:13). Could any Christian hear the name of the Roman without thought of the cross? When we think of the cross we think of the gospel and the need for its proclamation. Hence we read of Paul the apostle of Christ Jesus by command of both God and Christ (1:1). The Christ who with God the Father is the source of grace, mercy and peace is likewise with the Father the authority which commanded the apostleship of Paul. Paul the apostle was owned by Christ, was sent by Christ and testified to Christ when he preached the gospel—of God (cf. 1:11). Implicit in the language is the equality of Christ with God.

This brief outline concerning our Lord must now be elaborated in more detail. Christ Jesus came into the world (1:15); the world did not produce him. Could a companion of Paul like Timothy fail to recall such teaching as Philippians 2:6–8 and the fact that God sent forth his Son (Gal. 4:4)? The presence of our Lord in the world was not just a theophany or a Christophany; he became incarnate (3:16). The purpose of his coming, Christ's own purpose, was to save sinners (1:15). Once more he is united with the Father, for God too is Savior (1:1). Salvation may be described in terms of the context as eternal life (1:16; cf. 6:12, 19). In his work for men's salvation Christ gave himself as a ransom for all (2:6). In virtue of his cross he is the one mediator between God and men (2:5). This word "mediator" corresponds to the earlier Pauline expression "through Jesus Christ." It is through him that we have access (Rom. 5:2; Eph. 2:18, to the unapproachable God!), reconciliation (Rom. 5:11; 2 Cor. 5:18), peace (Rom. 5:1), salvation (1 Thess. 5:9), sonship (Eph. 1:5), confidence (2 Cor. 3:4). It is through Christ that worship is offered (Rom. 16:27), including thanksgiving (Rom. 1:8; 7:25); through Christ that victory is given (1 Cor. 15:57); it is through Christ that God will judge (Rom. 2:16).

The mediator between God and men is still the mediator and has a lively and continued interest in the gospel. Thus he empowered the apostle Paul for service (1 Tim. 1:12) after displaying all his longsuffering (1:16).

He who became incarnate has ascended (3:16) and he will come again in his second advent at God's good time (6:14 f.). In consequence he is our hope (1:1). This can only be so because he is the mediator. He has done for men what they could not do for themselves and he is (and will be) for men what they cannot be for themselves.

The Holy Spirit

The references to the Holy Spirit are scanty. This can be justified in two ways. If it is the specific "office" or task of the Holy Spirit to glorify Christ (John 16:14), then he has fulfilled his ministry in the epistle in the place accorded to Christ. Furthermore the statement that "the Spirit expressly says that . . ." (4:1) shows not only that the Holy Spirit was active but that Paul was sensitive to his promptings. The absence of explanation implies that Timothy would understand the allusion to the Spirit. He ought to have done so, because he himself had received a "gift" (4:14), the *charisma* of the Spirit (1 Cor. 12:1–11). From the tone of the epistle we can gather that he would thoroughly agree when the title of Lord was ascribed to Jesus by the apostle; and nobody can say that "Jesus is Lord" apart from the Holy Spirit (1 Cor. 12:3).

Salvation

The way of salvation may be summed up in the word "faith." The apostle Paul as a typical case is important here. Christ came into the world to save sinners. Paul was a sinner and he received mercy. He is thus a sample of a saved sinner, of a man who believes in Jesus for eternal life (1:15 f.). In accordance with this, God is stated to be the Savior especially of those who believe (4:10). The characteristic word for Christians is "believers," even though they need to have an example placed before them of what a believer really is (4:12). Thus we read of a believing woman (5:16) and of believing slave owners (6:2). It is a disaster when faith is shipwrecked (1:19). Faith must be sincere (1:5) and is more than intellectual assent, as it is associated with conscience and shows itself in love. From one point of view faith means knowing the truth (2:4, 7; 4:3). If emphasis is laid on the truth, we have inevitably a contrast with false teaching (1:3 f.; 4:1–7; 6:3–5, 20 f.). It is significant that the Christian religion is summed up in the expression "the faith" (3:9; 4:1). It is to be preached and taught (2:7) with a view to the creation of faith, for faith is the means whereby eternal life is received (1:16; cf. 3:16).

The duties of salvation, as we have termed them, cover all that saved men ought to do. They are comprehensively described by the two terms, piety and behavior. Piety means our duty to God, and it is preeminently faith in Jesus (3:16). He was "believed on in the world." Included in the mystery of piety are doctrinal statements about our Lord. Faith or trust in Jesus therefore has an intellectual element. The man who really trusts in him with saving faith has a belief that he gave himself as a ransom for all (2:6). He does not trust in a Jesus about whom he knows and believes nothing. This is confirmed by the apostle's words about "the teaching which accords with godliness" (6:3). In the exercise of piety, with a view to yet more piety, godless and silly myths are to be avoided (4:7).

An aspect of piety is holiness (2:15), for which the discussions on 1 Timothy 4:7 and 5:10 should be consulted. An aspect both of piety and of holiness is prayer (2:1–3, 8; 4:3–5; 5:5). Paul knew that piety has power (2 Tim. 3:5). How a man could have a saving faith in Christ, how he could live the life of holiness and prayer, how he could know the power of such piety and at the same time be a stranger to the mystical union of the believer with Christ, is a puzzle. Paul did not use the language here of the mystical union, but the experience is surely present—and through the Holy Spirit. We see holiness exhibited in the doxologies (1:17; 6:16).

The ethical side is summed up in the word "behavior" (3:15). Such conduct includes speech in all manner of situations, purity in thought and deed, and love towards all sorts and conditions of men (4:12). Love is the expression of a faith which is real and springs also from a conscience which has been informed by the Word of God and is unsullied (1:5; cf. 2:15). Love springs from faith and is manifested in good works (5:10; 6:18). Dress can be an indication of mind and attitude, and women have further duties also (2:9–15), as the rich have likewise (6:17–19). The abuse of speech is described (5:13) and an illustration of Christian love is given (5:16). Piety is an abstinence and an effort, a pursuit and a fight (6:11 f.). The reference to piety with self-sufficiency involves the mystical union with Christ, though Paul did not use these terms (see discussion on 6:6). Slaves have their specific duties (6:1–2). All kinds of impiety arise from false teaching (6:3–5).

The Church

The company of believers is the church (3:15; 5:16). It is the household or family of God (cf. 3:5), and its members are therefore brethren (4:6; 6:2). The intensity of the feeling of "brotherliness" is in proportion to the realization of God's fatherhood (1:2). Hidden here may be an allusion to the spirit of sonship (Rom. 8:15 f.). The members are characteristically called believers (4:12; 5:16; 6:2) and saints (5:10). The church is the pillar and bulwark of the truth (3:15), ethical as well as spiritual (1:10).

The church is cared for by the ministry in which three classes or orders may be distinguished. Bishops or supervisors are mentioned and their qualifications described (3:1–7). The duties of elders or presbyters overlap with those of the bishops (5:17–19). The qualifications of deacons are also given in some detail (3:8–13). Instructions concerning widows have been interpreted by some scholars as reflecting an order of widows who had a ministry as church workers (5:3–16).

Such in outline is the theology of the First Epistle to Timothy. It is not an Epistle to the Romans but to a surprising extent (surprising to some, at all events) it reflects the pattern of Christian truth. The situation did not call for an exposition in detail of Christian doctrine. When we consider the pedestrian nature of some of the necessary remedies—the organization of the ministry, the opposition to false teachers, or ethical guidance—we ought to be impressed by the extent to which authentic religion and sound doctrine have appeared. Some moderns could "organize the church" without much explicit reference to faith and doctrine. The man who could seek to settle a disagreement between two women by a soaring statement of Christian doctrine (Phil. 2:2–5; 4:2) could not keep Christ out of "church government" and kindred matters.

OUTLINE

1 Timothy

COMMENTARY

1 Timothy

I. GREETING (1:1-2)

The form of greeting is conventional but Christianized. It identifies the author and underlines his authority. The recipient is warmly addressed and blessing is invoked.

Verse 1: Paul, an apostle of Christ Jesus: An identity and an authority. The term *apostle* is used in the narrower sense (Acts 1:21-26). At first sight it seems unnecessary to use the word at all. We do not emphasize our official position when writing to an intimate friend. On the other hand the situation is altered if our letter is to be read or quoted as authority for some belief or practice of the church. So it is here. Paul had in mind a larger audience than one man, and he ended his letter with a prayer for grace to be with "you people" (6:21—plural). Hence his reference to his apostolic status, which needed no elaboration. *Apostle* was no mere title of honor but indicated a task to be performed and an obedience to be maintained. It thus anticipates the word "command" shortly to be used. (Cf. Mark 3:13-15; Luke 6:13.)

The order of the words *Christ Jesus* is of some significance. The first word emphasizes the office and deftly draws attention to the point of view from which Paul was writing. The revelation of God had come to Paul after, not during, the days of the Lord's ministry on earth. He was not denying the historic *Jesus* but was implying that he was now the exalted and glorified Lord. Paul was the apostle of the one who had been crucified, raised, and exalted, and was now forever in glory: the same Jesus, enthroned. From his conversion onward, Paul's knowledge of Christ was not "after the flesh," "from a human point of view" (2 Cor. 5:16, KJV, RSV). (Cf. 1 Tim. 3:16.)

By command of God . . . our hope: A ministry without options but with ample authority. Paul frequently referred his ministry to the will of God, as we see from a number of his greetings (1 and 2 Cor., Eph., Col., 2 Tim.). Here, however, he uses an even stronger term. God's will may be exercised invisibly in his providence, but *command* issues from a royal source which demands obedience. It comes from the King of kings (1:17; 6:15 f.) and the duty is "by order" as we say. The original command was addressed to Paul personally, and "I was not disobedient to the heavenly vision" (Acts 26:19; cf. vv. 16-18; in v. 17 note the word "send," *apostellō,* cognate with *apostolos,* "apostle"). Paul thus became an apostle by order. The Lord commanded his turbulent soul (cf. Luke 8:25), and he could have answered, "Lord, what you commanded has been done" (cf. Luke 14:22); he had entered office. The command continued in force and he was still an apostle "by order." The necessity to preach beat upon him like a tempest (cf. 1 Cor. 9:16 with Acts 27:20; cf. 1 Cor. 7:6).

God our Savior is a recurrent theme in the Pastoral Epistles (1 Tim. 2:3; 4:10; Titus 1:3; 2:10; 3:4). The fact that Christ is also termed Savior requires explanation (2 Tim. 1:10; Titus 1:4; 2:13; 3:6). According to Joachim Jeremias (p. 45), the Messiah is never characterized as Savior in the Old Testament and Jesus himself never referred to himself in this way; nor is he ever so called in the older strata of the New Testament tradition which originated on Palestinian soil. The term appeared increasingly, however, in Hellenistic circles, where there were already many "saviors," Asclepius, the god of healing (the Latin Aesculapius), Isis, Serapis, and preeminently the Roman emperor. "Caesar is savior" would be repugnant to Christians, inside or outside a temple erected for Caesar-worship. What would be more natural than for the term to be transferred to Jesus? Certainly Christians proclaimed "another king" (Acts 17:7).

Spicq (p. 2), however, finds salvation associated with the Messiah in 1 Enoch 48:7, the relevant words being "For in his name they are saved" (cf. v. 10, "His Anointed"). R. H. Charles points by way of comment to 1 Corinthians 6:11 and Acts 4:12.[1] Spicq is more impressed by the usage of the Old Testament than by Hellenistic influence. (See Luke 1:47 quoting Hab. 3:18, LXX; cf. Deut. 32:15; Pss. 24:5; 61:7; 64:6, [65:5]; Isa. 12:2, all in LXX.) In the Old Testament God is Savior and it is from the Old Testament soil that the Christian usage grew.

The best explanation of the application of the term *Savior* to Christ would be on the following lines. In the Old Testament God is Savior. The salvation of which he is the author is achieved in Christ, is present in Christ, and is offered to men in Christ. The term was therefore naturally transferred to him (cf. Matt. 1:21; Luke 2:11), the process of transference and use being accentuated and sharpened by the prevailing atmosphere of Caesar-worship. The very watchword (Caesar is savior) of the imperial cult would encourage a practice already begun: Jesus is Savior. We can almost see it happening in Philippians 3:20.

Salvation, originally conceived as deliverance from danger or from enemies, has found its deepest meaning in the Christian revelation. It may be described as all that believing men possess in Christ, which they would not have had apart from him and do not and never will deserve. It includes redemption and propitiation, justification and pardon, adoption and sanctification, Christian hope and certainty, and heaven itself. It is individually appropriated, and corporately and individually enjoyed. It begins in repentance and ends in glory.

Christ Jesus our hope is another example of transference of a term from God to Christ. Paul spoke elsewhere of "the God of hope" (Rom. 15:13). The progress of thought is as follows. (1) We hope in God that something will happen. The "something" may be the resurrection (Acts 24:15) or the redemption of the body (Rom. 8:20–25; cf. Gen. 3:17–19). (2) It is through Christ that we hope that something will happen; through him we hope to

---

1. R. H. Charles, ed., *The Apocrypha and Pseudepigrapha of the Old Testament* (Oxford: Clarendon Press, 1913), 2:217, note on 1 Enoch 48.7.

attain to the glory of God (Rom. 5:2; contrast 3:23) and to the resurrection (1 Cor. 15:19–23). (3) We hope to see Christ himself (Titus 2:13). (4) Christ himself is our hope and he is both in us and "laid up for you in heaven" (Col. 1:27; cf. v. 5).

Christ Jesus our hope thus combines two meanings. He is the ground of hope: he is the sufficient reason why Christians should hope. He is the only reason: "separated from Christ . . . having no hope" (Eph. 2:12). And he is the object of hope. John used the word hope when he said that "we shall see him as he is" (1 John 3:2 f.).

The succinct use of the abstract term *hope* is paralleled by a similar use of the words "peace" and "love." We should enjoy peace with God through our Lord Jesus Christ (Rom. 5:1) and be at peace among ourselves (1 Thess. 5:13) because "he is our peace" (Eph. 2:14). John tells us that "God is love" (1 John 4:8, 16). The deceptively simple terms should not blind us to the profound wealth of meaning.

The fact that Paul was made an apostle and continued to work as an apostle "by order" of both Father and Son is of theological significance. It points to the deity of Christ, just as the use of the term Savior does. Spicq (p. 3) helpfully finds implied in "Savior" a revelation of deity, a blessing in his deeds and a time of salvation in his reign. Salvation is immediately granted when a man believes (cf. 2 Tim. 1:9) but the eschatological *hope* looks to its future implementation (Rom. 5:9).

Verse 2: To Timothy, my true child in the faith: The convert's faith was real. The word *true* literally means "born in lawful wedlock" and distinguishes a son so born from a "natural son" who is illegitimate or a "legal son" who has been adopted. Paul was speaking metaphorically and using a figure of which he was fond. He spoke of his "child, Onesimus, whose father I have become . . ." (Philem. 10). He clearly regarded himself as Timothy's spiritual father, and it is likely that he had been the means of his conversion. Timothy had been brought up on the Old Testament (2 Tim. 3:15; cf. 1:5), and he may well have been converted during Paul's early visit to Lystra (Acts 14:6 f., 22), as he was later a well-known disciple there (Acts 16:1 f.). (See also 1 Cor. 4:14–17; Phil. 2:19–22.) It is plain that Paul did not regard Timothy as his true child. To think this would be guilty of an unwarranted literality. Paul looked upon Timothy as his true child-in-the-faith. Comparison with 1 Corinthians 4:17 suggests that *in the faith* means "in Christ." Timothy not only had been greatly influenced by Paul, but he was also an authentic Christian believer. A partnership of old and young can yield a fruitful ministry. Here the older man seems to have had the vigor and the younger the quiet reserve and even timidity.

Grace, mercy, and peace: Note the significant addition to Paul's usual greeting (cf. 1 Thess. 1:1). *Grace* [1] is one of the great New Testament words. The original is Greek (*charis*); it is flavored with the *hen* of the Septuagint and has been born again, like the apostle himself, on the road to Damascus. Grace moves from the superior to the inferior, from the greater in character and power to the lesser, from God to man and not from man to

---

1. For a profound study of the meaning of grace, see T. F. Torrance, *The Doctrine of Grace in the Apostolic Fathers* (Grand Rapids: Wm. B. Eerdmans, 1959), pp. 1–35.

God. It is entirely undeserved. God is not in any sense obligated to be gracious, a fact which is illustrated in the doctrine of election (1 Thess. 1:4; 2 Thess. 2:13) and in Paul's rejection of the picture of an employer paying wages. Wages must be paid for work done—a debt. Grace is free—*gratis* (cf. Rom. 4:4).

The term itself is abstract though convenient for use. It means that we are concerned with a gracious God who acts personally in dealing with men. We must not make *grace* a thing-in-itself, working impersonally. Grace means God himself working for and in men; and he thus works in Christ. In fact grace is alive in Christ, who embodies it. When we speak of it we should think of Christ-crucified-and-risen. Thus we should never isolate grace from Christ, and should never isolate Christ from his cross and resurrection; and never isolate Christ from God. Grace is thus a particular case of love. It is love loving the unlovable and pardoning the unpardonable. It is utter purity cleansing the defiled. It is the perfectly clean touching the leper. It is the exalted coming down to lift up the fallen. There is love between Father and Son but never grace. How could there be?

Salvation is due to grace (Eph. 2:5, 8; 2 Tim. 1:9). It is through grace that we receive the call to accept salvation (Gal. 1:15). Christian service is the gift of grace (Eph. 3:8). Equipment for the varying tasks is a grace-gift (Rom. 12:6; Eph. 4:7; 1 Pet. 4:10), diverse though the tasks may be. Justified men stand in the new territory of grace (Rom. 5:2), in which soil the Christian can grow to maturity (2 Pet. 3:18). It is grace which makes the Christian what he is and grace which gives him any success he may have in evangelistic and pastoral toil (1 Cor. 15:10). In grievous personal situations which need to be interpreted in order to be endured, grace is enough (2 Cor. 12:9). Grace means—the Christ of the cross (Rom. 3:24–25, 2 Cor. 8:9).

Mercy has behind it all the wealth of the Old Testament *hesed*. It is a word associated with the covenant, and it may be described as God's persistent and loyal love; it is what Scottish people call "leal love." This steadfast love is everlasting and unshakable and is not to be thwarted (cf. Isa. 54:10). The Greek word means pity or compassion, and it is exemplified in Jesus, in whom God's mercy is present and active. (Cf. Mark 5:19.) There is no deficiency in God's mercy, for he is "rich in mercy" (Eph. 2:4). It is dependent on his will and not on any emotion which he may be supposed to have (Rom. 9:15, 18). Mercy is thus God's settled purpose. It can anticipate the covenant relationship and thus, paradoxically, "loyal love" can be shown in advance, when we could hardly have expected the word "loyal." Thus Saul of Tarsus before conversion "received mercy." In this situation mercy is very close to grace (1 Tim. 1:13 f.). Paul was writing out of his experience. Regeneration is in virtue of mercy (1 Pet. 1:3), like salvation itself (Titus 3:5). Old scholars used to draw a distinction between compassion merely felt, as in the presence of hopeless suffering, and compassion felt and active. Certainly God's compassion has been active in the deeds of Jesus and through him in the providential care of his people. The German equivalent of *mercy* is the pleasing *Barmherzigkeit*, "warmheartedness."

Peace is an apparently simple word but one with deep undertones. In the normal Greek sense it is the opposite to war (Luke 14:32) or danger (Luke

11:21). But it was used in the Septuagint to represent the Hebrew *shalom,* which contains the idea of completeness, wholeness or welfare. (It is easy to see the connection with the absence of war. In war there are obviously *two* parties, fighting each other. When they are at peace there is *one* circle of friendship—obviously a "whole.") In particular the prophets saw such peace as a mark of the Messianic kingdom, and the Christian concept of peace was correspondingly filled out. It is almost the same as salvation (Isa. 52:7; Acts 10:36). In other words the Greek word (through the Septuagint) has taken on a Hebrew meaning. Three elements may be distinguished. The believer has peace *with* God (Rom. 5:1): the divine opposition has ended and in Christ God is "for us" (Rom. 8:31–32). By the combination of petition and thanksgiving he may dispense with anxiety in the knowledge that he is protected by the peace *of* God (Phil. 4:6–7). This is no mere subjective feeling, which as feeling might be a fool's paradise, but is grounded in God's work in Christ. There is no turmoil in the inner citadel of his heart, whatever happens outside (Matt. 10:34–36). It is the fruit of the Spirit (Gal. 5:22). The believer should also work for peace *among* men (Rom. 12:18; 14:19; Eph. 4:3). This goes back to Jesus (Mark 9:50). Paul prays that the "peace of God" may not have even the slightest crack (Rom. 15:13— "all . . . peace").

Thus the believer has peace with God; he may have the peace of God; and he ought to work for peace among men.

As in Galatians 6:16, Paul may here have borrowed from Jewish greetings. *Mercy* is inserted in place of the Thessalonian "to you." The latter may have been omitted for reasons of rhythm. The loss is not great and the replacement is rich. It is worth reflecting that however much Christians have received already of the divine grace, mercy and peace, God is always ready to give more, and prayer is a form not only of asking for it but of taking it.

The salutation *grace and peace* is thought by some to combine Greek and Hebrew greetings: *grace (charis)* from the normal *chairein* (to greet), and the Hebrew *peace.* But the Jews tended to identify them, even translating *shalom* on occasion by *chairein* (Isa. 48:22; 57:21, LXX; cf. Luke 1:28 [1]). The decision on this question does not greatly matter in comparison with the doctrinal message. The greeting is no mere form of words. The world gives a mere salutation; Jesus actually gives his peace (John 14:27). For how many does "goodbye" really mean "God be with you"?

There is no verb in the Greek. We may understand the thought as a statement, a hope, or a prayer. "Grace, mercy, and peace are actually yours." This is true in fact. But the hope and prayer are appropriate, for grace and peace may be multiplied in men's experience (1 Pet. 1:2), and God is rich in mercy (Eph. 2:4). To all comments should be added the extensive use of the concordance.[2]

From God the Father and Christ Jesus our Lord: The eternal source and the actual manifestation. Every word has doctrinal implications. (See above on v. 1.) The Father and the Son are on the same level. In the context of the

---

1. Theodor Zahn, *Introduction to the New Testament,* 2nd ed., rev. (New York: Charles Scribner's Sons, 1917), 1:119, note 7.

2. A convenient study will be found in Leon Morris, *The Apostolic Preaching of the Cross* (London: Tyndale Press, 1955), pp. 210–17.

New Testament—and the qualification is crucial—it is no argument to quote Acts 15:28, "For it has seemed good to the Holy Spirit and to us . . . ." The point there is that "we" responded to the Spirit's leading; and that in any case we are not called "the Lord." "*Our* Lord" points to the whole Christian fellowship or community. The Lord of the whole church is the Lord who is common to every member. Compare "common faith" (Titus 1:4) and "common salvation" (Jude 3).

There is perhaps an added reverence in the order *Christ Jesus*. *Christ* is Greek for the Hebrew Messiah, the Anointed One. It is instructive to look at Psalm 2:2 and Acts 4:26 in both KJV and RSV. The king who was the subject of prophecy has actually come (Mark 8:29; 14:61–62). Popular expectation had thought of a deliverer from the Romans, but for Jesus, Messiahship was a task involving the cross—the supreme service. He linked the Messiah with the Servant (Mark 1:11; Ps. 2:7; Isa. 42:1).

Jesus is the name of the historic person who was seen in Nazareth, Jerusalem, and elsewhere in Palestine. It is the Greek for a late form of the common name Joshua (compare the KJV and RSV of Heb. 4:8). We are so familiar with the sacred name that we miss its impact. But if we imagine the Savior's name to have been John instead of Joshua, we can savor the feelings of unbelieving Jews at hearing the sound of *Lord* John. The divine is linked with the common—quite rightly, because "God sent forth his Son, born of woman" (Gal. 4:4), and he was "the man Christ Jesus" (1 Tim. 2:5). The name *Jesus* is appropriate (Matt. 1:21).

Lord (Greek *kurios*) is the word used in the Septuagint (Greek) version of the Old Testament for the divine name traditionally rendered Jehovah, now Yahweh. It is of the deepest significance that the word used to translate the ineffable name of God should be applied to *Jesus* (Exod. 3:14–15; Phil. 2:11). The name of *Jesus* is *Lord*.

II. FALSE TEACHING AND THE GOSPEL (1:3–20)

Doctrinal error is to be forbidden. False doctrine is not only untrue but also unprofitable. Pretensions to teaching the law do not justify an ignorant use of it. Its lawful use accords with the gospel, of which the author has deep, personal experience. The solemn charge to Timothy is renewed: he must continue his Christian warfare.

1. False Teaching Considered (1:3–11)

Doctrinal distortions and irrelevant theories must be abandoned. Such activities do not promote Christian faith and life. On the contrary they result in fruitless discussion and a misuse of the law. There is a right use of the law which is in line with the gospel with which Paul has been entrusted.

(1) False teaching banned (1:3–4a)

Timothy is urged to stay at his post at Ephesus with the specific task of silencing those who propagate false doctrine and diverting them from irrelevant academic pursuits.

Verse 3: As I urged you when I was going to Macedonia: Oral persuasion made permanent in writing. Paul's Greek verb, "I exhorted," "I encouraged," "I appealed to you," implies persuasion with authority. The journey is later than any recorded in the Acts. *Macedonia* was the Roman province in the north of Greece. The cities of Thessalonica and Philippi were in Macedonia. The place of the conversation between Paul and Timothy is not mentioned. It need not have been Ephesus. The Greek sentence is a difficult example of an anacoluthon, that is, a construction involving a break in grammatical sequence characteristic of animated conversation or dictation. The rsv has given a workable rendering.

Remain at Ephesus: Stay on. It is not quite "go on staying" but rather "decide to stay where you are" when his heart was with Paul. The verb marks more than the temporal extension of residence, like prolonging a vacation or other visit. It is used in two texts which suggest moral and spiritual challenge. In Acts 11:23 Barnabas urged them all "to remain faithful to the Lord with steadfast purpose"; and similarly in Acts 13:43 Paul and Barnabas were exercising suasion on them to remain in the grace of God. Why urge, why try to persuade, if there is no temptation or no challenge and they will *remain* anyway? Timothy was faced with a decision.

Ephesus was in Asia Minor, a governmental, judicial and religious center (Acts 19:34 f., 38). Paul had ministered there for three years (Acts 20:31). It was a strategic point for the preaching of the gospel (Acts 19:26).

That you may charge certain persons: An ecclesiastical sergeant major? Not quite, but near enough to be startling. The timid and emotional young man (2 Tim. 1:3–7) was to give orders, for such is the meaning of *charge*. The names of *certain persons* are not given. Their faith had not yet been shipwrecked, to name them would give them unnecessary advertisement, and it would irritate and antagonize and deepen the breach rather than heal it.

Not to teach any different doctrine: A Christian pattern or standard is implied. (Cf. 6:3.) If a man mounts a pulpit or seeks in other ways to influence his fellows, his *different doctrine* may be of various kinds. It may not be specifically Christian doctrine at all. If a man taught mathematics from the pulpit, every word he said might be true, but it would be *different*. On the other hand, he may express Christian truth and then either deliberately give it a flat contradiction or else consciously or unconsciously imply its falsity. Again, his point of view may be so extreme that his perspective is wrong and his doctrine out of proportion. A man might preach the sovereignty of God in such a way that no room is left for repentance and faith. *Different doctrine* may thus be irrelevant, contradictory, or distorted; it cannot be "applied" in the true preacher's style, and it will be barren if not worse: it will edify none or it may pervert. Paul was here mainly concerned with the teaching given. In Acts 20:30 the emphasis is on the teachers (cf. 1 Tim. 6:3–5). In every case the effects should be observed.

Verse 4a: Nor to occupy themselves with myths and endless genealogies— a wasted concentration. They were paying attention to what did not deserve to be the focus of their thought. *Myths* may be used in a narrower and in a wider sense. Myth proper may be defined or described as facts naïvely understood and imaginatively explained, like a story to explain the thunder or the origin of the song of the nightingale. Myth has been called "the history of the gods." Some modern theologians seem to assume that anything concerned with the supernatural or the transcendent realm must be in the form of myth. This is unfortunate. The gods have never existed. The blessed and only Sovereign (6:15) has revealed himself in his Son.

In a broader sense myth means an invented story or an untrue fable. Herodotus (2. 45) regards a myth about Heracles (the Roman Hercules) told by the Greeks as ill-considered and silly, based on ignorance. Aristotle in the *Meteorologica* (2. 3) says of one of Aesop's fables that it is hardly suitable for those who are looking for the truth, and he calls it a myth. In the *Poetics*, a series of university lectures in which he examined the factors which led to the successful performance of plays,[1] Aristotle called the "plot" a myth. The plot of a tragedy or comedy is the arrangement of incidents. Together they should form one action and should so cohere that the transposition or removal of any one of them dislocates and destroys the whole. The incidents are obviously selected and the whole action is the product of the creative gifts of the dramatist. However refined the plot may be in the literary sense,

---

1. *Poetics* 6. 8; 8. 4. Cf. Dorothy L. Sayers, *The Mind of the Maker* (London: Religious Book Club, 1942), pp. 11 f.

it is fiction. On a lower level Aristotle refers in the *Metaphysics* (12. 8. 19 f.) to a traditional myth that the heavenly bodies are gods. Later mythological tradition was added to influence the common man in the interests of expediency. Plato (*Republic* 2. 17) refers to the use of myth in early education and calls it false, though it contains truth. It is not a dogma, formally proclaimed as official teaching, but expresses what cannot be expressed rationally.[1]

The danger is that myth may be used without reference to historicity, and the New Testament accordingly sets its face against it on religious grounds. (Cf. 4:7; 2 Tim. 4:4; Titus 1:14; 2 Pet. 1:16.) God has revealed himself in historic facts; even Old Testament propositions are part of the historical scene; and he has revealed himself completely and finally in his Son. For the New Testament the revelation can be received by the regenerated man. It can be "understanded of the people." [2] Men may excel in scholarship and be far advanced in saintliness, but there is no spiritual elite in principle who can understand, in distinction from the common herd which needs the mythical approach. The gospel is addressed to all; all may come, and all who do come have access to the unsearchable riches of Christ. It is perhaps in unconscious anticipation of this that the Septuagint translators avoid the use of the term *myth*. In both the technical sense and in the wider sense of "invented tale" the myth is out of harmony with the spirit of biblical religion.

The *genealogies* have been referred by some to the Gnostic speculations of the second century. According to these, God is separate from matter, which is evil, and yet is connected with it by a series of aeons or emanations, much as the contents of a telescope are pulled out. The aeons emanate from God and at the furthest end there is the possibility of contact with matter. This is much too developed for the situation in the Pastorals, which seems to be Jewish and savors of rabbinical speculation. An example of the latter is the Book of Jubilees, a rewriting of the Book of Genesis elaborated with much traditional lore. As a manifesto of legalism, it expresses the supremacy of law—with the suppression of prophecy. *Myths and endless genealogies,* taken together, would aptly suggest the invented stories of patriarchal pedigrees and their inconclusive results. A further possibility is the factor of personal pedigree. There were Jews and a synagogue at Ephesus (Acts 19:8, 17), and the question of descent from Abraham may have been raised (John 8:33; Gal. 3:29).

It is not possible to state precisely what Paul had in mind. What must not be forgotten is the fact that Christians start—or should start—with something given. The life of the church is not a search for God; he has already come in Christ. Even the approach, "Thy face, Lord, will I seek," is not a search but a response to a prior divine call: "Seek ye my face" (Ps. 27:8, 9). If we do not start here we have nothing left but speculation, which will be *endless*.

(2) False teaching unprofitable (1:4b–7)

Attention to myths and genealogies yields speculation rather than Christian

---

1. Cf. Rudolf Bultmann, *Primitive Christianity: In Its Contemporary Setting* (New York: Meridian Books, 1956), p. 125.

2. The phrase comes from Article 24 of the Thirty-nine Articles of the Church of England.

faith and life. The result is no more than vain discussion and the claim of ignorant men to be teachers of the law.

Verse 4b: Which promote speculations rather than the divine training that is in faith—wasted time and a missed opportunity. Arndt and Gingrich (*A Greek-English Lexicon of the New Testament*, p. 239) translate the first noun by "useless speculation" and Liddell-Scott-Jones (*A Greek-English Lexicon*, 1:506) by "research." The implication is that there is no significant breakthrough. Instances of the corresponding verb in the New Testament are instructive. "No one seeks for God" (Rom. 3:11). God's purpose in the church of the Messiah, the fulfillment of the church of Israel, is "that the rest of men may seek the Lord" (Acts 15:17). "He rewards those who seek him" (Heb. 11:6). The speculation is useless because it really belongs to past history. All the searching for the Lord ought to have been done already. The prophets searched (1 Pet. 1:10); believers should proclaim. It is a sad day when members of the visible church seem to be muddled men in search of a message. "We have found the Messiah" (John 1:41). When a Jew becomes a Christian, he ought to read the Old Testament through Christian eyes (1 Cor. 10:6, 11—the warnings were "types" or patterns). When a philosopher is converted, he retains his philosophic equipment but uses it all under the sovereignty of Christ.

The *divine training* is an attempt to render a difficult expression which means "God's stewardship" or "God's economy." This does not mean his thrift or parsimony. The revenues of an estate are administered, dispensed (not "dispensed with"), by a manager, steward, or even executor. It suggests a giving out to various people of what does not belong to him personally. He is administering a trust. Now Paul had been given "God's stewardship" (Col. 1:25, RSV, gives "divine office" for virtually the same expression as in 1 Tim. 1:4), and it was a stewardship of God's grace (Eph. 3:2). God's grace had been given to him and he in turn was to administer or dispense it. He did so by preaching the Word of God (cf. Matt. 13:19; Acts 20:24 f.). Other members of the church can share in this work. Just as Paul could administer not the revenues of an estate but grace by preaching Christ in uttered words, so the ordinary Christians could administer grace by the utterance of words in godly conversation (Eph. 4:29). Paul was justly indignant that men should spend their time and energy on fanciful interpretations of Scripture which yielded no final satisfaction but only further questions, when they might have paid the closer attention to what they had heard of God's final Word (cf. Heb. 1:1–4; 2:1), and shared in the task and joy of making him known. It was essentially the same attitude as that shown by Spurgeon in more recent times, when he complained of Christians who would rather devote themselves to solving the intricacies of the Book of the Revelation than to teaching poor illiterate children in a ragged school about Jesus. (See also Luke 16:1; 1 Cor. 4:1 f.; 9:17.) Such stewardship is God's work: "God's stewardship that is *in* the realm of *faith*."

Verse 5: Whereas the aim of our charge is love—the final goal of theological intervention. The word *charge* recalls the corresponding verb in verse 3. Paul was thinking of Timothy's charge to the false teachers. His ultimate purpose in the prohibition of "different doctrine" was not only theological correction but the inspiration of love. Speculation promotes friction, but gospel preaching creates love. Though it was Timothy who gave the charge, it was Paul who suggested that he should give it, and it was no doubt this reflection which led to the RSV *our charge*. *Our* is not present in the Greek. *Love* in the Christian sense is theologically motivated (1 John 4:10 f., 19), practically exhibited (Luke 10:25-37; 1 Cor. 13:4-7) and emotionally felt (1 Cor. 13:3). *Love* is both commanded and inspired.

That issues from a pure heart and a good conscience and sincere faith: Love is not self-created, and it is not secular. It springs up in a believing man whose faith in Christ is real. He is not playing a part and deceiving himself or others. Such a faith is expressed in life, in which he is obedient to God. The reception of salvation clears his conscience, and as he grows in sanctification he is more and more obedient to the command to love his neighbor. Such is the pattern of the Christian life from which Paul was deriving his argument.

Heart, conscience and *faith* all deserve special study.

The use of the term "heart" in the New Testament is a study in itself. As in our modern usage it is the seat of the emotions, both good and bad (Rom. 1:24; 10:1). But it is far more. It is the seat of the intellect, from which come thought and reflection (Mark 11:23; Acts 7:23; Rom. 1:21, where the RSV's "minds" translates the Greek "heart"). It is the seat of the moral consciousness and of the will (Acts 11:23, "with purpose of heart," KJV; 1 Cor. 4:5; 2 Cor. 9:7, KJV), and even the scene of the imagination (Eph. 1:18). It stands for the ego, the whole personality. God has put the "earnest," the first installment, of the Spirit "in our hearts" (2 Cor. 1:22), that is, he has given it (the earnest) to *us* (2 Cor. 5:5). The heart is the seat of religious experience from which springs moral conduct. The "hidden person of the heart" (1 Pet. 3:4) is that to which God looks for the truth about men (Luke 16:15; cf. 1 Sam. 16:7).[1]

Conscience is a term of Greek origin (though of course the actual *conscientia* is a Latin word). *Suneidēsis* originates either with the Stoics, as many scholars have thought, or in Greek popular thought. The earlier meaning of "consciousness" became "moral consciousness" or *conscience*. It is a natural endowment of the non-Jew and reflects that which has been given more precisely in the law. The conscience of the Christian is taught by the Holy Spirit, who does not teach from an absolute beginning but brings vividly to remembrance what our Lord has taught (Rom. 2:14 f.; 9:1; cf. 12:2). In conscience there is an individual recognition of obligation and approval of obedience to it (2 Cor. 1:12), or disapproval of disobedience (Rom. 13:5; cf. 7:15 f.). Conscience may be weak and unable to come to a decision; or defiled, so that it is less sympathetic to the good; or wounded, when it is made less capable of working properly (1 Cor. 8:7-13; cf. 1 Tim. 4:2).

In itself, conscience is an abstraction. In real life it indicates a man with the mental and moral characteristics just described. It is thus subjective. On

---

1. See Johannes Behm in G. Kittel, ed., *Theological Dictionary of the New Testament* (hereafter referred to as TDNT), 3:612. Cf. also W. David Stacey, *The Pauline View of Man in Relation to Its Judaic and Hellenistic Background* (London: Macmillan & Co., 1956), pp. 194-97; and H. Wheeler Robinson, *The Christian Doctrine of Man* (Edinburgh: T. & T. Clark, 1913), pp. 104-107.

the other hand, in a sense a man stands over against himself, passing a verdict on himself in the light of his previous spiritual experience, good, bad, or indifferent. Insofar as he has been educated by the law of God, either as a Gentile or as a Jew or Christian, the man as judge stands in contrast to himself as judged. Conscience is thus objective as well as subjective. It does not imply a merely personal oddity, like a refusal on principle to take the medicines prescribed by a physician.

A bad conscience means a consciousness, a reminder, of sins (cf. Heb. 10:22 with 10:2 f., and note "sins," plural, in spite of RSV). It implies a knowledge of personal responsibility and a sense of guilt. A *good conscience* is so called because guilt has been put away and sins forgiven. The blood of Christ cleanses the bad conscience (cf. Heb. 9:14). It may also be good in the day-to-day sense of having a conscience clear in regard to some accusation. If behavior is good, conscience is good (1 Pet. 3:16).

A *pure heart* is a Hebrew concept and is a rough equivalent of the Greek *good conscience*. Reference to the previous discussion on *heart* will show that it stands for the moral consciousness and for the whole personality. Just as the conscience is cleansed by the blood of Christ, so the heart is cleansed by faith (Acts 15:9). But faith in what? ". . . by the word which I have spoken to you" (John 15:3). The heart is cleansed; men are cleansed; and it is done when men receive the Word. When the conscience is good and the heart is clean in the manner described, then no cloud impedes the believer's vision of God and he is blessed indeed. For "blessed are the pure in heart, for they shall see God" (Matt. 5:8).

The overlap of *heart* and *conscience* is suggested by 1 Samuel 24:5, "David's heart smote him."

Faith must come first and must be real, not a pose. In all true faith, credence and trust mingle. Credence means that there are certain statements which are regarded as true, however simple (e.g., "Jesus is Lord"). This is implied by the fact of preaching: the preachers must say something *about* the Savior. If this element is lacking, the sermon has little content and the believer's trust is hazy. On the other hand, trust means that the believer confidently hands himself over to Christ, puts himself into his hands. If this is absent, we have no more than "signing on the dotted line," a mere intellectual assent. On faith depends the one experience, doubly expressed, of the *pure heart* and *good conscience*. From this is born love.

Verse 6: Certain persons by swerving from these have wandered away into vain discussion: A wrong aim ends in hitting the wrong target. Their object of concentration was wrong (v. 4) and their consequent achievement no more than idle talk. When speculation and discussion are animated, tempers are roused and love is forgotten. The *certain persons* should know that they were keeping odd company (Rom. 1:21; 1 Cor. 3:20; cf. 2 Tim. 4:4).

Verse 7: Desiring to be teachers of the law—with all the esteem with which the office was regarded. Judaism could produce a Gamaliel (Acts 5:34) and also others of different caliber (Luke 5:17, 21). But should *law* be the characteristic of any man of prominence in the Christian community?

Without understanding either what they are saying or the things about which they make assertions—ambition without the necessary qualifications. They said so much, but did not understand their own statements. They made *assertions*, they "insisted," as Titus was supposed to do (Titus 3:8), but did not understand the subject of their own emphatic teachings and could not identify it. If they had been asked, "About what matters are you speaking so strongly?" they would have found it hard to reply. They were not qualified, as the Lord had not "opened their minds to understand the scriptures" (Luke 24:45). They were not being constantly transformed by the renewal of their minds (Rom. 12:2). They no longer had the mind of Christ (1 Cor. 2:16). The men who were guilty not only of heterodoxy but of "heterodidachy," of teaching different doctrine, of teaching "otherwise," were depraved in mind (1:3; 6:3–5). This is not an honest mistake about a matter on the circumference of Christian doctrine. It touches the fundamentals of the faith and involves a persistence and self-will which is moral and spiritual as well as intellectual. The deposit of Christian truth must be guarded and godless chatter avoided (cf. 6:20).

(3) False teaching contrasted (1:8–11)

In contrast to the law wrongly expounded and wrongly applied, and therefore brought into disrepute, the law is good if its function is understood. Legislation is aimed at the impious and criminal, sinners against God and man in thought, word, and deed. This interpretation of law accords with Paul's gospel.

Verse 8: Now we know that the law is good, if any one uses it lawfully —in spite of its misuse by the false teachers. This would forestall any thought by Timothy, or the church at Ephesus, that in view of all the strange exposition and discussion, Paul was advocating the abandonment of the law. Paul's statement here does not contradict his earlier utterances on the subject. *The law* is holy and good (Rom. 7:12, 16). But it must be used *lawfully,* that is, not "legally" but "in accordance with its original purpose." It must be used "as law." Its goodness depends on its right use. This was common knowledge among instructed Christians: *we know.* The *we* is not limited to the apostolic circle.

Verse 9: Understanding this, that the law is not laid down for the just but for the lawless and disobedient—the persons to whom the law is directed. *Just (dikaios)* means "righteous" as in 1 Peter 3:18 (cf. KJV and RSV), and there is more than one logical possibility. *Law* is not enacted for its effect on the man who is righteous in himself. He does not need it. This is a principle, even though such a man may not exist. Just as a healthy man does not need to summon the doctor, so the righteous man does not need the law—or the gospel (Luke 5:32). It is not therefore enacted for him. When Paul, however, used the word *just* or "righteous" he was not thinking of the religiously self-made man, the Pharisee (Luke 18:9 f.). He filled the term with the content of the gospel. Through the obedience of the one Savior the many who believe are ranked as righteous (cf. Rom. 5:19). This righteousness is not their own, whereas the Pharisee's is. It is God's, and in Christ he has given it to believing men. In the cross, God made his Son to be sin for us, in order that we might become the righteousness of God in him (2 Cor. 5:21). (Cf. Rom. 4:1–5.) In speaking of the *just*, Paul clearly had justified men in mind.

The law, then, is aimed at the wrongdoer. It defines or delineates sin, showing it up with precision and in its true colors (Rom. 4:15; 5:13; 7:13).

Its purpose is to restrain the wrongdoer, either before he has done wrong or after it, so that it may not be repeated. In one sense it seeks to restrain the potential wrongdoer. If the law fails to restrain him, its purpose is to condemn him. "The law brings wrath" (Rom. 4:15).

This is not for the Christian, for he is "not under law but under grace" (Rom. 6:14). It had its place before we became Christians (Gal. 3:24), but we are now no longer under it. How then can we be so sure that "the law is good" (v. 8)? It is good because we recognize its purpose in relation to the wrongdoer and in relation to the man who may be driven by it to repentance and faith. And further, it is good because, though we are no longer under law, we are "in-lawed" to Christ (1 Cor. 9:21; it is impossible to render adequately Paul's play on the words *anomos* and *ennomos*, "God's out-law" and "Christ's in-law," here. The RSV does not greatly help. There is no "under" in the Greek as in Rom. 6:14). The Christian is not under law as a means of justification, though Paul recognized the place of law in the life of Christian discipleship, the necessity for "keeping the commandments of God" (1 Cor. 7:19). The law of ancient Israel was civil, ceremonial and moral. The moral law, interpreted by our Lord in the Sermon on the Mount (Matt. 5:1–7:29), is a guide to love's fulfillment of the law (Rom. 13:8–10). For it makes up for the deficiencies in the inclination of even the regenerated heart. For further guidance the reader is referred to Dr. Ernest F. Kevan's [1] profound study, *The Grace of Law.* He examines thoroughly the Puritan teaching on the place of the law in the life of the believer.

For the ungodly . . . for manslayers: A typical catalogue of vices. (Cf. 6:4 f.; 2 Tim. 3:2–5; Titus 3:3.) The list, which continues into the next verse, approximates the Ten Commandmants. *Ungodly, sinners, unholy* and *profane* characterizes those who transgress against the First Table and commit sins specifically against God (Exod. 20:3–11). They are described comprehensively. The Second Table covers sins against men (Exod. 20:12–17) and is followed in detail. According to rabbinic interpretation honoring father and mother involves an obligation to care for aged parents. To fail to feed, clothe and shelter them is murder. This is one form of breaking the fifth commandment. *Manslayers* obviously break the sixth. Immoral persons they certainly are in the broadest sense. But the English term is used in the next verse more narrowly.

Verse 10: Immoral persons . . . perjurers: This completes the list of "external" sins against fellowmen. *Immoral persons* means those who are guilty of any form of sexual sin, particularly fornication or prostitution. A special case is that of the *sodomites* or male homosexuals (Gen. 19:4 f.). The two groups break the seventh commandment, interpreted as covering all activities of sex. *Kidnapers* are guilty of stealing, and *liars* and *perjurers* bear false witness. The tenth commandment, "You shall not covet," is missed. Paul was concentrating on the external acts rather than the inner attitude. The breaking of the ninth commandment by lying and perjuring is not to be regarded as of minor importance. These acts tend to undermine social life.

And whatever else is contrary to sound doctrine: And so covetousness is

---

1. Ernest F. Kevan, *The Grace of Law: a Study in Puritan Theology* (London: Carey Kingsgate Press, 1964).

included after all. But the scope is wider still. Included is anything which is forbidden by the law but not specifically mentioned in verses 9 and 10. The *contrary* may cover an extension or distortion of the law, like the prohibition of marriage and certain foods (4:3). It may apply to the activity of teaching or to a body of doctrine; and to the attitude in word or deed which denies the validity and authority of the moral law, either in the nonbeliever or the believer.

Sound means "healthy." The implication is that from *sound doctrine* no disease can be caught by contagion or infection. Disobedience and sin produce their own disease, from which "with his stripes we are healed" (Isa. 53:5). By association with the healthy moral law the healed Christian stays healed. The idea of heresy lurks in the background, primarily in relation to law but perhaps also the heresy of confusing law and grace.

The *doctrine* under discussion is moral doctrine, as it is concerned with the law imposed on wrongdoers. It is not theological doctrine as such. The word of the cross is not imposed on all men as law. But it is theological doctrine insofar as it teaches the moral obligations of discipleship. The doctrine of justification by faith does not imply antinomianism. "Are we to continue in sin that grace may abound?" (Rom. 6:1).

Verse 11: In accordance with the glorious gospel of the blessed God with which I have been entrusted: Such an understanding of the law was inspired by the gospel. The *gospel* sets the law in its right context and assigns to it its function. Paul's words, literally rendered, read; "the gospel of the glory of the blessed God." The meaning is that the *gospel* "consists of" *the glory. . . . Glory* is that which reveals God—his being, his character, his majesty and his might. The gospel is the manifestation—not merely the argument— that God exists; it reveals his character as holy, righteous, wise and loving; it inspires worship and demonstrates God's power. Paul had been *entrusted* with the gospel (cf. 1 Thess. 2:4). His thought here has gone back to the Damascus road. (Cf. Acts 22:15, 21; 26:16–20; Gal. 1:15–17.) In 1 Corinthians 9:17, "I am entrusted with a commission," he was thinking more of the present moment. "I have the gospel in my hands as a trust, to offer it to men."

In the present verse God is *blessed* not in the sense that men give him the blessing of which he is worthy. God is blessed in himself, and though he may require much from men, he does not need anything from men in order to complete his perfection. He needs neither their service nor their worship (Acts 17:24 f.). All perfection is present in the living God, and infinite joy. The source of all satisfaction is within himself. The word *makarios,* blessed, is rarely used in the Bible for God (cf. 6:15), though not infrequently for men, as in the Beatitudes (Matt. 5:3–12). It is significant that the blessed are told to "rejoice and be glad" (Matt. 5:11 f.) and thus to actualize their blessedness. Human blessedness is the gift of God. The divine blessedness is inherent and eternal, the everlasting bliss which is the logical (not chronological) consequence of his own character and power. This must not in any circumstances be compared with human complacency.

2. The Gospel Experienced (1:12–17)

Mention of the gospel entrusted to Paul inspires gratitude for the power which equipped him to discharge his trust. The former opponent had been adjudged trustworthy for ministry after he had received mercy and abundant grace. The divine purpose of saving sinners had been remarkably fulfilled in Paul, who is to be regarded as a typical example. In him the patience of Jesus Christ is displayed to the utmost. The implication is that no potential believer need despair that his case is too hard. The section suitably ends with a doxology.

Verse 12: I thank him who has given me strength for this, Christ Jesus our Lord: Experience of both law and gospel inspires thanksgiving. The logical connection seems to be as follows. Paul had been speaking of the law, and his interpretation of its function had been claimed to accord with the gospel. He could reinforce his argument by asserting that he had personal experience of both. He certainly knew the law, both in an academic way (Acts 5:34; 22:3) and in intimate, "existential" feeling. In the works of the law he became blameless (Phil. 3:4–6), and the same law beat him to death (Rom. 7:7–11). The road to Damascus gave him also a deep knowledge of the gospel. Logically he might merely have said that "I know what I am talking about," in contrast to the false teachers (v. 7). But the thought of the gospel sparked his emotions and he therefore expressed his knowledge in terms of thanksgiving.

Just before his conversion Paul was frustrated by the experience of spiritual weakness. The law killed him. In contrast Christ in the gospel "empowered him." We may well leave it at that. There is no *for this* in the Greek. For *Christ Jesus* see on 1:1; and for *our Lord* see on 1:2; (and cf. 1 Thess. 1:1).

Because he judged me faithful by appointing me to his service: Thanksgiving for the power given and the attitude expressed. He who had been entrusted with the gospel was deemed trustworthy. The personal, spiritual power now merges with ministerial, preaching power. Paul was thankful for the power and the position. The attitude of Christ Jesus had been expressed in the call *to his service.*

Verse 13: Though I formerly blasphemed and persecuted and insulted him: Blasphemer, persecutor, insulter as I was. The RSV turns nouns into verbs, with Christ Jesus as object, against which translation there is no objection in principle. Blasphemy is directed against God, and he is present in Christ. Persecution works to the distress of the church and in this Saul was persecuting Jesus (Acts 9:4 f.), for the church is "in Christ" (cf. Eph. 4:15 f.). Both blasphemy and persecution were saturated with insult (*hubris,* cf. 1 Thess. 2:2). By this time Paul knew the smart of receiving insult, and it colored his thought of giving it.

But I received mercy because I had acted ignorantly in unbelief: The negative cause of receiving mercy. (For *mercy* see on 1:2.) The positive cause is the grace and will of God. The ignorance and unbelief suggest that the door was still open. Saul of Tarsus had not committed the unpardonable sin (Mark 3:29). Once more the Damascus road is recalled.

Verse 14: And the grace of our Lord overflowed for me with the faith and love that are in Christ Jesus: The Nile overflows; the crops abound. Grace overflowed and faith and love sprang up. We should not think that grace overflowed with faith and love in the sense that the Nile overflowed with crops. Grace overflowed, in close connection with which came faith and love. (For *grace,* see discussion on 1:2; for *faith* and *love,* discussion on 1:5).

The almost artless simplicity of *the faith and love that are in Christ Jesus,* apart from the relation to grace, must not blind us to the profound Christian truth involved. *Faith* is in Christ in the sense that when a man first believes, faith is directed towards Christ and comes to rest in him. More simply, the man entrusts himself to Christ, hands himself over to Christ, and ends up and stays in him. He is clothed in his righteousness, in Christ the righteous, and is also a member of his body, the Christian community or church. As a subsidiary thought, Christ is his natural element, like air for the animal and water for the fish. Inspired by such an experience of faith, the man directs his love to Christ and to the other members of the Christian community, who are also in Christ. The whole expression is steeped in Christian experience, from the time of conversion onward. Notice that *faith* replaces ignorance and unbelief (v. 13), for faith is a form of knowledge (John 17:3), and *love* arises in place of persecution.

Verse 15: The saying is sure and worthy of full acceptance—credible without reservation. (Cf. 3:1; 4:9.) The idea is that the statement is not merely believable but also commands approval. Compare our remark, "he commands respect." The Greek for *sure* or "credible" (*pistos*) also means "trustworthy" (the faithful of v. 12). A statement is to be given credence or believed; a person is to be trusted. These two meanings correspond to the two levels of faith or to the two aspects of it. Statements of Christian truth, as here, are to be believed; God, or Christ, is to be trusted. (Cf. 1 Cor. 1:9; 10:13; 1 Thess. 5:24; 2 Thess. 3:3.) An instructive example is 1 Peter 4:19, "let them hand over their souls (as a deposit) to a trustworthy Creator." Christian faith is the commitment of a person (oneself) to a trustworthy person; a handing over of the human self to the divine; and the divine has been described.

The fullness of the *acceptance* should match the abundance of the grace (v. 14; cf. Rom. 5:20). The *saying* seems to be one known in the churches, perhaps from use in teaching or worship.

That Christ Jesus came into the world to save sinners: The purpose of the incarnation. The comprehensive statement points to the preexistence of Christ, universal sinfulness and the work of the cross. The language has a Johannine flavor (John 1:9–11; 3:17; 12:46 f.; 16:28), which is not unnatural if the provenance of the Gospel of John is Ephesus. In any case there are other points of contact (e.g., Luke 19:9 f.; Gal. 4:4 f.). He *came . . . to save sinners.* Did he do it? The answer is that he redeemed all and saved some. All that Paul taught about an objective atonement can be regarded as clearing the ground. The purpose of salvation is achieved every time a man puts his faith in Christ, and a notable example is now given. The atonement is effective in God and is available for all men; but it is effective in some men only.

And I am the foremost of sinners—the personal verdict of utter humility. Paul did not say "was." In his own view he still could say *I am . . . .* Before Damascus he was a sinner; after Damascus he was a saved sinner. He was the first (*prōtos*) (cf. Mark 10:44) not in time—there were sinners before Saul of Tarsus—but in status, *the foremost.* It would be speculative and unedify-

ing to ask if Paul were worse than Judas. His own black record, on which
the mercy of Jesus shone with such luster, made him view himself as "the sinner," like the tax collector in the parable who prayed that God would be
merciful "to me *the* sinner" (Luke 18:13; it is a pity that RSV still translates by
"a sinner"; the Greek has the definite article). The sinner in his time of deep
repentance could see no other sinner in the world but himself (contrast
Luke 18:11). Paul had been transformed from a self-righteous Pharisee to
a repentant sinner, and for ever afterwards he was "the sinner" in his own
mind—but it was "the saved sinner." This has consequences in his thought.

*Verse 16: But I received mercy for this reason, that in me, as the fore-
most, Jesus Christ might display his perfect patience:* The providential cause of
the mercy (cf. v. 13). It was the purpose of God's grace and will to save
Saul, and it was his further gracious purpose—for the sake of others—to use
him as a demonstration. The. *perfect patience* means literally "all his patience." Paul would not wish to limit the divine patience, but with this proviso
we can argue that in his thought it had been stretched to the uttermost.
He did not mean that he had experienced all the patience in such a way that
there was none left for others. He regarded himself, so to speak, as a sort
of thermometer or other means of measurement, which on the Damascus road
registered the highest point. It could happen again: a thermometer which
registers boiling point can register it again, though Paul did not think it would
be necessary. He was "the sinner." Any other man would be "a sinner" in
whom Jesus Christ could display some patience, though "all his patience"
would not be necessary. This could be a ground of hope for the despairing.
Other and perhaps better illustrations are available. A jet airplane which
has gone "all out" at top speed can repeat the process, and also can fly at
slower speeds. A hockey player who has battled on through extra time to the
limit of his powers can repeat the performance and also play less energetically
and for shorter lengths of time in more normal matches.

For an example to those who were to believe in him for eternal life:
The object of the demonstration. Paul's experience was to be a model
or prototype. His case was to be typical or normal. His conversion is not
therefore to be regarded as exceptional. It has exceptional features like the
light from heaven, but its essential pattern applies to all conversion—sin, the
merciful Jesus, faith, salvation. Paul must not be regarded here as under obligation to "set an example." He actually is an example, an example of conversion. If an Eskimo from the far north shyly asked someone in the
U.S.A., "What is an automobile?" an ostensible definition could be given
by saying "This [pointing to it] is an *example* of an automobile." If the question is asked, "What is conversion?" the answer can similarly be given,
"Saul of Tarsus is an example of conversion." *Example* has sometimes been
rendered by "outline sketch" or "word-picture." (Cf. 2 Tim. 1:13.)

Paul in his conversion was an outline sketch of those who *were* going
to believe in Jesus. It does not mean quite that they "had to." The verb may
express simple futurity, with or without some flavor of destiny. *Believe in him*
suggests putting one's faith on bedrock or foundation stone (cf. Rom. 9:33;
10:11). Faith in Christ is "with a view to" *eternal life* and results in it.

*Verse 17: To the King of ages, immortal, invisible, the only God, be honor
and glory for ever and ever. Amen:* At this point a natural outburst of praise
from "the sinner." The phrase *King of ages* may be derived from the

synagogue worship; the phrase is found in Tobit 13:7, 11, LXX (13:6, 10 in NEB), and its thought in Psalm 145:13, "a kingdom of all ages" (cf. Ps. 144:13, LXX). The intensive plural expresses eternity. In the premessianic age, God was King. In "the age to come," which in Jesus has broken into the present time (Mark 10:30; Heb. 6:5), even though "the present evil age" (Gal. 1:4) continues, God is King. In the interim or "dual" period of the church, upon whom the ends of the ages have overlapped (cf. 1 Cor. 10:11, KJV; note the plural "ends"), the first "end" being the termination of the premessianic age and the second being the beginning of the age to come, in this period God is King. And in the heavenly age to come which has left behind the present evil age (Matt. 12:32; Luke 20:34-36), God is King.

God is the *King of ages* in the yet deeper sense that he is King of eternity. It is not enough to say that his life is endless or that he lives a "timeless" life. He understands the duration of time, the passing of time, and men's impatience at having to wait for the elapse of time, but he is not subject to it. He is "above" time in the sense that he is Lord of time. He is not limited or impeded by time. His time span is infinite: the whole course of human history, past, present and future, lies before his eyes like a flash. This has practical results for the Christian.

A man was watching a telecast of a Graham Crusade, broadcast over the North American network some months after the actual evangelistic campaign in one of the major cities. During Dr. Graham's sermon he found himself praying that many would have come forward as a public profession of their faith in Christ. He was praying not only that men would respond in their homes as they watched the telecast, but that they would have come forward some months ago. He was well aware of the philosophic difficulties involved but he continued to pray. It is the inference of faith from the fact that God is *King of ages*, Lord of time. We pray for people remote from us at the other side of the world; why should we not pray for people "remote" in time? This is not to be taken as the advocacy of prayers for the dead, which cannot be justified by the New Testament. It is the living who are in mind.

Immortal: An echo of Greek philosophy with the meaning of "imperishable." God will never cease to be. Though *invisible,* as spirit (John 4:24), we have seen his glory in the face of his Son (2 Cor. 4:6), his image (Col. 1:15). He is *the only God.* This does not mean, as some sentimental preachers have occasionally suggested, that he is (or was) "the lonely God." Creation was undoubtedly due to grace but it was not to minister to a solitary God, as we learn from the doctrine of the Holy Trinity. He is the blessed God (see on 1:11). *Honor* is to be given to him from now onward and through all eternity. To give him *glory* is to recognize his being, character, majesty and might as he has manifested himself, preeminently in his Son, and humbly so to address him. (Cf. Rev. 4:8 f., 11; 5:9 f. See also 1 Tim. 6:16.)

Amen: Assent. Paul stops; the congregation speaks. (Joachim Jeremias, *Die Briefe an Timothy und Titus,* p. 14.)

3. The Charge Renewed (1:18-20)

The man who was to charge false teachers to desist is now himself solemnly charged to fulfill the prophetic promise by not withdrawing from the Christian warfare. Both faith and conscience demand this. The rejection of conscience, as certain incidents sadly show, means the shipwreck of faith followed by spiritual discipline.

Verse 18: This charge I commit to you, Timothy, my son—a summary and reaffirmation of verses 3–11. The *charge* recalls the same word in verses 3 and 5. Timothy was to charge others, and the duty was not self-imposed. Paul said, *I commit* it to you. It is a word which in other circumstances would be appropriate for making a deposit in a banking account. The charge was a deposit in Timothy's possession. If he guarded it well (cf. 6:20; 2 Tim. 1:14) it would be like a tape or record with an insistent message, "banish error; teach the truth."

My son represents the same Greek word as "child" in verse 2. It brings a warm affection into what otherwise might have seemed somewhat formal and official.

In accordance with the prophetic utterances which pointed to you: It was not Paul's whim but God's will. The prophecies may have *pointed* Paul to Timothy; certainly the earlier *prophetic utterances* had their bearing on Timothy. He was their subject. Paul did not mean that he had found predictions of Timothy in the Old Testament. Men who had gifts of spiritual sensitiveness and speech, New Testament prophets, had spoken of Timothy. Prophets had recognized in Barnabas and Saul the divine choice for missionary work (Acts 13:1–3). Timothy had excited comment and was well spoken of "by the brethren" (Acts 16:1–3); in the fluid state of the ministry at that time Paul may well have detected a prophetic note in the remarks made about the young man. At least one person may have suggested that Timothy had a "gift" for ministry, which ought to be exercised. When he was ordained (1 Tim. 4:14), prophetic utterance must have had regard to the promise which he had shown and must have looked forward to a fruitful ministry. Paul recalled these hopeful words, and in the light of them and indeed in reliance on them, he committed the charge to Timothy.

That inspired by them you may wage the good warfare: The vision must be recaptured. The earlier prophecies not only confirmed the rightness of the ordination which gave him formal authorization, but by remembering them afresh he would be emboldened to go into spiritual battle and be given the tenacity for a long war. *The good warfare* is more than an individual fight or even a private war. It is the common war to which all Christians are called—the one war, not "a" war. The term implies that there is constant opposition; thought and effort are required and hardship must be endured. The warrior must be a man of one idea (cf. 2 Tim. 2:3 f.). Motive must not be forgotten. The right weapons must be used (2 Cor. 10:3–6).

By them refers to the prophetic utterances and the plural should be noted. Either the prophecy was repeated more than once and came to its climax at the time of ordination, or there was more than one speaker. Both may be true. The remembrance of several occasions and several speakers could mean much to Timothy when he sought "to rekindle the gift of God" (2 Tim. 1:6).

Verse 19: Holding faith and a good conscience: The basic means of sustaining "military" morale. *Faith* and *conscience* are interdependent. There is a sense in which effort is required, which is suggested by *holding*. If we say that a person is "a man of faith," we mean that he goes on believing; otherwise we must say that he was (not "is") a man of faith. Faith has to be "exercised." Similarly *conscience* remains *good* if it is obeyed. The close association of faith and conscience (cf. 1:5 and discussion; 3:9) asserts the association of religion and behavior and, in the intellectual realm, that of theology and ethics. Either is impoverished without the other. Faith without works is dead (Jas. 2:17, 26). Conscience without faith lacks the instruction of the Word and the Holy Spirit, is in danger of insensitiveness, and in the keenest struggles has missed the deepest inspiration. God's commandments are not burdensome to the Christian (though they are weighty), for the victory that overcomes the seductive world is faith (cf. 1 John 5:3–5). But faith must be held and not waver (Jas. 1:6–8).

By rejecting conscience, certain persons have made shipwreck of their faith—the inevitable ruin of one-sided religion. This verse illustrates as well as exhorts. The unity of faith and conscience is shown by a brief reference to men who have rejected one of them—conscience. With some violence conscience was rejected and faith was wrecked. A man who continually disobeys God will find himself further and further away from him, until finally he does not want to say his prayers. His faith has withered and God has to seek him out (Gen. 3:8 f.). How much more will those who deliberately disobey in a grave decision against the light find that they have lost touch with God. Thrust aside the pilot on the bridge and be deaf to his instructions, and your ship will run aground and break up. *Rejecting* means "pushing aside" (cf. Acts 7:27, 39; 13:46). One can almost see the self-willed captain giving the pilot a push and himself taking the wheel—and the consequent wreck. Intellectual "difficulties" with Christian belief are often morally based.

Verse 20: Among them Hymenaeus and Alexander, whom I have delivered to Satan that they may learn not to blaspheme: Names of actual men heighten the seriousness. They may be the same as those in 2 Timothy 2:17 f.; 4:14. They had rejected conscience, but their act seems to have been involved with false teaching. They had been *delivered to Satan* as a sentence of excommunication. In the light of precedent we may say that it was done by the apostle and by the church, not by the apostle in isolation (1 Cor. 5:5). The expression may have originated in Job 2:6, LXX. The sentence, though severe, was merciful and remedial in purpose. We must not think of a person banned from a modern church yet still enjoying "religion on the radio" and a normal social life. The realm of Satan was a dangerous one, and absence from the fellowship of the early church a real deprivation. (Cf. 1 Cor. 11:30.) There is an approximation to Matthew 18:15–17. Notice that rejecting conscience and possibly teaching false doctrine may be interpreted as blasphemy. It is withholding from God the honor which is his due.

III. THE STANDARDS OF THE CHURCH (2:1–3:16)

1. Public Worship (2:1–15)

In the household of God, the church, there are certain patterns of conduct which should be observed. Public worship is considered first. Directions for prayer are outlined, for which a theological reason is given, and the demeanor appropriate to Christian women is described and their status defined. Paul next deals with the ministry. The qualifications of bishops or pastoral supervisors are listed in detail, followed by those of deacons, with a side glance at women. Finally stress is laid on behavior in the Christian community, the church of the living God.

Prayer is of prime importance and its range is wide. The objects of intercession are by no means limited to fellow members. The praying church should look out on all the world. Such a comprehensive view reflects that of God himself. Women should not draw attention to themselves by excess in dress. Modesty and moderation should be their guide and submissiveness in thought and conduct their attitude.

(1) Prayer (2:1–8)

Prayer of every kind is to be offered for all men, with intercession and thanksgiving mingled. Rulers are specially mentioned because of their wide influence. The object of prayer is social peace and godly life. The universal compassion thus implied recalls the universal sweep of the divine offer of salvation, the universal mediation between the one God and all men of Christ crucified, and the universal field for the proclamation of the gospel.

Verse 1: First of all, then, I urge that supplications, prayers, intercessions, and thanksgivings be made for all men: Prayer is the life blood of all worship. Without it there is only a skeleton or at best a beautiful body, and worship lacks vitality because it has no contact with God. *Then* is resumptive and not without some logical force. In company with *urge* it picks up the same word in 1:3, points to the "charge" of 1:18, and recalls Timothy to the directions which the letter gives for his guidance. *All men* is a natural development of the sinners of 1:15. It is plain that Timothy was an "officiating clergyman" as well as a preacher and teacher, and had the responsibility of conducting public worship and drawing up the "order of service." Paul was not unmindful of the necessity of doing everything decently and in order, and for the purpose of edification (1 Cor. 14:26, 40). Matters must not get out of hand, whether of doctrine or behavior. There are times and occasions when worship is spontaneous, but in general it has to be planned in advance, with thought given to its purpose and content.

The order of words is not of major importance. The *supplications* are requests made to God (cf. Phil. 4:6). *Prayers* may be of any kind. As a generic term the word covers petitions, thanksgiving and praise, together with the confession of sin. *Intercessions* conveys the idea of a man or a group putting a word into the ear of a superior on behalf of some other person. The Jews spoke to the Roman governor, Festus, against Paul (Acts 25:24), but the church has to approach God and be "for" men and not against them. "Intervention" is sometimes the fitting word. In the mercy of God it may be that the *intercessions* of the church prolong the patience of God with the sins of mankind (cf. Rom. 2:4; 9:22; 2 Pet. 3:15). *Thanksgivings,* prayers of thanks, are both a joy and an obligation (cf. 1 Thess. 1:2 f.; 5:18). Some scholars see in this word (*eucharistia*) a reference to the Eucharist or Lord's Supper. It was certainly regarded as a thanksgiving, and the reference is possible but not absolutely necessary. *Thanksgivings* are possible without the actual service of Eucharist.

Notice the absence of narrowness or exclusiveness. The prayers of every kind should *be made for all men.* Paul was again "persuading with authority" (see on 1:3). The student as well as the church at large should ponder the implications of giving thanks for all men. It is not only a question of giving thanks for conversions. Some men will never be converted, but some parts of their political administration or their social life may have been of benefit to their fellows. The church should give thanks accordingly.

This principle is capable of wide application. For example, the church could give thanks for scrupulous fairness on the part of a judge who was an atheist and whose private life would not bear examination, especially if judicial impartiality led to the vindication of an innocent church member being tried on a serious charge. From another point of view if the judge himself were providentially saved from a grievous accident, the church could give thanks in another way. In the first instance, thanks could be given for the judge's own attitude; in the second, thanks could be offered which the judge himself should have offered, and would have done if he had been a believing man. The former act returns thanks for the judge's behavior in court; the latter expresses thanksgiving on behalf of the judge, as he does not give thanks himself. Prayer, including the prayer of thanksgiving, should be as wide in its range as love. This verse may have special relevance and poignancy in times of persecution.

Verse 2: For kings and all who are in high positions—because of the burdens which they bear and the influence which they exercise. The plural of *kings* is deliberate. 1 Peter 2:17 is restricted to the emperor at the time of writing. Paul meant the emperor at the time of writing and his successors in office as well. He was not thinking of individuals in their private capacity but as office holders. *Kings* was used of the Roman emperors as supreme rulers, and of petty monarchs like Herod or Agrippa (cf. Matt. 17:25). Once more Paul had in mind the local kings and their successors. *All who are in high positions* would include governors and men of eminence in the law or the army, men of power and influence whatever their actual rank or authority—what is sometimes called "the ruling class." "Grandees," "magnates," "leading men" is the idea (cf. Mark 6:21; Acts 28:7).

Prayer for such men is wider than prayer for their conversion. The attitude to be adopted is not that of servility but reflects the Christian doctrine of the state as instituted by God for the welfare of men. However wicked the rulers may be, anarchy is worse (Judg. 21:25). The teaching of Paul is an elaboration of that of Jesus (Rom. 13:1-7; John 19:11). In John 19:10 f. "power" means "authority." The instructions which Paul gave to Timothy are therefore permanently binding on the church. The church is not a revolutionary force in the generally accepted meaning of the term, however the "leaven" of its gospel may work out in society. Nor is it a slavish supporter of the status quo. But it must not be guilty of treason. Historical circumstances and apocalyptic visions give a different emphasis in the Book of Revelation, and in any case the state is not eternal. Even non-Christian and evil men need the support and influence of prayer.

Further implications should be noted. Prayer should be made *for* the emperor, not "to" him. This is an implicit denial of Caesar worship. The emperor himself is under the law of God.

That we may lead a quiet and peaceable life, godly and respectful in every way: Peace for and in the church. *Quiet* means the opposite of "movement" (Acts 21:30, KJV; cf. 24:5, KJV). It is the contrast, in philosophy, between motion and rest. *Peaceable* (*hēsuchion*) seems to imply the absence of disturbance (cf. 1 Thess. 4:11; 2 Thess. 3:12). The result of the prayer, which is indeed its purpose, is not the stagnation of the church but the opportunity for worship, the growth in holiness and the work of evangelism. Some people, ecclesiastical agitators, seem to think that one of the marks of a living church is to be in a constant state of uproar. Paul did not look at it in this way. He had had his share of riots as well as revivals, but his aim was not to stir up strife or political dissension. Incompetent government and the consequent widespread unrest in the world may be a challenge to the work of evangelism, but it is no necessary condition for the essential life of believing men. (Cf. Acts 24:2.) Indeed the very uproar may be the occasion of temptation. The aim is the peace of the world and peace in the hearts of members of the church.

To be *godly* means to be aware of one's dependence on God, to give him worthy praise, and to conduct oneself in a manner which is pleasing to him: the discharge of duty toward God in every way. *Respectful* is a pedestrian term but hard to replace. It suggests the expression of the former godliness or piety. It means taking piety seriously, as befits citizens of heaven (Phil. 3:20). It is reverent not only toward God but "in church"—it does not throw Bibles about or treat pews or the Lord's Table in a secular manner. It is not flippant in divine matters. It manifests the depth of faith rather than the frivolity of heathenism. It is not solemn or humorless but is fundamentally serious, and is calculated to gain the respect, if not the imitation, of unbelievers and of the authorities. Some see here the Greek equivalent of the Hebraic Luke 1:75.

A literal rendering would be "in all piety and seriousness." On the analogy of the sentence, "He spent his quiet life in all North America," we may infer that no part of piety and seriousness is to be unexplored. There should be no lapses.

Verse 3: This is good, and it is acceptable in the sight of God our Savior:
Prayer for all is good in itself and it pleases God. It reveals an attitude of
love to all and a desire for all. *This* is a comprehensive reference to verse 1.
Good means "fine," "beautiful" (*kalon*), but it is perhaps a little fanciful
to think of God looking at the praying church (*in the sight of God*) and
finding it "beautiful." The point is that the universal prayer of the church
accords with God's will.

*Verse 4: Who desires all men to be saved and to come to the knowledge of
the truth:* The range of divine benevolence justifies the range of human
prayer. *Who* means "as one in fact who," "inasmuch as he," and introduces
the reason why universal prayer is acceptable to God. The *and* is epexeget-
ical or explicative, implying "that is to say." To *come to the knowledge of the
truth* is the means *to be saved.* If men have to *come* they obviously start by
being at a distance. *Knowledge of the truth* is not innate. There is a Johannine ring about this phrase (cf. John 17:3). It contains no suggestion of
Tennyson's "We have but faith, we cannot know." In all genuine faith there
is an exercise of the mind in which statements are apprehended. For example,
the preacher says that "Christ died for our sins." Some men do not know
this. After they have heard the preacher they do know it. Then they put
their trust in Christ and exercise "saving faith." They have not gone back on
what the preacher said. They have embraced it at a deeper level, at which
they have given themselves to the living Christ. In their very faith they had
knowledge, knowledge of a truth and of him who is truth. (Cf. John 14:6.)
Christ contains, and is in himself, the whole of God's revelation, God's reality
manifested in act. There is a Greek savor about the words *knowledge* and
truth, though the intimacy of the Hebraic "knowing" is not absent. "Samuel
did not yet know the Lord" (1 Sam. 3:7). For *saved* see on 1:1. It naturally
follows "God our Savior" of verse 3.

All men should receive some stress. It is contrasted with the exclusiveness
of Judaism, the emotional prejudice of which is seen in Acts 22:21–23, and
with the esoteric pride of the later Gnosticism, which reserved salvation for
those who had been initiated and had received special knowledge denied to
the vulgar herd. God does not shut out. His grace is free and his characteristic word is "come!" He *desires* all men to be saved. This raises profound
questions about the will of God, suggested indeed by the verb (*thelei*). Is his
will always accomplished and, in particular, will all men be saved? The New
Testament shows that God's will is not always done (Matt. 6:10; 7:21;
12:50). The will of Jesus was not always done (Matt. 23:37; Mark 7:24).

From this it is apparent that the will of God must not be considered in
abstraction. It is not naked will, going into action mechanically and overcoming all opposition like a bulldozer. It is related to the human situation
and has distinctions within itself. It may be regarded as absolute in regard
to the original creation. God spoke, and it was done; there was no question
of any opposition. But in dealing with men we must think of modifications.

Consider the death of Jesus. Who was responsible? It is common knowledge
that Judas (Matt. 26:14–25, 45–48), the Jewish leaders, and Pilate himself
delivered him up (Matt. 27:18, 26). It is not always remembered that Jesus
also delivered himself up (Eph. 5:2, 25; cf. Gal. 2:20) and that God delivered him up (Rom. 8:32; cf. Acts 2:23). Now if the actions of Jesus and
Judas are compared, we must say that they both did the will of God but in

a different way. Our Lord always did what was pleasing to his Father and in the cross acted in accordance with the divine decree. But the deed of Judas was sin and merited the "woe" (Matt. 26:24; 27:3 f.; Luke 22:22). Jesus did the will of God and received divine aid to help him do it (Luke 22:42 f.). Judas did the will of God in that if God had withdrawn the sustaining power which upholds the universe he could have done nothing but would have ceased to exist. Judas further did the will of God in that he was unconsciously furthering the plan of salvation. The act of Jesus was approved by God. The act of Judas was sin, but was overruled and used.

It is a significant fact that Paul's Greek word (*thelō*) is used in the Septuagint as one of the renderings of the Hebrew verb *haphētz*, "to delight in" ("He delighteth in mercy," Mic. 7:18, KJV). Similarly God delights in the universal gospel. And just as his Son on earth once "meant to pass by them, but . . ." (Mark 6:48–50), so God willed . . . but . . . Paul's statement is thus not an absolute, mechanical one. We may not speak of divine afterthoughts, but there may well be logical priorities in the mind of God. The final solution is not possible on earth. "The secret things belong to the Lord our God; but the things that are revealed belong to us . . ." (Deut. 29:29; cf. 2 Tim. 3:7.)

Verse 5: For there is one God, and there is one mediator between God and men, the man Christ Jesus: No opposition to the universal divine benevolence and no failure to communicate. The argument is: pray for all, because God is kind toward all; he has no rival to impede him or colleague to dissuade him; no indecision, no fickleness, no partiality. His purpose of salvation is manifested by Christ and is implemented in him. Christ bridges the gulf between the holy God on the one side and sinful humanity on the other. He is the complete embodiment of the purpose and the achievement of God. It would be incorrect to say that some men find their salvation in one way and others in other ways, and yet other men find it in Christ. "There is salvation in no one else" (Acts 4:12). No member of the human race could provide it: "all have sinned . . ." (Rom. 3:23). Salvation depends entirely on God. But it also depends on the cross. The Savior can only be God, but if he is to die he must be man. The only person to satisfy these requirements is the last Adam, who is "from heaven" (1 Cor. 15:22, 45–47; cf. Rom. 5:12–21, esp. v. 14). He includes within himself, just as the first Adam did, the whole of humanity. On the cross he bore men's sins. Individual men receive salvation when they repent of their sins and have faith in him. They are thus incorporated into the second Adam by faith, who is the head of the new spiritual humanity, and in him they have access to God. God and men are thus brought together. The gospel is offered to all and hence *there is one mediator between God and* (all) *men,* one "middleman," "intermediary" or "go-between." He is *Christ Jesus* (see on 1:1), himself man. The *mediator* is both God and man. On the cross he did what only God could do: offer a sinless life of obedience. On the cross he did what only man could do: as the second Adam he represented all humanity. But it was representative, for humanity suffered nothing. He was therefore men's Substitute. The reference to the cross here is in anticipation of the next verse.

Verse 6: Who gave himself as a ransom for all: God's universal benevolence in action. Notice the *all,* which should receive some stress. Prayer should be

for all (v. 1) and it is acceptable to God our Savior because salvation is for
all (vv. 3 f.). Salvation is made possible because there is a mediator who
unites two parties, God and men, i.e., God and all men. In his work of
mediation he gave himself for *all*. It is worth reflecting that our Lord *gave*
himself. In spite of the machinations of Judas, the malignancy of the Jewish
leaders, the fickleness of the mob, and the craven attitude of Pilate, the
Savior was not trapped but was master of the situation throughout the Passion. He was the victim of neither a trick of the subtle nor the force of the
violent. He *gave* himself.

His death was *for all,* and he is the mediator between God and all men.
This does not imply that all are automatically saved. It does mean that
anything which any man had to do has been done, and done by the mediator,
and that if they are to be saved they must come to God through him.

The word for *ransom* is *antilutron* and this is its only occurrence in the
New Testament. It must therefore be interpreted in the light of its simple
form, *lutron*. Its leading idea is that of deliverance by purchase. In a recent
learned study,[1] Dr. David Hill gives its meaning in biblical Greek as "the
ransom paid to gain freedom," or "the means by which release is achieved."
It has figured prominently in scholarly discussion of Mark 10:45 (cf. Matt.
20:28) and especially of the phrase *lutron anti pollōn,* "a ransom for many."
Its background, not so much of language as of ideas, is that of the atoning
value of the suffering of martyrs, and of the vicarious suffering of the Servant
of Isaiah (Isa. 53:4–12). (Even the language of 2 Maccabees 7:37; 4 Maccabees 6:29; 17:21 anticipates at some points that of Mark.) Dr. Hill feels,
with considerable justification, that *ransom* is best interpreted as "atoning
substitute." The "many" must not be regarded as a limitation; its contrast
is not "all" but "the one." A modern parallel is found in the words of Winston
Churchill after the Battle of Britain: "never was so much owed by so many
to so few." "Many," in felicitous contrast to the "few," really stands for "all."
Paul's use of "all" and "many" in Romans 5:18 f. is similar.

If we bear in mind the picture of deliverance by purchase, we are entitled
to dwell on the cost (cf. 1 Pet. 1:18 f.). Christ *gave himself,* his blood, his
life. But it is straining the metaphor unduly to ask to whom the payment was
made. On the other hand, if we are thinking of "atoning substitute," it cannot
be wrong to ask not only who benefits from the atonement but to whom it is
directed. Atonement concerns sin, and sin is more than vice or crime: its
primary relationship is to God. "Christ . . . gave himself up for us, a fra-
grant offering and sacrifice to God" (Eph. 5:2).

These reflections are stimulated by the fact that our exegesis is not of a
bare and isolated text. Verses 5–6a are regarded by many scholars as a
quotation easily recognized by the readers. It has the ring of a creed about
it, and a creed attempts to summarize Christian truth. It points to something
further, like a signpost. It is a means of identification, whereby like-minded
men may recognize one another and have fellowship together. It is a battle
cry, to rally the true disciples.

Mark 10:45 links the Suffering Servant of Isaiah with the Son of Man

---

1. David Hill, *Greek Words and Hebrew Meanings: Studies in the Semantics of
Soteriological Terms* (Cambridge: University Press, 1967), pp. 76–81.

(cf. Dan. 7:13 f.). The latter term was used by Stephen (Acts 7:56) but does not appear in the epistles. The term "Lord" sums up all his glories, not the least of which is the forgiveness of sins (Mark 2:10). Timothy and other readers (or listeners) would understand what Paul was saying.

The testimony to which was borne at the proper time—by Christ. It is possible to drop the *to* and make *the testimony* a summary in apposition to verses 4–6, evidence of God's saving aim. The cross is Christ's testimony to God, the evidence of God's universal benevolence. It is also God's own testimony to his own benevolence, because he sent his Son. It all happened *at the proper time* (cf. 6:15; Titus 1:3), that is, at the time of God's own choosing (cf. Rom. 5:6; Gal. 4:4; Eph. 3:5, 9–11; Col. 1:26 f.).

Verse 7: For this I was appointed a preacher and apostle (I am telling the truth, I am not lying), a teacher of the Gentiles in faith and truth: Paul was commissioned to proclaim what would otherwise have been unknown. (Cf. 2 Tim. 1:11.) The New Testament *preacher* is aptly termed a "herald." As Spicq puts it so engagingly (p. 62), he is not entrusted with delicate missions. He must not alter the message which has been given to him, and he has no room to maneuver. He does not suggest but proclaims. He does not lead men to think, but "tells them." He is not a diplomat completing a whispered deal on the back stairs or advancing arguments in order to obtain better terms. He shouts from the housetops. He must not be given to garrulity or to exaggeration; nor must he understate his message. Such is the spirit which animated Paul in his continuation of the testimony for which he *was appointed.*

The nature of the testimony or evidence should be noticed. Christ himself in his work is the testimony; Paul in his preaching is the testimony. In one sense the testimony is thus repeated; in another sense it is not. Christ died once for all. Paul's testimony tells of that event and its meaning; he does not do it all over again.

There is clearly a distinction between the work of the preacher and that of the pastor. The preacher is characterized by publicity; the pastor often does his best work in private. The preacher does not discuss; he proclaims. In the privacy of counseling, the pastor may enter into discussion in order to show sympathy, to find out what the difficulties really are, and for other similar reasons. Both preacher and pastor are inflexible in refusing to alter the message; but the pastor will listen when the preacher will not. When the pastor ascends the pulpit he assumes the robe of the preacher, with all the knowledge gained in the counseling room. It does not affect his vital message but it may give it a warmth and sympathy otherwise lacking, or an intimate knowledge of the needs of the (or "an") individual. His approach may be more strategically worked out, but his goal remains the same—to glorify Christ in bringing men to him or in bringing them closer to him, in trust and obedience.

For *apostle* see on 1:1. *Preacher* implies that in relation to the congregation the herald has the initiative. *Apostle* tells us of his authority, because he has been commissioned and sent. *Teacher* suggests that something new is being brought; we do not normally teach what is already known. Even a "refresher course" carries the implication that much has been forgotten.

The fierce asseveration, *I am telling the truth . . . ,* coming as it does immediately after *apostle,* revives hot memories (Rom. 9:1; 2 Cor. 11:31; Gal. 1:20) and perhaps nips in the bud any opposition which Timothy might encounter (cf. 1:3–7). *A teacher of the Gentiles* would not be limited to Jews. Paul's ministry was thus universal in scope, and this reinforces his argument hitherto. Prayer should be for all men, because all men are within the divine benevolence, the mediation and work of Christ, and the range of Paul's ministry. Therefore pray for all! Paul was a teacher *in* the subjects of *faith and truth* (see on v. 4) and he taught as a believer himself who knew God in Christ, without misunderstanding or altering his message—i.e., sincerely and truly.

Verse 8: I desire then that in every place the men should pray, lifting holy hands without anger or quarreling: The conclusion of the whole argument, with directions added. *Then* summarily introduces the conclusion and recalls verse 1. *Desire (boulomai)* is not the same as in verse 4. "It is my wish" brings out the aspect of authority—not "I should like." It is not so strong as part of the subtitle of some British editions of the King James Version, "translated . . . by His Majesty's special command," but the authority is there.

Two interpretations are possible. (1) "I wish then that in every place (where the gospel has been preached and the church planted) prayer (for all men) may be offered by the men (as usual—not the women), lifting holy hands . . . ." This accords with other Scriptures (1 Cor. 1:2; 2 Cor. 2:14; 1 Thess. 1:8). (2) "I wish then that prayer (for all) may be offered by the men, lifting holy hands in every place without anger . . . ." If the second interpretation is right, Paul was giving directions for worship, a rubric, to be followed everywhere. He was not blind to the value of uniformity. (Cf. 1 Cor. 4:17; 7:17; 14:33.) On the other hand he was no formalist and seems to have recognized the place of spontaneity in worship (1 Cor. 14:24–32).

On the whole the first interpretation is preferable. It coheres better with the general argument of the section, through which the theme of "all" runs. Prayer for all men would be matched by prayer in all the church. (Cf. Mal. 1:11; John 4:21.)

Standing and *lifting* the *hands* was a characteristic attitude in ancient prayer (cf. Exod. 9:29, 33; 17:11 f.; Pss. 63:4; 141:2). The gesture was combined with kneeling when Solomon prayed (1 Kings 8:54). Psalm 44:20 is rightly rendered by Briggs, "Have we . . . spread forth our palms to a foreign god?" [1]

There is a rich symbolism here. The outstretched palms eloquently picture the longing felt by the worshiper to receive the divine blessing. Apart from prayer the *hands* are the instruments of human action, into which is concentrated the guilt or innocency of the man who did the deed (Gen. 20:5; Ps. 24:4; Mark 9:43; Acts 2:23). The whole personality, so to speak, is present in the hands, whether or not those Old Testament scholars are right in seeing consciousness diffused over the whole body.

Now Paul was not insisting that every time prayer was offered the hands must be held up; nor was he emphasizing the hands as such. He would ob-

---

1. Charles A. Briggs and Emilie G. Briggs, *A Critical and Exegetical Commentary on the Book of Psalms* (Edinburgh: T. & T. Clark, 1909; reprint ed. Naperville, Ill.: Alec R. Allenson, 1951–52), 1:381.

viously hope that they would be as clean as soap and water could make them, but this was far from being his main point. In his desire for the hands to be *holy,* he spoke of them as expressions of the mind and spirit. He was not advocating ritual without reality. Men must not offer the prayer of intercession from a position of unholiness. They must not exercise the ministry of disciples without possessing the spirit of true discipleship themselves. "The hand of him who betrays me is with me on the table" (Luke 22:21). Intercession no less than the Communion Service demands holiness. (See also Isa. 1:15 f.; Jas. 4:8.) This is not only a divine requirement. In actual experience unforgiven sin, including *anger or quarreling,* blocks prayer. The man who tries to pray is aware that he does not "get through." (For the "blocking" of prayer cf. 1 Pet. 3:7. Obvious comments are Matt. 5:22–24; 6:12–15; Mark 11:25; Phil. 2:14.) Wiclif (Wyclif) renders part of the last text by "without grucchingis and doutingis." A church of men given to questioning, doubting, debating, "grutching" and *anger* and *quarreling* will not be a church of prevailing prayer.

The classical illustration of unholy hands is found in Shakespeare's *Macbeth.* The sleepwalking Lady Macbeth speaks: "Here's the smell of the blood still: all the perfumes of Arabia will not sweeten this little hand." The doctor in attendance speaks a little later: "More needs she the divine than the physician." (Act 5, scene 1.)

(2) Women (2:9–15)

Women's dress should befit their Christian profession. They should manifest modesty in mind and a sanity in dress which spurns excess. Women should accordingly avoid ostentation in fashion or expense. Their best adornment is good works. They should be submissive, not teachers but taught, for which there is biblical authority. The normal life of womanhood does not deny them salvation.

Verse 9: Also that women should adorn themselves modestly and sensibly in seemly apparel: The outer dress is the index of the inner mind. There is clearly place for some adornment: Paul was not asking for sackcloth. *Modestly* implies a certain fear of self-assertion against society. "Loud" clothes shout against society's aesthetic sense; scanty attire offends the feeling for moral decency. In the present "mini" age (mini-car, mini-skirt) Paul's attitude may not always be appreciated. *Sensibly* would suggest that thought has been given to the clothes to be worn and the decision taken "not to go too far." There is a golden mean between a mere utilitarian covering, a dowdiness or even a slovenliness, and an excess which would make onlookers think of a fashion parade to elicit money from the purses of wealthy women or of a ball or formal dance where the socially ambitious may draw attention to themselves. An overdressed woman is in danger of resembling an embellished tomb (Matt. 23:27–29) rather than a place of worship (Luke 21:5; cf. Isa. 3:18–24; 1 Pet. 3:3–5). This must not be regarded as a scheme of "directions for dress," unrelated to the context. The *also* (*hōsautōs*) carries on the atmosphere of the previous section. "My wish is likewise that the women may pray and adorn themselves. . . ."

Not with braided hair or gold or pearls or costly attire: Examples of the previously mentioned seemliness. The *braided hair* is more than the simple plait of the schoolgirl. It corresponds more to the elaborate coiffure or "hairdo" of today. Paul had more interest in basic principles than in philistinism, and it is principles which should be kept in mind in applying the text to a modern congregation. Is thought being given to the effect on women of slender education and immature spiritual experience? Is femininity so exaggerated that the thoughts of the men are diverted from the prayers? In Christ the distinction of sex is not obliterated but sublimated (cf. Gal. 3:28), and nothing should be allowed to work against this. Is too much attention being drawn to the differences between rich and poor? (Cf. 1 Cor. 11:20–22.) It would be different if all the women of a country dressed in the way that Paul forbade. To be the exception then would defeat the purpose of his rule.

Verse 10: But by good deeds, as befits women who profess religion: Not barefaced dazzle but character and conduct. The "seemly apparel" changes from time to time, as clothes wear out. The *good deeds* are to be the permanent adornment. Paul was not only concerned with the thought of the obedience of Christians; he thought also of the "fitness" of things. Some actions no more suit a Christian than a dress of the wrong color or ill cut. We all know what is meant when a friend says: "That does not suit you." (Cf. 1 Cor. 11:13; Eph. 5:3.) *Profess* represents a Greek word meaning "promise." It is well to remember that a "profession of faith" is a promise that the faith will be exhibited in life (cf. Jas. 2:14), as in 5:16.

Verse 11: Let a woman learn in silence with all submissiveness: Feminine without being feminist. The *silence* (*hēsuchia*) is more than the absence of noise. Even a chair is silent. Paul's aim was to avoid "disturbance." (See on 2:2 and the references there given.) The implication is that *woman* needs to learn and is capable of it. The *submissiveness* here includes a willingness to be taught—without any breakdown or exception. *All* submissiveness suggests that women may not choose the subjects in which they are willing to be taught.

Verse 12: I permit no woman to teach or to have authority over men; she is to keep silent: This is less drastic than it appears. The background and Paul's whole experience must be kept in mind if we are to interpret fairly. To begin with, Paul was thinking of public worship. Even here he could think of a woman prophesying (1 Cor. 11:5), and he knew of the four women who prophesied, the unmarried daughters of Philip the evangelist (Acts 21:8 f.) at Caesarea. The remarkable woman, Priscilla, had some part in the instruction of Apollos (Acts 18:1–3, 24–26; cf. Rom. 16:3 f.; 1 Cor. 16:19; 2 Tim. 4:19). Euodia and Syntyche labored side by side with Paul in common Christian service (Phil. 4:2 f.). Paul was no misogynist. "I am not permitting . . . ."

He had adopted the same policy in writing to the Corinthians (1 Cor. 14:33–36). Women could teach the children at home (2 Tim. 1:5; 3:15); how otherwise can we explain Timothy's early knowledge of Scripture? "From whom" (previous v. 14) did he learn it? Older women were to teach the younger (Titus 2:3–5). Paul seems to have shrunk from the thought of women teaching the church as such. And in any case there was the possibility of discredit being brought on the church. There were wicked women in Corinth and in Ephesus, and many an outsider would be glad to think that women inside were no different from women outside of the church.

Women had been raised by our Lord from their inferior position in

Judaism, and Paul would have heartily concurred, and did indeed concur gladly, with their new status. All the church was one in Christ Jesus, with no emphasis on sex as such. In consequence there was something of the spirit of feminism in the air, and Paul saw its dangers. It is not unknown today for some women to be enthusiastic members of Bible study groups, with the consequent neglect of their homes (cf. Titus 2:4 f.). It can be a short step from study group to group without study, and from a regular meeting to a succession of calls—and gossip (1 Tim. 5:13). Women in the church can thus lose their balance. Instead of holding fast to the truth and being glad to be taught more about it, they will listen to anybody in the gossiping sessions and thus become a prey to anybody with a theory to sell. False teachers get invited into homes and capture the ears of credulous women. (Cf. 2 Tim. 3:6–7.)

Now does it make sense to allow any and every woman to interrupt the preacher or pose an awkward question to the teacher, when the whole church is gathered together around the Word of God? Paul would not take the risk. His policy was to exclude the silly, the credulous, and the masterful women by excluding all women from the opportunity of addressing the church. He would not allow false teachers to speak in church, even by proxy (2 Tim. 3:6 f.). It may be that his ruling caused some dissent, but the dissension could have been greater and far more serious if any crank claiming women's rights were given the floor.

To have authority over men means to domineer. The *silence* is the same as in the previous verse. There must be no disturbing element.

The circumstances of today are different. Careers and independence are open to women, many of whom have had a first-class education. Women, or some women, would today be prevented from speaking in church not on the grounds of their sex but of their incompetence to teach the faith. Some women are competent and some are not. In Paul's day most of them were not competent and he summed it up in the word "women." Today we should make a selection. In either case those who are not competent to speak should *keep silent.* The able Christian woman of today would not fall into the errors of doctrine to which the women of Paul's day were prone. But suppose she were a gossip? The question would have to be dealt with on its merits, in the light of guidance from the apostle Paul. (Cf. 1 Tim. 5:13.)

Verse 13: For Adam was formed first, then Eve: A biblical foundation for a practical policy. The woman was chronologically later than the man; physically dependent on him; and mentally oriented to him (Gen. 1:27; 2:7, 22; 1 Cor. 11:8 f.).

Verse 14: And Adam was not deceived, but the woman was deceived and became a transgressor: Woman taught man once. Never again! For Adam and Eve were looked upon by Paul as typical as well as historical. The woman was credulous and *deceived.* The punishment of womankind is pain in childbirth and subordination to her husband's rule. The force of the Greek perfect tense *(gegonen)* implies that the woman has fallen into transgression and is still in it. This reinforces Paul's argument: still credulous, still in transgression, still under the husband's rule (Gen. 3:6, 16; 1 Cor. 11:3). Paul knew that Adam was a sinner as well (Rom. 5:12–14) as Eve, but it is not part of the present argument. The woman *became* and still is *a transgressor;*

the punishment is childbearing and subordination. The fact of subordination is relevant to the question of behavior at public worship; that of childbearing is not. But Paul could not merely leave it in the air. He could not leave the Christian woman with no more than the thought that bearing children is punishment. That might make them seek careers for themselves without marriage! He therefore pointed out that the sentence was not God's last word. The career of wife and mother may lack attractiveness to the feminist but there is more to be said.

Verse 15: Yet woman will be saved through bearing children, if she continues in faith and love and holiness, with modesty: The career woman has no monopoly of salvation. We should dismiss all thoughts of attaining to salvation by bearing children; this would be a very odd form of justification by works. The same applies to the education (as opposed to the bearing) of children. Reading the sentence as an allusion to "the Childbearing," i.e., of the Messiah, is too obscure and isolated to warrant serious consideration. Paul means (or seems to mean) something like this: "You want to teach in church and be equal to men? It is against the order of creation. You do not want marriage and a family? The pressure of the 'curse' is off. Salvation will be enjoyed in the life of motherhood." This takes *teknogonia* in the widest sense, not merely in the sense of a "confinement." *If she* (literally "they," women in general) *continues* expresses the life of discipleship. Here is an answer to 4:3.

For *faith* and *love* see on 1:5. *Holiness* here is an activity, a "living for God." It arises out of holiness as a gift, which is received when a person first believes, and qualifies him to approach God. Believers are "holy ones" or "saints" (5:10; cf. Heb. 10:10, 14; "to sanctify" means to make holy). *Modesty* combines "sanity" and "moderation." Christianity does not banish thoughtfulness ("sensibly" v. 9).

We see today many instances of notable careers and of shining examples of public service to church and state in which highly gifted women lavish on others what in different circumstances would have been concentrated on their family. They deserve all recognition and praise. There have been unmarried heroines on the mission field. It may not be out of place to observe that their natural instincts have been sublimated, and in their situation rightly so. Some have a vocation to be unmarried. Yet Paul's words are a salutary reminder that the deepest satisfaction for women is to be found in the life of a Christian home. For there, too, Christ dwells; and its members, in this case particularly the mother, may enjoy salvation through faith in him, even though their "career" finds its outlet only in the care of husband and children.

2. The Ministry (3:1-13)

The seriousness with which Paul regarded the ministry is revealed in the detailed qualifications required by those who were to be appointed to the office of bishop or deacon. Bishops must be men of mind and character, with social and academic gifts, ripe in Christian experience and commanding the respect of non-Christians. Deacons are to be men of integrity, sobriety and conscientiousness. Both bishop and deacon should be the husband of one wife and a model *paterfamilias*.

(1) Bishops (3:1–7)

The office of bishop is a noble one and the qualifications required are high and of permanent significance. The bishop must be a man of able mind and excellent character, socially adaptable and tactful, and able to teach and lead. In everything he must be above reproach, including marital and family relationships, deeply grounded in the faith and commanding the respect of all.

Verse 1: The saying is sure: If any one aspires to the office of bishop, he desires a noble task: A timely word, to magnify the ministry. (Cf. Rom. 11:13.) The ministry is always in danger of being undervalued when false teachers take it upon themselves energetically to spread their doctrines in the church (cf. 1:3). The statement of the nobility of the ministry is enhanced by its introduction, *the saying is sure* (cf. 1:15). It is to be believed. The emphasis is not on personalities but on the nature of the work to be done. It may well be that the people of Ephesus needed to be convinced. It is uncongenial to think of a man "wanting" to be a bishop. Paul was no doubt thinking of official candidature for office rather than mere ambition. The Greek word behind *aspires* is neutral: it is used in a bad sense in 6:10 and in a good sense in Hebrews 11:16. The same is true of *desires* (Acts 20:33, "coveted"; Luke 22:15).

The office of bishop (*episkopē*) is not the later monarchical episcopate. What is meant is pastoral oversight in the widest sense. At this period the best word for *episkopos* is not "bishop" but "supervisor." "Overseer" would be acceptable if it were not for its objectionable associations with slavery on the plantations. Whereas in the later episcopate there was one bishop for each region, vested with complete authority, the situation was much more fluid in New Testament times. Thus the church in Philippi had a plurality of supervisors (*episkopoi,* cf. Phil. 1:1), like the church at Ephesus (Acts 20:17, 28). In the latter text the RSV gives "guardians" for the same Greek word.

It is clear that in Ephesus the elders were also supervisors, and certainly the duties of the two bodies resembled each other (1 Tim. 3:1–7; 5:17–20). The appointment of elders in every church (Acts 14:23; cf. Titus 1:5) was in line with the practice of Judaism (cf. Acts 5:21) with its "senate" (*gerousia*) or "council of elders" (*presbyterion,* Acts 22:5). In the earlier days "gifted" men exercised a varied ministry (1 Cor. 12:4–11, 28–30; cf. Eph. 4:11); the movement at the time of the Pastoral Epistles was towards an "official" ministry. To this day, some faithful men in office shine more in "routine" duties than in the manifestation of "gifts." To have the oversight of the church of God is not only to bear office; it means that there is work to be done, which is the meaning of *task,* and it is *noble.* It is fine ministry, and because of its nature the holder of the office should be given respect. Duty well done will command respect (cf. 3:13).

Verse 2: Now a bishop must be above reproach . . . an apt teacher: The qualifications to be held by candidates for office. This is shown by verse 6. Once in office a new bishop could not dedicate himself to not being a recent convert! Obviously he should exercise the moral qualities outlined. *Above reproach* dominates the whole list. Its meaning is best seen by a reference to Luke 20:20, 26. It must be impossible for the candidate to be "caught out" in word or deed; in particular in failing in any of the characteristics set out.

He must be *the husband of one wife.* Various attitudes have been taken by commentators to this somewhat unusual expression. Some have thought that it requires clerical, and in particular, episcopal marriage. No bishop must be a bachelor! But Paul was hardly the man to make such a demand (cf. 1 Cor. 7:7 f.; 9:5). Others see a prohibition of polygamy; but in New Testament times it would have been as unthinkable if not as absurd to forbid polygamy as to forbid a Christian life devoted to murder. A superficially convincing theory regards the words as forbidding second marriage on the death of the first wife. This anticipates the later disapproval of second marriages and reflects the high estimate later given to celibacy. Paul, however, could make room for second marriages (Rom. 7:1–3; 1 Cor. 7:39), and it is doubtful if he would countenance a "higher" moral standard for the ministry than for the church members generally. It may be that a man who had divorced his wife was in danger of being "caught out" by gossips or even by serious critics. Innocent or not, he could be charged with "hardness of heart." It could be suggested that he was inflexible in thought, rigid in will, cold in emotion and possessed of a conscience which could never learn (cf. Mark 10:2–9). The charges might be entirely wrong and his conduct might have been exemplary. But the fact that they could be made at all would be enough to spoil his candidature.

In spite of the attractiveness of this interpretation, however, it would seem that there is another one which is even better. Light is thrown onto the subject by Ephesians 5:25–33. A husband should love his wife. In so doing he loves himself, for husband and wife are one. When a man has *one wife* there is a community with two members who in a deep and real sense are one. Paul was thinking of a man at the time of his candidature for office. The appropriate questions would be: Is he married? Does the marriage "work"? Does it fulfill the ideal of marriage? If it does, the two are one and in particular the man is *husband of one wife,* to whom he is completely joined. Second marriage is not contemplated and rejected; it does not come into the picture at all. The question is: What is his married life now, at the moment of candidature? It must be remembered that the candidate "must not be a recent convert" (v. 6). Long ago he might have belonged to the company of whom it could be said, "And such were some of you" (1 Cor. 6:11), like many in the church. But that was long ago. He cannot now be "caught out" on the grounds of his marriage, which in any case is not recent (v. 4; cf. v. 12: Titus 1:6).

The candidate must be *temperate.* The literal meaning has reference to wine, but as this is covered by "no drunkard" in verse 3 it is better to take the word figuratively. It thus suggests that a prospective bishop should be clear-headed, self-possessed, sound in judgment and not an extremist. He must not be the kind of man who in everything goes off at the deep end.

Sensible and *dignified* imply individual and social qualities respectively. *Sensible* means that the man is level-headed, discreet in his decisions. Aristotle described him in the *Nicomachean Ethics* (1119b. line 16) as desiring the right things in the right way and at the right time. The *dignified* man reflects his inner life by his outward dress and behavior. His character is controlled and no "disorderly" element is seen. His outer life is decent, as is appropriate to his office. "Respectable" is not always a happy word today, but it is sound if it suggests that such a person does not degrade the position which he occupies. The conduct of some people may be within the boundaries of morality and if they are ordinary folk they may "get away with it." In a bishop it would cause eyebrows to be raised. As *dignified* he will not create a scandal. The term does not suggest pomposity.

The bishop's character must not be that of the hermit. The door of his house—and of his heart—must be open to strangers. He must be *hospitable*. In this aspect he is the spearhead of the "social program" of the church, for hospitality is sought in widows (5:10) and in Christians generally (Rom. 12:13). In an age which had no hotels as we understand them, the bishop would be the host to traveling preachers and other Christians. In the care of the poor and needy he would take the initiative in providing shelter. It should not be assumed that he had to have a palace. If his heart were right, it would satisfy the requirement if he were concerned and if he took steps to provide board and lodging either in his own home or in that of a member of the church. It is the attitude which is important. (Cf. Titus 1:8.)

If the bishop is to be *an apt teacher* he must himself know God and the gospel; he must know Christian truth—which includes doctrine—and with it he must be no stranger to experimental or experiential religion. There are men who have these qualifications but cannot teach. They have knowledge but cannot express it. They have their reasons for believing (cf. 1 Pet. 3:15) but cannot state their reasons. Teaching the faith is more than a natural talent; it is one of the "gifts" of God (cf. Rom 12:6 f.). In appointing a bishop the church must therefore look for a man with the "gift." A man may be a "natural" teacher but may not know God. He may have a sort of book knowledge of the gospel and to that extent be capable of giving religious instruction. But a bishop must work at a deeper level than that of the purely academic. He will need knowledge of both mind and heart if he is to lead his people into a deeper experience of God and if he is to confute the unbelievers who contradict. (Cf. 1 Cor. 2:12–14; Titus 1:9.)

Verse 3: No drunkard, not violent but gentle, not quarrelsome, and no lover of money: Virtues required in any Christian must not be absent from a bishop. The word *drunkard* must not be pressed too hard. The candidate might never get drunk but it would disqualify him if he were "addicted to wine." The point is not the advocacy of total abstinence but the undesirability of having as a bishop a man who drinks too much. We have here an illustration of the previous word "dignified."

An episcopal bully would not be a pretty sight. Even under provocation a man with pastoral oversight must not be *violent* and strike another man. On the other hand the church is not well served by a bishop who is a weakling. *Gentle*, however, does not imply weakness. It suggests here a certain elasticity in supervision, not in the sense of relaxing what is required of Christians but in applying it less rigidly. The *gentle* bishop does not say roughly, "Now my man, right is right and that is the end of it." He listens to the other's point and then applies the Christian call to duty on a broader front. He does not insist on his rights but leads the other man to yet higher duty. This corresponds to what is known in civic life as equity. In a certain famous lawsuit between two denominations, the verdict awarded to a tiny sect all the buildings and resources of a large denomination. It was legal justice but was obviously wrong. Equity demanded some modification. Equity thus is a sort of rectification of justice, when justice has an unjust result. Similarly, for example, a bishop will not—or should not—rigidly apply a church rule in such a way that hardship and injustice will result. This does not mean that he can tamper with the law of God. It does mean that he represents him who said, "My yoke is easy, and my burden is light" (Matt. 11:30). (*Gentle* in Matt. 11:29 is not the same word as in 1 Tim. 3:3. Our Lord's expression suggests restrained strength, not the flabbiness of the jellyfish. Paul was thinking of something like "restrained law"—in order to attain what would be even better.)

The *quarrelsome* man is always ready to fight, and probably enjoys it. The bishop should be longsuffering. He must be *no lover of money*. If he is, he will be subject to unnecessary temptations. He will not be the best person to handle any of the church finances, even partially, and in time he may lose the confidence of the members. And he may give a handle to "outsiders" (v. 7; cf. Luke 16:11–14). He should be "absorbed in the Word" (cf. Acts 18:5, Greek) because he loves the Lord (Matt. 22:37 f.).

Verse 4: He must manage his own household well, keeping his children submissive and respectful in every way—partly for the sake of example and partly as a "trial run" for the candidate. The father is clearly envisaged as the head of the house. Any possible sting in *submissive* is removed by Ephesians 6:1–4. *Respectful* . . . recalls 2:2, where see discussion. The Greek has a noun. Either the children show respect for their father or the meaning is that his character and demeanor call it forth. The mother would set an example to the children in being *submissive* (2:11; Eph. 5:21–24). This is not the martinet's paradise but is the Christian home, in which the husband exercises love, as the context in Ephesians shows. The standard set is old-fashioned, according to the thought and practice of today; but there can be little doubt that society would be improved by a return to such domestic virtues.

Verse 5: For if a man does not know how to manage his own household, how can he care for God's church? The home is the test of faith, love and skill. An analogy may be drawn with Luke 16:10; 19:17. The spirit in which a bishop can *care for* the people of God is beautifully illustrated in the story of the Good Samaritan (Luke 10:34 f.). To *care for* the church is to "take care of" it. The parallel between home and church should be noticed. The bishop should be no stranger exercising his compassion. *God's church* is a home and a *household,* a family derived from God and ideally a pattern for society (cf. Eph. 3:15).

It will be observed that a candidate for the pastoral office will be "caught out" (v. 2) if he falls short of any of the qualifications listed in verses 2–5. In particular a man is always tested when he is given any kind of authority. There are ministerial temptations arising from the fact that God has given "governments" (KJV) or "administrators" (RSV) to the church, according to 1 Corinthians 12:28 (cf. the modern study of "cybernetics"). This suitably introduces the next verse.

Verse 6: He must not be a recent convert, or he may be puffed up with conceit and fall into the condemnation of the devil: Promotion which is too rapid may spell disaster. It takes time to achieve Christian maturity in faith, knowledge, and character. Apart from the "old man" or "old Adam," a man's background has to be to some extent faded out. A convert who was a Gentile might have to learn Christian ethics as a completely new subject; and if he came from the synagogue it would take time for him to adjust from legalism to freedom, from law to grace. It would be no help to the church if it awoke to find an episcopal antinomian or an episcopal Judaizer.

Or he may be does not quite bring out the force of the original. The thought is: "The bishop must not be a new convert (and a new convert must not be appointed) in order that he may not be puffed up with conceit and. . . ." *The condemnation of the devil* may be the condemnation which the devil suffers or, more likely, that which he inflicts. He is the accuser of the brethren before God (Rev. 12:10).

The possibility that a *recent convert* should be even considered may be due to a number of reasons. Older men may shrink from the responsibility or may not be very prepossessing. They may decline office because they prefer their home and a quiet life of domesticity. A younger man may have taken the church by storm, and it may have been dazzled by his natural gifts or his social prominence. It is worth observing that the Protestant churches which at the Reformation declined to insist on clerical celibacy were on sound scriptural ground. The rejection of the new convert in favor of older men of spiritual maturity does not mean that the epistle must be so late as to prevent Pauline authorship. There must be a period of about eight years between Paul's arrival at Ephesus (Acts 19:1–10) and his arrival in Rome for his first imprisonment there (Acts 28:16). Candidates could have been chosen from men who had been Christians for about a decade. In the newly formed church of Crete it might have been necessary to appoint a new convert owing to the infancy of the church. At any rate no prohibition is stated in Titus 1:7–9.

Verse 7: Moreover he must be well thought of by outsiders, or he may fall into reproach and the snare of the devil: The best cause should have the best representative. Every Christian should be a witness to the faith that is in him and to the Lord who bought him. Even so there are occasions, some "official" and some not, when the church must be represented by a single individual. In any dealings with the authorities or with non-Christians generally, the church would start with a disadvantage if its spokesman did not command respect. The text does not mean that the bishop should be popular with the *outsiders* because he is "one of the boys." As a general rule even unbelieving men can recognize character when they see it. The thought in *or he may* is similar to that in the previous verse: "in order that he may not fall . . . ." The *fall* pictures vividly the regular pursuit of duties and the sudden crash. Such a man is reviled—and with reason; unlike Jesus (Mark 15:32). Paul was concerned for the good name of the church (1 Thess. 4:12), and in that the church is the people of God he was reflecting the teaching of Jesus (Matt. 5:16). For the distinction between "those inside" and "those outside," cf. 1 Corinthians 5:12 f. The logical order in the New Testament would be: "in Christ"; then "in the church."

The snare of the devil will entrap the man whose character is not an open book and able to bear the searching light of unbelieving investigation. He will be forced to defend and justify himself—if he can. Pride and temper may be roused. Scandal may result. And further it is part of the strategy of the

devil to base his temptations on previous ones. Stronger temptations follow
an earlier yielding. The *snare* pictures the devil as a hunter, catching his prey
by guile.

(2) Deacons (3:8–13)

Deacons should be proved blameless through examination before entering
office. Desirable characteristics are sincerity in speech and faith, sobriety and
unselfishness. Their private life ought to manifest a true Christian home.
Good service in the diaconate results in higher position and confidence, with
consequent influence.

*Verse 8: Deacons likewise must be serious, not double-tongued, not
addicted to much wine, not greedy for gain:* High qualifications are
needed even for subordinate office. The *deacons* are associated with the
bishop (*likewise,* cf. Phil. 1:1) though they do not seem to have been
given oversight or supervision; they are more like "helpers" (1 Cor. 12:28).
The word "deacon" is used both in a restricted sense, as here, and in a wider
sense of "minister." Even Paul and Apollos were deacons (1 Cor. 3:5) or
servants, and they had a ministry or service (*diakonia,* 2 Cor. 4:1). The
word is appropriate to menial service (Luke 17:8; 22:27) and has not the
romance associated with, say, a cabinet minister in civil government. But it
has its greatness for those with eyes to see, and our Lord used the term to
describe his work for men (Mark 10:42–45). Deacons do not seem to have
been specifically charged with the duties of teaching or of hospitality, though
a warm heart might have inspired it. Stephen was appointed one of "the
seven" for "the daily ministry" (Acts 6:1–6; 21:8), but he could not keep
silent. It is open to question whether Acts 6 marks the formal origin of
deacons as they appear in 1 Timothy. "The seven" are not described by that
name.

For *serious,* see the discussion on "respectful" (2:2). The *double-tongued*
say one thing to one person and another thing to another. This can be
quite innocent: we may talk of the weather to one person and discuss politics
with somebody else. But Paul had in mind inconsistency, the adoption of
different attitudes about the same subject, and therefore insincerity. (Cf.
Matt. 5:37; 2 Cor. 1:17 f.) The qualification is important to men who do
much pastoral visitation. *Not addicted to much wine* implies not only that
they should not actually be heavy drinkers but that they should not be interested
in the subject. They must not only not be *greedy,* but they must be above
making money on the side with no questions asked. "Easy money" must have
no attractions for them. If deacons had the handling of money, it should be
known in advance that church finances were perfectly safe with men who were
not interested in feathering their own nests.

Verse 9: They must hold the mystery of the faith with a clear conscience:
Utterly sincere believers in thought and life. They must not be examples of a
flash in the pan. They should not merely have grasped the truth but should
be maintaining their hold on *the mystery* which consists *of the faith.*
Mystery is the open secret of God's truth hidden to man's unaided reason but
revealed in Christ. *The faith* means the objective Christian religion—"the
Christian faith," as we say. It is not quite right to say that it means the whole
body of Christian doctrine. It does mean that, and more. It means
Christian truth as revealed in Christ, and Christ trusted and obeyed. It has

been thought by some that this use of *faith* (*pistis*) is late. Such a development from faith as trust to *the faith* no doubt took time. Even so the "late" meaning appears surprisingly early in the Epistle to the Galatians (3:23–26), mingled with the normal meaning. Justification springs from faith and adoption is through faith, but *the faith* "came" and was "revealed" (note the connection with *mystery*). The Greek does not here explicitly say that Christ came (like *the faith*), but he did come, because "God sent forth his Son" (Gal. 4:4). The "late" meaning is thus Pauline: Paul preached "the faith he once tried to destroy" (Gal. 1:23). For *conscience* see discussion on 1:5.

Verse 10: And let them also be tested first; then if they prove themselves blameless let them serve as deacons: The "unknown man" is not to be given office. This is a command, though expressed in the third person. There is no question of "permission." Men are not to hold office as deacons until examination has shown that they are *blameless*. This is a relative word here. In one sense all Christians are blameless. "Who shall bring any charge against God's elect? It is God who justifies" (Rom. 8:33), whose Son "will sustain you to the end, guiltless . . ." (1 Cor. 1:8). On the other hand believers know in their hearts that entire sanctification belongs to the distant scene. Sin is not to go on reigning within them; it must stop (cf. Rom. 6:12). If they sin "Christ Jesus . . . intercedes for us" (Rom. 8:34; cf. 1 John 2:1). Prospective deacons are to be *blameless* in the sense that other, even mature, Christians cannot bring charges against them which can be substantiated. Obviously nothing can be said or done about inner sins of, say, envy or covetousness. Admittedly it is hard to prove that a man "holds . . . the faith with a clear conscience" (v. 9). Yet in the living fellowship of believing men uncertainty, doubt, or hypocrisy will eventually come out, not because spiritually minded men are suspicious detectives, but because in time they will find that "he does not ring true." In one sense, then, all Christians are blameless; in another sense all are unworthy; but in the mercy of God some men, though they feel their own unworthiness, are adjudged fit by their experienced fellow believers. God uses men before they are completely sanctified, and the church perforce must do likewise. But in that same mercy, some men have progressed far enough in discipleship to hold office in the church.

Verse 11: The women likewise must be serious, no slanderers, but temperate, faithful in all things: Even when subordinate, women can do damage in a church. The *women* are either the deacons' wives or, more likely, deaconesses, like Phoebe (Rom. 16:1). Paul could hardly be here inserting an injunction with regard to women generally, and though the Greek noun can mean "wife" or "woman," it should have the article if "the wives (of the deacons)" is the meaning. The Greek has no article. The word for "deaconess" (*diakonissa*) does not appear in the New Testament (but it does appear later), and the word for men (*diakonos*) has to serve (cf. Rom. 16:1). This is a small evidential item which prevents us from dating the Epistle too late. In A.D. 112 Pliny wrote to the Emperor Trajan from Amisus and spoke of "(ancillae) quae *ministrae* dicebantur," "(slave girls) who were called deaconesses." The church found that women were necessary for women's work. At times only women could visit, and they would certainly be needed when women were to be baptized if immersion were still practiced.

They should be *serious,* like the men (v. 8 and discussion). Maliciously to bring charges against people is devil's work, for the devil is the accuser *par excellence*. Women will be no help to the Christian cause if they are *slanderers*. Like the bishop they must be *temperate* (v. 2 and discussion). Wild extremism of any kind can be dangerous. They must be always trustworthy, always reliable, *faithful in all things* (cf. 1:12). There may be an undertone of "maintaining their faith in all circumstances."

Verse 12: Let deacons be the husband of one wife, and let them manage their children and their households well: They are to be like the bishop in this respect (vv. 2, 4 and discussions).

Verse 13: For those who serve well as deacons gain a good standing for themselves and also great confidence in the faith which is in Christ Jesus: Public opinion and private spirit. The *good standing* suggests a "step upwards" from which higher position an influence can be exercised. This is a second "test" (v. 10), largely unconscious. The character already revealed in the first test has to face the experience of actually holding office in the church. No "private member" bears quite the same responsibility or the same burden; and as a general rule he does not receive so much criticism. When the newly appointed deacon has been in office for some time and has come through all the hazards which are incidental to his office, he finds that his influence has increased. As a new deacon he was something of an unknown quantity: known indeed as a man and as a Christian but unknown as a deacon. Now he has been tried and proved—and people trust him. That is indeed influence.

There is also the effect on the man himself. If he has served well he gains *great confidence* or "much boldness." There is no doubt a sense in which we can speak of an experienced minister not having a "fit of the nerves" as he did when he was but a fledgling fresh from the seminary nest and with wings untried. But Paul meant far more than experience or self-confidence. "Boldness" is one of the great New Testament words. It may characterize access to God in Christ (Eph. 3:12; Heb. 10:19–22); prayer (Heb. 4:16; 1 John 5:14 f.); preaching (Eph. 6:19 f.); the attitude of the believer at the Parousia, the Second Coming of Christ (1 John 2:28) and in the Day of Judgment (1 John 4:17). *Those who serve well as deacons* have inevitably found that in themselves they were quite inadequate and that "our sufficiency is from God" (cf. 2 Cor. 3:5). Men may conceivably serve as deacons and not do it well. It is the fact of doing it well that implies that they have walked closely with God; and in that experience their boldness has grown. This is not in any sense of the word self-confidence, and it must never be interpreted as a familiarity with God which has lost the sense of reverence. It is the deep intimacy of sonship, and there is no place in it for impertinence. Boldness in the New Testament sense is found only *in the faith which is* exercised in the realm which is *Christ Jesus*. It is faith in Christ indeed; but it is the faith of those who are *in Christ Jesus*. Ultimately boldness is the result of the cross.

It has at times been suggested that the qualifications to be sought in bishops and deacons are very ordinary. Certainly it is not laid down that they are to be great preachers or great scholars. But if we work thoughtfully through the list of "virtues," we shall find that the standard is high indeed.

3. Behavior (3:14–16)

Paul anticipates a visit to Timothy but he has taken the precaution of writing the above instructions about behavior in the Christian community in case he is delayed. The importance of behavior is emphasized by a brief statement of the nature of the church and a hymn celebrating the work of Christ.

Verse 14: I hope to come to you soon, but I am writing these instructions to you . . . : Wise anticipation. The ground would be prepared for any further discussion and it might help Timothy to have the mind of the apostle in writing. It is at times better to show a document than to report an opinion. A critic can argue that the spoken word has been misunderstood; the text stands fast. The prospect of a visit would mean encouragement. The role is reversed in 2 Timothy 4:9, 21.

Verse 15: If I am delayed, you may know how one ought to behave in the household of God, which is the church of the living God, the pillar and bulwark of the truth: Not faithlessness but precaution. Any delay would be under the providence of God. The door of opportunity might be open so wide to the apostle that it would be wrong not to stay where he was and continue his work of evangelism. In the meantime, Timothy would have the letter as a start. The possibility of delay was the primary reason for writing, though this does not invalidate the comments on the previous verse.

The "behavior" is expressed impersonally because it does not apply only to Timothy. It is a standard for the church and the churches, and it is determined by the holiness of God (cf. 1 Cor. 3:16 f.; 11:22). It is right that men should *behave* "in church," but this is not quite Paul's meaning. He was thinking of the fellowship of believing men and women, united in a common allegiance to Christ and in worship together. *The household of God* is not a mere collection of people, a crowd; it is *the church,* the assembly, owned by *the living God,* called by him and made distinct by him from all sociological groups. Other companies, nations, societies, service clubs and the like are owned by him as Creator, but however distinct any of them may be they have not been called into the fellowship of his Son. They may contain Christians, but as groups they cannot be described by the word *church. The living God* is in contrast to every false god. The Christian faith is different from and superior to all "other religions," because God is completely revealed in Christ, and the church is distinct because it is not only called by God but indwelt by him. The church has thus great responsibility, in particular for its "behavior." This is a general term, because the "instructions" of verse 14 cover the whole letter. It includes the conduct of individual Christians, the qualifications required in ministers, and sound doctrine in contrast to the doctrine of false teachers.

The church is the earthly origin from which God's revelation in Christ makes its impact on the world. There are truths of God written in the universe: "the heavens declare the glory of God . . . ." But Christ is *the* truth, the ultimate reality of God made manifest in speech and action; God in Christ has made himself open to men's awareness of him.

Now the truth is not in danger of collapse. We must not think that if the church does not act as a buttress the truth will lie in ruins. Paul was using a metaphor by which to express the task of the church in the world, and he rightly chose a robust figure. The church is not a twittering little bird to sing the Redeemer's praise; it is not a gentle breeze to waft the message over the countryside; it is not a kindly cloud to rain refreshing mercy on the earth beneath. At least Paul did not here so describe it. It is *the pillar and bulwark of the truth*. If these are the means to the continued existence of a building, so the church is the means to the continued presentation of the truth to the world. Paul was not thinking of shoring up a tumbledown building, and it is open to question how far he thought of the church as an integral part of the truth. The world must be told the gospel and the church is the means chosen by God for this purpose.

Some will remember dark periods in history and will reflect that the church in her corruption was the last place where the truth would be found. But what men termed "the church" in those days was hardly *the church of the living God* as the New Testament understands it. The world sees an organized society, either on a world or denominational scale or in a local setting. God who looks on the heart knows those who are his, and organization or no organization they constitute the church.

Verse 16: Great indeed, we confess, is the mystery of our religion: The authentic human response to the truth. Contrast 2 Timothy 3:5. There is something of revelation in a genuine believer which cannot be accounted for by human standards. Just as the truth of God would not be known if he had not revealed it, so the truth of believing men ("Christ in you") cannot be known apart from the Holy Spirit. There is a *mystery,* an open secret, about God and an open secret about his people. (Cf. 3:9.) The language resembles that of Ephesians 5:32, "this mystery is great." The preacher will see in it the triumphant answer to the pagan cry, "Great is Artemis of the Ephesians!" (Acts 19:28, 34). *Our religion* is frequently translated by "piety," "godliness."

He was manifested in the flesh . . . glory: A quotation from a Christian hymn. The six parts are balanced and rhythmic and the ends of the Greek verbs are very much alike. The last syllables are identical and the penultimate ones are allied in sound. The verbs all come first in their strophe and the result is a pleasing assonance. The best attested reading in the first strophe is *hos,* "who" (the one exception to the priority of the verbs), which the RSV quite naturally translates by *He.* It is a relative pronoun meaning "and he." "Who" at the beginning is a sure sign, since it is not interrogative, that there was something earlier, an antecedent, but it is not given. Hence the strong certainty that we have a quotation, which from its form suggests a hymn. Now a creed can be cold but a hymn is warm. We may expect some sound doctrine, or Paul would not have inserted it. It may well be that his motive was to elicit a response from those who had earlier used the hymn. All ministers know how a hymn may revive memories and soften hearts. (Secondary variants are *ho,* "which," referring to *the mystery;* and *theos,* "God." Apart from the relative value of manuscripts, the latter is unlikely. It is true that God was manifested in the flesh, but the rest of the hymn quoted more naturally refers to Christ. The one subject is related to all six verbs.)

The first strophe clearly describes the incarnation. *The flesh* in which *he was manifested* exhibits human personality and has not here the pejorative undertones sometimes associated with the word. *Flesh* in the New Testament is of course a Greek word, but it is a Hebrew concept and an important one for the purposes of exposition. It may have the ordinary, literal meaning of "animated flesh" (as in Rom. 2:28, KJV; 1 Cor. 15:39). It may stand for the body (Eph. 5:29) and for the man himself (Rom. 3:20; 1 Cor. 1:29; cf. KJV and RSV). At this point we should notice the famous text, "the Word became flesh" or human (John 1:14). *Flesh* is used of physical descent and would be appropriate in genealogies (Rom. 4:1). It may imply human standards (1 Cor. 1:26, cf. KJV, RSV) and the pre-Christian life, the life before conversion (Rom. 7:5) and also the Christian life—or rather the life of Christians—which has fallen below the Christian standard (1 Cor. 3:1–4), immature and "ordinary." It is associated with sin (Rom. 7:18, 25; Gal. 5:19–21, 24) though not to be identified with it. Still less is it to be thought that it is evil simply because it is material. It is the instrument of sin, cooperative even if unwilling, the accomplice of the criminal and not the master mind which originates and plans the "crime." Or it may be likened to the base of operations from which sin's army sets out, the beachhead which the invading forces from overseas have captured and from which they will spread out in their advance. Just as freedom can be the beachhead for the flesh (Gal. 5:13), so in turn the flesh can be the beachhead for sin (cf. Rom. 7:8 f., 11). Calvin described *the flesh* as whatever is not in Christ.

Paul started with the Old Testament idea of *flesh* and, no doubt unconsciously, developed it. The climax is seen in Romans 8:5–8. "Fleshly" people are "fleshly" in mind, and this means death, because they cannot please God but are insubordinate and hostile to him. It is clear that this can hardly be the meaning of *the flesh* in 1 Timothy 3:16, which accords more with John 1:14. This is no inconsistency on Paul's part, if the hymn is a quotation; and it may tie the hymn down to Ephesus, the probable provenance of the Fourth Gospel. Apart from quotation, Paul would speak of the Son of God as coming "in the likeness of sinful flesh" (Rom. 8:3).[1]

Christ came, then, in the flesh and as *he was manifested* he might have been recognized as such. But he was crucified. This seems like rejection by God as well as by man; but he was *vindicated in the Spirit*. He was "justified." This is the word normally used for the justification of sinners and at first sight does not seem appropriate here. But "justify" means "to deem to be in the right." In the case of sinners who believe in Jesus, God counts them as being in the right, just as "faith was reckoned to Abraham as righteousness" (Rom. 4:9), even though they are sinners. From the point of view of language, however, it is possible to deem a person to be in the right when he is actually so. Thus the word is used of God himself, "that thou mayest be justified in thy words" (Rom. 3:4). God is in fact—right. And so was Jesus. (Cf. Matt. 11:19; Luke 7:29, 35.) He was vindicated by the resurrection.

The vindication *in the* realm of *Spirit* balances the manifestation *in the flesh* (cf. Rom. 1:3 f.). Paul did not mean that the Lord came only in the body or that the resurrection was a purely spiritual occurrence. The two lines of the hymn thus far exhibit the contrast between *flesh* and *spirit*. The question now to be faced is whether *the Spirit* is the human spirit of Jesus or the Holy Spirit. In a hymn and in a terse line it is likely that both are applicable. In his sacrifice Christ offered himself to God through eternal spirit: his act was

---

1. Cf. W. David Stacey, *The Pauline View of Man* (London: Macmillan & Co. Ltd; New York: St. Martin's Press, 1956), pp. 154–180. Rudolf Bultmann, *Theology of the New Testament* (London: SCM Press Ltd, 1965), 1:232–46.

rational, voluntary, and loving in contrast to that of the dumb beasts of animal sacrifice. The sacrifices were offered and offered at best with animals' acquiescence (Isa. 53:7); he for the joy that was set before him endured the cross (Heb. 12:2). By that act eternal judgment was averted, eternal redemption secured, an eternal inheritance promised and an eternal bond between God and men established, the eternal covenant (Heb. 6:2; 9:12, 14 f.; 13:20). His work was absolute and final. Nothing more needs to be done. The means of such a sacrifice was essentially not his body (though his body suffered), as with the sacrificial animals, but his spirit. It was eternal in the sense that the attitude and motive of Jesus was not a temporary impulse. In eternity "he set his face to go to Jerusalem" (Luke 9:51) and he went there. He holds eternal office as priest and can forever save those who come to God through him, because he is forever alive—to make intercession for them (Heb. 7:23–25). How natural it is that his resurrection, his final vindication, should find him of the same mind! (For "spirit" in the sense of "will," cf. Matt. 26:41; Mark 14:38; Acts 19:21, KJV. Luke 9:54 f. and footnote is the opposite of the eternal spirit of Jesus.)

On the other hand *the Spirit* may be interpreted as the Holy Spirit. The Suffering Servant possessed the Spirit (Isa. 42:1). If he did so in his life there is no reason why he should not have continued to bear the Spirit in his resurrection. The Spirit is the giver of life (Rom. 8:11), even though it is God who raised Jesus from the dead.

There is a further factor. The resurrection which *vindicated* Jesus was private. The actual "rising" was witnessed by nobody and the risen Lord appeared only to chosen witnesses (Acts 10:40 f.). How then did the resurrection vindicate him? Apostolic testimony proclaimed it, and "this was not done in a corner" (Acts 26:23, 26). The world could receive the evidence if it liked. The final vindication comes when men believe in Jesus. They know then that he is the Savior and they know that God raised him from the dead; and they have so learnt because of the ministry of the Holy Spirit. For them the crucified Lord was *vindicated*. They knew it when they found themselves *in the* realm of the *Spirit*.

Both of these interpretations are applicable. By contrast the sacred stone at Ephesus that fell from the sky (Acts 19:35) was not a person, was not a revelation of God, and was not in any sense vindicated.

He was . . . seen is a single Greek verb *(ōphthē),* and it appears in the Old Testament with God as subject and in a context of worship. "Then the Lord appeared to Abram. . . . So he built there an altar to the Lord, who had appeared to him." ". . . the Lord appeared to Abram. . . . Then Abram fell on his face" (Gen. 12:7; 17:1–3; cf. 26:24 f.; 31:13; 35:1; Exod. 3:2–5). This Septuagintal use offers a clue for the purposes of interpretation. We do not need to ask when the Lord appeared to angels, whether immediately after the resurrection or after the ascension. (The latter is covered by the last clause in the verse.) Whenever he appeared to angels we may assume that they fell on their faces in worship. This accords with other parts of the New Testament. "And again, when he brings the first-born into the world, he says, 'Let all God's angels worship him'" (Heb. 1:6). Certainly the event at Bethlehem was celebrated by angels, for "a multitude of the heavenly host [was] praising God . . ." (Luke 2:13). And in consequence of obedience to the ultimate length—death, death of a cross—God gave to his Son the name which is above every name, the Name of Lord, that every knee should bow in worship, beginning with the knees of heavenly beings (cf. Phil. 2:9 f.). Some scholars see the angelic worship given to Christ while he was actually ascending into heaven. A reference to Acts 1:9–11 may possibly be included, but there seems no need to limit the worship to the time of the Ascension. Without doubt the Lord will receive angelic worship at his Second Coming— the Parousia and the Judgment (Matt. 25:31; 1 Thess. 4:16; 2 Thess. 1:7)— but the past tense of the verb, (he was) *seen by angels,* shows that this is not the main thought.

Preached among the nations emphasizes the universal scope of the gospel. It is not restricted to the Jews but is for the Gentiles also; *the nations* must mean all mankind. It is with some piquancy that we recall Galatians 2:15, "Gentile sinners." Paul did not mean that world evangelism had been completed. The principle had been asserted and the work had surely to be continued. Hitherto it had not been unsuccessful: he had been *believed on in the world.* The last term, *the world,* repeats *the nations* and thus reaffirms the scope. But something is added. If we consult the concordance we shall see how many times *the world* appears in the Fourth Gospel (with Ephesus as its provenance!); and *the world* is characterized by its hostility to God. Here then in the hymn the church sees enmity turned into faith. Time after time the love of Christ when preached has broken down every barrier. In triumph it sings its climax *he was . . . taken up in glory.* This means the Ascension, which was prior in time to the proclamation and the faith but comes fittingly at the end of the hymn as quoted. More is meant than the bare ascent, though even in this it should be noticed that he was *taken up.* Who thus took him up? It can only be God, just as it was God who raised him from the dead, and gave him glory (cf. 1 Pet. 1:21). Paul was referring to the exaltation of Jesus and to his authority at the right hand of God (cf. Acts 2:33–35; 3:13; Heb. 2:9). It is almost impossible not to think of Philippians 2:5–11 in this connection. A preview of this was given in the Transfiguration, which combines the glory of revelation and of radiance, and of authority. (See on 1:11, 17; cf. 1 Pet. 5:1, where Peter may be referring to the Transfiguration.)

We do not feel it necessary to comment on the technical question of the structure of the hymn. It may consist of two stanzas, each of three lines, as suggested by the RSV; or it may consist of three couplets, as set out in the Greek Testament edited by Nestle and Aland. The reader may be able to discern patterns and contrasts.

IV. DANGER: FOREWARNED AND COUNTERACTED (4:1–16)

1. Error and Apostasy (4:1–5)

The Spirit clearly teaches a partial apostasy through misguided attention to demonic doctrine. Examples are given of the negative teaching of liars and the Christian position is positively affirmed. Everything in creation is good and may be received, for it is consecrated by the prayer of thanksgiving.

Verse 1: Now the Spirit expressly says that . . . doctrines of demons: The divine precision of realism rather than the vagueness of human pessimism. *Expressly* is an adverb which would imply the explicitness with which the conditions were listed in a legal document, or (in mathematics) a statement in rational numbers. We all know what is meant by, say, the numbers 6 or 84 or 983 as opposed to the square root of 17 or of minus 1. The warning could not be plainer. The human agency is not stated. It is enough that the Spirit has spoken, either through the apostle himself or through some unknown prophet. The *later times* foreshadow the gathering eschatological storm, warnings of which had already been given (Matt. 24:11 f.; Acts 20:29 f.; cf. 2 Thess. 2:3, 10 f.). The apostasy is partial (*some*) and those who *depart from the faith* (see on 3:9) may be compared with the people in the parable of the sower who have no root but likewise abandon the faith (the Greek verb is the same). If we set Luke 8:13 against Matthew 7:24 f. the thought is suggested that the Christian should be founded on the rock but not planted on it. (Cf. 1 Cor. 3:11; Col. 1:23; Heb. 3:12.) Those who *depart* ought not to be deacons (3:9)! The thought is entertained that believers may become unbelievers. The prophecy may or may not be absolute but it is certainly a warning —to avoid its own fulfillment. It is like a mother's "prophecy" to a son climbing a dangerous tree: "you will break your back." The remedy is plain. Just as deacons should not attend with interest to much wine (3:8), so believers should not pay attention to, *give heed to, spirits* which lead astray and *doctrines* which *demons* teach.

This is heady stuff. Its origin is satanic but the spokesmen are human (v. 2). The parable of the tares or weeds (Matt. 13:24–30, 36–43) is a partial parallel, the difference being that in the parable the weeds were present at an early date; in the epistle the "wheat" becomes "a weed." It may be inferred that the devil has a theology, and that believers should be selective. It is one thing for a theological professor in the course of his duties (which include the defense of the faith) to read anything and everything himself and to supervise the wide reading of his students so that they face problems in seminary as a preparation to meeting them in the ministry; it is quite another to tell the mass of the faithful to read anything and to come to their own conclusions. Most Christians are theologically untrained and time is limited. Let them read the best! This is no more brainwashing than telling a young child not to touch the medicine bottles on the top shelf.

Verse 2: Through the pretensions of liars whose consciences are seared: Three parties are apparent, the demons, the liars, and those who depart from the faith. The *liars* are characterized in three ways: their *pretensions* (they are not what they seem); their moral insensitiveness; and (v. 3) their negative teaching. At first we might be surprised that such teaching should lead men to apostasy. Is it impossible for a vegetarian bachelor to be a Christian (v. 3)? The answer is that the practice of vegetarianism and celibacy is here theologically based and it is but a beginning which leads to other errors. Once such false teaching has been accepted, a door has been opened to yet further error. This is suggested by the Greek preposition *en* rendered naturally enough by the RSV by *through*. This takes it in a largely instrumental way, a use of the Greek vernacular which came easily to the Aramaic mind. But it need not be interpreted instrumentally. It may be broadly local. If the phrase is taken in close association with "doctrines" the result is "doctrines of demons present in the *pretensions of liars.*" On the other hand it may be taken with the participle "giving heed to." The final construction would therefore be: "Some will depart . . . by giving heed . . . in the atmosphere of the sham of liars." When the liars talk and teach, it is the opposite of being "in Christ."

The *liars* teach others but their own *consciences are seared,* branded with a red-hot iron. Either they are marked as belonging to their master, the devil (contrast Gal. 6:17), or their conscience has been put out of action. Both thoughts are applicable. If the church is to be indeed "the pillar and bulwark of the truth" (3:15), its members must be alert to recognize the brand mark and so sensitive themselves in conscience that they can detect false teaching when it appears. This does not require them to become incessant heresy-hunters, sometimes in sheer suspicion condemning innocent men and making mountains out of molehills. A sentry must challenge before he shoots.

Verse 3: Who forbid marriage and enjoin abstinence from foods which God created to be received with thanksgiving by those who believe and know the truth: Not marriage guidance and food inspection but absolute prohibition. The teaching is unscriptural. Marriage is a divine institution. The Old Testament teaching (Gen. 1:27 f.; 2:24) was reaffirmed by our Lord (Matt. 19:4–6; Mark 10:6–9) both explicitly in his teaching and by implication in his presence at a wedding (John 2:1–11). Paul recognized marriage in the same way (1 Cor. 7:28, 36; Eph. 5:22–31). Marriage is in principle open to all or at any rate is the normal, not the abnormal. But it is not so "normal" that celibacy is a sin. In fact it is "well," i.e., honorable for a man not to touch a woman (1 Cor. 7:1), because both marriage and celibacy are a gift (1 Cor. 7:7; cf. Matt. 19:11 f.). In principle, then, "all things (including marriage) are lawful" but not all are advantageous (cf. 1 Cor. 6:12). It is right for some people not to marry. But it is wrong to make a rule of the exception; indeed marriage can be the solution to a difficult situation (1 Tim. 5:14). (Cf. Heb. 13:4.)

To enforce *abstinence from foods* seems very much like the reimposition of the Old Testament food laws. These have been abolished in the gospel. The Gospel writer was intelligent enough to notice that our Lord's teaching revealed him as "making all foods clean" (Mark 7:19; cf. Acts 10:13–16). Paul was in line with this: "everything is indeed clean" and "the weak man eats only vegetables." Christian love and care should inspire abstinence not because the food as such is unclean but in order to help the weak brother. The decisive factor in abstinence is not the food but the brother. A sweeping rule to abstain is therefore wrong (Rom. 14:1–4, 13–23). Food in itself is a thing indifferent (1 Cor. 8:8), but it may be a test of discipleship. If the false teachers thought that food, as matter, was evil, they might as well starve. In any case God's creation is good (Gen. 1:31).

A partial asceticism may be a spiritual discipline or an act of pastoral care. But as part of the universal program of the Christian faith ("asceticism always for everybody") it is without biblical foundation. If we ask again how celibacy and abstinence from foods can lead to a departure from the faith, the answer is clear. The principle is unscriptural, speculative, and it leads on to something further. Paul would not prohibit the "thinking out" of a theological or ethical problem, and to that extent would not be unsympathetic to the speculative; but it must be rooted in the "givenness" of the Christian faith and its results—which should certainly not be the results of pure speculation—must not be equated with the deposit of Christian truth. Once speculation is regarded as being on a level with revelation, then any wild idea may enter and the result is a departure from the faith. Therefore: do not give too much attention and interest to speculation. "Take heed what you hear" (Mark 4:24); "take heed . . . how you hear" (Luke 8:18); "test everything; hold fast what is good" (1 Thess. 5:21). Failure in the early stage may have dire consequences: "Peter began to sink" (Matt. 14:30).

This is a wholesome precaution, not a prohibition of thought. The use of the word "therefore" in the New Testament shows us something of the place of inference in the Christian life. "Therefore, since we are justified by faith . . ." (Rom. 5:1). Even so care must be exercised not to regard our conclusions as automatically part of God's revelation in Christ. The inference may in itself be valid; but we may have omitted a vital part of the evidence which ought to have been included in the premises.

The question of *marriage* is not here further treated, but the rejection of the teaching about *abstinence from foods* is now given its justification. The *foods* are those *which God created*. They are therefore good (v. 4) and are within his purpose. He formed the earth to be inhabited (Isa. 45:18), and if men are to live on the earth they must eat. Provision is made for this (Gen. 1:29; 9:3). Food is to be eaten; it is not a means (by abstinence from it) of justification by works. It is *to be received with thanksgiving* by all men (cf. Matt. 5:45; Acts 14:15–17; Rom. 1:21) and therefore in particular *by those who believe and know the truth*. The latter phrase may expound the former. Believers are those who know the truth (2:4 and discussion) at the deepest level. But Paul might have been allowing for the weak brother who only partially knows the truth; even clean food "is unclean for any one who thinks it unclean" (Rom. 14:14). But he may still be a believer. The link between marriage and food lies in the fact that if both are abandoned the race will die out.

Verse 4: For everything created by God is good, and nothing is to be rejected if it is received with thanksgiving: A general principle concerning God's creation. Nothing is said or implied about quantities to be received, or when; and nothing is said about individual cases. The statement should not be used, for example, to justify pressing liquor on a rehabilitated alcoholic. Paul's language here recalls a proverbial saying which goes back to Homer. "Not to be tossed away are the splendid gifts of the gods" (*Iliad* 3. 65). But even a proverb must be put in Christian dress. Everything must be *received,* not demanded or exploited; and *with thanksgiving* (see v. 5).

Verse 5: For then it is consecrated by the word of God and prayer: The reason for the importance of the thanksgiving. Paul had in mind the pious practice of "saying grace" before meals. The food does not change its nature: it is already "good" (Gen. 1:31). The sincere prayer of thanksgiving marks off the food. This food, this meal, it is implied, comes from God and is for the sustenance of a man of God. It will enable him to continue his discipleship and it is therefore fit for his consumption. To that extent it is *consecrated.* Insofar as the word for *prayer* is used for petition, the thanksgiving may take the form of: "Bless, O Lord, this food to our use and thy glory, for Jesus Christ's sake, Amen." *The word of God* recalls the truth about the subject which God has revealed, and may refer, as some think, to the Jewish use of texts of Scripture in saying the grace. (Cf. 1 Cor. 10:30.)

The use of the word *consecrated* here illumines a difficult passage elsewhere. Paul says that "the unbelieving husband is consecrated through his wife . . ." (1 Cor. 7:14). It cannot mean that the husband is saved because he has a Christian wife. But what does it mean? It would seem that he is not to be regarded as unclean and therefore to be divorced; he can continue to be the husband of a Christian. It is odd to reflect that he is like the food which can be used by Christians, but this seems to be the implication. The difference is that he may become a convert; the food does not need it.

2. Countermeasures (4:6–16)

A good minister will instruct the people in sound doctrine, which is the diet of his own soul. Superstition is to be avoided. Spiritual as opposed to athletic training is advocated because of its wide range and long view, and its relationship to the living God. Such is to be the burden of Timothy's message, in spite of his youth, reinforced by the example of his own life. He is to exercise his ministerial gift until the arrival of the apostle, with thoughtful concentration and manifest progress.

(1) Living on one's own message (4:6)

The good minister is no theorizer. He teaches the apostolic doctrine which he has made his own both as nourishment by which to live and as standard by which to judge himself.

Verse 6: If you put these instructions before the brethren, you will be a good minister of Christ Jesus, nourished on the words of the faith and of the good doctrine which you have followed: The uncongenial task contributes to the making of a mature minister. *These instructions* are primarily the contents of verses 1–5, though the earlier words of guidance lie in the background. Even if they are *put before* the brethren, even if they are suggested in mild terms, there is the possibility of a clash. *A good minister* is not a mere record player. He is a person and deals with persons. The "handling" of persons reveals the minister and makes the minister. Timothy was thus given the task of dealing with a situation, and it imposed the sort of test which "makes or breaks." In his favor was the fact that he ministered to *the brethren,* the members of the family of God (cf. 3:15). They must have already had some Christian instruction and were not without Christian experience. Timothy could count on a measure of good will and of Christian love. Much would depend on whether he antagonized or adopted the wooing note. Sometimes the indirect approach is advisable, provided always that there is no toning down of the truth.

Also in his favor was the fact that he himself not only knew what he was talking about but had himself proved the reality of the Christian faith in his own life. He himself had been *nourished.* We rather expect to read "by the Word of God" but Paul wrote *the words of the faith.* It corresponds to the fact that "faith comes from what is heard, and what is heard comes by the preaching of Christ" (Rom. 10:17). *The words* do not replace the Word but express it, whether in Scripture or sermon. Timothy had been *nourished* and so lived "by every word that proceeds from the mouth of God" (Matt. 4:4; cf. 2 Tim. 3:14 f.). *The words* are more than an academic study; they give directions to be followed. Doing God's will nourishes the life (John 4:34). The more mature Christians would recognize that in his teaching—and even in controversy—Timothy was giving to them not only "food for thought" but spiritual sustenance. This he was able to do because his spiritual life was not only past history but present experience. He had *followed,* had "traced through," the good doctrine. Luke had similarly traced through the events of the life of Christ in his historical investigation (Luke 1:3). But whereas Luke had been seeking to discover or confirm historical facts and their meaning, Timothy was not a historian. He had followed the elements of doctrine as they had been unfolded before his mind. He had grasped them and made them his own both by deep understanding and by obedience in life. He had done more than take a course in theology. He had mastered the teaching. This may be regarded as part of his past. His early knowledge of Scripture had been given precision and perspective by Paul (2 Tim. 3:10, "Now you have *followed* my teaching . . ."). But it was not only a memory, something once learnt. It was living knowledge and he was *nourished* by it day by day.

Nourished is a present participle with the force of: "(you will be a good minister . . .), going on being nourished (day by day) . . . ." *You have followed* leaves the doctrine indelibly impressed on his mind up to the moment of writing. *The good doctrine* is true. There is such a thing as bad doctrine. It is to be disbelieved and avoided. See the next verse.

(2) Avoiding superstition (4:7)

Invented stories and untrue fables have no place in Christian proclamation. The faith is rooted in history.

Verse 7: Have nothing to do with godless and silly myths. Train yourself in godliness: Energy is to be concentrated. The base from which the apostle argues—or issues his orders!—is the givenness of the Christian faith. *Have nothing to do with* rules out the popular practice of today, discussion. Much time and energy can be wasted in this. Timothy by contrast was to teach the faith positively, no doubt with an occasional side-glance at false doctrines and a comment showing why they were false, but devoting most of the teaching time to exposition. The best form of defense is attack, and the best Christian apologetic is the affirmation of truth rather than the denial of falsity. For *myths* see discussion on 1:4 and note that they "promote speculations." *Godless* is rendered by "profane" in 1:9 and is very like "common" or "defiled" (cf. Acts 21:28 with 24:6). It describes that which has no religious value and is thus the opposite of "the words of the faith . . ." (v. 6). It has no place in a religion which is concerned with a holy God (1 Pet. 1:16) and with "thy holy servant Jesus" (Acts 4:27); with the Holy Spirit, with "holy apostles" (Eph. 3:5), and with "the holy scriptures" (Rom. 1:2; cf. 2 Tim. 3:15); with "holy people," the saints (see on 1 Tim. 2:15), with "holy faith" (Jude 20), with "holy commandment" (2 Pet. 2:21) and holy conduct (1 Pet. 1:15; 2 Pet. 3:11). The profane can be dangerous (cf. 2 Tim. 4:4). *Silly* ("old wives' fables," KJV) refers to the talk of old women and covers gossip and stories told to children. Be mature!

The last sentence means that Timothy should *train* himself so that (increasing) *godliness* is the result. The metaphor is that of the gymnasium. Hebrews uses the same figure in speaking of mature men whose faculties are "in condition," as the athletes say, because they have been brought into a healthy state (see Heb. 5:14). A runner brings himself "into condition" by running and by being "in training"; a man becomes thus able to run the more. Similarly a man goes into spiritual training and makes himself spiritually fit by being godly, and from this he advances into greater godliness. In the religious life it means taking discipleship seriously and devoting effort to it. Prayer does not just happen. It has to be done deliberately as a matter of choice and indeed of policy. A man must make his plans and give thought to them. The Bible does not come to a man and ask to be read. He must decide to read it regularly, with thought and prayer. And he must carry out his decisions. This may involve effort, like the training of the athlete. The figure of speech thus suggests seriousness of purpose and effort in performance. In a religion of grace it is a temptation not to pay too much attention to the need of effort, but the wrestler does not spend all the time of the bout in relaxation (Eph. 6:12). Before a man can even start his training in *godliness* he must be converted or regenerated. The "effort" of unjustified men may or may not yield practical results of value, but they are not the same as the works of a saved man. (See on 2:2; 3:16.)

(3) Self-training (4:8–10)

The minister's own spiritual life does not come automatically. He must train himself in spiritual exercises, for the prize of the good fight is both here and hereafter. Personal religion and evangelism alike are grounded in the living God in whom we hope.

Verse 8: For while bodily training is of some value, godliness is of value in every way, as it holds promise for the present life and also for the life to come: The long view is the standard of value. Paul could not have ruled out the body entirely, owing to the Christian doctrine of personality which is a unity of body and soul. (Cf. discussion on 2 Tim. 2:18.) The best body for a Christian is a fit body, even though God can and does use servants frail in body and shines through them. But the magnificent physique of an atheist or unbeliever may be an instrument of sin (Rom. 6:13, 19; 12:1). Hence is seen the need of *godliness*. It profits both body and soul. The godly man does not allow his body to run away with him and he spares it the ravages of, say, alcoholism. (Cf. 1 Cor. 9:24–27.) Godliness means true life now and true life for eternity—both in Christ. The training in godliness, which includes mastery of the body, is a means to an end, godliness itself. The harsh austerities of verse 3 are an end in themselves. (Cf. Col. 3:5.) The Christian life has its toils (v. 10), in which hope is an inspiration, without manufacturing a false asceticism.

Verse 9: The saying is sure and worthy of full acceptance: A solemn re-affirmation of the previous verse. See on 1:15, where the language is identical. Scholars are divided as to whether *the saying* points backwards or forwards. In 1:15 the reference is forwards; in Titus 3:8 it must be backwards. This leaves the present verse to be decided on its merits. The context seems to imply that "the saying (about godliness, v. 8) is to be believed, (and our ministry points in this direction) for (v. 10) we toil and strive towards the goal of giving life to men—the life spoken of in verse 8." *The saying* there-fore points backwards.

Verse 10: For to this end we toil and strive: The energy of the athlete's training is put into evangelism. *Toil* is the same root as the noun used in 1 Thessalonians 1:3, "labor of love." The verb means to work energetically, to the point of weariness. To savor its intensity see Luke 5:5. Jesus calls all those who toil wearily to come to him for rest—and then for further toil (Matt. 11:29, 30). *Strive* preserves the metaphor of sport and is translated by "fight" in 6:12. *To this end* (*eis touto*) is neuter and cannot refer specifically to any noun in the previous two verses. The *end* or goal must therefore be the offering of life in Christ to men—the work of evangelism. (Cf. John Wesley: "I offered them Christ.") This is confirmed by the later words about God as Savior of all men. Paul and Timothy (notice the partnership in the plural *we toil*) could each say with Wesley, "the world is my parish."

Because we have our hope set on the living God: The inspiration of their work. *The living God* is the foundation of their hope. The perfect tense, "we have set our hope," implies that "our hope is now in firm position on the living God." This was the motive power by which they endured the privations of toiling and striving. An idol can do nothing. An idea may inspire. Only *the living God* can own and bless their ministry and sustain them in adversity. Fitting illustrations of the divine "intervention" would be 1 Thessalonians 1:5, 9; 2:2.

Who is the Savior of all men, especially of those who believe—and there-fore sustains the work of evangelism. This passage raises profound questions because the title *Savior* has advanced from "God our Savior" (1:1 and discus-sion) to *Savior of all men.* This is not universalism. The key is in the words *especially of those who believe.* An attempt to deal with the matter will be found in the discussions on 1:15 and 2:4. The present text does not say that God actually saves all men but that he is the Savior. *Especially* divides the *all men* into two classes, *those who believe* and others. The believers are those who receive eternal life, and Paul himself was an example (1:16 and discussion)—the very life mentioned in 4:8. Nothing is here said about those who do not believe, though the toiling and the striving are directed toward them. *Savior* is a noun, and a clear statement that God actually saved *all men* would require a verb. A rough analogy may be found in the use of the word "King" as a noun (1:17) and the cognate verb in 6:15, "(the King of) those who are actually reigning as kings." Here, however, the King has more than a title; he himself is doing that which the title indicates. *The Savior* does that which the title implies when men believe in Jesus. He has already satisfied the divine righteousness in the cross. The only saving work which God does now is to sustain his evangelists, to overrule the lives of potential believers to bring them within the sound of the gospel and to speak to them through the Holy Spirit in the preached Word and in all the activities of prevenient grace. God is finally glorified as Savior every time a man believes. Cornelius is an example of God's saving activity before he was actually saved (Acts 10:33). (For significant uses of the verb "to save," see 1 Thess. 2:16; 2 Thess. 2:10; 2 Tim. 1:9; Titus 3:5; cf. Eph. 2:8.)

(4) Example (4:11–12)

Though Timothy is young he is both to teach and command the apostolic message. He is to be a living embodiment of what he says, believing in God and showing love in word and deed in an exemplary moral life.

Verse 11: Command and teach these things: Regularly, habitually, continually. Once only, just to get it on record, would not be enough. "Tell me the story often, for I forget so soon." It is likely that because of a natural diffidence Timothy was not sufficiently assured of his authority in the church, lacked self-confidence and needed an impetus to his faith. He may not have realized the strength of the challenge thrown out by the false teachers and was therefore unprepared for the shock which would come. In conscious or unconscious anticipation Paul directed him to a sustained course of ministry. The epistle would most likely be read out "in church" and it would strengthen Timothy's hand. It is always helpful (if not always successful) when a young preacher or teacher knows, and the listening church knows, that what he says and does represents the convictions of the highest authority. How many young preachers of the last century brought into their sermons the words, "Mr. Spurgeon says . . ."? There are men who from the depths of their own prophetic consciousness can expound and preach the Word of God without fear of any. There are others, among whom Thomas Cranmer has been named as a striking example, who must have some authority to which they can look. This may be regrettable but it is a fact, and Timothy seems to have approximated to this position. (See 1 Cor. 16:1, cf. RSV and KJV.) *These things* broadly covers the contents of the epistle. *Teach* gives information; *command* tells the people to carry it into effect.

Verse 12: Let no one despise your youth, but set the believers an example in speech and conduct, in love, in faith, in purity: The present answer to a problem which only time can solve! The situation could not wait for Timothy to grow up. But he was no child, even though Paul could affectionately, as the older man, regard him as such (1:2). Paul himself was a young man when Stephen was martyred (Acts 7:58) yet influential enough to get official authority to persecute (Acts 9:1 f., 14). His right to vote for the execution of Christians is thought by some to establish his age as about thirty years (Acts 26:10). It would not have been wrong to think of Timothy as young, even at the age of about thirty-five.

Who would *despise* his *youth?* Who would "underrate" (Kelly's helpful interpretation, p. 103) a minister simply because he was much younger? The obvious answer is "the elders," both those holding office (5:17) and those who were simply older (5:1 f.). It sometimes goes against the grain for older people to be instructed by younger, especially when they themselves have already been engaged in teaching. *Let* does not mean "Do not allow anyone to despise your youth." It is a third person imperative with the force of "No one must despise . . . ." The tense suggests "Every one (so doing) must stop despising your youth." Timothy himself can take steps to bring this about, not by issuing orders but by the quality of his own life. What he lacked in years could be replaced or made up for by what he actually was.

He was to *set . . . an example.* Obviously it was an example to *the believers* for them to copy; it was not meant to be a mere exhibition. Even so the meaning strictly is not "an example to imitate" but "an example of what a believer really is." The Greek is *tupos* (see on Titus 2:7). He was to manifest the essential strokes of a "pattern" or typical Christian as God meant a believer to be.

Speech covers everything said, in public or private, in conversation or in preaching. There is private talk which ill becomes a Christian and at times of frustration or even righteous indignation a sermon itself may fail to reveal the true Christian spirit. *Conduct* or behavior is a wider term and includes everything which comes under moral scrutiny, whether word or deed. It is hardly *conduct* if a man swings his arm in sleep and does damage; it is *conduct* if through carelessness or choice he strikes and hurts another. It was certainly *conduct* when Paul persecuted the church (Gal. 1:13, "life"). We have been redeemed from futile and traditional conduct (1 Pet. 1:18). The emphasis in *speech and conduct* is on the outward. *Love, faith* and *purity* are inner. This distinction is not absolute: the outward arises from the inner disposition, and the inner attitudes and qualities may be discerned by believers.

For *love* and *faith* see on 1:5; 2:4; 4:3. The idea of reliability or trustworthiness may also be included. *Purity* means the outworking of faith in holiness of life, which includes chastity and propriety (5:2) in thought as well as deed. Timothy must keep himself from too close an association with the world, which will leave its stains (Jas. 1:27). He must always be ready for an approach to God ("abide in me," John 15:3 f.). Ritual purity is not enough. John 18:28 is a lesson here.

(5) Spiritual ministry (4:13–16)

In the interim before the apostle's arrival, Timothy is to concentrate on his ministerial duties. In devoting himself to the exercise of his spiritual gift he must manifest his progress. Concentration means salvation for both teacher and taught.

Verse 13: Till I come, attend to the public reading of scripture, to preaching, to teaching: A summary of ministerial essentials. The apostle would be shocked at some ministerial activities today. The Greek gives the bare term, *the reading,* though the RSV interpretation is surely right. In the days of the early church, all reading, even when alone, was out loud as there were no spaces between the written words and the reader had to "feel his way forward" (cf. Acts 8:28, 30). Prior preparation was advisable and Paul no doubt had this in mind. This is early—and incidental—evidence that the church took over the practice of the synagogue. The Old Testament was read in the "church services." (Cf. Luke 4:16 f.; Acts 13:14 f.) A letter from an apostle might also be read (cf. 1 Thess. 5:27).

Preaching stands for the Greek word *paraklēsis,* often rendered by "exhortation," "appeal" or "comfort." See discussion on 1:3. It suggests preaching to Christians. Preaching to non-Christians is evangelism rather than exhortation, though in actual fact it is certainly "persuasion with authority." *Paraklēsis* is a gift (Rom. 12:6, 8). It has been said that Charles Simeon (1759–1836) demonstrated that it is possible to teach men how to preach. If this means that it is possible to take a callow youth and teach him to stand in the presence of men and state what is true, showing the meaning of a passage from the Bible and asking his hearers to obey its instructions, and to do it without making a fool of himself, then no doubt there is substance in the view. Even here the tutor must have something to work on. But is it preaching? The next verse draws attention to Timothy's gift, which is significant in the present context. If two men consecutively occupy a pulpit, and one has a gift for preaching and the other has not, and if in other respects— Christian experience, education, etc.—they are on the same level, a listener, one would surmise, would be able to tell the difference between them.

Teaching to some extent lacks the element of appeal, of emotion and to some extent also the dramatic which is associated with preaching. It seeks more to inform than to move the will. In preaching there must always be an inner core of information, the great facts of Christian truth; in teaching there need not always be the appeal to the will. Preaching has the threefold purpose: *docēre, placēre, movēre* (to teach, to please—not antagonize— and to move the will); *teaching* concentrates on the first. It may have special reference to members of the catechumenate, to those who, as we should say today, are under instruction with a view to full church membership. They would have to be given an outline of Christian truth.

Teaching is also a gift (Rom. 12:7). This does not imply that *reading* is an ordinary task which may be left to anybody. For one thing, the fact that Paul mentioned it carries some weight. For another, it is possible for the same Old Testament to be read and for a "veil" to be over the mind of some people (2 Cor. 3:14–16). Jewish Christians might need further persuasion, to say nothing of the false teachers. Timothy must so read that the veil is pierced wherever it is present. Finally all of the Old Testament was written for our *teaching,* and in that very context Paul spoke of "the encouragement of the scriptures" (Rom. 15:4). "Encouragement" is *paraklēsis,* or "exhortation." The Scriptures exhort us, and they cannot do so unless they are read. The reader must not murder their message. The *preaching* and the *teaching* of the Scriptures come in part from the *reading.* The former two are gifts; the latter may therefore be a gift also. The selection as well as the actual reading of passages of Scripture might be mighty weapons against error. It ought to be added that there is a preaching which is distinct from the reading of the lesson! Even so it should be based on the Scripture and steeped in it. This does not rule out the use of the language of today.

Verse 14: Do not neglect the gift you have, which was given you by prophetic utterance when the elders laid their hands upon you: Spiritual gifts do not work mechanically. What is here urged negatively is put positively in 2 Timothy 1:6. The *neglect* is not quite the same as that in Acts 6:1. There the widows of the Hellenists were "overlooked," because the church membership was increasing so fast. It was no doubt culpable, but pardonable. Here the possibility is more grave. *Neglect* savors of taking everything for granted. Its stock word would be "of course!" Some men, when given the invitation of the gospel, "make light of it" (Matt. 22:5). Their characteristic attitude is: "Of course! We'll see about that." And then they go off to something else. The temptation of some Christians is to neglect their great salvation (Heb. 2:3). If faced with the question of whether they are saved or not, their typical remark would be: "Saved? Of course!" And then through inattention to it they drift off into what absorbs their whole life. They do not glorify God and certainly do not "enjoy him for ever." If Timothy did *neglect the gift* it would mean that when asked if he were using it he would reply: "Of course! I can easily handle *that!*"—and then completely forget it, perhaps putting on some other "program" to entertain the church. It is significant that in verse 13 he was told to "attend to" certain activities. The sin behind the "Of course!" is inattention. The invitation is to be received; the consequent salvation, the source of unceasing thanksgiving, praise and obedience, is to be enjoyed; the gift is to be exercised.

When a man is ordained to the ministry he is given a formal authority to do what previously he was not entitled to do. Even the state recognizes this, when it asks if a man has been ordained and is entitled to solemnize marriage. Now as a matter of ascertainable fact before the service of ordination a man cannot do certain things and after the service he can. His authority dates from the ordination service when it was given to him.

This is all very precise, as it should be. But it may be doubted if it applies to gifts. They are gradually recognized by the church members and are the subject of talk. Finally, prophetic voices draw attention to a gift and its bearer, and the man in question is set apart for ministry. In the moving moments of the actual ordination service, the candidate may well feel that God has a work for him to do and has given him the equipment with which to do it. The belief that he has a gift may crystallize when *prophetic utterance* is confirmed by further action, when *the* presbytery or body of *elders* lay *their hands upon* him. *The gift* is not *given* in the absolute sense by the laying on of hands: the man in question could already preach or teach and possesed it already. It is given to be authoritatively exercised in the church as part of the ministry exercised by the church. Given to be exercised in the church: this is the meaning. Hitherto the gift has been used informally, in conversation or discussion, in which its bearer has already stood out from his companions, or on the exceptional occasion when he has addressed the church. Now he does it regularly, with authority.

See further on 1:18 (cf. 2 Tim. 1:6). The point is that an abstract authority, though it may be neglected and not used, hardly needs to be rekindled. A spiritual gift is apportioned to each individual who bears it by the Holy Spirit himself, as Paul taught elsewhere (1 Cor. 12:11). Our problem has been to combine two thoughts: the gift was made by the Spirit, and it was associated with prophecy and the laying on of hands. We attempted to solve the matter by the concept of "gift to be exercised in the church," with the subsidiary thought that the man being ordained takes hold of the gift afresh. If this is the wrong interpretation, either Timothy is a positively unique case of human beings giving a spiritual gift; or he is meant to be a typical case of ordination in the church, a pattern to be followed through the centuries. The latter raises historical difficulties. Ordinations have taken place which gave authority to minister but no gift to exercise. On the other hand there have been, and are, men who have received no kind of ordination whatsoever but who undoubtedly bear and exercise a *gift* of the Spirit. For laying on of hands cf. Numbers 27:18–23; Deuteronomy 34:9.

Whose hands were laid on Timothy, those of the elders or those of Paul? The traditional answer says that Paul was joined by the presbytery in the rite. Some recent scholars regard the Greek as the equivalent of a Hebrew technical expression which here means the ordination of an elder, not ordination by elders. This leaves Paul, as it were, in sole charge. The theory, if true, would support an early date for the epistle.

Verse 15: Practice these duties, devote yourself to them, so that all may see your progress: "This one thing I do" (Phil. 3:13, KJV). Versatility is excellent, for it means adaptability (1 Cor. 9:19–23; Phil. 4:11–13). But in it all there should be the one overriding purpose. *Practice* suggests prior thought, an actual doing (unlike the man who refused to enter the water until he could swim!), and the endeavor to improve ("practice makes perfect"). Herodotus (6. 105) speaks of a "day-runner," meaning a man who spends all day running, a long distance courier, who "practices" that profession. He has to do it frequently or he will not be able to do it at all. The way to preach and teach is—to preach and teach. *These duties* cover the activities of verses 12–14. *Devote yourself to them* is literally "be in these (duties)," with the implication of absorption. In the Church of England a newly ordained deacon is given a Greek Testament in which the bishop has written these three Greek works *(en toutois isthi):* they make a good beginning and a continuing motto for a young minister. The purpose is not selfish. The work will be aided, for if his *progress* spiritually (cf. Phil. 1:25) is plain for everyone to see, the disadvantages of youthfulness will fade away, and his words will carry the greater weight. The virtues of verse 12, not always attained by young people, will admit him into the company of the mature. Authority is more than that of office; it depends often on influence, i.e., on the man himself. Church members will often follow the lead in thought and deed of a man whom they respect and love when the bare authority of office would leave them cold. Character counts; known character counts still more; *progress* in character can disarm even those who "despise your youth" (v. 12).

Verse 16: Take heed to yourself and to your teaching; hold to that, for by so doing you will save both yourself and your hearers: Ministerial perspective and persistence benefits both minister and people. There should be a nice balance between self and people, one's own "progress" and the people's grasp of the faith. *Take heed* is a slight advance on "paying attention to" (v. 13). It means "aim at" yourself, "take pains with" yourself. If the minister is to be the embodiment of what a Christian really is (see on v. 12); if he himself is to be the living answer to the question, "What is a Christian?" then he clearly must take pains with himself, in thought, will and imagination. Christians are not always unkind; what seems unkindness is often just thoughtlessness. They have not used their imagination and pictured the life endured by others. Timothy must "take pains" with himself, deliberately imagining scenes and visualizing situations. If he could think out in advance the possible effect of certain words or behavior, he might modify his approach or reveal more of his faith and love. He must take pains! It is similar with his *teaching*. It is not only a question of "adequate preparation of the lesson," though this is important. He should imagine the background of his listeners, the sin and sordidness of their earlier Gentile lives. They needed the truths of the gospel and also the ethics of the gospel. When he teaches them he should be ready to exercise infinite patience with the slow and the difficult; he should plan in advance (and so be on his guard) never to hurt but always to be compassionate. "Jesus saw a great throng, and he had compassion on them . . . and he began to teach them many things" (Mark 6:34).

Hold to that: But what is *that?* The Greek is plural, with the meaning "them." It would seem that the first part of the verse, *Take heed . . . teaching,* must be taken in parenthesis; "them" will then refer to "these duties" and "them" of verse 15. *Hold to* calls for persistence and perseverance. Patience may be tried and disappointments encountered: never give up. The persistence may be illustrated by Peter who, when the girl failed to open the door, "continued knocking" (Acts 12:16); or by journalists who are faced with obstruction or evasion at a press conference and yet continue to "needle" their victim (cf. John 8:7).

Such conduct *will save* both Timothy and his *hearers.* This can hardly mean salvation in the sense of 2 Timothy 1:9 or Titus 3:5 (cf. Eph. 2:8). Timothy was not unsaved and the believers were not unsaved either. To admit this would bring uncertainty into the very religion which has it. Either Paul was thinking of the outworking of salvation (cf. Phil. 2:12) on the lines of 1 Timothy 1:5, the saving of everybody from the havoc which could be caused by false teachers; or the strictly soteriological sense has faded and he was thinking of keeping them all from the harm of spiritual ill health. The emphasis on teaching has some significance (1:3, 7; 4:11, 13, 16). If Timothy taught as he should, Paul was confident that speaker and listeners would be saved from shipwreck (1:18–20).

V. ATTITUDES AND REGULATIONS (5:1–6:2)

Wise counsel is given for dealing with people of different age and sex. Provision for widows is primarily a family responsibility, neglect of which is infidelity. Widows officially recognized by the church should bear the marks of piety as well as of age. Younger widows should not be thus enrolled, partly because of their tendency to a shallow and faithless life and partly because they should remarry and set up Christian households. The church must not be burdened unnecessarily if the family can help, so that its resources may be applied to widows in genuine need. Elders deserve honor and financial support. Guidance is given for their discipline in serious cases. Prejudice and haste are to be avoided as evidence of moral value may be delayed in its appearance. A word of medical advice to Timothy is inserted. Slaves are guided.

1. Different Age Groups in the Sexes (5:1–2)

People are to be treated according to their age as if they were blood relations: father, brother, mother, sister.

Verse 1: Do not rebuke an older man but exhort him as you would a father; treat younger men like brothers: All part of the process of disarming critics. If even to be taught by a younger man would go against the grain, how much more would *an older man* object to being the object of his *rebuke! Exhort* is rendered by "urge" in 1:3 (see discussion). The situation is reversed in Luke 15:28, where the older man "entreated" (same Greek word) the younger. "Appeal to him" sounds the right note. The *younger men* would warm to a man who really regarded them as belonging to the "household" or family of God (3:15) and brought into the church the spirit of true family relationships. Aloofness, coldness or authoritarianism would defeat Timothy's purpose. Yet even brothers sometimes have to stand up for themselves. Two extremes are thus to be avoided. Timothy was not to mete out rough treatment to the older men; and he was not to be trampled on by the younger.

Verse 2: Older women like mothers, younger women like sisters, in all purity—following Paul's own custom and spirit. He had sent greetings to Rufus and to "his mother and mine," though she was hardly his mother literally. She may have mothered him in some adversity (Rom. 16:13; cf. Mark 15:21). Cf. John 19:26, f. Paul's relation to *younger women* may be illustrated by Lydia (Acts 16:14 f., 40) and the four unmarried daughters

[80]

of Philip the evangelist (Acts 21:8 f.). For *purity* see on 4:12. *All* is a precaution against even a breath of suspicion.

2. Widows (5:3–16)

It is a religious duty for their children and grandchildren to care for widows. The genuine case is contrasted with one who is a widow in fact but not in spirit. Qualifications are given for those who are to be officially enrolled in the church's list of widows and reasons are stated for declining to include younger widows. They fall short of the spiritual qualifications and their widowhood is not to be permanent. The church should assist the widows who have no family help.

(1) Provision for widows (5:3–8)

Widowhood, which is a vocation as well as a state of life, is to be honored. Such a genuine widow continues to manifest living faith in contrast to "the merry widow" whose faith is dead. Disobedience to the religious duty of providing for widows in one's own family is to repudiate the faith.

Verse 3: Honor widows who are real widows: An unusual distinction but a valid one. *Real widows* have poignantly felt the impact of their bereavement, through which they have been brought closer to God rather than the reverse. For them widowhood has meant spiritual enrichment; for others it has meant spiritual collapse (vv. 5 f.). Anna was a *real widow* and the fact that she is called a "prophetess" suggests that widowhood is a vocation for which God gives the appropriate *charisma* or "gift" (Luke 2:36–38) as he does in marriage (1 Cor. 7:7).

The preacher and pastor will start from here and in his ministry to the bereaved will point out the opportunity which widowhood has brought. He will do it with charity and tact and he will be careful about his timing. It would be the height of folly and heartlessness to stand by the deathbed and tell the new widow what an opportunity she has now that her husband is dead.

To *honor widows* is to take on the duties of the Fifth Commandment (cf. Mark 7:10–13). It may give them public regard and respect. Widows were traditionally defenseless (Luke 18:3; 20:47; Jas. 1:27). And if necessary it may involve also some financial support. (The *honor* is financial with the elders, as vv. 17 f. show.) In the absence of assistance from her family the church would be rightly acting as the family of God (3:15; 5:1 f.; cf. Mark 3:31–35; 10:29 f.).

Verse 4: If a widow has children or grandchildren, let them first learn their religious duty to their own family and make some return to their parents; for this is acceptable in the sight of God: The children should learn their duty and therefore should learn to make some return. The *religious duty* means "the exercise of godliness" (toward God and therefore) toward *their own family.* The verb in question, "(learn) to exercise godliness," is cognate to "godly" (2:2), "religion" (3:16) and "godliness" (4:7 f.). This recognizes the Fifth Commandment. To *make some return* is a reasonable reciprocity. From parents they have received love, shelter, home and security. A *return* is but thankfulness.

True godliness or the discharge of *religious duty* could hardly fail to be *acceptable*. In this context the duties of the family, an institution of creation which has even deeper meaning in the realm of grace, have priority over the duties of charity. (Contrast Matt. 10:34–37.) The place of the Greek accent leads some scholars to prefer the rendering "pleasing" to *acceptable* (cf. 2:3). This avoids giving the impression of any kind of justification by works: men are "accepted" by God in Christ. Paul combined "acceptable and pleasing" in Philippians 4:18. In Romans 12:1 "acceptable" means "pleasing." Its spirit is illustrated by our welcoming of people. "When we had come to Jerusalem, the brethren received us gladly" (Acts 21:17).

In the sight of God is a hebraism, with the meaning of "in the opinion of, in the judgment of" (cf. 2 Cor. 8:21). It yields the pleasing picture of God watching men and giving a glad welcome ("acceptance") to their works when they come to his house.

Verse 5: She who is a real widow, and is left all alone, has set her hope on God and continues in supplications and prayers night and day: Isolated on earth but never alone. She has no husband and no relations. The two perfect tenses suggest a crisis in her life. "She who has been made solitary" means that "she is now *alone*." This obviously refers to the death of her husband. "She *has set her hope on God*" implies that "her hope is now resting firmly on God." See on 4:10. When did she *set* it *on God?* It must be when her husband died or just afterwards. But as a Christian wife she must have already been hoping in God (cf. Eph. 2:12; 4:4; Col. 1:23, 27). After her husband had died there was no one in her immediate circle to whom she could turn, and she turned to God in renewal of her hope. The shattering effect of bereavement was a deep experience in itself and did not automatically bring its own alleviation. She found that the object of her earlier hope was nearer, more tender, than she had ever realized. The "hope of sharing the glory of God" became for her a hope which "does not disappoint." God's love flooded her life. After the death of her husband she clearly drank more deeply of the wells of salvation from which she had drunk at her conversion and once more she *set her hope on God*. The pattern of her experience is outlined in Romans 5:1–5.

From the time of this renewal of her hope up to the present moment she had been hoping without cessation. *Night and day* she kept the hope alive because night and day she *continues in supplications and prayers. Night* may hint at the overcoming of sleeplessness; *day* shows her at her normal duties or in any intervals of relaxation, not indeed forgetting the past but growing in the joy of an outlived sorrow, because her hope continues, parallel to her prayer. As long as the prayer lasts, so long does her hope abide, as days pass into months and months into years. The hope of eternity has a new appeal, and as a result of her life of prayer she is at home with God—long before her "homecall."

Verse 6: Whereas she who is self-indulgent is dead even while she lives: "Seeing life" means death. *Self-indulgent* points to revelry and dissoluteness. Just as widowers at times seek to drown their sorrows in drink, so some widows try to forget an earlier happiness in living a wild social life. They join the smart set, with its glitter and its looseness, and think that an earlier dullness, as it now appears, has gone forever. "This is life!" But in spite of all appearances, "the merry widow" is *dead*. She has cut herself off from the Christian community, either by deliberate choice or by neglect of its worship and fellowship, and has forfeited any claim to its care. She has undoubtedly forgotten her prayers, in contrast to the "real widow." Her rightful place would be at funerals. "Leave the dead to bury their own dead." She has ceased "to keep on following Jesus" (Matt. 8:22). (Cf. Jas. 2:17; 5:5a.)

Verse 7: Command this, so that they may be without reproach: Additional instructions for the church (cf. 4:11). Widows must be as much *without reproach* (see on 3:2) as bishops. This suggests that widows must be carefully screened, and prepares the way for verses 9–15.

Verse 8: If any one does not provide for his relatives, and especially for his own family, he has disowned the faith and is worse than an unbeliever: The Christian faith does not cancel but emphasizes the claims of kinship. See on verse 4. It seems to be implied that all the parties are Christians.

Men have *disowned the faith* in two ways. The one class does it with words and explicitly repudiates it, emphasizing either the rejection of a person or the denial of Christian truth. A classical example is Peter, who denied his Lord (Matt. 26:69–74). A man who denies that Jesus is the Christ is a liar and is antichrist (1 John 2:22 f.). Denial may be stated by one who formerly professed the Christian faith or by those who have never believed. The Jews of Antioch of Pisidia contradicted what Paul was saying and thrust the Word of God from them (Acts 13:45 f.).

The other class implicitly disowns the faith by what it does rather than by what it says. "They profess to know God, but they deny him by their deeds" (Titus 1:16). The Jews denied Jesus, the Holy and Righteous One, and killed him, the Author of life (Acts 3:13–15).

As Paul saw it, the person who *does not provide for* the widows who are related to him has *disowned the faith* whatever he may actually say. Deeds speak more loudly than words. *Relatives* may be more "distant" than members of *his own* immediate *family*. Such a man is *worse than an unbeliever*. He sins against the light; the unbeliever has little light. The man who switches off the light is worse than the man who has never known anything brighter than a candle. In conversion he has undertaken obligations which the unbeliever has not. The unbeliever may even put him to shame by following the light which he has (Rom. 2:14 f.)—the Fifth Commandment! (Cf. 2 Pet. 2:21.)

(2) "Official" widows (5:9–10)

If a widow is to be formally enrolled as such, she must have a reputation in the church for a long life of Christian service. Though busy as wife and mother, she must have entertained guests in her home and aided the distressed outside, in the humble and constant versatility of doing good.

Verse 9: Let a widow be enrolled if she is not less than sixty years of age, having been the wife of one husband: Not any and every widow is qualified. The "real" widow has high spiritual qualifications (vv. 5, 10). She is to receive assistance (v. 16), but she is more than merely a name on a list of beneficiaries. It would seem that the real widow had the duties roughly corresponding to that of a deaconess. Some scholars speak of an order of widows, much like an order of deaconesses. The age is significant: at *sixty* the widow can be trusted to devote her time to the service of Christ, without hankering after remarriage (v. 11; cf. 3:11).

The wife of one husband is reminiscent of 3:2, 12 (see discussions). It may here imply that her marriage must have been a happy or "successful" one. The view is held that the expression is directed against the remarriage of the divorced, not of the widowed (cf. v. 14). More likely it reflects the possibility that a woman twice married may have more relatives to aid her in her needs, so that she will not need the financial help of the church (v. 16). She need not therefore be *enrolled.* Inevitably this would mean one less on the roll of "church workers" in receipt of money; but it would not necessarily mean one less worker. A woman with the character described in the next verse would surely go on "doing good in every way." At the age of *sixty* she has proved her Christian experience and reliability and has not been the disappointment revealed in verses 11–13.

It is worth reflecting that a "real" widow is more than a woman whose husband is dead. It is a vocation, a calling, which is not heard or at least not heeded by all. We are reminded of this from an unexpected source. It is said that when Lenin's widow was proving somewhat lacking in cooperation, the authorities threatened to appoint someone else to the position! Widowhood is a task as well as a sorrow.

Verse 10: And she must be well attested for her good deeds, as one who has brought up children, shown hospitality, washed the feet of the saints, relieved the afflicted, and devoted herself to doing good in every way—her life an open book, read and approved by all. Even in humble circumstances such a woman would be a city set on a hill, letting her light shine before all (cf. Matt. 5:14–16). She shares the testimony of the bishop once more (cf. v. 7; 3:2, 7). (Cf. Heb. 11:2, 4, 5, 39, KJV.) Merely to be sixty years of age is not enough. "Samples" of good works (2:10) are given, summed up in the comprehensive *doing good in every way.*

If she *has brought up children* they must now be dead (vv. 4 f.) or she would not qualify. She may, however, have looked after the children of others or orphans. *Hospitality* again links her with the bishop (see on 3:2). Even the poor can open their door to the stranger; and traveling evangelists might be more at home with simple souls than with the wealthy. The scene is drawn from her married life, not her widowhood. If she had *washed the feet of the saints,* she had shown both hospitality and humility (1 Sam. 25:41; Mark 1:7; Luke 7:44–46; John 13:1–15). *The saints* are fellow Christians, however much or little they have advanced on the road of holiness. The Epistle to the Ephesians was addressed to the saints there (Eph. 1:1). The Epistle to the Romans was sent to "all God's beloved in Rome" (Rom. 1:7). They were not merely "called to be saints" but were "saints by calling," "saints by vocation." Some of them had a long way to go (cf. Phil. 1:15–18), and the word "saint" may emphasize destiny rather than performance. The point is that "every saint" (Phil. 4:21 f.) is a way of speaking of any Christian. Some Christians are not very saintly, and may not be attractive in behavior; even so the real widow *washed the feet* of such people.

When she *relieved the afflicted* she did what believers were supposed to do to "assist" (same Greek word, v. 16) widows. This may be an example of a "return" (v. 4). The verb has the flavor of being "sufficient," being adequate in meeting needs. Part of her ministry to *the afflicted* may have been counsel concerning the place of affliction in the Christian life; this at times could be quite as important as food, drink and shelter. (See 1 Thess. 1:6; 3:3 f., 7.) She may even have shown them that affliction confirmed their election.

Devoted herself to: Literally "follow" every good work. It is the same word as in "follow in his steps" (1 Pet. 2:21). The good works are the footprints of Christ, which good works "God prepared beforehand, that we should walk in them" (Eph. 2:10). The real widow is an example to all Christians.

(3) Younger widows (5:11–16)

Younger widows are not to be enrolled. Their plight tends to lead them away from Christ instead of closer to him and they are likely to degenerate into idle and dangerous gossips. It would be spiritually more profitable for them to remarry and set up Christian households. A Christian woman with widowed dependents should undertake the responsibility of caring for them and thus relieve the church for more necessitous cases.

Verse 11: But refuse to enrol younger widows; for when they grow wanton against Christ they desire to marry: If they were enrolled they would give up their Christian work. This is an interpretation of the Greek, which means literally "have nothing to do with" younger widows (as in 4:7; 2 Tim. 2:23). Paul might have been warning Timothy that they would seek to entangle him. If he kept apart he would not enroll them anyway.

Paul was not here betraying an antagonism to marriage or to second marriage. A little later he advocated it (v. 14). He was thinking, realistically and perhaps as a result of what he had seen in church life, of the dangers of younger widows giving themselves to the work of the church and then, with a greater or less degree of blameworthiness, giving it up owing to the emotional strain. They were still in the flower of life and the tide of their instincts was running high. This is what is meant when the text says that they *grow wanton*. It does not necessarily mean that the apostle was accusing them of sexual sin. Everything within them cried out for marriage and it was *against Christ* in that it diverted their attention from his service to their own needs. "He who is not with me is against me" (Luke 11:23).

Verse 12: And so they incur condemnation for having violated their first pledge: It is to avoid this that they are not to be enrolled. They had been given support and they were pledged to serve. They were regarding—or would be regarding—their original consent to minister as no longer of any significance. (Perhaps cf. 2 Cor. 11:2.) Paul may even have felt that in some way they would be slighting their "first faith" in Christ. It is not apostasy but deficiency which he had in mind. They would not be denying the faith but not living up to it in their situation. He wanted to save them from this. Their emotions would lead them into other dangers also (v. 13).

Verse 13: Besides that, they learn to be idlers, gadding about from house to house, and not only idlers but gossips and busybodies, saying what they should not: Once complete devotion to Christ is abandoned, a chain reaction starts. Other interests begin to take the place of the once dominant purpose. Notice that they *learn;* they have not always been *idlers*. When the Lord filled their life there was plenty to do. There still is, but they do not do it.

What in the days of real ministry had been a circuit of purposive visitation has become the flitting of a butterfly. They are itinerant speakers without an itinerary or a message. They are *gadding about* without the excuse that they "went about" under persecution (Heb. 11:37).

Their life is a study in the mismanagement and misuse of a privileged position. Ministers and Christian workers more than most people have the entrée into people's homes. These women take the familiar road into well-known houses where they show themselves as *gossips and busybodies.* As *gossips* they do not talk about subjects appropriate to their high calling. When they could be bringing the word of life they talk nonsense. They pry into affairs which do not concern them; they are inquisitive and meddlesome and express opinions which at the very least should have been left unsaid: they say *what they should not.* Such a "ministry" of *busybodies* could not be tolerated as it plays into the hands of the enemy (v. 14). The fair Name of Jesus must not be sullied or blasphemed (cf. Jas. 2:7).

Verse 14: So I would have younger widows marry, bear children, rule their households, and give the enemy no occasion to revile us: Marriage and the domestic life should keep them out of mischief. *I would have* (*boulomai*) expresses authority, as in 2:8; it gives a ruling to solve a difficult problem. The decision recognizes the realities of the situation and the causes which give rise to it (1 Cor. 7:9), and ultimately appeals to the natural vocation of women (see on 2:15). When wives *rule their households* they are not giving up their submissiveness (see on 2:11 f.) but are acting as the female counterpart of their husband, the householder (Matt. 24:43). They preside as hostess, manage the housekeeping and look after and bring up the children. In such an innocent occupation the adversary, "the one who opposes" (2 Thess. 2:4), will find no base of operations from which to launch a verbal attack on the church. Such wives are to give him no "handle." *To revile* is to abuse, to hurl obscene epithets at a person. (Cf. 1 Pet. 2:23.)

Verse 15: For some have already strayed after Satan: Paul was not theorizing. Bitter experience led him to his decision. Some widows had turned away, had gone over to the other side, and followed the enemy (v. 14). There is an echo of the call of Christ in *after Satan. After* is *opisō,* used by our Lord when he said, "Come after me" (Matt. 4:19), "follow after me" (Matt. 10:38). When they should have continued to follow after Christ, some changed direction and went *after Satan.*

Verse 16: If any believing woman has relatives who are widows, let her assist them; let the church not be burdened, so that it may assist those who are real widows: Funds are limited and must not be diverted. The *relatives* is an inference as the Greek says "has widows." It may include dependents, widows of men employed by the *believing woman,* who could be brought into her household. This would not be impossible if there were a Christian woman at Ephesus with a position equal to that of Lydia at Philippi (Acts 16:14 f.). See on verse 10 for *assist.* Paul was quite capable of pointing out to believers what he deemed to be their Christian duty. The great preacher and defender of the doctrine of justification by faith had a considerable place for works (1 Cor. 7:19). Works do not justify but are evidence of having been justified, evidence of a living faith. Cf. Rom. 13:8–10.

3. Elders (5:17–25)

Elders deserve respect and financial support, as the Bible teaches. No accusation against an elder is to be entertained except on the strongest evidence, but persistent sin is to be publicly rebuked as a deterrent to others. Timothy is solemnly charged to follow the line set out by the apostle without prejudice or partiality. Speed is frowned upon as it involves action without full knowledge. A medical remedy is prescribed.

(1) Financial support (5:17–18)

Notable service in the eldership, especially preaching and teaching, is to be recognized with double honor. Scripture is quoted to justify payment.

Verse 17: Let the elders who rule well be considered worthy of double honor, especially those who labor in preaching and teaching: Preachers and teachers shine among the elders. Reference should be made to 3:1–7; 5:1; Titus 1:5–9 and discussions. *The* first *elders* were most likely chosen from among the older men, so that a man who was "older" became an "elder." The core of their work was pastoral supervision. The word for *rule* is used in 3:4 f., 12 for the management of household and children. This ministry of oversight is described as episcopal (3:1), as the Epistle to Titus makes clear. Elders of certain character are to be appointed, "for a bishop ... must be blameless" (Titus 1:5, 7). The "for" is very significant. There is thus no precise distinction between elder and bishop. The ecclesiastical structure is primitive. This points to the early date of the epistle, which does not reflect the monarchical episcopate as Ignatius advocates it. It is doubtful if Paul would have gone so far as to say, with Ignatius, that whatever the bishop approves is also pleasing to God (*Epistle to the Smyrnaeans,* 8).

The *double honor* includes respect and financial support (cf. 5:3 and discussion). Verse 18 must involve finance or some kind of material assistance. *The elders* are not only to be *considered* ... but actually given the *double honor.*

Pastoral supervision comes to its climax and makes its impact *in preaching and teaching.* For *teaching* see discussions on 1:3, 7, 10; 4:1, 6, 11, 13, 16. The Greek word behind *preaching* is *logos.* Paul could not have meant merely "speech," which is what it could mean in other contexts. He was referring to men *who labor* in the Word. "Preach the word" (2 Tim. 4:2). It may be doubted if Paul made a distinction between those who preached and taught and those who "labored" in the work. To preach and teach is to *labor* (cf. 1 Thess. 5:12).

Verse 18: For the scripture says, "You shall not muzzle an ox when it is treading out the grain," and, "The laborer deserves his wages": Interpretation and literal statement combined. The first quotation is from Deuteronomy 25:4. In the threshing of grain the sheaves were laid down to a depth of about a foot. An ox walked backwards and forwards or round and round on top of the sheaves. The repeated pressure of its *treading* separated the grains which fell to the bottom with broken pieces of straw. When this stage had been completed the winnowing began. Grains and pieces of straw were together shoveled up and thrown into the air, particularly when the wind was blowing. The heavier grain fell to the ground but the straw was the "chaff which the wind drives away" (Ps. 1:4). The grain, now separated from the straw, was itself shoveled up and taken away to the granary. The Old Testament law was a beneficent provision to allow the ox to eat some kernels as it was *treading out the grain*. Paul was not calling a minister an ox—though even if he were there would be no legitimate grounds for complaint. Our Lord spoke of his sheep; and even "pastor" is the Latin word for a shepherd. If the Lord himself is the Lion of Judah (Rev. 5:5) there is no reason why his ministerial servants should not be oxen. All this, however, is not the main point. In the Old Testament law Paul detected a principle which he had applied before (1 Cor. 9:9 f.; in v. 10 render "entirely" by "certainly"). If sustenance is to be derived even by animals from their work, how much more by humans? The agricultural metaphor is used in the words to the Corinthian church, "You are God's field" (1 Cor. 3:9).

The second quotation is identical with Luke 10:7b. (Matt. 10:10 has "food" instead of "wages." Cf. 1 Cor. 9:14.) Now it may or may not have been possible for Paul to have quoted from Luke's Gospel *as we now have it*. But it is not impossible for him to have quoted from the Gospel of Luke during its formation. Paul had close associations with Luke, as the "we" passages in the Acts testify. "We . . . came to Caesarea" (Acts 21:8), where Paul later spent two years (Acts 23:33; 24:27). From there it was decided that "we" should sail for Italy (Acts 27:1). To judge from his preface, Luke must have taken a long time in the necessary research for, and writing of, his Gospel (Luke 1:1–4). What is more reasonable than that Luke should have discussed his work with Paul? What is more reasonable than that Luke should have read extracts to the apostle or that Paul should have dipped into Luke's writings? Spicq (p. 177) regards this as the oldest quotation from the Gospels as Scripture. Some scholars dissent from such a view, in spite of the significant *and*. But Paul could speak of men who "read the old covenant" (as we say, "the Old Testament," 2 Cor. 3:14) and he was obviously referring to a book. He also believed in "the new covenant" (1 Cor. 11:25). He knew that the apostles would not live forever. Is it utterly impossible for him to have conceived of a written record, on a level with the Old Testament, especially when it contained the words of Jesus? The argument that the second quotation is floating evangelical tradition is not in itself impossible, apart from the problematic *and*.

The "we-sections" in Acts are: 16:10–17; 20:5–21:18; 27:1–28:16.

The principle that "what *the scripture says,* God says," is not to be used mechanically or against the general teaching of Scripture or indeed against plain commonsense. It would be ridiculous to assert that "there is no God" (Ps. 53:1) on the ground that "this is what *the scripture says.*"

(2) Discipline (5:19–20)

Honor is to be accorded to elders by the rejection of insinuations against them. Any accusation must be formally substantiated by two or three witnesses. Persistent sin should be publicly rebuked as an example to others.

Verse 19: Never admit any charge against an elder except on the evidence of two or three witnesses: Correctness is to be established before being influenced. A *charge* may be idle gossip or may arise out of an individual's misunderstanding or prejudice. It would be a strange minister who never had a word said *against* him. Frivolous accusations or even serious ones arising from isolated people should not determine Timothy's action. Either such talk should be completely ignored or, if *two or three* people unite in a common testimony, a discreet inquiry should be made. Such a *charge* should be dealt with and innocence or guilt established. The refusal to *admit* the single *charge* would be part of Timothy's "example" (see on 4:12), and would express part of the "honor" (v. 17) due to an elder. *Two or three witnesses* is an allusion to Deuteronomy 19:15. Apart from the justice of the matter, Timothy's continued attitude might help to stamp out idle talk.

Verse 20: As for those who persist in sin, rebuke them in the presence of all, so that the rest may stand in fear: Not censoriousness but pastoral discipline in the interests of all. The force of the impact would depend on the rarity of the occasion of *rebuke. Those who persist* must mean the erring elders from time to time. *All* refers to the whole church and *the rest* may mean either the other elders or the church. Paul's scheme is midway between an intolerance which is always pinpricking and a tolerance which neglects to deal with a grave situation.

(3) Avoidance of prejudice and haste (5:21–25)

The apostle's directions are to be strictly observed. There is no place for prejudice or partiality. Hasty action may involve Timothy in the sins of others, for the moral evidence is not always apparent at first sight. A little wine is recommended for Timothy's ailments.

Verse 21: In the presence of God and of Christ Jesus and of the elect angels I charge you to keep these rules without favor, doing nothing from partiality: Not ecclesiastical despotism but apostolic fortification. Paul was not laying down the law in an objectionable way but putting backbone into a timid young minister. If the words were read in church they would strengthen his position. The solemn *charge* has as its background the very Day of Judgment, though not as a mere idea. The act of writing such a charge was *in the presence of* the One who sees all—and approved the charge. Timothy must not fail to carry it out. For *Christ Jesus* see on 1:1-2. The *elect angels* may be contrasted with the angels who had sinned (cf. 2 Pet. 2:4). They do not detract from the majesty of the Lord but enhance it (see 2 Thess. 1:7; cf. Mark 8:38; 2 Tim. 4:1). The situation was such as to inspire awe: Timothy represented the Judge and would himself finally stand before him. *Without favor* means "without making decisions in advance" of the due examination of witnesses—without "prejudice." The absence of *partiality* is well illustrated by the old Wiclif rendering of Hebrews 10:23, Let us hold fast the confession of our hope, "bowing to no side." No private preference for individuals should make Timothy "bow" to a guilty man.

Verse 22: Do not be hasty in the laying on of hands: Do not ordain anyone in a hurry. This fairly obvious interpretation (cf. 4:14) accords with the requirement that a bishop must not be a recent convert (3:6). The view that the text refers to the readmission of penitents into church fellowship is an anachronism. The restoration to communion through the laying on of hands does not seem to have started until the third century. It is just possible that

Paul was thinking of laying (violent) hands on people, but it is unlikely. The context favors the thought of ordination, and violence is not the best interpretation of the Greek. Young men in a hurry to become ministers and chafing at the slowness of the church in coming to a decision should reflect that it is not always due to negligence. Ancient wisdom is supported by Scripture, and the ability to exercise patience may be part of the test (cf. 3:10).

Nor participate in another man's sins—by giving him the opportunity to sin. A minister has the temptations common to all men, and he has also those which arise from the office which he holds. To be a shepherd of the church of God is a solemn responsibility, and a minister has opportunities for sin which he did not have as a layman. Men listen to his public utterances: does he deny the truth or mislead the faithful? Does he make inflammatory speeches which raise tempers but fail to edify? Does he merely entertain when he ought to be an influence for holiness? Almost as a matter of course he can enter a hundred homes. Does he abuse hospitality? Does he resist the charms which may begin in innocence but are fraught with dangers? Does he loaf and chatter and piously call it pastoral visitation?

Any ecclesiastical authority which recklessly and hurriedly sets apart for ministry men who are untested and unproved is guilty. Such careless men *participate in* or share the *sins* of those to whom they have given the opportunity, even though they themselves have not committed the actual sins. The thought is analogous to that of 2 John 11. The admonition not to *participate* is an extension of the former prohibition of hasty ordinations.

Keep yourself pure—by following the instructions just given. This is in addition to 4:12; 5:2 and means "go on keeping yourself pure." Notice the place of effort in the Christian life. It is inspired by John 17:11 f., 15. (See also 1 Thess. 5:23.) Timothy was himself an ordained man and had received a "gift" (4:14). It should be recognized that any blessing which came to him because he was a minister, any "grace of ordination" as it is sometimes called, did not work like a machine. Like all ministers he had to *keep* himself *pure*.

Verse 23: No longer drink only water, but use a little wine for the sake of your stomach and your frequent ailments: A realistic appreciation of the situation. The verse is not so irrelevant as it might seem and no forger, trying to pass himself off as Paul, would have inserted so "unspiritual" an injunction. The operative word is *stomach*, which is no more than a transliteration from the Greek. It was taken over into Latin, where a "good stomach" means a good digestion. As a deponent verb (*stomachari*) it is used in the sense of "to be peevish, out of humor, to fume," and it can mean "to quarrel with."

As Timothy had weighty responsibilities on his hands he would have to guard against dyspeptic choler and the possibility of losing his temper and starting a quarrel. Paul's robust commonsense is here united with his spirituality. Take a little remedy; the water may be impure anyway. The quantity advocated is small and the reason is clearly stated. It would be quite unjustifiable to use the verse as an argument for heavy drinking.

Verse 24: The sins of some men are conspicuous, pointing to judgment, but the sins of others appear later: All the more reason to avoid hasty ordinations. *The sins of some men* are so blatant that the dullest person cannot help thinking of *judgment*. *The sins* point to it as surely as prophetic utterances had pointed to Timothy's future ministry (1:18). The contrast between the two kinds of sin is remarkable. The sins of some are obviously leading them on to judgment. They are out in front, heading in the direction of judgment. In the rear, following as inevitably as if tied with unbreakable rope, come the men. In the other case the men themselves are out in front, thinking that they are alone. But hot on their heels, relentlessly refusing to let them get out of sight, come their sins. In grim contrast the sins follow in their steps (cf. 1 Pet. 2:21). (See on 5:10, "devoted.") Seen or unseen, sins are never separated from those who commit them until they are forgiven. *Appear later* is a paraphrase. Read literally: "some (men) their sins follow."

Verse 25: So also good deeds are conspicuous; and even when they are not, they cannot remain hidden: The previous verse in reverse. Just as hasty ordinations are to be avoided, so candidates for the ministry, even when unprepossessing, should not be rejected without allowing plenty of time to find out their worth. There is no reference here to judgment. A parallel to *good deeds* which are *conspicuous* is "a city set on a hill" (Matt. 5:14–16). Other good deeds which do not strike the eye may have been done in secret without fanfare, even the left hand not knowing what the right hand is doing (Matt. 6:1–4). Sooner or later, Paul implied, the story would come out; Timothy would hear about it—and perhaps another timid man, like Timothy himself, would be saved for the ministry.

4. Slaves (6:1–2)

Slaves should respect their masters and not take advantage of them if they are Christians. On the contrary they should serve them all the better.

Verse 1: Let all who are under the yoke of slavery regard their masters as worthy of all honor, so that the name of God and the teaching may not be defamed: The great object is not the maintenance of the status quo but the glory of God. *Their masters* are not Christians. If, contrary to practice, the slaves do not respect their owners, it will be assumed that their conduct is due to their Christian faith. God will be blasphemed and men will say that it all comes from *the* new, foolish *teaching*. Their criticisms will be made to appear reasonable. Slaves should be witnesses to the gospel which means so much to them, not so much by talk as by deed, withholding not even the slightest form of respect: *all honor* is to be given, not "some honor." For *yoke* cf. Genesis 27:40. The figure eloquently likens the slave to an animal which cannot go where it likes or do what it wants. Paul's great concern was the glory of God, not to perpetuate the institution of slavery (cf. 1 Cor. 7:21). The lesson for today is that the Christian employee should commend his gospel by the quality of his work and his respect for those who issue the orders. He may be the only Christian witness the "boss" is ever likely to see. For *name of God* see 2 Thessalonians 1:12. It means God as revealed, present and active. (Cf. Titus 2:9 f.)

Verse 2: Those who have believing masters must not be disrespectful on the ground that they are brethren; rather they must serve all the better since those who benefit by their service are believers and beloved: Christian faith means more respect and service, not less, to fellow Christians. Equality before God does not always mean equality before men. This has to be carefully expressed in order to avoid the charge of snobbery. A man's social position is largely determined by what other people think of him. If he is an aristocrat by birth, he has social eminence only because society is pleased to recognize aristocrats—not every society does. If he carries weight as a highly educated man, it is because society values learning. Some sections of society could not care less. If he is a very ordinary person, he occupies a humble position because society does not see anything higher in him. If he is a slave he is virtually a nonentity because society so regards him. Now in the community of believers high and low meet together in Christ as brethren in him. Slave owner and slave go to the Lord's Table together, each equally dependent on the Lord for salvation. In the life of society, society's distinctions are to be observed. The slave who takes advantage of *believing masters* puts fellow slaves into a difficult position and perhaps himself into a privileged position. It would not be the best form of Christian witness. Serve the master all the more: you are giving benefit to one who is among the *believers and beloved.* Thus even the slave becomes a benefactor. And he saves his master from an awkward dilemma. If he is *disrespectful*, is the master to punish him (*brethren!*) or tolerate the offense? If he tolerates it, it is unfair to the other slaves; it might encourage cheekiness, insubordination or careless work; and its logical end would be anarchy and even the horrors of a slave war. Christian slaves who *serve all the better* are an example to the other slaves and they might help to sweeten their common lives. *Believing masters* would surely be responsive.

The other side of the picture is seen in the Epistle to Philemon (cf. vv. 15 f.).

In case it is thought that the position of Christianity in general and of Paul in particular was reactionary and accepted the social order when it ought to have opposed it, certain statements must be appended. The approach of the social gospel would have led to violent argument and bloodshed and would not have succeeded. Persecution would have been intensified and the slaves would have gained no benefit. And the chief truth of the gospel would have gone unpreached. It was largely a question of policy and Christianity chose a better way. It concentrated on preaching the gospel and living the Christian life. The owners of slaves were taught their Christian duty towards their property (Eph. 6:9; Col. 4:1). In Christ man was valued as man, whether slave or free (Gal. 3:28). The Christian spirit was in time followed by legislation to mitigate the lot of slaves and finally to abolish the institution. It is a case of the leaven working secretly. A direct attack would have brought utter chaos. Social redemption follows individual conversion.

Critics of the historic Christian method do not always remember that the church was under persecution when the problem of slavery was at its height. It is one thing today for a preacher of the social gospel to denounce the government and to seek to undermine the present structure of society. He is fortunate: it is the very society under his criticism that gives him the right so to speak. He might find it very different if he were a hunted man in a totalitarian state which had vowed to stamp out the Christian faith. Even if men heeded his message, would it be a profit to gain a new, secularized world and to lose the soul, because Christ himself is unpreached because unknown?

There is a place today for the church to be the conscience of society and to protest against social ills. But it is not the first place. Seek first God's kingdom, which is not the material eating and drinking, and all the rest will follow (cf. Matt. 6:33; Rom. 14:17). The obvious course is to get devout Christians into politics; but how far could they legislate if they depended on the votes of an unbelieving, secularized populace? The message of the ancient church is still relevant: evangelize—or two generations will see the end of the church and the rise of the secularized state with the slavery of its freedoms.

VI. MINGLED OBSERVATIONS (6:3–19)

False teaching arises from conceit and ignorance and love of controversy, with disastrous moral consequences. It is even thought that piety is profitable. It is profitable, if combined with contentment. Desire for wealth leads to temptation and ruin; indeed in the love of money all evils are rooted. It leads to departure from the faith and great sorrow. In contrast the man of God should have spiritual aims and continue the Christian warfare. He is called to eternal life. A solemn charge is laid on Timothy in the light of the coming of the Lord. The grandeur of language culminates in a doxology. The rich are not to be haughty but should set their hope on God, and by generosity and good works prepare for the future and for the life which is life indeed.

1. A Verdict on False Teachers (6:3–8)

A teacher whose doctrine impiously conflicts with the apostolic principles laid down and with the Lord's words is inflated with ignorance and bent on controversy. The result is that depraved men devoid of the truth find further expressions for their social enmity. They think that piety is mere gain, forgetting to add the qualification of contentment.

Teach and urge these duties: This concludes the foregoing and introduces what follows, thus doing double duty. The words strictly belong to verse 2 but are considered here because they begin the paragraph in RSV. Continued activity was in the mind of Paul. He was far from saying, "Have a go at it." He rather meant, "Keep on teaching and . . . ." Hearers were to be informed about the truth and its claims and urged to obey. The behavior of slaves was in the foreground of the apostle's thought but behind it was the whole message of the epistle. For *urge* see discussion on 1:3.

Verse 3: If any one teaches otherwise and does not agree with the sound words of our Lord Jesus Christ and the teaching which accords with godliness: Not a medication but a virus. *Teaches otherwise* recalls 1:3, with the same Greek verb. (Cf. 4:1.) *Agree with* is literally "approach." Such a person does not investigate the evidence but leaves it severely alone. His teaching in consequence does not even "approach" the truth. *The sound words* are both healthy and healing (see on 1:10), and afford nourishment (cf. 4:6; the discussion there is relevant here). *The sound words of our Lord Jesus Christ* suggest the Lord's own words to be found in the Gospels, but it is far from certain. For one thing the meaning might be "words about our Lord" (on the analogy of "the word of the cross," 1 Cor. 1:18). For another, *sound words* has no article, the effect being "does not agree with sound words, those of our Lord Jesus Christ." The *sound words* in fact stand for the apostolic message which Paul implied was the message given by Jesus. Two texts from the Gospels give us a clue: ". . . if any one will not . . . listen to your words . . ." (Matt. 10:14); "He who hears you hears me . . ." (Luke 10:16). For *Lord Jesus Christ* see on 1:1–2, and cf. Romans 14:11 with Philippians 2:11, noticing the common background of Isaiah 45:23. For *godliness* see discussions on 2:2; 3:16; 4:7 f. *Teaching* comes through but does not originate in Christian experience.

Verse 4: He is puffed up with conceit, he knows nothing: Size—huge; contents—nil. (Cf. 3:6.) "Knowledge puffs up, inflates; love builds up" (1 Cor. 8:1). But here it was not even knowledge but speculation deeply embedded in pride, for the one source has been ignored (1 Cor. 2:2—and the whole context).

He has a morbid craving for controversy and for disputes about words: He runs berserk into many a verbal battle. He has ignored the only healing words (v. 3) and is still ill, *craving* not for liquor but for *words*. *Controversy* is verbal or it becomes a fight; and when it is petty it becomes *disputes about words*. When he needs nourishment he looks for stimulants (cf. 4:6).

Which produce envy, dissension, slander, base suspicions—a crescendo. Controversy and disputes have their children and grandchildren, as it were, each succeeding generation being worse than its predecessor. First to be born is *envy*, the inner attitude towards other teachers who have their following; perhaps towards orthodox Christian teachers and even Timothy himself. The child of envy is *dissension*, which is envy brought out into the open. It is possible at times for men to be envious and to say nothing and do nothing. But not in the present instance. Envy here is vocal. The object of the envy objects to what is said and the result is division and strife. The first words of envy may have been near to the truth, though sufficiently direct and relevant to catch the opponent on the raw. But the resultant *dissension* begets its own child, worse than itself. Hitherto the argument has been about theories and speculations, principles and doctrines. But now *slander* has been born. Hidden animosity is brought out into the open. Personal remarks are made. The attack is pressed home, no longer on the opponent's theories but on his personal life, and truth is conveniently forgotten in the heat of the moment. It is legitimate in discussion or controversy to say, "Your theory is wrong." But slander goes further and says, "You are a liar." The child of slander is even more inventive than its father. *Base suspicions* imagine—and state—deeper motives, twist the opponent's words so as to show him up as a villain, impute to him what he never said or thought and maliciously cast aspersions on his character. This is not godliness and it does not accord with godliness; and it is not contending for the faith.

Verse 5: And wrangling among men who are depraved in mind and bereft of the truth, imagining that godliness is a means of gain: The final monstrous birth. The "perpetual collisions" which constitute *wrangling* are illustrated by Chrysostom in the picture of sheep with the mange which infect the healthy ones by rubbing against them. Certainly he who "teaches otherwise" (v. 3) is a sick man (v. 4) and has sired an ailing race: mind, truth and sense of values have all gone from them. They are *depraved in mind* in that their mental and moral consciousness is ruined. No doubt something "goes on in their head" or they would not be able to say anything at all. But they have lost the power of significant thought, have no apprehension of the truth, and conscience has throbbed its last. (Cf. 1:5, 19; 3:9; 4:2 and discussions.) They are as *bereft of the truth* as a man who has had something stolen from him. They may be described as "completely without it." But the truth has not been actually stolen from them: it has ebbed away. It begins to leave when a man neglects his own devotional life; he becomes a prey to false theories and pride, in time, welcomes them, especially if they are of his own creation ("I do my own thinking."). Allied with this is the loss of a sense of values; religion has become commercialized. Such men are of the opinion that *godliness is a means of gain*. No doubt they charged fees for giving lectures to Christians who ought to have known better. (Cf. Titus 1:11.) Insofar as the divine came into their picture, they were making use of God for their own material gain and turning the church or part of it into just another business house with which to trade.

It is important to recognize the gravamen of the charge. It was not in the mere fact of taking money; presbyters or elders and widows did that. And it was not exactly in the mere fact of trade. There are men of God whose trade and livelihood is to be printers and they have set out to do "religious printing" almost exclusively at the cheapest possible rates. In some cases a man who has for some reason or other not entered the ministry finds his work for God in such printing. Books, calendars, pamphlets and the like aid the people of God in their own spiritual lives and in their universal mission. This cannot be wrong. A religious printing business does not have to be a non-profit charity. Paul's point was that the false teachers exploited the church for their own ends, without caring what havoc they created. The religious printer works for the kingdom of God and incidentally gets a moderate living from it—like any minister.

Verse 6: There is great gain in godliness with contentment—the false teachers outmaneuvered. Their own word is taken up and reinterpreted. They thought of godliness as a means of procuring wealth for themselves. So it is, if wealth is rightly understood (cf. Heb. 11:26). Grace, the very keyword of the gospel, consists in the fact that "though he was rich, yet for your sake he became poor, so that by his poverty you might become rich" (2 Cor. 8:9). In consequence, "in every way you were enriched in him" (1 Cor. 1:5), and there is ample to give away. Paul himself counted it a gift of grace to have the opportunity "to preach to the Gentiles the unsearchable riches of Christ" (Eph. 3:8).

Gain is here a "means of getting." The English word is used elsewhere in the sense of "business." A slave girl with a spirit of divination was exploited by her masters and brought them "much business," and the hope of yet more of it "went out" with the spirit which Paul ordered to "go out" (Acts 16:16, 19). The English *gain* may be used as the opposite of "loss." "Whatever gain I had, I counted as loss for the sake of Christ" (Phil. 3:7). Or it may be used to express an advance on what hitherto had seemed the supreme good: ". . . to live is Christ, and to die is gain" (Phil. 1:21). It speaks of profit, advantage, of what is helpful or better. "I must boast; there is nothing to be gained by it . . ." (2 Cor. 12:1). "It is better" to lose one limb than for the whole body to be thrown into hell (Matt. 5:29 f.; do "be thrown" and "go," in v. 30, stand for the divine and the human activities?). "It is to your advantage that one man should die for the people, and that the whole nation should not perish" (John 11:50, literal). "It is to your advantage that I go away . . . I will send him to you" (John 16:7). The former is cynical political expediency; the latter means spiritual profit. Paul recognized that "all things are lawful" but he saw as well that "not all things are helpful" (1 Cor. 10:23).

The false teachers were successful in their object—to "get." In simple terms it meant hard cash. The man of *godliness* also "gets," but with a difference. He gets: what he did not have before; what is better than anything he had before; what will help him at his deepest level; and what is capable of infinite exploration. The false teachers may gain the whole world —but at what cost (Mark 8:36; Luke 9:25). The true believer gains— Christ (Phil. 3:8). Even with a strict balance sheet he has *gain*.

For Christians it could hardly be otherwise. "For all things are yours . . ."— including "the world" (1 Cor. 3:21 f.)! (Cf. Rom. 8:32.) Yet Paul felt it necessary to add *with contentment*. We should not limit this to a mere psychological feeling. Contentment (*autarkeia*) is a Stoic word which has been brought into the church to be baptized and used in Christ's service. The last two syllables of the Greek word suggest "sufficiency," and the first syllable means "self." The latter provides the key. The Stoic wise man lived in detachment from the world and was independent of it. He himself was the source of his own independence, for he was self-sufficient. But the word "self-sufficiency" is rather different in Christian use. In contrast to the Stoic use, the "self" is not the origin or source of the sufficiency but merely the place where it is located. "My grace is sufficient for you" (2 Cor. 12:9). Paul received the power of Christ whereby he was able to triumph over adversity. The method is "through his Spirit in the inner man" and this is closely associated with "Christ [dwelling] in your hearts through faith" (Eph. 3:16 f.). The inference is that wherever the true believer goes, Christ goes, for he dwells within—"Christ in you, the hope of glory" (Col. 1:27). The objection that "you" here is plural and that our treatment errs by too much individualism is answered by reference to Paul's deep personal religion. "If any man [singular] has not the Spirit of Christ, he is not his" (Rom. 8:9). The believer is self-sufficient in the sense that he has his resources within him. He does not carry them round in a traveling bag. They are within his "self" but they are not to be identified with the "self." "I have learned, in whatever state I am, to be self-sufficient. I know how to be abased, and I know how to abound" (Phil. 4:11 f., literal). The context is instructive.

Verse 7: For we brought nothing into the world, and we cannot take anything out of the world: We can take only the "self." (Cf. Job 1:21; Luke 12: 20.) The text explains why godliness is a great gain: there is no other permanent gain. (Cf. 4:8.) We shall face our Maker alone, with no baggage. Everything will depend on whether we are in Christ. Godliness is a sign that we are. See discussion on 6:3.

Verse 8: But if we have food and clothing, with these we shall be content: The identity of the *we* makes all the difference. The *clothing* represents a Greek word which means a covering. It is used mainly of clothes but not exclusively so. Aristotle uses it of a house, "a covering consisting of bricks and stones put together in a certain way" (Met. 1043a.32). "Food and shelter" conveys the idea.

We shall be content sounds very optimistic to modern ears but it fits the context. If *we* are people of godliness (v. 6) we are not secularists, tied down to our own age. Our eyes are on the distant horizon, for we are pilgrims with a heavenly destiny as well as witnesses to our own times. The spirit of the passage has been caught by Clement of Rome who speaks of "being content with the travel allowance given us by Christ" (1 Clement 2:1). A travel allowance is by definition for the purposes of travel. Other arrangements have been made for the time after "arrival."

The optimism to which reference has been made may reflect the apostle's confidence in Christians, or, more likely, it may express the logical result of a genuine godliness. On the other hand it may be a disguised exhortation. When addressing others, a speaker who is giving a command normally says "Do this," an imperative. The cold expression of relentless authority, like that of an administrative machine or of military command, merely says "You will do this." The imperative is not used but the simple future indicative. The bare statement of future fact is sufficient. This usage is reflected in Greek, and Paul may have transferred it to the first person. "We shall be content"—I am going to be; you must join me. There is an alternative explanation: the Greek may represent a Hebrew cohortative lurking in Paul's mind. (The cohortative expresses an exhortation in the first person plural with an added touch of emotion: let us be content.")

If we are tempted to think that he was advocating a Spartan regime for Christians we ought at least to consider the other side of the picture. "Spartan" suggests asceticism, to which Paul was opposed (4:3–5). God richly supplies us with everything for our enjoyment (6:17), and we give him thanks. But we can manage on iron rations—without complaint.

2. Dangers of Seeking Wealth (6:9–10)

Desire for wealth involves temptation in which men are entangled in ruinous ambitions. From the love of money grow manifold evils attended sometimes by the abandonment of the faith and many sorrows.

Verse 9: But those who desire to be rich fall into temptation, into a snare, into many senseless and hurtful desires that plunge men into ruin and destruction: The glittering vision proves to be worse than tinsel. It is important to identify *those who desire.* Paul was not thinking of the many light-hearted people who say, "Wouldn't it be nice to be rich?" and then do nothing about it. After all, this is only a way of commenting on some of the amenities of life and the pleasure of being able to have them and enjoy them. *Desire* (the first time) is a word which we have noticed before (2:8; 5:14). It carries the idea of authority, and we must picture certain people giving a ruling to themselves as it were. A point has come up for decision and they make their decision. The flavor is almost that of a newspaper report of a legal action. "Mr. Justice So-and-so laid it down that . . . . His decision means that in future . . . ." In other words the men in question have a settled policy, not merely a vague attitude. They want to be rich and they are going to be rich, if by any means they can bring it about. Their methods are not described in the verse but their moral declension is vividly brought before our eyes in three main stages.

First they *fall into temptation*. In this case they need not have done. All Christians are indeed tempted, but if they had not desired to be rich they would not have encountered this particular temptation. The fact that they fall into it implies that there was a time when they were distant from it. The decision to seek wealth brought them within the influence of a temptation which otherwise they would not have known. Now temptation in itself is not a sin; but it is a danger. They fell into it. Our Lord knew the perils to the soul when he taught his disciples to pray, "lead us not into temptation" (Matt. 6:13). If the would-be rich thought about it at all, they were confident in their own ability to stand and not to fall. God did not let them be tempted beyond their strength but provided a way of escape (1 Cor. 10:12 f.). They did not take it. One way of escape is to take advantage of the sustaining power of Christian fellowship. "You are those who have continued with me in my [not "trials" but, with Arndt and Gingrich, p. 646] temptations" (Luke 22:28). We may surmise that in their quest of wealth they had little time for Christian friends. "The pleasant illusion of riches chokes the Word" (Matt. 13:22, TDNT 1:385) and "in time of temptation they fall away" (Luke 8:13; cf. 1 Tim. 4:1 and discussion).

What is the *temptation* into which they *fall?* As we have seen, it was self-confidence, desertion of the fellowship of Christians, and a delight in being dazzled. But it was more. Men whose heart is set on wealth begin to see the benefits of what in business circles is called "sharp practice." It does not precisely break the law but it is dangerously near to doing so. It keeps the letter of the law but not its spirit. It is in fact within "one letter" of breaking the law, so narrow is the distance between observation and offense. It is significant that sharp practice is frowned upon by men of integrity.

The would-be rich are tempted by sharp practice. It pays off and money comes in. It is but a short step from this to a downright lie. A traveling salesman who carries his goods with him can boost his sales by false claims, and be in the next city before he is found out. He can act unjustly and, for example, may charge twice for the same item. A plausible tale or a hectoring manner may force some timid soul to sign the "small print," as we say, and take on unsuspected and unwanted obligations. Payment may be exacted unfairly and advantage may be taken of unprotected widows. Many people, like tellers in banks or those who operate the cash register in a store, handle large sums of money and feel no temptation to steal it. But a man who is set on wealth and is amassing it, and who is already acting as we have described, will feel the smart of temptation as an ordinary person will not— in respect of money. Here are sums of it. Take some; nobody will know.

These are temptations which arise in the gaining of money. There are others involved in the use or enjoyment of it. It brings with it a certain power, like that of an employer. Many people depend on his slightest whim for their very livelihood. In the world in which we live, money adds to his prestige and to his social acceptance. It will open many doors, not all of them calculated to build him up in his most holy faith. The factor of rivalry comes in. The "other man" has a motor cruiser; he must have a yacht. Whatever social eminence is reached at any particular stage, he is a junior on attaining it. Is he ennobled? Even so he cannot compete with "the oldest families." He must go higher yet. Does he seize the crown and make himself a king? He is but the new member, a *novus homo,* compared with those who sit on settled thrones. Thus he always has rivals and never really reaches the top. And always he is discontented.

There was once a man who became a millionaire. His friends gathered round at some social function to celebrate his success and to drink his health. "Congratulations, George; now for the second million." Such a tale needs no comment. In all this progress from temptation to temptation there is an atmosphere present all the way: neglect of wisdom and of the spiritual life. One day he will awake to find that his soul has died. It has had no nourishment and done no work. Its essential spirituality has drained away and has left at best a shriveled husk.

We have interpreted Paul's words according to the modern scene. But the principles applied in the ancient world no less than in our own.

The second stage of the moral declension has begun to emerge in our survey of the development of temptation. The man whose policy is to seek wealth not only falls into temptation but succumbs to it. As he advances in his financial pilgrimage he comes within the "fall-out" area of successive temptations and is infected. Some practice appeals to him and he carries it out. Some business method holds out the prospect of quick profit and he adopts it. In the end—if not before—he shows no resistance. Temptation has but to show itself and he is caught. He has not merely fallen into temptation; he has taken up residence in it. It may or may not be against his will. But he cannot escape.

This is expressed by Paul's verdict that he has fallen *into a snare.* He did not start there. At one time he was not even near to the temptation to make money at any cost. He is vividly illustrated by the dumb beast which first enjoys its freedom, is then enticed by the bait, approaches it and is trapped (cf. 3:7 and discussion).

The third stage is *ruin and destruction.* The way to this is through *many senseless and hurtful desires.* These are not a development later than the *temptation* and the *snare* but are coincident with them. "Each person is tempted . . . by his own desire . . . desire . . . gives birth to sin" (Jas. 1:14 f.). The expression, *fall into . . . desires,* is a metaphor which is quickly followed by another one, *plunge.* It shows us a picture of men totally enfolded by desires, and in its own way tells us again that they are trapped.

This is the second "desire" in the verse. The first is a verb (*boulomai*). This is a noun (*epithumia*) which sometimes has a good meaning and sometimes means no more than "lust" (cf. 1 Thess. 2:17; 4:5; see 1 Tim. 3:1 and discussion). *Many desires* converge on, and are subordinate to, the one overriding purpose; and they hint at the deep discontent all along the line. They are *senseless* as being characteristic of the pre-Christian life (Titus 3:3) and not expressing the mind of Christ (1 Cor. 2:16). They are *hurtful* because of their consequences. The aspirant to wealth may or may not "feel" the hurt, but they do him final damage: they *plunge* him into ruin.

The verb *plunge* is used in Luke 5:7 of boats. The passive voice there means "to be sunk." The active voice recalls news reported during war to the effect that "our fleet has sunk a battleship and a destroyer." The present tense of repeated action suggests that the desires "sink" the would-be rich men one after another. There is an awful finality when a ship is sunk on the high seas. Salvage is impossible. Here the "ocean" is *ruin and destruction.* These two words go closely together to sound the final chord of doom. But *ruin* may include the temporal as well as the eternal, as in "the destruction of the flesh" (1 Cor. 5:5, though it is eternal in 2 Thess. 1:9. For *destruction,* cf. 2 Thess. 2:3, "perdition").

Verse 10: For the love of money is the root of all evils; it is through this craving that some have wandered away from the faith and pierced their hearts with many pangs: The explanation of the previous verse. "Those who desire to be rich" are obviously suffering from *the love of money.* We have seen where it led them: temptation, snare, and ruin. This thought is now expressed in another way. From *the root* grows a luxuriant crop. Once a man has in his heart *the love of money,* any sin may be committed to get it, because it is a *root* and not a stone. It grows and spreads. Because of the love of money, men have told lies, have defrauded, have exploited their fellows, have adopted violence as a policy, and have done everything from bullying to murder, with torture in between. They have betrayed their country, made money out of slums, and even married an innocent woman for the sake of her fortune. The love of money is a ghastly parody of "the love of Christ" which "controls us," hems us in (cf. 2 Cor. 5:14). A man so dominated has a kind of inverted likeness to the man in the parable who sold all that he had and bought the field containing the treasure or bought the one pearl of great value (Matt. 13:44 f.). He gets rid of any and every moral scruple in order to obtain the "pearl" of great price—money. He is truly a slave to mammon (Matt. 6:24), for it dominates his every thought and deed.

It is important to notice that the love of money is not the only root. Paul's point is that it develops and has effects. It was all but inevitable that the RSV should translate the Greek word by *the root* in order to bring out the fact that the one dominant desire can lead to *all evils.* The one root by itself is enough. To have written "a root" might have suggested that the love of money is insufficient of itself to produce all evils but needs some other motive to assist it. In actual fact, however, Paul wrote "a root"; there is no definite article.

Antiochus Epiphanes is called a "sinful root" in 1 Maccabees 1:10. Moses warned the people against idolatry when he said: "Beware lest . . . there be among you a root bearing poisonous and bitter fruit . . ." (Deut. 29:18; cf. Heb. 12:15). Lust for power, pride, or sex can be a root the luxuriant fruit of which can be poison for others and ultimately merit the term *all evils.* The world's dictators have not always been animated by a love of money, but all evils have flowed from them. And obsession with sex has led to dreadful crimes and sins. There is the so-called sexual maniac on the one hand; and the cynical exploiters of the human instinct on the other. Undercover agents trap a sex pervert and blackmail him into revealing secrets of state. The alarming thought is clear. Any one dominant desire, apart from obedience to "Hear ye him," can be a root which leads to all evils.

We now read of precise effects which *some* have experienced. No names are given but they might be well known to Timothy and the members at Ephesus. They *have wandered away from the faith.* This is not deliberate apostasy. Some such people in modern times even continue to believe that they are good church people, though they attend rarely. They have not observed their own spiritual condition. Their soul needs to be nourished and it has been starved (4:6). It needs to be challenged, and they have not recently heard or read the Word of God. They do not so much attack the faith as neglect it. They have had "more important things to see to," and this judgment of value they have expressed in deed and in life rather than in word. The prelude to their ruin and destruction (v. 9) is sounded in their wandering away.

They are now, after having wandered, distant *from the faith.* They do not consciously exercise their trust in Christ; they are not deliberately following him; they are certainly not testing their lives by his; and they are avoiding the stimulus of genuine believers for they have no time for their company. *The faith* is thus the Christian faith, known, obeyed, practiced. (See 3:9; 4:1, 12; 5:8 and discussions.) It is more than a body of doctrine. There is some significance in the fact that the whole Christian religion is summed up in one of its most characteristic words. If its crucial doctrine were justification by works, Paul could have written that the men in question had wandered away from the works—as indeed they had. But that was not quite what the apostle meant. The works had gone because the faith was dead or at least dying.

Paul did not use the word "conscience" at this point, but consideration should be give to the presence or absence of conscience in the lives of the men who seek wealth. (See 1:5, 19; 3:9; 4:2 and discussions.) His words literally rendered are: "they spitted themselves." The picture is of meat impaled on a spit in readiness for being held over a fire. Two interpretations are possible. They may be impaled not by one spit but by many; but it is not many thin pointed rods which impale them; they are impaled by *many pangs.* Or they may be surrounded by the impaling points, as if they wore a studded belt—with the sharp studs on the inside. Perhaps it is somewhat far-fetched to see them metaphorically wearing a crown of thorns. Whatever picture Paul had in mind, the thought of spikes or of the pointed spit must suggest how sharply their conscience has pricked them.

There is yet another possible method of treatment. The language may describe God's dealing with them. In figurative speech it has been well said that when God wishes to gain a man's attention he taps him on the shoulder, like a man approaching a group from the rear and getting the attention of one man with a view to a whispered consultation. Then, if the man does not listen, God plucks his coatsleeves, like the chairman of a meeting trying to convey to a speaker that he has been going on too long. Finally, if the man still persists and will not listen to God, he finds in his life that— anything may happen. He has to stop what he is doing; he is pulled up short. For he is beset by *many pangs.* The "pains," whatever they may be, are God's method of bringing the man at least to begin thinking of a renewed repentance and faith. This interpretation is supported by the fact that it is here said that *some have wandered away from the faith,* not that they "have made shipwreck of their faith" (see on 1:19). There is no time to be lost; but there is still time.

Paul did not say that God had *pierced their hearts*. In fact they brought it on themselves. But with a deep conviction of the divine providence Paul could have said that God had pierced them. ". . . many of you are weak and ill . . . when we are judged by the Lord, we are chastened . . ." (1 Cor. 11:30, 32; see also Heb. 12:3–11). This truth has to be expressed— and used—with great care. It must not be taken as the ground for "spiritual bullying" whenever we visit someone in hospital. "Do you think that they were worse offenders than all the others who dwelt in Jerusalem?" (See Luke 13:1–5.) Adversity, illness, hospitalization are all challenges to re- flection and self-examination; they may be opportunities as well. The awakened conscience sees more than this: "Unless you repent you will all likewise perish." It is the awakened conscience that knows that God is speaking in the sudden emergency. In that respect God has indeed *pierced* the heart *with many pangs*.

It is inadequate to understand the *pangs* as consisting of the mental strain involved in the acquisition of wealth, apprehension in taking care of it, and anguish at its loss.

3. The Program of a Man of God (6:11–16)

The man of God will choose rather the inner spiritual activities and over- come all opposition to his hold on the eternal life to which he has already been called. In the sight of God the giver of life and of Christ Jesus the faithful witness, Timothy is charged to keep the commandment unsullied until the Lord's coming in God's good time. Honor and dominion is ascribed to the only sovereign and Lord.

Verse 11: But as for you, man of God, shun all this: Constant evasive action. In a man's first act of profession he manifests repentance towards God and faith in our Lord Jesus Christ (cf. Acts 20:21). He turns from *all this* in a decisive act and "renounces the devil and all his works." In a sense it is done and done forever. " 'Tis done, the great transaction's done, I am my Lord's and he is mine." But it is not "done with." He has to keep on running away from the devil and *all this* work of his. It is not the flight of cowardice but the swift movement of obedience, as we shall shortly see in considering *aim at righteousness*. It is the negative aspect of the positive "keep on following me." Christianity has its negatives, its avoidances, its abstentions, its selections, as well as its priorities. (See 1 Thess. 4:3; cf. 1 Cor. 6:18; 10:14; 2 Tim. 2:22.) Flight is not only obedience; it is sound spiritual in- stinct. The sheep will flee from a stranger because they do not know the voice of strangers (John 10:5). Timothy is thus to "keep on running away" from *all this. As for you* is very emphatic and is in marked contrast to "those" and "some" of the previous two verses, and to "any one" of verse 3.

The *man of God* is not a man of wealth, though he may have to minister to such. There seem to have been wealthy men at Ephesus (Acts 20:33–35; 1 Tim. 6:17–19). At the very least he is the opposite of a "man of lawlessness" (2 Thess. 2:3). The description is used in the Old Testament for Moses, David, Samuel, and Elisha. To some is given great prominence and vast influence. Others are minor characters, like Timothy himself (see on 1 Tim. 1:2), and hardly known, such as Shemaiah (1 Kings 12:22) and Igdaliah (Jer. 35:4). Some catch the imagination by the high drama of their acts, like

Elijah, and yet others are quite anonymous (1 Sam. 2:27; 1 Kings 13:1). If Timothy knew his Bible—and he did (2 Tim. 3:15)—he would derive encouragement from the fact that even the obscure and unknown can be a *man of God.* The humble minister in a remote rural area can similarly take heart.

The title is one of honor, but not empty honor. There is work to be done (2 Tim. 3:17). The man of God has received the Word of God and has been sent by God to bear it as his representative. He brings blessings and warnings. He lives with God and walks with God, a fact which brings freshness and vitality into his message. Even though he first received it years ago, it is renewed in his daily dealings with God.

Aim at righteousness, godliness, faith, love, steadfastness, gentleness: A goal to be approached with energy and speed. *Aim at* is not quite the best rendering for the verb *diōkō.* It means to "pursue" or to "persecute" (see 1 Thess. 5:15). It is used in the sense of "pressing on" in the hope of overtaking (Phil. 3:12, 14). Similarly the "Gentiles who did not pursue righteousness" have caught up with it, have overtaken it (Rom. 9:30). This must surely be an unusual illustration of grace: to overtake what you have not pursued! This association of "running after" and "overtaking" is seen in a story told by Herodotus (2. 30). Some Egyptian guards revolted and made their way to Ethiopia. Their king pursued them and overtook them. Similarly Timothy should pursue *righteousness.* All his powers should be exerted because it is a serious matter.

Righteousness is one of the major terms in Pauline doctrine, and we have met the concept before (1 Tim. 1:9; 3:16). The discussions already given should be consulted. In one sense Timothy did not need to *aim at righteousness.* If his Christian experience tallied with that of Paul he could reecho the apostle's own words, "not having a righteousness of my own . . . but that which is through faith in Christ, the righteousness from God that depends on faith" (Phil. 3:9). He possessed it already for it had already been imputed to him when he first believed in Christ (Rom. 3:21 f., 26; 4:5).

To possess righteousness, however, is not only to stand in a right relationship to God. It is to be under obligation. In a celebrated question, Paul once rhetorically asked if we were to continue in sin in order that grace might abound (Rom. 6:1). He was shocked at the very thought. The purpose of our baptism was that we might walk in newness of life and not still live in sin. We must count ourselves as dead to sin and alive to God in Christ Jesus. "Consider yourselves!" It is not a thought with no bearing on reality, least of all the reality of moral and spiritual effort. We must not yield our "members" to sin as tools of unrighteousness. We must not, for example, present our hands to sin as to a false king and say with a low bow: "I place these at your disposal, your majesty; use them as you will for your own purposes." We must present ourselves to God, as if we had come through a resurrection, and must present those same hands to him and to him alone as tools for him to use, "instruments of righteousness." Liberated from sin, we have become "slaves of righteousness"—which means doing as we are told. The sixth chapter of the Epistle to the Romans teaches that the man who has been deemed righteous as a result of his faith in Jesus must now serve righteousness. His righteousness of faith must show itself in righteousness in life. It must produce the fruit of righteousness (Phil. 1:11). He used to "bear fruit for death" but now serves "in the new life of the Spirit" (Rom. 7:5 f.; cf. 8:9 f.). Hence comes the fruit of the Spirit (Gal. 5:22 f.). Timothy must clearly not continue in sin or sluggishness. He must pursue righteousness. He must do it in his capacity as a Christian and a member of the people of God; and he must do it as a minister and as an example (4:6; see on 4:12).

Righteousness means the doing of God's will particularly in dealings with fellowmen. *Godliness* or piety is the practical life of the Christian in his personal dealings with God. The former means, for example, that he pays his debts and is not a parasite on other Christians; the latter means that he says his prayers. These are only examples and many more could be found; but they show the kind of difference that is involved. When we love our neighbor we do righteousness; when we love the Lord our God we manifest godliness. (See further on 2:2; 3:16; 4:7 f.) Godliness determines right teaching (6:3) and is true gain (6:5 f.).

Faith, standing alone, can take the widest interpretation. Perhaps the best comment would be to refer to a concordance. Timothy already had faith (see on 1:2; cf. 2 Tim. 1:5). In some way he was to "pursue" it. It is not implied that faith is elusive but that it is capable of development. Timothy must not take it for granted but must give it attention. He must ponder, and learn more of, the truths which are the common property of the believing church. He must understand them better and grasp them more firmly and feed on them regularly. He must believe them more and more. And his trust in Christ must become deeper, more intimate. He must be more sensitive to the divine guidance. He must pray increasingly with reliance on the divine answer and must be alert to recognize the answer and to give thanks for it. He must do it regularly, frequently, for this is the method of gaining a closer intimacy with Christ. If he shrinks from exercising authority in the church, knowing that to teach as Paul directed would involve a clash with false teachers, he must launch out in reliance on the fact that God owns his Word and aids his servants. His prayers must be the prayers of faith rather than of desperation.

If he feels something of the desolation of the evangelist who has made an appeal and waits—alone in the world as it seems to him—for the first stirring of response, then he must trust himself more and more to the living God and really believe that God speaks to men's hearts when the gospel is preached and taught. In faith he must put some of his doctrines to the practical test. If, for example, after his association with Paul he believes in the divine election (1 Thess. 1:4), he must preach in the conviction that there are people in his congregation who are among God's elect and will therefore respond to his preaching of the gospel. There may be those who will be deaf to his most persuasive notes; but there will be those who gladly receive the Word. In this spirit he must stand before men, if necessary for years, if necessary alone.

Reason will have its due place in his life, and knowledge likewise. But faith must loom larger, for it will take him further. He must not postpone prayer, or the recognition of answers to prayer, until in every case he can give a philosophic justification for it. William Temple, one of the acutest minds of the Christian church in this century, was once asked if he could justify prayer philosophically. He is reputed to have answered in these terms:

"I know that when I pray, coincidences happen; and when I stop praying, the coincidences stop." It is a wise, practical answer. Faith recognizes the "coincidences." And if on any occasion they do not occur, faith does not abandon prayer but realizes that God is either bidding his servant to wait yet longer, or in loving wisdom is answering "no." It is a negative "coincidence," and faith recognizes it as such. This is not the unreality of fairyland, because in the succession of "coincidences," both positive and negative, the believing soul increases intimacy with Christ. (Cf. Eph. 3:17–19; 1 Tim. 6:20 f.)

The apostle's exhortation to *aim at . . . faith* is a legitimate extension of our Lord's comparison of faith to a grain of mustard seed (Matt. 17:20; Luke 17:6). The power of faith does not lie in its smallness (as if it were an atom) but in its ability to grow (Mark 4:31 f.). The literal seed may grow "of itself" (cf. Mark 4:26–28), but faith does not. It has to be cultivated. This may explain the insertion of Matthew 17:21 into the text (see RSV footnote) from Mark 9:29, "this kind cannot be driven out by anything but prayer." ("Fasting" is a later gloss.) Paul's *aim at* means cultivation. Faith itself has to be cultivated by prayer.

But faith must be influenced by another factor also. There are people who have some vague attitude of trust in a higher power, and they address it in an attitude of prayer. If they claim to believe and to pray, what is missing? Is not such faith and prayer enough? It should be realized that faith can have an almost secular meaning. When Paul tried to join the disciples at Jerusalem, they "did not believe" that he was a disciple (Acts 9:26). It does not say that they did not believe the Christian faith, because they did. The difference consists in the object of belief. "Faith [in the Christian sense] comes from what is heard, and what is heard comes by the preaching of Christ" (Rom. 10:17). Timothy could not spend his time listening to sermons; but he could hearken to the Word of God. To *aim at . . . faith,* then, means to cultivate it by constant subordination to the Word of God and by prayer which accords with the Word of God. Without the Word, faith is amorphous, shapeless and vague, or it may even be belief in wrong statements with no vital relationship to God in Christ; without the Word, prayer has no deep knowledge of God and may be no more than an utter vagueness on wrong lines.

The Corinthians were also told to *aim at . . . love,* to pursue love (1 Cor. 14:1). *Faith, love, steadfastness* occur together once more in Titus 2:2 (see also 1 Thess. 1:3). The famous triad of faith, hope and charity are suggested here to Timothy, because hope is the motive power of steadfastness. For *love* see on 1 Timothy 1:5. To love a person involves both feeling ("caring") and doing. Their proportions may vary in different individuals and one may come into existence before the other. God would hardly command us to have an emotion, but he did command us to love: "Thou shalt love . . . thy neighbour as thyself" (Luke 10:27, KJV). This means at the least that we must do something. But what must we do? Obviously thought is necessary. If Timothy must love his church members, and indeed those who are not yet members, he must give thought to their needs and his best way of meeting them. "Doing things for people" may give birth to "feeling for people," "caring for them." Timothy had much scope for thought and prayer on this subject as a preparation for action.

So far we have been thinking of human love. In the context this must be prominent. But there may also be the thought of "cultivating" the love of God. This is not like "cultivating" a rich man in the hope of gaining his confidence—and access to his pocket. Our Lord told his disciples to abide in his love (John 15:9 f.). He cannot mean that they can ever put themselves outside the scope of his love or that he will ever stop loving them. But they can forget his love for them. Even if they do not forget, they can fail to keep his commandments and thus lose the consciousness of his love. If they sin they grieve the Holy Spirit within them, through whom the love of God has been poured out into their hearts (Rom. 5:5). The warmth of the realization of the divine love may thus be cooled. The experience has to be guarded and cultivated. *Aim at . . . love:* pursue the divine love. The exhortation and the human activity which would follow in obedience to it may be taken as an answer to Paul's prayer concerning the Thessalonians. "May the Lord direct your hearts [more deeply] into the love of God" (2 Thess. 3:5, KJV). This is a spiritual journey which may be compared with a literal journey: "May [he] direct our way to you" (1 Thess. 3:11).

Steadfastness conveys the idea of standing one's ground. The steadfast man is "like a tree planted by streams of water" (Ps. 1:3). The rains may fall and the winds beat about it; thunder may roll and lightning may strike; but the tree stands in its appointed position, unlike the animals which are free to seek safety and shelter. "Storms" of various kinds were likely to fall upon Timothy. He might lack many of the amenities of life and his "frequent ailments" (5:23) might have a debilitating effect. The trial of strength with the false teachers might even bring him to the verge of nervous prostration. The sorrow and anguish which are the hazards of the ministry might well tempt him to give up: the opposition of the powerful, the indifference of some, and the dullness of others tend to drag down the spirit of all but the resilient. When a truth which brings a sparkle to the minister's eyes leaves hearers unmoved and entirely lacking in interest, he has to renew his own spirit in order to remain steadfast. Where was Timothy to look?

In addition to the "pursuits" already mentioned—righteousness, godliness, faith, and love, the benefits of which would be cumulative—Timothy must exercise his memory. He has an inspiring example. "Jesus . . . for the joy that was set before him endured the cross, despising the shame" (Heb. 12:2). Timothy must lay aside every weight as well as the enfolding garments of sin which trammel his movements and must look away to Jesus who pioneered the course before him, intent on his immediate task and its fulfillment at whatever cost to himself (Acts 20:24; Heb. 12:1 f.). "Considering" is an antidote to crumpling up (Heb. 12:3).

Timothy has a glorious hope. "If we endure, we shall also reign with him" (2 Tim. 2:12). He must keep this in mind, remembering that the pressure upon him is to be interpreted as the opportunity for endurance, from which is born the sterling quality of the veteran (Rom. 5:3 f.; cf. 1 Tim. 5:10). *Steadfastness* is the soil of fruit-bearing. "They hold the word fast . . . and bring forth fruit in [*en*] steadfastness" (Luke 8:15).

Timothy has advantages open to other men but at times declined by them. Paul linked steadfastness with the encouragement of the Scriptures. Through them God inspires steadfastness, for he is "the God of steadfastness" (Rom. 15:4 f.), and leads his people into it through their communion with his Son.

(See above, and 2 Thess. 3:5.) Steadfastness is the badge which authenticates the minister (2 Cor. 6:4; 12:12).

It is at first a little surprising to find so timid a man as Timothy urged to *aim at . . . gentleness.* But in the heat of controversy and kindred situations even quiet people have been known to "lash out." With the authority of the apostle behind him, he might feel an access of strength; he must remember that *gentleness* is restrained strength. He had the vision of his Master to inspire and restrain him. Our Lord was gentle (Matt. 11:29) even though a king, and rode on the ass of peace not on a war horse (Matt. 21:5). Timothy must exercise this spirit. He would have an opportunity in controversy, for he should correct his opponents with gentleness (2 Tim. 2:25). As a spiritually minded person—and possessed of the Holy Spirit—he should restore (that is, "mend," cf. Matt. 4:21) a man detected in some trespass "in a spirit of gentleness" (Gal. 6:1). In the work of apologetics he should speak with gentleness (1 Pet. 3:15). He should always watch himself, to keep his conscience clear by avoiding a fall into temptation. In this way he will tend to conciliate rather than antagonize, and will find in a new way that the gentle "inherit the earth" (Matt. 5:5).

Verse 12: Fight the good fight of the faith: The purpose of his training (4:7). Notice especially that it is *the good fight,* not "a good fight." The latter would imply something like "give a good account of yourself" or the common "give them a good run for their money." The point is that there is only one fight, and all Christians are called to take their part in it. Timothy must not be A.W.O.L., as they say in the armed forces—away without leave. The wider conflict was suggested by Paul to the Philippians. They were "engaged in the same conflict which you saw and now hear to be mine" (Phil. 1:30). This is an aspect of Christian fellowship or communion. We have a common faith (Titus 1:4) and a common salvation (Jude 3), a common task of evangelism and service, a common equipment in the Holy Spirit, and a common enemy. We belong to a community, the people of God, the family of God, or simply the brotherhood, and we celebrate the Holy Communion or "do this" in remembrance of our common Savior in a service of holy fellowship. We are exhorted to be of a common mind (Phil. 2:2; cf. 4:2). ("Common" means "shared," not "vulgar.")

The word *fight* must not be limited to military activities such as battle. The noun *agōn* is cognate with the verb (*agōnizomai*) and is drawn from athletics rather than the army. It means a "contest" in which competitors contend for a prize, as in the Olympic Games. What is called a *fight* may refer to a race as well as to a boxing match or a wrestling match (1 Cor. 9:24–27). In using such a figure of speech Paul implied the need of training and the abstinence involved in it; a sure knowledge of the purpose—to knock out a boxer, to pin a wrestler to the floor, or to reach the winning post first—and an ability and a willingness to "take punishment" and to strain every nerve at any cost in order to win. The contest must be taken seriously—it is more than "a mere game"—and the prize highly valued. In the Olympic Games today the competitors are rivals but hardly enemies; but Paul would not dissent from the view that in speaking of a contest he had in mind the whole forces of evil which are ranged against the church. In a celebrated chapter in which he spoke of "the whole armor of God," he could still say that our "wrestling" is against ". . . the spiritual hosts of wickedness in the heavenly places"; we have against us "the wiles of the devil" (Eph. 6:11 f.). Part of the Christian contest is seen in a text to which reference has already been made (Jude 3). Jude appealed to his readers to "contend [a compound of our present verb] for the faith which was once for all delivered to the saints." This was precisely what Timothy would have to do in dealing with the false teachers. His ministry was not limited to this, however. He would have to give himself to the urgent task of dealing with the "rival" in his own heart which would divert him from his own swift pursuit (v. 11); and he had to preach and teach, to comfort and guide, and to pray with and for his people. He had to be as forgiving as his own Master and Savior, who in virtue of his own temptations could sympathize with our weaknesses (Heb. 4:15), and yet inflexible in maintaining the standards of Christian faith and morals. It was an unending struggle. That is why Paul used the present imperative. He did not exhort: "one big effort!" He rather said: "Keep on straining every nerve."

The whole figure implies not only effort but mastery. If we think of the foot race, Timothy must run to win: to reach the sinner before some further evil influence could do further damage; to reach the suffering saint before some other person could suggest a complaint against God. If we think of boxing or wrestling, Timothy must outthink and outlive his opponents who advocated false theological and ethical doctrine; he must beat them in argument and in the quality of his own life. And if we think of some such event as throwing the discus, he must manifest the love of Christ which "throws further" than the pretentious knowledge of the false teachers (cf. Eph. 3:19); must manifest the grace of God which likewise "throws further" than any rival remedy for man's ills (cf. 2 Cor. 9:14).

The contest is the contest of *the faith,* that is, the contest which is characteristic of the Christian faith as such and which it wages. The faith is the rival of all evil, and its task is to conquer it. The struggle may be hard; it may be a "close finish." Now if there were no believers at all, there would be no Christian faith—only perhaps Bibles tucked away in libraries and churches as buildings tolerated as museums. In other words every believer is, or ought to be, a typical Christian and a typical Christian engaged in struggle. It is not a purely private contest to maintain the holiness of his own soul, though it is that. In him *the faith* is present and he makes the contribution of his effort to overcome all evil.

Take hold of the eternal life to which you were called: A duty even for a minister. This at first is a surprising word. Of all the people at Ephesus, one would think that Timothy possessed eternal life! He is to preach and teach; is he a mere theorist? He has to oppose false teachers; is he no more than a pamphleteer in a war of words? Was the advice wrong which told preachers to tell of what they "smartingly" felt? Timothy was a believer (see on v. 11, "faith") and his faith was sincere, not an adopted pose. Can a genuine believer be devoid of eternal life?

There can be but one answer to these questions. Our problem is to show how a man possessed of eternal life can still *take hold of it.* Plato has a story of a man who owned an aviary. The birds were in safety in their home and could not escape. They belonged to their owner and by right of ownership he may be said to have possessed them. But if one day he himself entered the aviary and took hold of one of the birds, he then possessed it in a deeper sense. It was really in his hands. Preachers used to speak of "possessing your possessions." On these lines we can understand the apostle's thought.

The owner of the birds entered more deeply into possession when he took one of them into his hands. In like manner Timothy was to enter more deeply into the possession of eternal life. It is analogous to the "journey" more deeply into the love of God (see on "love," v. 11; cf. 2 Thess. 3:5). Eternal life is a gift from God (John 3:15 f.; 5:24; Rom. 6:23), received by faith. If Timothy would *take hold of it,* he should meditate on it, for it affords much scope for meditation. It cannot be fully expounded or expressed. "Thanks be to God for his inexpressible gift! " (2 Cor. 9:15; cf. v. 14). This outburst of thanksgiving on the part of the Apostle Paul surely reveals him entering more deeply into eternal life. The spiritual eye can see him *take hold of* it as he writes in such exultation.

Our Lord said that "he who eats my flesh and drinks my blood has eternal life" (John 6:54). The text means at the least an appropriation of Christ. The words are strongly sacramental and their background may be the thought of the Lord's Supper. Now we should not normally think of participants being converted at the communion service; that ought to have happened some time ago! It is a service for believers. Yet as a Christian eats the bread and drinks the wine he remembers the Lord's death—for him. Would it be surprising if he found himself uttering the same words of thanksgiving as Paul? Would it be wrong to say that he had entered more deeply into *the eternal life* which became his when he first believed?

As a matter of fact, Paul has himself given us the clue to the understanding of his language. Timothy had been called to eternal life, as Paul went on to say, and he had heard the call and had obeyed it. We have already seen that God calls us to conversion, and after we have been converted he still calls us. If we are sensitive to the promptings of his Spirit, we do not merely remember the call which came at our conversion; we hear his voice still. We are still called to follow Jesus. Paul's words thus imply that Timothy should watch and pray, should be on the alert to hear and to hearken to God's call. If he thus responded and "came closer" to God in Christ he would enter more deeply into eternal life. Once more, with maturer grip, he would *take hold of* it. (See 1 Thess. 2:12; 4:7; 5:24; 2 Thess. 1:11; 2:14.)

Our difficulty arises because "taking hold" suggests to us the first response to the gospel, though this cannot have been the apostle's meaning. It is a suitable figure because it points to a decisiveness and to a conscious effort. The effort has nothing to do with justification by works but implies the mental bracing of attention for decision. Men do not drift further into eternal life. The life of the believer is a conscious response to God in Christ; a journey consciously continued into the love of God; a deliberate further feeding on the bread of life; and so, at any given moment, a decision to *take hold of* yet more of God's free gift which is eternal life in Christ Jesus our Lord. It is plain that Paul was speaking of the human side of the fellowship between God and men.

Eternal (aiōnios) life is the life which pertains to the *aiōn,* the final age of God's consummated purpose. It is thus an eschatological concept. By faith believers have entered into that age. This is analogous to justification, the picture of which is the Day of Judgment. But when a man repents and believes in Jesus, the Day is, as it were, brought forward and he receives by grace a favorable verdict here and now. He does not have to wait. When Christ says that "thy sins are forgiven," then there is now no condemnation for him. Similarly, the life which is characteristic of the age when God has completed his saving purpose is given here and now to the man who trusts in Jesus. He has much to learn, but in principle all is his. He is justified and he has life—which is *eternal.*

This life used to be called "everlasting life" (as the KJV translates it), but an emphasis on the *aiōn* has brought an emphasis on "the life of the age to come." It has been pointed out that mere longevity is an inadequate description of the life which is in Christ. This is perfectly true. Mere survival forever might not always be a welcome prospect. The length of life is not enough to describe all that we have in Christ. We must add the concept of depth. Eternal life is life which is life indeed. It is not bare existence. It finally involves complete sanctification and the closest fellowship with God in Christ in the company of the redeemed and saved, and all in a perfect environment: a dynamic (not a static) life of perfection with scenery to match. Even so, we must retain the idea of length as well as depth. If it ever stopped we should be of all men most to be pitied. But "they shall never perish." We shall be forever with the Lord.

When you made the good confession in the presence of many witnesses— at his baptism. Some have thought that the reference is to his ordination, but evidence for this is lacking. It could recall an examination before magistrates, like that of our Lord before Pilate (cf. v. 13). Such a public examination is hardly an evangelistic service in which sinners are called to repentance; but if, as we have seen, God repeats his call to his own people, there is no reason why an ordeal before the court should not have drawn Timothy "further into" eternal life. "I am with you" (Acts 18:10). Could he not have reflected in prison that the prospect was bright? He had confessed the Lord before men and the Lord would confess him before the Father in heaven (Matt. 10:32 f.; Luke 12:8 f.). Might he not have felt that such an experience was the occasion of God's calling him in closer? He may or may not have "felt" and reflected thus. But when in prison, Paul and Silas were praying and singing hymns to God (Acts 16:25), was God completely unresponsive to his servants? Or was he drawing them yet closer to himself?

Such memories might have crowded into Timothy's mind. But *the good confession* is almost decisive. "A good confession" might be made anywhere. The definite article *the* draws attention to some well-known occasion, and Timothy's baptism seems the most likely. The main objection is that Christ Jesus also made *the good confession,* which was not quite the same. The *presence of many witnesses* suggests a measure of formality. Timothy no doubt confessed Christ at his conversion, either in his home or elsewhere. The *many witnesses* could be the people who heard Paul preach and saw Timothy respond. In any case his earlier confession was gathered up, concentrated, and made public in his baptism.

Why is the confession *good?* It is because some confessions, though necessary, when taken in themselves do not go far enough. For example, we are urged to confess our sins (cf. 1 John 1:9). The word here means "admit."

It is one of the most difficult tasks of the evangelist to persuade sinful men to admit that they are sinners. Conviction of sin is a first step towards conversion. Some Christians also have a struggle before they will make the admission, even though unforgiven sin raises a cloud between them and Christ. It is good to confess our sins but it is better to confess Jesus. ". . . if you confess with your lips that Jesus is Lord . . . you will be saved. For man . . . confesses with his lips and so is saved" (Rom. 10:9 f.). (The evangelist exercises suasion on men—cf. 2 Cor. 5:11—in order that the Holy Spirit may convict them of sin and lead them to "admit" it.) The confession of Jesus presupposes the confession of sin. Sins should be confessed once; Jesus must be confessed all the time (cf. Heb. 3:1; 4:14; 10:23).

Confession is part of the witness of the church to Jesus the Savior. It has also a certain psychological value to the person who confesses. It crystallizes his own decision and expresses his own "first faith" publicly. It is thus no longer a private matter between him and God. It is still a personal relation; he is still united to God through Christ, but after public confession there is a sense in which he cannot go back on it. This has nothing to do with backsliding or falling away. We are thinking of people who think that they have begun to believe in Christ but never admit it openly. When temptation comes they are not reinforced by the fellowship of kindred minds, and they find it easy to persuade themselves that they were never Christians anyway. In public confession a man burns his boats. He crosses his Rubicon. He has taken a stand. That is why counselors after an evangelistic service tell inquirers who have made a decision to "go and tell someone about it."

Verse 13: In the presence of God who gives life to all things, and of Christ Jesus who in his testimony before Pontius Pilate made the good confession: Two greater witnesses. *The presence* would remind Timothy of the earlier occasion mentioned in the previous verse. But this is not a congregation of men, devout and faithful but perhaps of simple mind and of servile status: ". . . not many . . . wise . . . powerful . . . of noble birth . . ." (cf. 1 Cor. 1:26–31). This is the presence of the living God and of his Son. Timothy must have been awed by the words. Both he and Paul stood before God. An appropriate comment would be Hebrews 4:13. (See on 1 Tim. 5:21.) Both God and Christ had been confessed by Timothy, for in Christ God is known and present.

The *God who gives life to all things* is the Creator and Sustainer. We must not press *things* too hard, as if Paul were trying to exclude human beings. *All things (ta panta)* can mean the universe. All living creatures owe their life to God. He gave life in the first place, and while they live, their continued life is due to him. A new generation is likewise due to him. This says nothing about parents or natural law, and it is not here necessary. Without God parents could not be parents, and there would be no offspring of man or beast, nor would the seed of vegetable life have vitality. Even the new spring flowers each year come ultimately from God. Earlier thought is here reflected. It was a living God who made all that is in heaven and earth and sea, and he witnesses to himself in giving rains and fruitful seasons to sustain life (Acts 14:15–17; cf. 17:24 f., 28). If Timothy were disposed to tremble before the forces arrayed against him, whether false teachers or persecuting civil authorities or even an angry populace, he could reflect that even those against him derived their life and power from him whom Timothy had himself confessed and whom he represented.

Creation is prominent here but Paul may also have had in mind the fact that God is the giver of life in another sense to those who believe in Jesus. He could speak of men being dead through trespasses and sins and of how God made them alive and raised them up with Christ (Eph. 2:1, 5 f.). Life in the widest sense comes from God the Creator; in the "salvation" sense it originates in God the Redeemer. It was not necessary to elaborate. "God sent forth his Son . . . to redeem . . . " (Gal. 4:4 f.). Behind Timothy and Paul, to steel them in hardship and adversity and to add solemn weight to apostolic injunction, stood God the Redeemer as well as God the Creator. In spite of popular—and political—religion it was not Caesar who was the author of life.

Christ Jesus . . . made the good confession though not in the sense in which Timothy had done. Timothy confessed because as a sinner he had been called to repentance and faith and had responded to the call. Christ was no sinner but was the Savior himself. In one sense our Lord and Timothy made the same confession. Timothy would have taken his stand with all those who affirmed that Jesus was the Christ, the appointed deliverer whom God had sent. Our Lord's own words, "You have said so," may be taken as a cautious admission that he was indeed the messianic King, not in the popular sense but as a witness to the truth (Matt. 27:11; Mark 15:2; Luke 23:3; John 18:37).

The meaning of the *testimony* of Jesus depends to some extent on how we interpret the phrase *before Pontius Pilate*. *Before* (*epi* with the genitive) can mean "in the time of," as in Mark 2:26, "in the time of Abiathar the high priest"; or it can mean "in the presence of" with special reference to legal authorities, as in Mark 13:9, "You will stand in the presence of governors and kings for my sake, with a view to testimony to them." There is a parallel between Timothy in the presence of many witnesses and Jesus in the presence of Pontius Pilate. But it must not be pressed. Timothy's witnesses were not trying him; and the two Greek words are different (*enōpion* and *epi*). On the whole it seems best to think of the testimony of Jesus as having been given generally in his life on earth and in particular in his appearance before Pilate. This does justice to the ministry "in the time of" Pilate and to other evidence also. Our Lord did witness apart from the testimony at his trial (John 3:11, 32 f.; 8:13 f.). He is called "the faithful witness, the firstborn of the dead" (Rev. 1:5; cf. 3:14).

Thus Timothy had an inspiring example before him as he read the apostle's charge (v. 14) and the encouragement which comes to every evangelist who realizes what is meant by the thought of Christ Jesus as witness. When his servants preach the Word there are some men who reject it outright; there are some Christians who do not add their witness to that of the preacher; but there is one Witness who never fails to give his testimony. When the Word is preached, the Lord Christ through his Spirit attests it in the hearts of listeners. Timothy's confession had been a solemn statement of faith in the setting of worship—perhaps a baptismal origin to the Creed; and it had been a self-dedication to heroism in the Lord's service. Now the earlier emotions return with the new vision of the Lord as witness; and with them surely Timothy gained new vigor and refreshment of spirit from Jesus, the Prototype of Confessors. For the whole life of Jesus was testimony. His Person, words and work summed up the revelation of the living God.

Our Lord suffered under Pontius Pilate and comment has frequently been excited by the presence of this notorious man in the Apostles' Creed. The fact that he is mentioned there—and by the apostle Paul—is of high significance. It ties the revelation of God to history (cf. Luke 3:1 f.). The Christian faith is not a religion of ideas; certainly not of ideas alone. It is a religion of fact. The sermons in the Acts of the Apostles are very factual and tell what God has done in Christ. An idea may simply be contradicted, but facts are stubborn things. Christian origins are indeed open to historical investigation, but the data differ from those of secular history. The Gospels "talk back" to those who read them. And even the critical historian, whose business it is to sift evidence, if a believer and possessed of the Holy Spirit, finds that the Jesus of the Gospels is the same as the Lord of the epistles; and that this same Lord Jesus Christ is known to men even in this very day. The record is enshrined in a book; but from the book the living Lord speaks to his listening and obedient people. He has no new message for them except the old one applied in the modern age. Thus the gospel and all the unsearchable riches of Christ are not merely "something in a book." They are indeed there. But he who was upon earth and is present in the book is also the Lord of glory, exalted in heaven—and dwelling in our hearts.

Verse 14: I charge you to keep the commandment unstained and free from reproach until the appearing of our Lord Jesus Christ: A soiled Christian implies a soiled commandment. The nature of *the commandment* is at first not clear. The term might mean any one of the Ten Commandments or the Decalogue itself, though it is unlikely here. A wiser course of interpretation is to consider the term in itself and then to work backward. Now whatever the reference, a commandment suggests some sort of obligation. It is not merely a piece of information or some good advice. It calls for obedience; it brings to the mind something which ought to be done. What, then, ought Timothy to do? A course of action has been laid out in some detail in verses 11 f. This may be illustrated by the various instructions given throughout the epistle. And if the "atmosphere" is Timothy's confession and the strenuous "fight of the faith" to which he was committed, *the commandment* summarizes his Christian duty and task. In his own life he should maintain the faith: its doctrines should not be cut down, distorted or denied, and he should not neglect his personal fellowship with the Lord. The demands and disciplines of faith must not be lost in the enjoyment of its consolations. There were duties of worship and witness and the need to manifest Christian character in conduct and behavior. The life of faith must be seen as well as unseen. It was "hid with Christ in God" (cf. Col. 3:3), but men must "see your good works" (Matt. 5:16; cf. 1 Cor. 7:19). All this would be the duty of Timothy as a Christian, the duty to which any believer was obligated. He was a minister also, with pastoral responsibilities. He must teach the faith and ensure that his own work is not undermined by false teachers. He must both proclaim and defend and exhort. He must rally the discouraged and restrain any who would break through the moral restrictions on disciples. Christian faith and Christian behavior: Timothy must guard it in himself and in his flock.

It is just possible to translate: "I charge you to keep the commandment, yourself unstained and free from reproach." It is possible; but unnatural and awkward. This leaves an exegetical problem. God's *commandment* stands high over men and cannot be touched by them. How could it ever be stained? The same question could be asked about Jesus. But at the Passion the soldiers spat upon him (Matt. 27:30; Mark 15:19), and his fair Name may be blasphemed (Jas. 2:7). In himself he remains untouched, but the blasphemy, the spitting and the stain express what men think. If Timothy had failed to meet his Christian obligations, men would have thought little of God's *commandment*. It may be irrational and may arise from the senseless, darkened minds of men (Rom. 1:21), but the fact remains. Jesus was entirely innocent and men rejected him. A Christian who fails may make irrational and sinful men spit at him—and at the *commandment* of God as well. For in their view it is not *free from reproach*. They forget the impotence of law (Rom. 8:3).

For *free from reproach* see 3:2 and discussion; 5:7. It would have been enough for the apostle to charge Timothy just *to keep the commandment,* for this means observing it and obeying it. The wider reference adds to the solemnity of the charge. Paul hardly "trembled for the ark of God" (1 Sam. 4:13) nor did he merely want Timothy to obey "because of what people think." The thought of putting a stumbling block into the way of others, however, could be an added incentive. God must be obeyed because God is God and for the sake of Christ who died. But for the sake of others also Timothy should sanctify himself (cf. John 17:19).

Charge is a strong word (see on 1:3; 4:11) and it raises the question of how far a minister of Christ can go in commanding people. It is all the more striking here because Paul had not become so passionate that he had forgotten the existence and claims of God. On the contrary he was consciously standing in the presence of God the Creator and of Christ Jesus. In these circumstances is it seemly for a man to issue orders? If it is said in answer that Paul was an apostle and therefore had authority to do this, the "ordinary minister" cannot complain. But even Paul was a man: can even an apostolic man give orders, and in particular can he do so when in the presence of God? The answer is that he can give them only when they are God's orders and not his own; and he can test himself by asking if he would be prepared to give orders in God's presence. Certain reflections are called for. A minister is a minister of the Word. If the Word for any particular occasion is an order, then the minister must give it, because he is transmitting the Word, the commandment, of God. The gospel is to be obeyed as well as enjoyed (1 Pet. 4:17; cf. Rom. 10:16). This is a note which is not sufficiently struck today. Preachers point to the relevance of the gospel, defend its claims and invite listeners to its benefits—all of which is to the good. But the gospel comes to men with all the authority of God behind it. Therefore it should be proclaimed with authority; men should be called and summoned to hearken; and they should be told their duty to obey. This does not mean that a minister must be known as a man who is always barking out orders; it does mean that with ringing voice or with quiet impressiveness he must press upon men the rightful claims of Christ. Whether he adopts the wooing note or the clarion call he must always appear as one who brings a message from on high. Tidings from such a source should be obeyed.

The orders are to remain in force *until the appearing of our Lord Jesus*

Christ, that is, the Second Advent or Parousia. Here the term "epiphany" is used (see 2 Tim. 1:10; 4:1, 8). After the *appearing* there will be no possibility of attack on the commandment; it will be beyond stain or reproach in any sense. Like the Lord himself after his cross and resurrection, it will be exalted. Timothy's struggle will be over. Faith and life will continue, even though we shall see him as he is. Even though faith will have passed into sight and knowledge, we shall still believe and we shall still trust. It is quite possible to trust a person whom you fully know and whom you always see before you. But at—or at any rate after—*the appearing* the *charge* will not be necessary.

Paul did not here say "keep the commandment . . . until you die." If, as some suggest, his hopes of the Second Advent had begun to recede in his later days, it is remarkable that he could still refer to it as he did. Too much weight should not be attached to this; but it should not be ignored. In earlier days Paul could speak of the day of the Lord as coming like a thief in the night (1 Thess. 5:2); in earlier days also Paul could think of delay (2 Thess. 2:3). If his hopes did indeed recede he was only emphasizing the delay of which he had spoken earlier. Then why mention *the appearing* here? We must always distinguish between the speculative construction of a future calendar (Mark 13:32), which is forbidden, and the spirit of expectancy which is both relevant and obedient all through the centuries.

The thought of *the appearing* was yet another incentive to Timothy. It would mark the great climax of his good fight of the faith; and it would also mean that he would have to render an account of his ministry. He would stand before the judgment seat of God (Rom. 14:10–12) and of Christ (2 Cor. 5:10). All believers are free from condemnation (Rom. 8:1; John 5:24) but differ in their rewards. The "appearings" are linked: Titus 2:11.

Verse 15: And this will be made manifest at the proper time by the blessed and only Sovereign, the King of kings and Lord of lords: "My times are in thy hand" (Ps. 31:15). *This* refers to "the appearing" of the previous verse. *The proper time* is the time of God's choosing. It does not mean that God found out what the right time would be and then decided to act at that moment. The time of his choice would in itself be the proper time. On the other hand he does not act in an arbitrary way. He has his reasons for his choice, for he does not act from whim or fancy. They arise from his nature as righteous, loving and wise; from his omniscience whereby he knows the whole course of history, including the secret thoughts and purposes of men; and from his omnipotence whereby he is at all times in control of everything. (See on 2:6.) *The proper time* means God's own seasons which the Father has retained in his own authority (cf. Acts 1:7). When he sees fit, then our Lord Jesus Christ will "appear."

God is *blessed* in that he knows himself and finds his deepest joy and satisfaction within himself. (See on 1:11.) This does not in any way detract from the joy which is his over one sinner repenting (Luke 15:7, 10). He is the *only Sovereign.* Others may have the name, but in comparison with him they only seem to be "the mighty" (Luke 1:52). Petty princes may be called *sovereign* and the mighty Roman emperor ruled the world: but not apart from and only under the living God (cf. Prov. 8:15 f.). The word rendered *Sovereign* is *dunastēs,* connected with *dunamai,* "I am able, I can." The *sovereign* is one who, as we say, is able to get things done. Its two other uses in the New Testament are interesting and significant. In the one already mentioned (Luke 1:52), God has "put down the sovereigns from their thrones." They are not able to resist him. The other *sovereign* is the Ethiopian eunuch (translated "minister" in Acts 8:27, RSV), whose story exhibits a delightful coincidence. He must have been a powerful man in his home state, because he was what we should call a Cabinet Minister or Secretary of the Treasury. He was in charge of all the queen's treasure. This potentate, this person who can get things done (cf. 1 Tim. 6:15, KJV), was asked by Philip if he understood what he was reading from the Book of Isaiah. The astounding reply from "a man who can," a *dunastēs,* was "No; how can I . . . ?" and his words express but the remotest possibility. "How should I be able to, unless . . . ?" The man who can, cannot.

The two examples may be regarded as typical. In the one case the sovereigns are dethroned; in the other—he cannot. This is not proof, of course; but they are interesting pointers, illustrations of the fact: there is but one, the *only Sovereign.* The one concrete example in the New Testament of a *dunastēs* being described by that name is shown as not being qualified to hold the title. Ultimately only God "can." He and only he is the *Sovereign.*

The primary reference in the use of the word *sovereign* is to rulers and government. God is the supreme and *only* ruler. The derivation of the word, however, has useful lessons if we consider the concept of power. It is said that God is omnipotent, and some critics have asked if God can really do everything. It has been thought that if there is anything he cannot do, he has lost both power and prestige. But there are "things" which God cannot do: he cannot die; he cannot change; he cannot make the false true; he cannot deny himself. These are not "disadvantages." They suggest that omnipotence must not be considered in the abstract. God is omnipotent in being in control of all things. The "almighty" of the Book of the Revelation is the All-Controller (e.g., Rev. 1:8; 19:6; cf. 2 Cor. 6:18). Our present word, *dunastēs,* enables us to retain the term omnipotence, the ability to do anything and everything provided we define it correctly. It is not the concept of abstract possibility before which God must bow, a possibility in existence before the very creation. Omnipotence means that God is the *dunastēs,* the one "who can do everything that he wills." In philosophical language, he can invest his will with reality. All existence, including all individuals in their mutual relations, depend on his sustaining activity. They cannot even close an eyelid apart from his will. He is the *only* one thus able.

His sovereignty is illustrated in his control of rulers. He is *the King of kings and Lord of lords.* There is a vivid actuality in Paul's language here. A king is a man of royal blood, and the term thus describes him by his character and office. But Paul gave us a picture of kings on their thrones, carrying on their work. God is *the King* of "those who are actually reigning as kings and *Lord* of those who are actually 'lording it'" (cf. 2 Cor. 1:24 for "lording it"). On the human level these men are not merely men with empty titles. They are not deposed monarchs living in exile or men of royal blood seeking a throne. They are actually in power and are actually doing something—they are really ruling their fellowmen and imposing their will on them. All these men in their turn, whether they know it or not, are under God's kingship and lordship. They can do nothing but what his will allows. They are never out of his control. Each man, as Paul suggested elsewhere, is "God's servant" (Rom. 13:4).

Paul was obviously thinking o. earthly rulers. Caesar did not have the last word. He might be over millions but he was under God. (Cf. Acts 17:7.) Somewhat similar language in the Old Testament speaks of God as "God of gods and Lord of lords" (Deut. 10:17; cf. Ps. 136:2 f.). The contrast here is with false gods, not human rulers. Paul was a monotheist, yet he recognized the power and the danger of polytheism (1 Cor. 8:4 f.). The Lord God is over all. Caesar as emperor or as Lord—and any such—are characterized in Isaiah 14.

The title *King of kings and Lord of lords* is attributed to Christ in Revelation 17:14; 19:16. It is the outcome of his ascension and exaltation to the right hand of God. God rules everything through his Son. God is not absent from this rule. To be under the rule of Christ is to be where God's rule holds sway.

At the end of the next verse is a short doxology. It should be observed that in verse 15 Paul was beginning to move into the doxology. In one sense it is not quite clear where it begins. Strictly speaking it ought to be the short ascription, "To him be honor. . . ." But the elevated language of verse 15 and the earlier part of the next verse is appropriate to a doxology. All the great epithets, blessed and only Sovereign, King of kings and Lord of lords, immortal, unapproachable, invisible are summed up and, as it were, concentrated in the brief "To him." Perhaps it would be safest to say that the atmosphere of awe and of worship begins with the word "blessed," is intensified as the apostle proceeds, and comes to the climax of the introduction with the words "can see." Then the formal doxology begins, "To him . . . ." It is sometimes said that in his epistles the apostle "bursts forth into a doxology." However true this may be elsewhere, in the present passage it is not so. The apostle was ascending in thought and when he reached the summit he did not suddenly utter an exclamation of praise; he found that he was already praising God in his heart. It only remained to say so: "To him . . . ."

It is sometimes said that the spirit of worship is created by music. We go to church and the first hymn takes hold of us, inspiring us to utter the praise of God which we did not seem to possess while we were traveling to the service. The singing "warms our heart" indeed; but there would be no worship without the knowledge of the truth. Great music may move the emotions but the inner core of praise is centered in the Word. The hymn either contains the Word or reminds us of it. In like manner the spirit of worship rose in the apostle as he dwelt on divine truth. This is not an argument for the abolition of music in the worship of God. It does mean, however, that there must be a steady and regular ministry of the Word if even the greatest music is to have a significant place in worship. Without the Word there may be change of mood, elevation of spirit, new resolution and strength; but without the Word there will be no worship. Without the Word there will be no utterance of thanksgiving and praise from the hearts of redeemed men—which is the object of our gathering together.

Verse 16: Who alone has immortality and dwells in unapproachable light, whom no man has ever seen or can see. To him be honor and eternal dominion. Amen: Because in Christ he himself has broken down the barriers. God is the source and ground of his own existence. Any "explanation" of why he exists is to be found within himself. This means that God is immortal in both directions. We look back and there never was a time when the self-existent one did not exist; we look forward and there never will be a time when God is no more. God's *immortality* is inherent. That of men is given to them by him. "This mortal nature must put on immortality" like clothes (1 Cor. 15:53). The metaphor is clear. Clothes do not belong to the nature of man; they do not belong to him like arms or legs; they have to be "put on." In like manner human immortality comes from outside; it is not a natural endowment. The divine *immortality* is in strong contrast to the "immortality" ascribed to deceased Roman emperors. (Cf. 1:17.)

God is his own home. He who is light *dwells in . . . light*. (Cf. 1 John 1:5.) Though the metaphor has been changed, the thought of Psalm 104:2 is repeated: "who coverest thyself with light as with a garment." The term suggests God's complete spirituality. "God is spirit" (not "a spirit," John 4:24). He is not material, and has no body. He is not limited by matter. He is creative and life-giving. And he is truth. In him is no error, falsity or deception and he never changes (Jas. 1:17). This is a pure order of existence which is beyond us. The nearest we can get to it is to think of the saint upon his knees, rapt in meditation and worship, "lost" in fellowship with God, for whom the world and even his own body has fallen away. But even he has to come back; even he may find his body stiff; and he receives God's gift of life and does not impart it. Human spirituality is a reality but it cannot create a universe.

The *light* in which God *dwells* is *unapproachable*. This is in contrast to all those, from the Gnostics onwards, who have their own secret way into the divine which they are prepared to give to those willing to be "initiated." God is *unapproachable* metaphysically. If flesh and blood ever found it possible to draw near, the strain would be intolerable. Man could not draw near and live. It would mean passing from the immanent to the transcendent, because God transcends all created existence. God is also *unapproachable* morally. It is not only that man cannot approach God; he must not. On all sides of the *light* which is God's home notices are to be seen bearing the familiar words: "keep out." In his infinite holiness God has no place for sinful men. "The face of the Lord is against those that do evil." "God opposes the proud" (1 Pet. 3:12; 5:5).

This is the background to the gospel. If God's holiness is forgotten, men create the concept of a sentimental, indulgent divine love which makes the gospel unnecessary and wastes the very blood of Christ. The heart of the gospel lies in the fact that the unapproachable God himself has provided a way of access in Christ. Paul was not merely filling up space when he wrote the word "access" in Romans 5:2. There is only one way "in," and that is Christ crucified.

No man has ever seen God as he is in himself. The thought goes back to Exodus 33:18–23. God has been seen in vision (Exod. 24:9–11; Isa. 6:1–5) and there have been what are called theophanies, occasional manifestations of God in human form. "The angel of the Lord" had no permanent personality but appeared as if the Lord himself. The angel of God said, "I am the God of Bethel" (Gen. 31:11–13). The emphasis is on temporary appearance. Theophany must not be confused with incarnation, in which there took place a permanent union of the divine and the human. The New Testament repeats the thought that no man has ever seen God (John 1:18; 6:46; 1 John 4:12; cf. Col. 1:15; Heb. 11:27). Yet in the new era of the gospel he has been seen.

"He who has seen me has seen the Father" (John 14:9). Christ is the image of God and "gave an exegesis, an exposition, of him" (John 1:18). In Christ God is seen, known and experienced. (Cf. further Matt. 11:27; 2 Cor. 4:6.) Just as believers see in Christ the invisible God, so in him they enter the unapproachable light (Col. 1:12; 1 Pet. 2:9).

No man . . . can see God because God is spirit and spirit is not manifest ("subject to awareness") to the human eye. Jesus was seen as a man by many, including such characters as Pilate. He was seen in his divinity by the eye of faith and we can still "look away to Jesus" (Heb. 12:2, literal). Unbelievers looked upon him who was and is the Son of God and they saw only a man; believers see more because their eyes have been opened (cf. Acts 26:16, 18 f.).

At this point the apostle put his feelings—in distinction from his thought—into words. To such a God *honor and eternal dominion* is to be ascribed. He is worthy of the *honor;* the *dominion* is his whether acknowledged or not, for he is the *pantokratōr,* the All-controller. The invitation to worship, to join the apostle in praise, is a call to ascribe all *dominion* (*kratos*) to him who has the sovereignty over all things. It is a call to all who exercise their lesser sovereignties: to auto*crats,* techno*crats* and demo*crats;* even to Caesar himself and his imitators. And it is a reminder to Satan himself, who wields the *kratos* of death (Heb. 2:14). For "you would have no power . . . unless it had been given you from above" (John 19:11).

The Jewish flavor of the mounting doxology must not blind us to the fact that Paul was writing as a Christian. The blessed and only Sovereign is the Father of our Lord Jesus Christ in whom we have seen what God can do. The King is the author of the kingdom of God, to preach which is to preach the gospel of the grace of God (Acts 20:24 f.). The Lord is the one who has given this name which is above every name to his Son Jesus in acknowledgment of his cross and passion (Phil. 2:9–11). He who alone has immortality has given immortality to those who believe in Jesus, an immortality which is not a mere survival but is eternal life. Though he dwells in unapproachable light he has sent his Son into the world as the light of the world (John 8:12; 12:46) and in him he bids men come to him. No man can ever see him but "he who sees me sees him who sent me" (John 12:45). It is unthinkable that Paul should have offered up any sacrifice of praise to God except through Jesus Christ our Lord (Heb. 13:15).

The listeners to the epistle might well have asked themselves if they were among the pure in heart who see God (Matt. 5:8); and remembering the cleansing power of the Word (John 15:3) when applied by faith (Acts 15:9) they may have joined with the reader in the final *Amen.*

4. The Duties of the Wealthy (6:17–19)

The rich are to give up arrogant behavior inspired by wealth. They should set their hopes on God, who amply supplies all things, and be rich in kindness and generosity. This is the foundation of their future with its promise of life indeed.

Verse 17: As for the rich in this world, charge them not to be haughty, nor to set their hopes on uncertain riches but on God who richly furnishes us with everything to enjoy: Right faith, right behavior. The wealthy *in this world,* in the present *aiōn,* are so characterized in contrast to the coming age which will be consummated—and inaugurated—by the "appearing of our Lord Jesus Christ" (v. 14), which should be the horizon and background of every Christian. This should appeal to *the rich,* if they are sincere when they speak of "our" Lord Jesus Christ. *In this world* contrasts also with the "eternal" (the adjective is from *aiōn*) dominion of verse 16. The power which wealth gives is still under the divine *kratos.* (Cf. 2 Tim. 4:10; Titus 2:12. The thought is parallel to that of Luke 12:21; Jas. 2:5.) When we speak of the world (*aiōn*) our emphasis is on time; "the world" in the Fourth Gospel (*kosmos*) implies hostility to God. The time element prepares the way for the later reference to the uncertainty of riches. The *aiōn,* here rendered by *world,* means "age" (for which see discussion on 1:17).

The language of *charge them* is strong and authoritative. It is not infrequent in the epistle (1:3; 4:11; 5:7; 6:14) with its variant of "command." Timothy was clearly to take a strong line. The present tense here suggests a long term policy: Timothy was not merely to "tell them" and the matter would be ended. He had to keep on telling them, because as long as *the rich* remained rich they would be under pressure from temptation. When men become wealthy they go up in the social scale. They enter a higher class of society, and because they have gone "up" they are tempted to be "superior." The key to the interpretation of *haughty* lies in the word "high." Men may look up to them, but the damage is done when *the rich* look for it, expect it, and are disappointed and annoyed when people fail to look up to them. If *the rich* do not guard against the temptation they will be "high and mighty." Paul had previously used similar language (Rom. 11:20; 12:16). Our Lord said that "what is exalted among men is an abomination in the sight of God" (Luke 16:15). To be "superior" is to stand on dangerous ground. The classical warning against what is "high" is found in Isaiah 2:11–17. When the church is as it ought to be, the question of wealth does not determine fellowship, which is in Christ and not in wealth or in the absence of wealth.

If "superiority" is to be avoided, the rich must have a right outlook. There would be little point in looking for the appearing of the Lord who is "our hope" (see on 1:1) if by their lives they showed that in actual fact their hope was not in the Lord but in their wealth. They were therefore to be continually commanded not *to set their hopes on uncertain riches.* The verb is in the perfect tense and implies that the rich should not have their hopes firmly resting on—an uncertainty. ("I have set my hopes on something" means that "my hopes are now 'in position on,' or 'firmly embedded in' something.") *Uncertain riches* is literally "the uncertainty of wealth." It is *uncertain* in that it may deteriorate to an alarming extent or be stolen (Matt. 6:19). In modern times we think of inflation, of maintaining property in good repair or "maintaining the equity," of bank or business failures or even of revolution. In any case wealth may give a man a splendid funeral but it will not prepare him for the Day of Judgment (Luke 12:20 f.; 1 Tim. 6:7). Hopes should be "in position" on the one great certainty, *on God.* This would follow the example of the apostles (see on 4:10) and would bring the same blessing. God is the living God and he does not change (Jas. 1:17; cf. Heb. 13:8).

It should be noticed that there is a Christian "theology of wealth." There is a Christian mode of behavior appropriate to a rich man. Paul himself said, "I know how to abound . . . I have learned the secret of facing plenty . . . abundance . . ." (Phil. 4:12). The "theology" may be summed up by saying that God supplies everything, his purpose is beneficent and it entails obligation. Although the rich may be self-made it is ultimately *God who richly furnishes* them with all that they have. He it is who supplies *us,* all of us, rich or poor, *with everything.* The scale of his giving is measured by *richly* (cf. Acts 14:17; 17:25; Jas. 1:5). Inasmuch as Timothy's congregation included slaves (6:1 f.) it is clear that everything depends on the point of view. The secret is "contentment" (see on 6:6). After the experience of regeneration the converted man can make the twofold affirmation that the world about him is new and that he himself is new (cf. 2 Cor. 5:17; 1 Pet. 1:3). In Christ even the slave can see that *God . . . richly furnishes us.* This is not the opium of the people; it is this alone which sets the people free.

We have been supplied with *everything to enjoy.* An advance is here made on the "to be received" of 4:3. The gifts of God in creation are not merely for the support of human life; they are for men *to enjoy.* The distribution of God's gifts is uneven, largely through men's sins. The slave-owner possessed far more than the slave. On the other hand some, through the exercise of integrity and thrift, become men of substance. In every case privilege involves responsibility; wealth brings obligation with it. This further point is considered in the next verse. See further on 6:1 f. for slavery and how far the church should go in asking for the redistribution of wealth. In the service of Harvest Thanksgiving, recognition is given to *God who richly furnishes us with everything to enjoy.*

Verse 18: They are to do good, to be rich in good deeds, liberal and generous: Duties following the doxology (v. 16) are as pedestrian—and as necessary—as the "collection" after the resurrection (1 Cor. 16:1). After the great chapter on the resurrection and after the soaring worship of the doxology, we seem to come down to earth: a collection for the poor and duties towards the poor! But this should be the outworking of faith. The resurrection sanctifies the collection and the doxology desecularizes the duties. The rich should be like God and *do good* (Acts 14:17). The whole church is called to good works, minister, religious women, widows, every one (2:10; 5:10, 25; 2 Tim. 2:21; 3:17; Titus 2:7, 14; 3:1, 8, 14). It would not be good works, and the rich could hardly be said *to do good,* if in a cold-blooded way they merely made a gift of cash. To qualify as a good work, a gift from the rich should come out of recognition that it was God who had richly furnished them with everything they have (v. 17)—"we give thee but thine own"—and should thus be a thank-offering; it should be the natural expression of Christian faith; and it should be inspired by love. "If I give away all I have . . . but have not love, I gain nothing" (1 Cor. 13:3). Love and good works are closely associated (Heb. 10:24), even to the apparent neglect of the poor (Matt. 26:10; Mark 14:6). The rich must give not only cash but themselves (cf. 1 Thess. 2:8).

By a pleasing paradox those who are already "rich in this world" (v. 17) are to be told repeatedly to be rich in a new way. The tone is moderate: there is no suggestion of violent revolution or of the abandonment of wealth. It is to be rightly used. The former command *to do good* is put in another form, with an addition. The rich (who by definition have much) are *to be rich in good deeds.* They are to have a large quantity of them, just as they have a large quantity of money or property. In other words, they are to keep on doing good. This has been implied already in the present infinitive but it is here brought out into the open. They are to keep on doing good—many times. No limit is imposed any more than a limit is imposed by our Lord on forgiveness of others (Matt. 18:21 f.). Great scope is here afforded to the sanctified imagination both of the rich and of the expositor. The obvious *good deeds* are gifts of cash, but the advantage of wealth is the variety of ways in which money can be used for the benefit of others. The rich can afford to take time and to take a journey to visit in prison; they can take time to choose the gift which is most appropriate to the needy: not only clothes in bulk but the kind of clothes which are suitable; they can educate the orphan as well as feed him; they can provide amenities for the widow as well as the bare necessities of life. They can quietly step in and handle funeral plans on behalf of those who are dazed. They can relieve the minister by undertaking some of the duties of hospitality. They can spare the time just to be with people and to give them friendship. All of these *good deeds* are to be done without thought of acquiring merit. They are to be the overflow of Christian faith and love, not wooden and mechanical but nourished by prayer and worship.

The meaning of the paradox is not yet exhausted. By their repeated *good deeds* the rich will still be *rich.* When the deeds are done they are not lost. The rich still "have" them if they are *rich in good deeds.* This must be because "God is not so unjust as to overlook your work and the love which you showed for his sake in serving the saints, as you still do" (Heb. 6:10). They will be blessed when they die, "for their deeds follow them" (Rev. 14:13).

The two final adjectives, *liberal and generous,* speak of the character to be manifested by the Christian rich. If they have grown in grace and have expressed their faith and love in many good deeds, then acts of mercy should flow naturally from their developed character. They will tend to share the good things which they possess with their less fortunate fellows, and thus will be *liberal.* They will realize that they belong to a Christian fellowship and that we are members one of another. Deeds of kindness openly express that in Christ Christians belong to one another. They will be "sociable" in property as well as in personality, for this is the meaning of the Greek word (*koinō-nikos*) behind *generous.* Fellowship will be seen.

Verse 19: Thus laying up for themselves a good foundation for the future, so that they may take hold of the life which is life indeed: A true and lasting treasure. The thought of *laying up* or storing up is not inappropriate when the rich are under discussion. If they heed the apostle's words, as men of sincere Christian faith, they will store up *for themselves* treasures in heaven (Matt. 6:19–21). These will not be wrath (Rom. 2:5; cf. Luke 12:21). But the apostle did not say "treasures" but continued an earlier motif. He had been speaking of where hopes should be set: to build on riches is to build on sand; only God is the sure foundation of the Christian's hope. The Christian rich whose faith is seen and expressed in kindly works will continue to have hopes set on God—*a good foundation for the future.* Their hopes will still be based on him and when in *the future* they arrive in heaven they will find their hopes were not misplaced (v. 17; cf. 2 Tim. 2:19).

So that expresses the purpose of "charge them" (v. 17). With hopes set on such a *foundation* the rich would enter more deeply into the experience of eternal life (see on 6:12), *the life which is life indeed.* The *indeed* calls attention to the life which is real. It is not coming into existence, for it exists already. It is not mere appearance which attracts by its glitter but rapidly becomes dull. It is not the life of pleasure which is supposed to delight but turns sour in the mouth. It is not wealth. It is Christ himself (Col. 3:4).

VII. FINAL CHARGE AND FAREWELL (6:20–21)

Timothy is to guard the Christian deposit entrusted to him in preference to the empty talk and contradictions of so-called knowledge. The fate of some men is a warning. They have professed the knowledge and missed the faith. A farewell prayer is offered for grace upon all the recipients.

Verse 20: O Timothy, guard what has been entrusted to you. Avoid the godless chatter and contradictions of what is falsely called knowledge: With deep feeling the contents of the epistle are summarized. *What has been entrusted to you* is literally "the deposit." In the ancient world valuables were deposited in temples "for safe custody" and the custom illustrates the meaning of the word. Paul had deposited a charge with Timothy (1:18) and he now reaffirmed his words with a deeper meaning. The deposit in Timothy's care was no less than the gospel, the message of salvation. It was his task and responsibility to see that it was kept intact: not diminished by being toned down, not increased by speculative additions, and not distorted by false perspective or proportion. (The "deposit" appears again in 2 Tim. 1:12, 14; cf. 2:2.) The punctiliar aorist, *guard,* sees Timothy's whole life concentrated into one activity. (For a definition and a discussion of the aorist tense, see on 2 Tim. 4:2.) He is a sentinel whose one duty is to see that the deposit entrusted to his care is not lost, stolen or altered. Those who would tamper with it must be warned off. It should never be forgotten that the believing church starts with what has been given. A church in search of a gospel or wondering what the gospel really is would not be a church in the New Testament tradition. The gospel has come by divine revelation. It is not man's discovery and still less is it man's speculative invention.

The *godless* or profane (see on 1:9; 4:7) has no religious value even if the *chatter* is about religion. The *chatter* says nothing about the value of a "chat" (cf. Roosevelt's "fireside chat" over the radio). The word means "empty talk." Its spirit is caught by such comments as: "he spoke for half an hour and there was nothing in it" or "he talked a lot and said nothing." Highfalutin speculation may impress the shallow but it will not bring them nearer to God. The *contradictions* are equally *godless.* They are objections to the Christian faith and the opposition which arises from them. They have no connection with Marcion's *Antitheses* except the mere name.

When Christians, and especially ministers, are presented with *knowledge,* they must be on their guard. The Christian faith and experience is a form of knowledge (see on 2:4). Eternal life consists in knowing the true God

[125]

and Jesus Christ whom he sent (John 17:3). Paul himself spoke of "the surpassing worth of knowing Christ Jesus my Lord" (Phil. 3:8). This knowledge is partly propositional, for it includes statements of truth; and it is partly personal, akin to the close acquaintance of friends. After years of friendship we know our friend with a deep, intimate knowledge which goes beyond "book knowledge." We can recognize certain alleged acts as consistent or inconsistent with his character. Analogous to knowlege of this kind is that of an elderly judge who has administered justice for a generation. He knows human nature through and through and few defendants in the dock can deceive him. Yet he might find it hard to reduce his knowledge to the contents of a textbook for budding lawyers. Even so what he has is worthy of the name of knowledge. The knowledge of God in Christ comes to Christians partly through the usual channels of everyday knowledge such as books and people—the preached Word, the spoken or taught Word and the written Word—and partly through the Holy Spirit interpreting this and mediating the presence of Christ. Through the Holy Spirit, believers encounter God in Christ and they can say, "I know him" (2 Tim. 1:12). The operation of the Holy Spirit cannot be rationalized but it is self-authenticating to the believer. When a man meets with God he knows it.

But there are others who also say that they have knowledge, though it is *falsely called* by that name. Hence comes the need to be on our guard. The false teachers call their speculative doctrine knowledge, though it is not derived from revelation and its appeal depends on an overestimate of the competence of the human mind. Timothy must not be entangled in speculalation when he has the responsibility—and the joy—of positively teaching and preaching the unsearchable riches of Christ. This is ample. *Avoid* all else.

Verse 21: For by professing it some have missed the mark as regards the faith: False doctrine has practical results. Paul was not content with pointing out the fact of intellectual error, though it is bad enough. Men who claimed to be experts in what was falsely called knowledge placed far too much emphasis on their own theories. They neglected accordingly all the treasures of wisdom and knowledge which are hidden in Christ (cf. Col. 2:3). This means that they rated their own theories higher than the doctrines of the Christian faith. Imperceptibly but surely the spirit of pride gains the upper hand in such cases. Prayer is neglected and finally abandoned. The worship of the church is no longer the joyful uttering of thanksgiving and praise for what God has done in Christ; at best it is an opportunity for the false teachers to introduce their "contradictions" and perhaps reduce the proceedings to uproar. Their spiritual life, if they ever had one, withers away. As far as *the faith* is concerned they *have missed the mark*.

They have not hit the target because they did not take accurate aim. Their failure can be interpreted by the use of another metaphor used elsewhere by Paul. He said once that he was pressing on "toward the goal..." (Phil. 3:14). He knew what the goal was and he wanted to reach it. He heard the call of God in his soul bidding him come "upward." He put all his energy into his advance. All his powers were concentrated in the "one thing I do." If the false teachers had taken God's revelation seriously and in the light of it had chosen their one dominant purpose; if they had nourished their own life of devotion and maintained the spiritual glow; if they had regarded all the advantages of ease as sheer loss and thus to be abandoned for the sake of Christ: then it would have been another story. As it is *some* men are a melancholy example of a wrong aim and a missed target— and a shipwrecked faith. (Cf. 1:6; 1:19; 6:3–5.)

Grace be with you: With all of you. The epistle was addressed to Timothy (1:2). *Grace* was for all his people. The letter was surely to be read to the church for its own edification and to support the young minister. The final word transcends all the charges and all the answers to the false teachers. Grace: lay hold of it and keep it and preach it. It sums up the infinite worth and character of what God has done and given in his Son.

2 Timothy

INTRODUCTION

2 Timothy

DATE

Most of the questions normally raised in the "introduction" to an epistle have already been considered in the Introduction to the First Epistle to Timothy. The three Pastoral Epistles belong to one another and we have attempted to deal with them as a group. It is thus not necessary to go over the ground again and think in detail of such matters as attestation, historical situation, language or authorship. All that needs to be said is that 2 Timothy was written by the apostle Paul a few weeks or months before his death (4:6), and written from Rome (1:17; 4:20–21). It must have been in the late summer or early fall, but the actual year depends on finding an answer to the vexed questions of Pauline chronology, especially that of the last few years. Dates assigned to the epistle vary between A.D. 64 and A.D. 68. One theory inclines to the view that Paul was executed in the reign of terror which followed the great fire of Rome, when Nero was looking for scapegoats and the Christians were "framed." This would indicate A.D. 64, the date of the fire (cf. 1 Clement 5:7; 6:1), as the time of the composition of the epistle. Others postpone his death until the last year of Nero's rule, A.D. 68. The uncertainty is to be regretted but it has to be accepted. It cannot detract from the value of the epistle, with the apostle's moving last words to Timothy— and to us.

THEOLOGY

The new ground to be covered is the theology of the letter. Once more we must disentangle its leading ideas.

God

We begin with the teaching of the epistle, explicit or implicit, about God. He is the living God, for Paul stands in his presence (2:14; 4:1). He is the Father (1:2) and from him come grace, mercy and peace (1:2; 1:18; cf. 4:22). Grace is the attitude, the purpose, and the action of God and meets the situation created by two factors, the holiness of God (1:9) and the sin of men (3:6; cf. 2:19; 3:13; 4:14 f.). Grace is the very purpose of God. We can say, if we wish, that God had a purpose, but we should add that he still has a purpose. This is reflected in his will, which is still alive and operative. Paul was an apostle by the will of God (1:1).

God promised life (1:1) and he took the steps to carry out his promise. He elected (2:10) and he speaks to men and calls them (1:9). When they respond to his call they repent, but even in this experience of men, divine grace is at work because God is the giver of repentance, and true repentance leads on to a knowledge of the truth (2:25). When men thus respond to God's call he saves them (1:9). The Scriptures are an instrument which may be used to tell men the good news of salvation offered to them and all that they need to know to lead the life of salvation already received. With this dual purpose God inspired the Scriptures (3:15–17). The living God makes gifts to his ministerial servants for the purpose of their ministry of grace and he makes gifts also to those who are his people but not ministers. He gives the spirit of power and of love and of self-control (1:6 f.). God is to be addressed in prayer, thanksgiving is to be offered to him, and he is to be worshiped (1:3; 2:19, 22; 4:6). He is to be served, both in and outside the ministry (1:8; 4:5). When a man presents himself to God, he receives him (2:15), for this is the very attitude of grace. He knows those who are his (2:19): he knows their identity and he knows them in fellowship. And he may be known (1:12).

This is anticipating the discussion of the Mediator, but it ought to be said here as part of the doctrine of God. He is not unknowable but is known in Christ. He is "able" and he keeps his people. He is to be obeyed, a fact which is suggested by Paul's mention of conscience (1:3). He will judge (1:18), and the purpose which arose in eternity (1:9) is a long-term "policy" and culminates "on that Day." He has a Word (2:9) and it is to be preached to all men (4:2, 5, 17).

The Gospel

The contrast between the apostle in fetters in the service of the gospel and the Word of God which is not in fetters (2:9) suggests that the Word of God is the gospel. It is the subject of apostolic testimony, and of others who are not apostles (1:8). The gospel is to be served, that is, preached at any cost because it is of supreme importance. The gospel demands the preacher's concentration, exertion and persistence. He must yield to no distractions, succumb to no half-heartedness and must never allow himself to give up. Nothing can take the place of the gospel (2:3–6).

The gospel is important because it is the outworking of God's purpose and grace; and its importance can be seen in the fact that through it life and immortality have been brought to light (1:10). Like the Word of God—and as the Word of God—the gospel is to be preached. The apostle, the man who has been sent, is a preacher, a herald. And it is to be taught (1:1, 11). It is to be taught to "the man in the pew," and to potential teachers also (2:2). The teaching is to follow the preaching, and the message is to be disseminated throughout all the world (4:17). This is a natural inference, parallel to apostolic practice, from the appointment of the faithful men who will be able to teach others also. It is through the apt and gentle teaching of the gospel that God gives repentance and knowledge of the truth (2:24 f.; cf. 4:3 f.). Such teaching is healthy and wholesome.

Jesus Christ

The gospel is preached and taught in words, but it is never to be forgotten that it is more than statements or propositions. These are necessary both to formulate and to preach the gospel; but the gospel in its essence is—Christ. This is illustrated by a remarkable parallelism in the apostle's words to Timothy. "Do not be ashamed then of testifying to our Lord . . . take your share of suffering for the gospel . . ." (1:8). The gospel is Christ, described indeed and preached in words but still Christ; and Christ is living, not a mere memory. Grace, mercy and peace derive from him (1:2; cf. 1:16, 18). He is Lord. The significance of the title of Lord and of the association of Christ with God the Father is noticed in the commentary.

Grace not only comes from Christ but is in Christ (2:1), and life also is in him (1:1). We can go further. The grace which God gave to us in Christ Jesus ages ago has been manifested. It has been made "subject to our awareness" through the appearing of the Lord (1:9 f.). He is the embodiment of grace. He himself is grace. When he "appeared," it was as a man "descended from David" (2:8). The incarnation was real. He did not merely appear and seem to be human. He actually was a man, a Jew, though he was and is still the Lord. His humanity, as thus taught, meets the standard set by "my gospel."

He was raised from the dead; in fact he "has been raised" and is therefore still "up." Behind this apparently simple statement lies all Paul's teaching about the meaning of the resurrection of Christ (see discussion on 2:8). In particular it should be noticed that he could not have been raised if he had not died. Implied in the verse is the fact and indeed the meaning of the cross. God saved us and Christ Jesus is called our Savior (1:9 f.). Our salvation is not received by us in virtue of our works but through faith (3:15).

This is already drawing near to the Pauline pattern of doctrine, and we pause to comment. Charles Haddon Spurgeon once rebuked "some of our extremely orthodox brethren" for what he deemed to be over-subtlety in criticism. "Paul did not write for those who must have all the creed in every sermon, and require all statements of the truth to be cut into one shape." [1] The judgment is just and wise. And when we see the Pauline pattern emerge we should not demand the slavish repetition of his every thought and all the characteristic words of his technical vocabulary.

Christ is the Mediator between God and men (see on 2:12). He is faithful to his people and consistent in his purpose (2:12 f.; 4:17 f., 22). The meaning of "the Lord" seems at times to oscillate between God and Christ. In the last cited references some see a reference to God because of the doxology. (In 2:11–13 Paul was thinking of Christ: "died with him . . . reign with him.") If Christ reigns and "his heavenly kingdom" means God's kingdom, then the oscillation is illustrated. The fact that certainty is not always possible emphasizes the mediation of Christ. God saves and rules in him.

---

1. Charles Haddon Spurgeon, Sermon no. 1170, page 241 in the 1874 volume (vol. 20). Preached in the morning of 26 April 1874, in the Metropolitan Tabernacle.

Christ will appear at the Second Advent as the righteous judge (4:1, 8), and as judge he will also be Mediator (1:18; cf. 4:14, 16). Paul could speak of "our Lord" (1:2) and at the same time imply that the Lord deals with individuals (2:7; 4:22).

The Christian Life

Not all men are Christians. Those who are are under obligation to live the Christian life. This may be considered under two aspects, though they merge in actual life. The duties of a Christian man may be broadly distinguished as religious and as ethical. He must exercise faith and practice love. He has his duties towards God and his duties towards man. The former are summed up in the word piety or godliness. Profane chatter is one of the causes of ungodliness; by implication godliness is created by the word of truth (2:15 f.). The heart of godliness is true faith, which is to be pursued (2:22). Its importance lies in the fact that without faith salvation is not received (3:15); its weight is illustrated by Paul's attitude to Timothy. In his longing to see his young friend, he was reminded of his faith—not his good looks or his brilliant intellect but his sincere faith (1:5). The continued response to God in faith, from conversion onward, is an attitude of trust in a holy God (1:9), who requires holiness in his people. In the description of men who cause stress in the last days we should notice the unholy and those who love pleasure rather than God. The implication is plain: believers, men of faith, should be holy and should love God (3:2, 4). Love of God is seen in the life of prayer, and Paul himself is an illustration of this (1:3; 4:16).

The union of faith and love (1:13; 3:10) is an indication that "pure" religion cannot omit right conduct. If faith is to be pursued, it must not be pursued in isolation; righteousness must also be the object of pursuit. This is not the righteousness of faith but that which springs from it, righteousness in life. It means that which God requires of his people in their dealings with their fellowmen (2:22). It has its negative side: certain activities should be avoided. Worshipers must depart from iniquity (2:19). The "content" of righteousness, the details of Christian behavior, are love and peace, (also to be pursued, 2:22), patience and steadfastness (3:10). To take the matter into even greater detail we should have to work out the opposites of the attributes of men in the last days (3:1–5). Their mere form of godliness is not able, has not the power, to produce a genuine Christian conduct. Real godliness is evident in real righteousness. (Cf. 2:24 f.) Such piety has power (3:5), and is "useful" and "ready" (2:21). There is always room for improvement (3:16; 4:2). Men of genuine piety must have a certain thrustfulness or assertiveness, because they are subject to persecution (3:12). Without such persistence they would abandon the faith. A particular case of the negative in Christian life is the duty to avoid certain people (3:5). This is not quarantine but the true separatism. The snare of the devil should be avoided, as otherwise it will be necessary to escape from it (2:26).

The Church

The Lord deals with individuals, as we have seen, but he gathers them into the church. The word "church" itself does not appear in the Second Epistle, but there are pointers to it. Believers participate in "the faith" (3:8; 4:7) which is common to them all. The fellowship of the one good fight and the race which they all run is the fellowship of the church. "The brethren" (4:21) means members of the one family of God, the family of which God is the Father, which again can be only the authentic church. "This present world" (4:10) implies by contrast the church. In that same company the Holy Spirit dwells (1:14; cf. Eph. 2:22).

It is because Christians encounter opposition that "the deposit" is to be guarded (1:14). There may be differences of expression: the church in the New Testament is both the flock under the care of the Good Shepherd (John 10:11) and the family which belongs to the one Father. But there is a central core of truth which must be guarded. Paul could thus speak of "my teaching" (3:10) and could tell Timothy to "continue in what you have learned and have firmly believed" (3:14). It is possible for men to swerve from the truth (2:18) and indeed to resist it (3:8). Men of corrupt mind will not come up to the standard of belief required by the faith. Doctrine can be distorted (2:18; 3:13) and faith upset.

For the care of the church the Lord has given the ministry. It appears in a rudimentary form in the Second Epistle and seems to be still fluid. Faithful men are to be appointed teachers of "what you have heard from me" (2:2). Timothy himself is to do the work of an evangelist (4:5) and fulfill his ministry. Whatever degree of uniqueness attached to Timothy's position, he was a minister (1:6). An apt comparison would be Ephesians 4:11 and perhaps 1 Corinthians 12:28–30. It is all for the glory of the Lord (cf. 4:18).

OUTLINE

2 Timothy

I. GREETING (1:1–2)

II. THANKSGIVING (1:3–5)

III. THE RENEWAL OF TIMOTHY'S MINISTRY (1:6–18)
1. A Gift Recalled (1:6–7)
2. Uninhibited Endurance Advocated (1:8–10)
3. An Example Presented (1:11–12)
4. A Method Indicated (1:13–14)
5. Timothy's Knowledge Revived (1:15–18)

IV. POWER THROUGH UNDERSTANDING (2:1–13)
1. Personal Power to Be Received (2:1)
2. Ministry to Be Extended (2:2)
3. Hardship to Be Understood (2:3–7)
4. Power Exhibited (2:8–10)
5. Principles to Inspire (2:11–13)

V. TASKS AND CHARACTERISTICS OF A MINISTER (2:14–26)
1. Ministerial Tasks (2:14–19)
2. Ministerial Characteristics (2:20–26)

VI. THE LAST DAYS (3:1–9)
1. The Character of Men in the Last Days (3:1–5)
2. A Typical Example (3:6–9)

VII. APOSTOLIC STIMULUS (3:10–17)
1. Paul's Known Experience (3:10–11)
2. Inevitable Opposition (3:12–13)
3. The Authority of Teachers and of Scripture (3:14–17)

VIII. THE FAREWELL GLORY (4:1–18)
1. Summary Exhortations (4:1–5)
2. The Threshold of Glory (4:6–8)
3. Several Requests (4:9–13)
4. A Warning (4:14–15)
5. Alone But Not Alone (4:16–18)

IX. GREETINGS AND FAREWELL (4:19–22)

COMMENTARY

2 Timothy

I. GREETING (1:1–2)

The framework is similar to that of the First Epistle and falls naturally into the threefold division of writer, recipient, and blessing. The style is also similar though the apostle did not merely repeat himself in a stereotyped way. The verbal differences breathe the living spirit of the author.

Verse 1: Paul, an apostle of Christ Jesus by the will of God: No private enterprise. In the previous letter Paul had said that he was an apostle "by command of God," which is more precise and more personal; the command was addressed directly to Saul of Tarsus, and addressed on a given occasion. On his response to the divine call he entered office and continued an apostle "by order." The will of God came into the experience of the road to Damascus but was not limited to it. It works invisibly and has all time at its disposal. The command was not uttered before the creation of the world but the will of God was active in a past eternity. God elected Paul for salvation (cf. 1 Thess. 1:4; 2 Thess. 2:13), an election which is logically prior to his election for service. God would hardly choose as an apostle a man who would be permanently unsaved. He set him apart before he was born (Gal. 1:15) and then called him. In distinction from the experience of some other men, Paul's call to salvation coincided with his call to service. God's will, which had elected Paul before time was and had set him apart before his birth, converged on his call. Many elements of God's will were operative in the circumstances which led up to the call. They include everything which made Paul the man he was and any knowledge he had of Jesus and his people— and all the factors which are classed under divine providence. All these "units of God's will" were gathered up and concentrated in the one compelling call to salvation and to apostleship. Paul's apostleship was not derived from men. He did not choose to be an apostle and he was not chosen by men as a bishop may be chosen (cf. Gal. 1:1; 1 Tim. 3:1–7); nor did his call come "through man" (Acts 9:10–19; 22:12–16). The call came and he was made *an apostle of Christ Jesus* through the will of God. (See further on 1 Tim. 1:1.)

According to the promise of the life which is in Christ Jesus: God is faithful to his promise. He made the promise ages ago (Titus 1:2) and he fulfilled it in Christ. But the fulfillment would have been of little avail if men had known nothing of it. In his mercy therefore God raised up his servant Paul to tell the story. He was thus an *apostle* in virtue of *the promise. The promise of the life* is none other than the promise of the gospel (Rom. 1:2), the word of life (Phil. 2:16), indeed of Christ himself who is our life (Col. 3:3 f.). Paul had earlier made mention of the promise (cf. Acts 13:23, 32 with 2 Sam. 7:11; 22:51; Ps. 132:11, 17; see also Acts 26:6). The Old Testament was the Bible of the early church, and the Christians found Christ "in all the scriptures" (cf. Luke 24:25–27). It is likely therefore that Paul had no definite promise in mind but was thinking of the general testimony of the Old Testament to "him who should come" (Luke 7:19 f.). This afforded him great scope in his choice of language. He might have spoken of *the promise* of the gospel, of the Savior or of any of the terms which sum up the message. Instead he chose *the life,* a term in which the Pauline gospel overlaps the Johannine (cf. Rom. 6:23 with John 5:24).

It is *the life which is in Christ Jesus.* An analogy may help us here. If we spoke of "the promise of the money in the bank" we should mean that the money is going to be ours. So we may begin by saying that we are promised *life. The life which is in Christ Jesus* is to be given to us. But *the life* is not separate from *Christ Jesus.* It is received when we put our trust in him (cf. 1 Tim. 1:16). Paul spoke elsewhere of being sons of God in him through faith and of putting on Christ like a new robe. The believer is thus *in Christ Jesus.* The phrase thus expresses the forensic status of the Christian before God. But inasmuch as faith, if it is real faith, is living, we have here more than an abstract status. A healthy faith encounters the living Christ, trusts him, prays to him, worships him and obeys him. In short *in Christ Jesus* implies the fellowship of the believer with Christ, the fellowship which is open to all who put and keep their trust in him. This is the meaning of "the mystical union with Christ" of which commentators speak. It is sometimes said that "Christ gives us his own life" because he is the vine and his people are the branches (John 15:5). Great care must be taken in the interpretation of such an expression. Christ does not give anybody his own metaphysical life, the life which he has as a member of the Holy Trinity. If he did he would be giving them a place in the Godhead, which is impossible. He has redeemed them from death and given them access to God and fellowship with him in newness of life (cf. Rom. 6:4). In Christ they have come home to God (cf. John 17:3).

For *an apostle of Christ Jesus* see further on 1 Timothy 1:1. Once more a letter to an individual must be understood as being written for a community as well as for Timothy himself. Once more it ends with grace for "you people" in the plural (4:22).

Verse 2: To Timothy, my beloved child: An attitude to be expected toward "my true child in the faith" (1 Tim. 1:2). The love may be seen in the prayers which Paul offered, in the longing which he had to see Timothy and the joy which a reunion would bring (vv. 3 f.). There are few bonds which are closer than the love between a spiritual father and his spiritual child. A convert cherishes all through his life the memory of the man who was the means of his conversion; and if the two work together in the interests of the kingdom of God the love between them grows.

Grace, mercy, and peace . . . our Lord: A repetition of 1 Timothy 1:2. This is no empty greeting. Its use recalls what God has done for us in Christ and what in consequence he offered us in Christ. When we became Christians we received *grace, mercy, and peace.* When Paul used these words in the

First Epistle he implied that, though Timothy had already experienced *grace, mercy, and peace,* God was offering him more and he could receive more. Now in the Second Epistle he implied that he could receive still more. And so, it may be inferred, it goes on through life. It might have been expected. "The grace of our Lord overflowed" in a constant stream (1 Tim. 1:14). "The grace of God . . . abounded" (Rom. 5:15; cf. 2 Cor. 9:8, KJV, RSV). "God . . . is rich in mercy" (Eph. 2:4). "May the Lord of peace himself give you peace at all times in all ways" (2 Thess. 3:16). *Grace* and *peace* may be multiplied (1 Pet. 1:2). The rightness of our expectation is proved by John. "*Grace, mercy and peace* will be with us . . ." (2 John 3).

II. THANKSGIVING (1:3–5)

The remembrance of Timothy inspires the apostle with thanksgiving to God. The picture of the young man's tears makes Paul long to see him again. He is moved by Timothy's manifest love but dwells more on his sincere faith and the background of the faith of his grandmother and mother.

Verse 3: I thank God whom I serve with a clear conscience, as did my fathers, when I remember you constantly in my prayers: To think of Timothy is to give thanks for him. This statement would encourage him and therefore prepares the way for what is to follow. The thanksgiving is sincere. It is a part of worship, which is what Paul had in mind when he said that he served God. To *serve* is here a cultic term. The thanksgiving is sincere because the worship is sincere. It is *with a clear conscience*. For *conscience* see discussion on 1 Timothy 1:5, 19; and cf. 3:9; 4:2. The worship contained nothing of calculation. Paul was following a long-established family tradition, and his *clear conscience* attests both the sincerity of his thanksgiving and his innocence even in bonds (1:16; cf. Acts 23:1; 24:14–16). It should be noticed that Paul's conversion did not mean that he ceased to worship a false God and began to worship the true God. In his Jewish days he worshiped God according to the Old Testament; on becoming a Christian he worshiped the same God in and through Christ the Mediator, the one who had been sent by the God of Israel (cf. Acts 13:16 f., 23).

There is a difference between remembering a person and remembering him *in my prayers*. Paul mingled intercession with thanksgiving. *Constantly* implies that in his life of prayer he remembered Timothy—it was his regular habit. (Cf. 1 Thess. 1:2.) One of the tests of friendship is prayer, and when it is offered *constantly* it affords an opportunity not only for repetition but for variety. Frequent supplication on behalf of the same person enables us to go into detail about his needs, his particular temptations, his immediate dangers or the disappointments or sorrows of the hour.

Verse 4: As I remember your tears, I long night and day to see you, that I may be filled with joy: A "human interest" story. When the time came for separation, it was too much for Timothy. The situation recalls that of Acts 20:37 in its poignancy, though it must have been some years afterwards. It may well have been the occasion of Paul's arrest, leaving Timothy on his own in a yet deeper sense, with the added knowledge that Paul was in danger. The verse reveals elements in the apostle's character which ought not to be forgotten in a final estimate of the man. The fiery controversialist who could write the Epistle to the Galatians was a man of tender love. He may have

[142]

been more "tough" than Timothy, though he was no stranger to *tears* (Phil. 3:18; cf. Acts 20:31). He could later tell him to take his share of suffering (1:8; 2:3; cf. 4:5), but there is no sign in the verse of rebuke. He did not roughly and unsympathetically tell him to "pull himself together." Let the tears flow: they will do no harm; "see how he loved him!" (John 11:36). The tears of Timothy may have sustained the apostle in his imprisonment; and his highly strung, emotional nature could have been the making of him as a preacher, provided it was controlled. A preacher whose intellectual grasp is strong has added power when it is suffused with emotional warmth. Cold intellect does not sway multitudes; hot passion does not give them anything to take away; intellect on fire teaches them, moves them, feeds them with the truth of God. Timothy was soon to be reminded to rekindle the gift of God within him (1:6). Can the purely phlegmatic rekindle anything?

Quite apart from considerations of the place of emotion in preaching, the attitude of the apostle to the tears of Timothy is a true expression of Christian behavior. We are not called to a hard Stoicism which condemns all emotional experience. There is nothing to be ashamed of in a good, honest cry and it may have a cathartic effect. It may reveal an intensity of belief or the depth of love. In it may be detected the bonds of fellowship and the reality of sympathy.

At any rate Paul did not condemn it. The vision of tears prompted the wish, *I long night and day to see you.* There is as little calculation in Paul's longing for Timothy as there was in his worship of God. He had no ulterior motive. He longed to see him (cf. 4:9, 21). It would be highly artificial and quite contrary to the spirit of the verse to assume that Paul wanted to see Timothy merely for the sake of the cloak, the books and the parchments (4:13).

The verse may be regarded as a classic example of fellowship between ministers in general; and between the senior and the junior. Ordained men have in common a certain authority and a certain field of duty. It is easy to become formalists and to dwell on a correspondence of mechanical duties. But here we have a "flesh and blood" relationship. To say the least we see a warm friendship between men who are working for a common Savior and Lord. Their mutual affection was more than the natural attraction of different personalities. Their friendship was "in the Lord" and it grew out of their common service to him.

As to questions of seniority, Paul was not like some men who are in a position of authority and cannot forget their office. There is a right and a wrong attitude here. It is sound advice to say to a man: "Never forget that you are an apostle, a minister of Christ. Every introduction, every social event, every occurrence may be an opportunity for witness to Christ or for pastoral care; at every moment there is a standard of behavior to be maintained so 'that the ministry be not blamed' (2 Cor. 6:3) and occasion for blasphemy given." A senior man, however, who cannot forget his seniority when in the presence of a junior and throws his weight around even on social occasions like a private meal or a visit to a family in a parsonage, will never be drawn close to his subordinate and will deny himself the deeper intimacies of Christian fellowship when man meets with man as man—in Christ. Paul longed to see Timothy as a Christian brother. He had advice and encouragement to give, to be sure. But in the present verse we see Paul the Christian man, hungry for fellowship. He wanted to see Timothy for his own sake. He was not summoning him "to my office at headquarters for an interview." He just cried from his heart: "Try hard; come soon." It is as poignant as the tears of Timothy and it reveals the man—not the official.

Little comment is needed on the final clause, *that I may be filled with joy.* The man who knew that the secret of joy is "in the Lord" (Phil. 4:4) knew also that it sometimes comes through his servants. There is no contradiction. Some scholars take *night and day* (note the Jewish order; cf. 1 Tim. 5:5) with "remember . . . in my prayers" in the previous verse, partly because the punctuation is fluid and partly because *night and day* is a stock phrase conventionally connected with prayer. It is not a point of great importance and either interpretation will suit.

Verse 5: I am reminded of your sincere faith, a faith that dwelt first in your grandmother Lois and your mother Eunice and now, I am sure, dwells in you: The ultimate ground of Paul's thanksgiving. Paul may have been *reminded* by receiving some news of Timothy, though it is not strictly necessary to assume it. When he was praying for him the thought of his *sincere faith* could have struck him. When faith is sincere there is no question of its being adopted for the sake of appearance. It is really faith and the believer is not pretending in any degree (cf. 1 Tim. 1:5). Demas could have been in the apostle's mind (4:10). If it is true that the test of faith is the action which should express the obedience of faith, then Timothy undoubtedly passed the test. He was not only willing to leave home and accompany Paul but also to submit to the painful rite of circumcision (Acts 16:1–3). His faith was proved sincere in the temporary pain and the permanent plodding of the ministry.

Timothy's background, like that of the apostle, was a religious home. He had been brought up on Scripture, which can instruct for salvation through faith in Christ Jesus (3:15). The Old Testament must have been interpreted in a Christian, not a merely Jewish, way. *Lois* and *Eunice* are both Greek names, but Eunice his mother was a Jewess and the grandmother may have been Jewish also (Acts 16:1). The father was a Greek and Timothy was therefore the product of a mixed marriage. His upbringing in the Christian faith was aided either by the early widowhood of Eunice, which is likely, or otherwise by the fact that she was a stronger character than her husband, especially if he were neglectful of the boy's religious interests; or by being skilled in the methods of secret education. The reference to "home and mother" would not be without a stimulating effect on Timothy. Memories of childhood can sometimes have a religious value, which is why "the old hymns" are often used in evangelistic meetings. It has been remarked that Germans dying on the battlefield have often moaned for their mothers rather than for their wives.

Paul's conviction about the quality of Timothy's faith was stronger than our translation might suggest. *I am sure* is at times used half-heartedly or as a mere concession: "Mr. X is a good man, I am sure, but his best friend could not regard him as a good president." Paul's certainty was far deeper than this. It is of the same order as his conviction about the love of God in Christ Jesus our Lord (Rom. 8:38). His perfect tense, "I have been persuaded," means "I am now certain, I am convinced" (cf. Luke 20:6). The faith had first taken up residence in the two women, Timothy's mother and grandmother; it had not "come on a visit" but had come to stay permanently; and then it had also taken up residence in Timothy—without leaving Lois and Eunice. Even in speaking in a simple, nontheological way, the apostle did not deviate from Christian truth. Faith, as it were, comes from outside and comes to stay. It is not produced in the home, either in the kitchen (home-baked bread is not the bread of life) or in the study (human theories do not save). It is the gift of God and not man's meritorious service. The language is of course metaphorical but it expresses truth. It means that when a man puts his faith in Christ it is not an act for which he is entitled to a reward. He would not have been able to believe apart from the work of the Holy Spirit. Hence even faith, the faith of men, is the gift of God.

III. THE RENEWAL OF TIMOTHY'S MINISTRY (1:6–18)

Paul recalls the charismatic gift which Timothy had received. With its ardor renewed he should testify without shame and even suffer for the sake of the gospel. He has the power of God, measured by what he has already done for us in Christ. Paul is himself the evidence of God's power at work in and through him. He indicates to Timothy a method whereby he may guard the deposit entrusted to him and in a noble spirit reminds him of apostolic isolation and refreshment.

1. A Gift Recalled (1:6–7)

Paul reminds Timothy to kindle afresh his charismatic gift. This should mean an access of power and love and self-control.

Verse 6: Hence I remind you to rekindle the gift of God that is within you through the laying on of my hands—because it does not work mechanically. It is because (*hence*) Paul was convinced that Timothy was a man of faith (and not merely had been) that he saw fit to *remind* him. It may be questioned if an unbeliever has a spiritual *gift*, though he may have a natural talent. If a man's faith is dormant he is hardly likely to exercise his gift. Faith is therefore of first importance. But even a man of faith may at times be idle or even lazy. He may not take the opportunities to preach and teach. He still believes, but instead of guarding and using his gift he neglects it (cf. 1 Tim. 4:14). In a "dry period" he may succumb to fear, boredom, or even temporary doubt. His *gift* may then be likened to a fire which has burned low. It has not gone out but it needs attention: a poker and a bellows may turn embers into a blaze. So Timothy is to stir his gift into flame. The renewed experience of mind and heart may be compared with that of Jacob. When he heard that Joseph was still alive and was ruler of Egypt "his heart fainted." But "when he saw the wagons . . . [his] spirit . . . revived" (cf. Gen. 45:27, LXX).

There are certain prerequisites if a man is *to rekindle the gift of God*. He must first remember that he has such a gift. Paul's reminder was of value here. Then he must determine to use it. He must give himself to the Word of God and to prayer. He must associate with other Christians in their varied experiences of joy and sorrow and watch for any and every situation to which his particular knowledge of the Word is appropriate. He must study the needs of men. Then he must prepare his sermon or teaching material. If his heart is not burning by this time he must faithfully plod on until it does; or else wonder if he ever did receive the gift. But apart from the burning heart, he must continue his work of preaching and teaching; and he should discover that the gift is manifesting a renewed vitality.

As Paul saw it, *the gift* was not a matter of past history. *The gift of God that is within you* is not "the gift that was in you." It raises the question of the permanency of spiritual gifts. Are they given for as long as life lasts? Can they fade away or the fire go out? Are they ever withdrawn? They are given by the Spirit "as he wills" (1 Cor. 12:11), and he does not act in an arbitrary manner. He does not give the gift of preaching for a year and then withdraw it. So far, then, we may regard the gift as permanent. But if a man neglects it he has to rekindle it. The longer he neglects it the harder it may be to rekindle it. With some the neglect may be extended over a long period and the time required to rekindle it may be too much. The gift, for him, has been lost; the fire has gone out; in fact the gift has been withdrawn. He has passed the point of no return.

This is a particular case of a general spiritual rule, and it may be seen in those who have no specific ministerial gift. If a man neglects the life of prayer he gradually prays less and less; then he does not pray at all; finally he does not want to pray. The ability to pray has atrophied—from another point of view it has been withdrawn. Similarly a man who hears the voice of God calling him and continues in sin finds that the voice becomes a whisper and then falls silent. He did not come to Christ when God called him and it becomes harder and harder to come to him. In the end he cannot come. In the end he may face death and judgment and become alarmed. In the end he may find it impossible to repent even though he seeks it with tears (cf. Heb. 12:17). There is an analogy in Romans 1:24, 26, 28. The one case may be called the unpardonable sin and its end is death. The other case is the unpardonable neglect, and its end is unfruitfulness. If faith is alive at all, the man is saved but "only as through fire" (1 Cor. 3:15). If a minister is thus guilty of continued neglect, he may possibly continue in office and perform his duties in an uninspired way, though his people may vaguely suspect that something is missing. His authority to minister may be permanent, unless he is guilty of grave moral offence. But with *the gift* permanently neglected, can he really minister? Timothy had not reached this dangerous position.

For the expression, *through the laying on of my hands,* see discussion on 1 Timothy 4:14. (Cf. also 1 Thess. 5:19.)

Verse 7: For God did not give us a spirit of timidity but a spirit of power and love and self-control: Nothing to prevent the exercise of the gift and everything in its favor. The first use of *a spirit* can hardly refer to the Holy Spirit. Its sense is more akin to the reading of Luke 9:55 preserved in Codex Bezae (D), "You do not know what manner of spirit you are of" (see RSV footnote). It resembles the spirit of slavery which inspires fear (cf. Rom. 8:15). Timothy may have been timid by nature (1 Cor. 16:10 f., KJV) but he now has a new nature in Christ. Fear should not therefore suppress the exercise of his gift.

The second *a spirit* is of the same order as the first, with the underlying thought that God gave the Holy Spirit. It is through him that we have *power and love and self-control.* If we have *power* it means that we can make a spiritual impact on men. We have the will to preach and we do preach, and preach effectively. "Boldness" (cf. 1 Thess. 2:2) is implied and more than boldness, a spiritual effect (cf. 1 Thess. 1:5). The gospel itself is the power of God (Rom. 1:16). If Timothy were afraid to fan the flames of his gift, he should be encouraged. What an effect it could have!

The power is not to be misused or misdirected. A preacher who knows his power may be tempted at times to bully his congregation, but the presence of the Spirit within him will enable him to resist the temptation. If at times the thought of preaching is irksome, the same love will inspire him, not only not to bully but to spread the banquet before his people. For he has much to give them, the finest food and the richest treasure. From the Word on his lips may be derived encouragement even in slavery, comfort in bereavement, new vision to inspire, new power to overcome. If Timothy loved his · people, he must stir up his gift and bless them with his words.

The value of tears (1:4) is in proportion to their rarity. The upsurge of timidity or an attack of nervous dyspepsia (cf. 1 Tim. 5:23) must not frequently prevent Timothy from fulfilling his ministry. Emotion must not be ruled out of preaching, but "tears every Sunday" would be overdoing it. The Holy Spirit would enable Timothy to control himself. Hide the tears; trample down the fear; forget the stomach and the palpitations. Timothy was a minister of the Word and he had the equipment for his task. Therefore: what was to prevent him from stirring up his gift?

The identity of *us* has to be considered. It includes at least Paul and Timothy and some scholars would so limit it. Power is certainly the characteristic of the preacher but it is not limited to him. "May you be strengthened with all power . . ." (Col. 1:11). Love is the fruit of the Spirit (Gal. 5:22) and cannot be restricted to ministers. Self-control (v. 23) is likewise fruit of the Spirit. (Paul used two different Greek words translated alike by *self-control*. This fact hardly invalidates the argument.) It would seem that *a spirit of power and love and self-control* is given to all Christians but perhaps sharpened and intensified in those who also have received a gift. The gift is that of preaching and teaching, and is not given to all Christians; but it is exercised when the possessor draws on that which is common to all genuine believing men. The *us* therefore means "us Christians, especially you and me." In the face of all this, how could Timothy fail to rekindle the gift?

2. Uninhibited Endurance Advocated (1:8–10)

The inference is drawn that Timothy should show no shame but should manifest his membership of the fellowship of suffering. It is for the sake of the gospel, and he is equipped with the power of God, whose grace began ages ago and whose power has been disclosed in Christ.

Verse 8: Do not be ashamed then of testifying to our Lord, nor of me his prisoner, but take your share of suffering for the gospel in the power of God: A reasonable inference. *Then* means "therefore." Timothy had received the gift of God (v. 6) and in common with all believers the spirit of power and love and self-control (v. 7); therefore he should not be ashamed. Paul had set him a good example (Rom. 1:16) and gloried in the cross (Gal. 6:14). Even so a man of Timothy's natural sensitiveness and timidity would realize what is involved in preaching the cross. To some it is a stumbling block and to others it is folly (1 Cor. 1:18–25), especially when they want signs to be given on demand or mere philosophic theories to satisfy their speculative curiosity. It seems to be a tale of weakness, often told by uneducated men without pride of birth or influence. (Cf. Gal. 5:11.) Preaching to the unspiritual man finds him listening on a different wavelength; and communication is likewise difficult to establish with the immature (1 Cor. 2:14; 3:1). The very kingdom of God is construed as treason (Acts 17:7). If the preacher is sensitive to the atmosphere which surrounds an unbelieving congregation and dwells on it, like Peter who "saw the wind" (Matt. 14:30) when he should have kept his eyes fixed on his Master, then he will be sorely tempted to *be ashamed* of his own *testifying to our Lord.*

Yet *testifying* is apostolic work. Paul's testimony at Jerusalem had to be followed by testimony at Rome (Acts 23:11). " . . . we testified of God that he raised Christ . . ." (1 Cor. 15:15). The preaching of Christ is the telling of a story and the asserting of meanings rather than the development of an argument. Argument has its place in apologetics but the prime task is the preaching of the gospel. In this testimony even apostles have their exemplar (1 Tim. 6:13).

If Timothy rekindled the gift of God within him and opened his heart afresh to the Spirit from whom comes power and love and self-control, then he would be so absorbed in preaching, like Paul himself in earlier days (cf. Acts. 18:5), that the temptation to *be ashamed . . . of testifying to our Lord* would be overcome in the exhilaration of the task. And with it he would take in his stride the awkward fact that the apostle himself was a *prisoner.* A leader of the church in the chains of a malefactor could be as much a stumbling block, a scandal, as the execution of the Lord himself. Snobbish heathen would not relish association with a community under such an influence; and the love of some Christians might grow cold (cf. Matt. 24:12). Some would fail in understanding and wonder why the Lord had abandoned his servant.

Paul would have none of this and by implication swept it aside. In chains as he was, he was not the emperor's prisoner. He spoke of *our Lord* and *of me his prisoner.* He did not escape from jail but he changed his jailer. He was the Lord's prisoner, brought into jail because of what he had done in the Lord's work and in the providence of God for what he could do in the jail. Apart from his testimony to fellow prisoners and to his guards, he has been the inspiration of many through the centuries. The Word of God is not in chains (2:9). It is an instructive lesson in both faith and providence to contrast Paul's present imprisonment with that of Peter (Acts 12:1–11) and with his own earlier experiences (2 Tim. 3:11). The Lord does not always "rescue" his servants. But against the dark background of what they endure they themselves may shine as lights in the world. Timothy could be emboldened by such reflections.

Timothy, then, was *not* to *be ashamed* of the testimony to Christ (cf. 1 Cor. 1:6) either as a ministry which he must fulfill or as a message which he must give. He must not be ashamed of doing the work or of the content of the gospel. It would be confirmed by the Holy Spirit when men repent and believe. In the meantime Paul told him to *take your share of suffering.*

This must not be interpreted as a vigorous assertion of ecclesiastical democracy. "Now then, young man, you must not be a passenger. Other people are carrying responsibility. It is not fair if you are slack." Paul was not drawing attention to the *share* which Timothy must take if he were to be fair to other workers. His meaning was first: endure suffering; you have the motive and you have the power (cf. 4:5). He was shortly to say that he himself was suffering (2:9). It is the common lot of all genuine Christians (3:11 f.). There is in fact a fellowship of suffering and this is what the apostle had in mind. The Greek verb which gave rise to the rendering *take your share of suffering* might be translated by one word in English to correspond to the one word in Greek: co-suffer. It is a "fellowship" word. Such "co-suffering" is one part of fighting the good fight of the faith (see on 1 Tim. 6:12). Our Lord himself is not absent from this company. Paul could speak of "the fellowship of his sufferings" (Phil. 3:10, KJV) and could rejoice in his own sufferings and in his flesh "complete what is lacking in Christ's afflictions" (Col. 1:24). The suffering of the atonement is not inadequate. Paul would never suggest such a thought and his meaning was quite different. He would agree that "in all their affliction he was afflicted" (Isa. 63:9). He could admit that "I persecuted this Way . . ." and still record the question put by the heavenly voice. "Saul, Saul, why do you persecute me?" (Acts 22:4, 7). But how could the exalted Lord suffer? He could suffer in the suffering of sympathy but not "in the flesh." That joyous experience was left to the apostle to "complete."

Timothy had the motive of suffering *for the gospel* and he could rely on *the power of God* already given (v. 7). There follows a rich description of what God has done which in itself is a commentary on his *power*.

Verse 9: Who saved us and called us with a holy calling, not in virtue of our works but in virtue of his own purpose and the grace which he gave us in Christ Jesus ages ago: A stupendous assertion of power inspired and directed by grace. *Who saved us* is a comprehensive statement which includes all that God has done for us in Christ, the *us* being "us believers." It marks the fact that the gospel (vv. 10 f.) has been accepted. (See further on 1 Tim. 1:1, 15; 2:4; 4:10.) The tense should be noticed. It is possible, in spite of the objection of some people, to say that we "have been saved." This does not imply an armchair but a program (Eph. 2:8, 10). Salvation is related to the hope which we have in Christ and is as sure as the promise of God (cf. 2 Tim. 1:1).

A further aspect of the tense should be observed. It is an aorist and it suggests all those paraphrases and illustrations of the order of "he plucked us as a brand from the burning." Our actual experience may not have taken place in a moment of time which we can remember, but the apostle views it as God's decisive act, of which the swift "plucking" from the fire of destruction is an apt and vivid picture.

Calling for the first time is logically prior to saving. The apostle was not reversing the order. (See discussion on 1 Tim. 6:12 and the further references there given.) His meaning is: *who saved us and* (when he did so) *called us with a holy calling.* Two meanings of *calling* coalesce. When we first heard his voice, we were not in the atmosphere of a bright and cheerful invitation to a new game nor did we catch the note of entrancing music which

lured us on to hear more. We were in the presence of the living God and the
solemn hush of holiness was weighing on our minds. The Word had penetrated
our heart and had discerned our inmost thoughts. Nothing was hidden; all was
laid bare before him with whom we have to do. (Cf. 1 Thess. 4:7; Heb.
4:12 f.) Our *calling* was in the atmosphere of holiness. And further God
called us to a life of holiness. Christians are saints, holy, by calling (Rom.
1:7).

God did *not* call us and save us *in virtue of our works*. To say that he did
would be to go back on all that Paul had written and would necessitate the
rewriting of the Epistles to the Romans and to the Galatians. Our calling and
salvation are not the natural development of our good deeds (cf. Matt. 7:
17 f.). They are not God's inevitable response to the life we lead. They do not
occur because they are caused by our deeds, and they are in no sense inevitable at all. Calling and salvation come *in virtue of* God's *own purpose*.
It is important to dwell on this before passing on to consider grace.

Purpose involves will. God willed to call and save us. It is sometimes said
that we owe it all to the love of God. This is true, provided our understanding of the love of God is correct. We sometimes think of the love of God
welling up like an eternal fountain, enough for all and enough for each for
evermore. This again is true, as long as we do not think of God's love for
men bursting forth because he cannot help it, because his love is so deep and
tender and compassionate that he has no option in the matter. He did have an
option. He need not have saved men. He was under no compulsion to save
them. He deliberately chose to save them. He willed to give them his love. It
was his *purpose*. This is not to be regarded as a cold-blooded calculation. The
point is that God is not dominated by an emotion sweeping over him. It may
be questioned whether it is right to use the word emotion in reference to God
at all. But in any case he always acts in the totality of his attributes. Those
who love God are "called according to his purpose" (Rom. 8:28), *in virtue
of his . . . purpose,* "the purpose of him who accomplishes all things according to the counsel of his will" (Eph. 1:11; cf. 3:11).

God's *purpose* was not abstract or arbitrary but was inspired by his
grace. Calling and salvation are therefore *in virtue of his own purpose and
. . . grace.* For *grace* see discussion on 1 Timothy 1:2. The RSV has adopted a
course unusual in English of speaking of *the grace*. This has been done in order
to bring out the fact that it was *the grace* (and not the purpose and grace)
which he gave us in Christ Jesus ages ago. This is a startling thought. We
did not then exist. Perhaps we can glimpse a dim picture of the meaning
by thinking of those wealthy men who set up a trust and settle large sums of
money on their grandchildren, perhaps even on grandchildren yet unborn.
We did not exist; but God did and Christ did. If we wonder why God gave to
men as yet unborn and with no apparent guarantee that they would accept
the gift, we reply that the gift was in the eternal purpose of God and that he
took steps to see that it would be accepted. This is surely the meaning of the
doctrine of election (cf. 1 Thess. 1:4; 2 Thess. 2:13). In eternity grace
was given to us *in Christ Jesus* and not apart from him. He is the one mediator
between God and men (1 Tim. 2:5). His mediation is seen preeminently
in the cross, but it did not begin at the cross. It began in eternity. "He set his
face to go to Jerusalem" (Luke 9:51) is in its context a record of the

decisive act of the historic Jesus. It could well represent his eternal acceptance of his mission.

It might be thought that belief in election would undermine moral effort. It seems to be a natural consequence. In actual fact the testimony of history does not support this view.[1] The Apostle Paul is himself an illustrious example of a man who believed strongly in election and in salvation by grace and who at the same time manifested a moral effort which is beyond human praise.

Verse 10: And now has manifested through the appearing of our Savior Christ Jesus, who abolished death and brought life and immortality to light through the gospel: Grace visible. All that existed in the mind of God in eternity came down to earth for men to see. Grace has been concentrated in *Christ Jesus.* His *appearing* or epiphany usually refers to the Second Advent (cf. 4:1, 8). Here it means the first advent, the incarnation.

The whole life of Jesus on earth, his early hidden years, his public ministry, his death and resurrection and ascension, are summed up in one comprehensive "moment" of vision as grace *now . . . manifested. Now* does not quite mean "this present instantaneous moment" or "the present time" at which Paul was writing. It is in direct contrast to "ages ago" (v. 9) and has three levels of meaning. It points to the time process as distinct from eternity, the time within which we all spend our days on this planet. It refers in particular to the duration of the life of Jesus from the birth to the ascension, for this is essentially the period in which God's complete revelation of himself was given in Jesus. It spills over into later times, for in Paul's evening and from then until now, the twentieth century, the revelation of God in the historic Jesus is still effective when we look back to him. God is still revealed in Jesus *through the gospel.* The historic Jesus becomes our contemporary through the Holy Spirit, though this does not mean that he is brought back to earth as in the days of his flesh.

The appearing does not mean a mere appearance as when a man "appears" on a television program; nor does it mean the appearance in which a man just "appears." "The President appeared in New Jersey yesterday. As his automobile flashed past . . . ." That appearance says nothing except that he was there for a short time. *The appearing* of Jesus means the activity of grace, and it is there for men to see if they will but look upon it with faith. We can still so look upon it. "When I survey the wondrous cross . . . ." *The appearing* includes the character of Jesus, his knowledge of God and intimate fellowship with him, his sinlessness, and his attitude to men; it includes his teaching about God and men, and his works of compassion for men, and especially his cross and passion. All this taken together was grace *manifested,* the gracious God in action for men.

It is remarkable that Paul could say that God saved us (v. 9) and go on at once without embarrassment to speak of *our Savior Christ Jesus.* Father and Son are united in the work of man's salvation. This, together with the adjacent mention of *our Lord* (v. 8; see on 1 Tim. 1:2; 6:3), points to the deity of Christ. As the embodiment of grace he has been given to his people.

---

1. Cf. F. L. Cross, ed., *The Oxford Dictionary of the Christian Church* (London, New York and Toronto: Oxford University Press, 1957), p. 444.

He *abolished death.* This may occasion a wry smile from some when they see huge funeral homes. Far from having been abolished, they may say, death is still with us. It has been commercialized. The observation is true but it is based on a misunderstanding. Paul did not mean that death had been abolished like an old custom or an antiquated law. He meant that it had been put out of action. The finest automobile on the market will take you precisely nowhere if it is permanently "put out of gear." An autocratic and tyrannical king can do you no harm if he has been effectively deposed (Rom. 5:14; cf. 1 Cor. 2:6 and 15:24, both KJV).

Death here is a chord of two notes. As the penalty of sin it will not be experienced by the believer. The wages of sin may be offered but the believer will not take them (Rom. 6:23). He has already passed out of death into life (John 5:24). He was once in a state of spiritual death, separation from God. Now in Christ he is free from this forever. For him indeed it has been *abolished.* But he will still experience physical death. He will still pass through the valley of the shadow. For him, however, as a believer the horrors have been removed. Let us suppose for the purposes of illustration that a trembling old lady has to pass through a large factory. She has heard of the roar of machinery and the crash of metal on metal and is most apprehensive. The terrifying plant will overwhelm her! But to her relief when she is conducted through she finds that all is still. Gigantic machines are as silent as sleeping babies. Everything has been turned off. Not a wheel is in motion. So it is with the Christian's death. The horrors of passing through and entering unknown territory have been switched off. Through his own death the Lord has put out of action the one who wielded the power of death as the weapon of a blackmailer (Heb. 2:14 f.). The sting of death is sin (1 Cor. 15:56) and sin has been dealt with by the Savior. There remains for the believer no more than a migration, and in this he is not unaccompanied. For he will be passing "through Jesus" (cf. 1 Thess. 4:14).

This is due to the fact that our Savior *brought life and immortality to light. Life* is more than existence. It is eternal life (see on 1 Tim. 6:12). When he *brought* it *to light* he was not like a man who fetches something from an inner room or from under the counter of his store and holds it up for inspection and even for admiration. Eternal life is not only to be inspected or admired. It is offered and it is to be received. Otherwise, though *brought . . . to light,* it will not be enjoyed. *Immortality* is represented by the word "imperishable" in 1 Corinthians 15:52–54. If anything were needed to make *life* everlasting, this word would do it. Paul was not thinking of the Greek immortality of the indestructible soul or of mere survival. *Life and immortality* depend upon and are *through the gospel. The gospel* means the gospel as preached to men. When they receive it they receive eternal life. But the gospel itself even when preached does not stand alone. It goes back to Jesus, or it is no gospel but merely words. Hence we must understand not only the gospel which the apostles preached; not only the gospel which Jesus preached (cf. Mark 1:14 f.); but also the gospel which Jesus was and is. Jesus, in Mark, could speak of "for my sake and the gospel's" (Mark 8:35; cf. 10:29); in the Acts of the Apostles they preached Jesus (Acts 5:42; 8:35; 11:20; cf. Gal. 1:16). To preach Jesus is to preach the gospel, for he is the gospel, just as the appearing of Jesus is the manifestation of grace. *Life* in him is enjoyed by the believer here and now. The *life* which he will have is *brought . . . to light* through the resurrection of Jesus. The Lord will restyle the Christian's earthly body to bring it into conformity with the body of his resurrection glory.

The thought and language of verses 9 and 10 are characteristic of Paul. Even Philippians 3:20 f., to which we have just alluded and which is not the strongest parallel, speaks of "a Savior, the Lord Jesus Christ." The verses may echo teaching material or a hymn but the stamp is Paul's.

3. An Example Presented (1:11–12)

Paul himself is also suffering but has no shame. He is intimately acquainted with the one whom he trusts and has confidence in him.

Verse 11: For this gospel I was appointed a preacher and apostle and teacher: Paul was in the same service as Timothy (cf. v. 8). The verb and the construction recall 1 Thessalonians 5:9. A combination of the two passages would result thus: "God did not appoint us for wrath but for the acquisition of salvation . . . ; I was appointed *for this gospel*('s proclamation) as a preacher . . . ." Paul's appointment is thus within a wider appointment of "us." The implication is that the preacher knows from his own experience the salvation which he offers to men to "acquire." (Cf. 1 Tim. 1:12, "appointing me for ministry," and see the following v. 15.) At any rate Paul knew; every preacher ought to know; otherwise it may be a case of the blind leading the blind.

For *apostle* see discussions on 1 Timothy 1:1; 2 Timothy 1:1. See further on 1 Timothy 2:7 for Paul's threefold office. The *teacher* elaborates the faith in detail and in perspective to believers; the *apostle,* like the evangelist, addresses the hitherto unbelieving world. Comment is sometimes made that the *preacher* or herald today has the congregation at his mercy: they cannot answer back, though the comment suggests a suspicion that listeners would welcome the opportunity. Contradiction of the man in the pulpit would be in order if his subject were a subject of discussion. But it should never be this. If the preacher really preaches the Word of God (and he has no authority to preach anything else), contradiction, comment and discussion are out of place. For he is preaching the Word of God, which is to be received and obeyed, not discussed; and in theory he is preaching in the modern church building to the believing church, which is gathered together for worship and for hearing the Word of God. From two points of view the Word of God should be heard without interruption: the preacher is giving it; and the believing congregation has assembled in order to hear it.

Verse 12: And therefore I suffer as I do. But I am not ashamed, for I know whom I have believed: The secret of unashamed apostolic suffering. This reinforces Paul's exhortation to Timothy not to be ashamed of the Lord's prisoner (v. 8) but to suffer for the gospel. Careful scrutiny should be given to the content of Paul's knowledge. The question turns on the nature of *whom.* Is it interrogative or relative? In form it is relative in the Greek, though there are instances of a relative being used in an interrogative sense. The problem can be best understood by the use of an analogy. A man may say, "I know whom I support (I voted for Mr. Nixon)" in reply to a taunt, "You have no political sense." On the other hand if he is told that "you have no political friends" he may answer, "I know whom I support (Mr. Nixon and I have been friends from boyhood)." In the former instance he claims to know the identity of the man for whom he voted: it was Mr. Nixon. In the second case he is asserting a knowledge which is personal acquaintance: I know Mr. Nixon. It is similar in Paul's language here. To take the relative pronoun in the interrogative sense would mean that Paul was merely asserting a knowledge of identity. I know who it is; it is Jesus. It is better to follow the normal Greek idiom of the "telescoped" relative, in which the relative "contains its antecedent within itself." That is to say, *whom* means "him whom." Paul thus meant: "I know him whom I have believed." This interpretation has behind it the great authority of A. T. Robertson (*A Grammar of the Greek New Testament,* pp. 720 f., 726), who specifically excludes the interrogative approach.

I know him: This was Paul's incessant quest from the time of his conversion (Phil. 3:10). The world did not know God (1 Cor. 1:21); the heathen do not know God (1 Thess. 4:5; cf. 2 Thess. 1:8). Even Paul's knowledge was partial (1 Cor. 13:9, 12), but it was real. He could speak of "the surpassing worth of knowing Christ Jesus my Lord" (Phil. 3:8). (Cf. 1 Cor. 2:2; Gal. 2:20.) His experience is that of eternal life, "that they may grow in the knowledge of thee" (John 17:3).

Belief here is more than belief of propositions, though this is included. The sense is: I know him whom I have trusted. The content of "him" is all that was stored in the mind of Paul about Jesus: the fact of Christ and its meaning. Hence the propositions are included. "I have trusted" means that "he is now the object of my trust." The expression covers a long history of Christian experience. He knew the Person; he could describe him by propositions.

And I am sure that he is able to guard until that Day what has been entrusted to me: Acquaintance means certainty. For *I am sure* see on 1:5. Paul was here taking a long view, as well he might, for it is indeed true that *he is able. That Day* occurs in 2 Thessalonians 1:10 and refers to the eschatological day, the Day of the Lord (1 Thess. 5:2). He who *is able* is also faithful and willing (1 Thess. 5:23 f.).

What has been entrusted to me is an interpretation, as the RSV shows with its footnote, "what I have entrusted to him." The Greek reads literally "my deposit" (see on 1 Tim. 6:20). Some scholars regard the deposit as the gospel (cf. v. 14) or as the souls in Paul's pastoral care. Others see in it a reference to Paul himself, to his soul. The latter view seems to accord better with the thought of the Last Day and with the idea of faith or trust, especially if faith means the handing over of oneself to Christ in trust. The link between "deposit" and "faith" may be seen in 1 Peter 4:19, ". . . let them deposit their souls with a faithful [trustworthy] Creator." Paul himself used the same verb (which is cognate with the noun "deposit") in Acts 20:32, literally, "And now I deposit you with God . . . ." Bengel aptly summed up the matter: "Paul, on the point of his departure, had two deposits, one to be committed to the Lord and the other to Timothy."[1] Thus for the apostle suffering

---

1. The famous J. A. Bengel (1687–1752) was a Lutheran New Testament scholar. His *Gnomon Novi Testamenti* (1742) is a classic among commentaries and is marked by deep insight and rich suggestiveness, expressed in pithy comments. The original Latin refers to the two deposits of 2 Tim. 1:12, 14: "Paulus, decessui proximus, duo deposita habebat: alterum Domino, alterum Timotheo committendum."

brought no shame and faith meant certainty. Notice how in verse 8 Paul began to "walk and not faint" as he considered his imprisonment, but in verse 9 he broke into a run considering the power and grace of God, and soon was mounting up with wings like an eagle (cf. Isa. 40:31). With such an inspiration he knew no shame. It could be the same with Timothy.

4. A Method Indicated (1:13–14)

The pattern of sound words already received by Timothy with the aid of the indwelling Spirit will enable him to guard the deposit entrusted to him.

Verse 13: Follow the pattern of the sound words which you have heard from me, in the faith and love which are in Christ Jesus: Practical advice at ground level (see above). Timothy must preserve the pattern and *follow* it in his own life and in his preaching and teaching. He would thereby nourish the spiritual life of himself and of his listeners (cf. 1 Tim. 4:6 and discussion). *The pattern* would give a right perspective and proportion to their thinking and a balanced diet for their souls. *Pattern* (see on 1 Tim. 1:16) means an outline which is to be regarded as a standard. It consists of *sound words,* not pictures. The unsearchable riches of Christ (Eph. 3:8) is illustrated by the inexhaustible depths of the New Testament. In a real sense Christian truth is unwieldy; it is too much for the preacher and teacher to handle. That is why he needs a summary statement of the faith as an aid to understanding and to proclamation. The *sound words* which form the constituents of the outline are "healthy" and spread no infection. (See discussions on 1 Tim. 1:10; 6:3; cf. 2 Tim. 4:3; Titus 1:9, 13; 2:1 f.) If our Christian lives are to be spiritually healthy, healthy words must not be neglected, especially those which form the doctrinal pattern. A single word may or may not have much effect, but groups of words, if not sound, can distort or deny the faith, lead astray morally, and even excite hatred.

Timothy had been well instructed: he *heard* the *sound words* from Paul himself. He must keep and hold their *pattern* just as deacons should "hold the mystery of the faith" (1 Tim. 3:9). He must not do it mechanically; must not observe the letter and forget the spirit; must not be orthodox—and dead. It must be all *in the faith and love which are in Christ Jesus.* The Greek here is very close to that of 1 Timothy 1:14 (see discussion). The *pattern* is not a mathematical formula merely to be remembered, or remembered and used in calculations. It should foster Timothy's own life of prayer and his discipleship generally; it should direct and test his moral behavior; and in this spirit he could teach others. Together they would grow in "the life which is in Christ Jesus" (1:1 and discussion).

The *pattern* leaves Timothy free to choose his own language, including that of illustration (word-pictures), in his preaching and teaching. Otherwise he would spend his ministerial time in little other than reciting a fixed creed. If he does it all *in the faith and love which are in Christ Jesus* he himself will be a living *pattern* (cf. 1 Tim. 1:16), not indeed of conversion but of Christian discipleship.

Verse 14: Guard the truth that has been entrusted to you by the Holy Spirit who dwells within us: Literally, "guard the good deposit." See on verse 12. The "deposit" is the gospel, which is formulated by the "pattern" of the previous verse. Timothy could *guard* it only through *the Holy Spirit who dwells within us*, like faith (v. 5 and discussion). The teaching recalls that of Romans 8:9–11. *The Holy Spirit . . . dwells* in individuals ("Any one") as well as in the believing church, and the presence of the Spirit mediates that of Christ ("But if Christ is in you"). The words must not be so grouped as to read *entrusted to you by the Holy Spirit*. The thought is: *guard* the fine deposit through the Holy Spirit . . . .

It would seem that in some sense Paul was designating Timothy as his successor. The exhortation to *guard* the deposit is no novelty. Paul had told the Thessalonian church to "hold to the traditions which you were taught by us" (2 Thess. 2:15). From the beginning the Christian faith was "handed down" and "received."

5. Timothy's Knowledge Revived (1:15–18)

Paul himself has kept the faith although he was at first deserted. This is clear from his prayer for Onesiphorus who had served him with selfless devotion.

Verse 15: You are aware that all who are in Asia turned away from me, and among them Phygelus and Hermogenes: A small place gained in history through a failure. Phygelus and Hermogenes did not abandon the faith (cf. Titus 1:14) but left their apostle in the lurch. A number of commentators refer to Matthew 5:42, "turn not thou away" (KJV). Equally apt illustrations would be the priest and the Levite who "passed by on the other side" (Luke 10:31 f.) because they did not want to be involved; or, more charitably, the disciples whose spirit was eager but whose flesh was weak (Mark 14:38). Apart from the bare mention Paul assigned no blame (cf. 1 Cor. 13:7). Timothy was already *aware* of the situation and he may have taken the words as a hint of the need of swift pastoral care (see on 1 Tim. 6:12). The *all* is a figure of speech (hyperbole), natural enough in the circumstances. We can imagine the vigor with which a counseling interview would have been conducted by James (cf. Jas. 2:15 f.). The text is a poignant example of a "ministerial disappointment." The occasion may have been the arrest of Paul. The verse is a silent plea to Timothy: do not likewise (cf. Luke 10:37); and a study in lost opportunity. Even repentance would not bring back the past. They would not meet Paul until the resurrection.

Verse 16: May the Lord grant mercy to the household of Onesiphorus, for he often refreshed me; he was not ashamed of my chains: A wish in form but really a prayer. For *mercy* see on 1 Timothy 1:2; 2 Timothy 1:2. Onesiphorus must have received *mercy* already, or why should he have identified himself with a Christian apostle? The divine reward of loyalty is yet more loyalty from on high. (Cf. Matt. 25:39.) It was Onesiphorus who "did the actual work." *He was not ashamed* (an object lesson for Timothy; 1:8), and *he often refreshed me. The household* endured his absence and possibly ran his risk and gave him encouragement (cf. Mark 9:41). His name means "bringing advantage" and the "refreshment" may be likened to that given to a weary athlete (cf. 4:7). The strain of the course had begun to tell (cf. Acts 20:24). At the sight of his friend, Paul must have found the reinvigoration of taking courage (cf. Acts 28:15). The reference to *the household* rather than to the man alone (cf. 4:19) has led to the conjecture that Onesiphorus was dead by the time the epistle was written. Disgrace is suggested by *chains* as well as discomfort and pain. The Greek has the singular, "chain." Mark uses the same word in both singular and plural (Mark 5:3 f.).

Verse 17: But when he arrived in Rome he searched for me eagerly and found me——: The simple words cover a moving story. Despite the possible fatigue of the journey he *searched* with seriousness of purpose and with care in his pursuit, not wasting time and *eagerly* following up every clue. Everything else was irrelevant and his persistence was rewarded. We know neither the rebuffs nor the cuffs which he may have received.

Verse 18: May the Lord grant him to find mercy from the Lord on that Day—and you well know all the service he rendered at Ephesus: The missing reference to *him.* Onesiphorus must have been alive still as it is hard to think of Paul praying for the dead. *That Day* recalls verse 12 (see discussion). There is a pleasing repetition in this second prayer (v. 16). Onesiphorus had found Paul in a Roman prison; in return for this and for *all the* other *service,* Paul prayed that he might *find mercy.* The words of two frequent short prayers may here have been conflated, if J. Jeremias is right. This would yield the following interpretation: *May the Lord* (Christ) *grant him to find mercy from the Lord* (God). This accords with Paul's thought of Christ as the Mediator (1 Tim. 2:5 and discussion). The obvious comment is 1 John 2:1. (Cf. Rom. 8:1, 34; Heb. 7:25; 9:24.) Paul did not list all that Onesiphorus had done at Ephesus because Timothy knew it "very *well.*" (The Greek comparative adverb here, *beltion,* is elative.) He knew how many services he had rendered and how great they were.

There is no reason to think that Paul had any doubts about the salvation of his friend. He had faith in Christ—or why the long journey to Rome?—and it was a living faith. The prayer is the natural expression of Paul's gratitude.

IV. POWER THROUGH UNDERSTANDING (2:1–13)

If Timothy exercises the intelligence which the Lord will give him he will realize that power is available from above and that he can widen his own ministry by training others to spread the faith. He will not question his own need to endure. The degree and the range of the power may be measured by the resurrection of Jesus Christ and by the fact that the Word of God cannot be imprisoned. Certain principles are laid down to increase Timothy's understanding and to inspire him in his ministry.

1. Personal Power to Be Received (2:1)

Timothy is to realize that power is not a matter of his own strength of mind or will. He is to be empowered.

You then, my son, be strong in the grace that is in Christ Jesus: The searchlight swings round and "spotlights" Timothy. *You* is emphatic: *you,* in view of God's action, Paul's unashamed suffering and certainty, and the out-standing service of Onesiphorus, *you* therefore *be strong. My son,* with its warm affection, turns an order into an exhortation (see on 1 Tim. 1:2; 2 Tim. 1:2). For *grace* see the same references and discussion.

Be strong does not visualize Timothy bracing himself to new endeavor nor does it urge him to "take a dose" of strengthening medicine. It means "keep on being empowered" and the *in* (Greek *en*) may be instrumental: "be empowered by *the grace that is in Christ Jesus."* But *grace* has been manifested (see on 1:10). It is not only "located" *in Christ Jesus* but may be regarded as "consisting *in" Christ Jesus.* This is on the analogy of "command-ments 'consisting in' *(en)* ordinances" (Eph. 2:15), an interpretation of the Ephesian text which has the authority of J. H. Moulton.[1] Moulton's new linguistic knowledge justified Henry Alford's earlier translation. We may therefore render: "be empowered in (the grace consisting in) Christ Jesus," that is, "in the gracious Christ Jesus." All the wealth of the formula, "in Christ" (1:1 and discussion) may be tapped here.

The verb "to empower" appears rarely in the Septuagint, but one instance may be relevant. It appears in the Codex Alexandrinus and the recension of Origen at Judges 6:34. The RSV has "the Spirit of the Lord took possession of Gideon." The Hebrew means: "put on Gideon (as a garment)," or "clothed himself with Gideon." Is it too fanciful to think of Timothy being exhorted

---

1. See his *Grammar of New Testament Greek,* Vol. 1, Prolegomena, p. 103.

constantly to be clothed with the gracious Christ? Someone must have thought that when Gideon became the clothes of the Spirit it was Gideon himself who was empowered. Paul had already told the Roman Christians to "put on the Lord Jesus Christ" (Rom. 13:14). He had told the Ephesians to "be empowered in the Lord" (Eph. 6:10, literal). There is a connection between clothing and power: be in Christ not only in status but in experience and the result is that you will *be strong*.

2. Ministry to Be Extended (2:2)

One man cannot do everything. If Timothy teaches other men they too will be able to teach and thus the gospel will be spread.

And what you have heard from me before many witnesses entrust to faithful men who will be able to teach others also: A deliberate policy, not to restrict but to safeguard the spontaneous expansion of the church (cf. Acts 8:4). The evangelistic testimony of laymen is good but it has its dangers. Sincere men may not fully grasp the meaning of the gospel; and false teachers may infiltrate their ranks. There must be some standard of Christian truth to check extravagances and to be an authority to which to appeal. Timothy would not last forever, and in any case his own position might be threatened (cf. Heb. 13:23).

The *many witnesses* may include the Christians present at Timothy's ordination or baptism (cf. 1 Tim. 4:14; 6:12; 2 Tim. 1:6), lesser known characters who could testify to the gospel (cf. 1 Cor. 15:6); perhaps even the Old Testament Scripture, or Paul's own converts. *Before* is an attempt to render the Greek preposition *dia,* "through," "by means of," which is hard to render in the present context. If Paul were thinking of the presence of Christians, Timothy could not later argue that he had not been told or had been taught inadequately. If the reference is wider he could hardly plead lack of authority.

Timothy was to *entrust* the gospel, that is, to "deposit" it in the care of *faithful men*. See on 1 Timothy 6:20; 2 Timothy 1:12, 14. When this had been done the recipients would themselves be under obligation: "guard the deposit." We have here a simple example of the fact that it is possible to deposit the gospel with someone else and at the same time retain it yourself. The *faithful men* are to be *faithful* in two senses. They must be men of faith, believers. So precious a treasure as the gospel would not be *entrusted* to anybody and everybody, agnostic, atheist, or just plain heathen. And they must be men in whom others, particularly Timothy, can and do repose their trust. They must be trustworthy, reliable.

The purpose is not only to ensure that "the pattern of the sound words" (1:13) which *you have heard from me* should not be lost and the gospel, thus formulated, kept safe in its purity, for the correction of possible errors and as a standard of reference and appeal. It is not only that the *faithful men* may pass on the message into the safe keeping of a later generation. They *will be able to teach others also,* partly as evangelists and pastors and partly as trainers of evangelists. The whole gospel is thus to radiate from Timothy. *Able* implies competence. Timothy was to look upon the whole body of believing men and choose from among them those who would be capable of teaching. It is not given to every believer to "grasp the pattern" even though he can testify (cf. John 9:1–38); not everyone can teach.

3. Hardship to Be Understood (2:3–7)

To exercise intelligence in suffering is to raise man above the level of the dumb beast. As a soldier Timothy should expect hardship and have the right priorities; as an athlete he should recognize the need of training and of maintaining a high standard; as a farmer he should expect the divine blessing on his labors. With the Lord's aid in such reflections Timothy will learn the secret of endurance.

Verse 3: Take your share of suffering as a good soldier of Christ Jesus: Suffering for the gospel is the true military glory. (See discussion on 1:8, where the Greek verb is the same as here.) *Soldier* and Timothy are unexpected companions: he is not the military type. In the spiritual warfare, however, it is not always the muscular and the aggressive who have the moral courage for the encounter. Even the timid by God's grace can prove more than conquerors.

The fellowship of suffering is part of a wider fellowship. An individual man may be a lone fighter, but a *soldier,* even if working alone as a sentry or on a secret reconnaissance, belongs to a company bigger than himself. The numbers are greater and the purpose is greater than that of any private ambition. A *good soldier* will obey orders promptly and without question or argument. "Suffering for the gospel" is part of the work of *a good soldier of Christ Jesus.* Notice how closely associated are the gospel and *Christ Jesus.*

The force of *as* is not easy to determine. The force may be: "suffer . . . just as a good soldier would," or perhaps "suffer as a good soldier does." This is a simple comparison, with a finite verb understood. The understood verb, however, might be a participle in the construction known as "*hōs* subjective." This would mean: "suffer, conscious that you are a good soldier." This would encourage Timothy. But was he a good soldier? It might be argued that all soldiers engaged in "the good warfare" (1 Tim. 1:18) are "good." Christ's servant is a fine (*kalos*) soldier in a fine (*kalē*) warfare. It might be wiser to extend the meaning of *as* and translate: "suffer, conscious that you are (called to be) a good soldier." Even if the subjective construction is rejected Timothy would have the thought of being *a good soldier of Christ Jesus.* Part of what is involved is described in the next verse.

Verse 4: No soldier on service gets entangled in civilian pursuits, since his aim is to satisfy the one who enlisted him: No distractions! The statement holds good whether the *soldier* is actually engaged in a hard campaign or is just *on service* and doing quiet garrison duty in some remote outpost. It applies even in the hours when he is off duty or supposed to be sleeping. At all times he is on call. He cannot indulge in moonlighting and, for example, run a business on the side. As a plain statement of fact the *soldier* has but one duty, to obey orders twenty-four hours in the day. As a statement of obligation it is implied that the interests of the *soldier* should be exclusively military. His dominant interest and only purpose should be the success of the army to which he belongs and his own contribution to it. He could have said: "to me to live is to be *on service*" (cf. Phil. 1:21).

Paul's words may reveal a situation in which Timothy timidly did not accept or ask for ministerial support and perhaps aimed at imitating the apostle (cf. 1 Thess. 2:9; 2 Thess. 3:8 f.; 1 Tim. 5:17 f.). He may not have relished taking money from members whom he had to oppose for one reason or another—inadequate doctrine or sub-Christian moral life. He may even have welcomed the need to work at some trade in order to be too busy to attend to some challenge from which he shrank. At any rate this may have been a temptation. No distractions! urged the apostle. Timothy must be absorbed in his work.

Common sense must not be left out in the interpretation of the text. Paul was thinking of a dominant purpose, not whether there can be such activities as part-time ministries. Even the man who earned his own living could live with the one purpose of preaching and teaching Jesus Christ. He could be like William Carey, who in his early days described himself as a preacher who worked as a shoe repairer to pay expenses!

This verse must be used with great care in the formulation of any ecclesiastical rule forbidding ministers to be members of other professions or to engage in trade. It may be questioned whether marriage was in Paul's mind at all. The text cannot and must not be used to justify clerical celibacy. For the minister, marriage of the wrong kind could be a distraction; but if it is a marriage of the right kind it can support his dominant purpose. "We are not without authority, are we, to take with us on our missionary circuit a Christian woman as wife, like the other apostles and the Lord's brothers and Cephas?" (1 Cor. 9:5).

Entangled is a highly expressive word for involvement in irrelevant matters. It carries the idea of interweaving, entwining or plaiting. The corresponding noun is used in 1 Peter 3:3 for the fashionable plaiting or braiding of women's hair. (Cf. 2 Pet. 2:20.)

The one who enlisted him is not to be regarded as a recruiting sergeant or a military clerk who took down the particulars of a man who voluntarily had joined the army. Even the keenest of new soldiers has wider ambitions than that of giving pleasure to a minor, military official whom he may never see again. The man in question is the commander-in-chief. Historians of times of stress sometimes say that "X raised a new army." They mean that an outstanding general called for men to follow him in a great cause, and from all parts they sprang up and placed themselves under his command—to fight. He it is who may be said to have *enlisted* them. Such is the spirit of Paul's word. No entanglements—in order to please the chief.

Verse 5: An athlete is not crowned unless he competes according to the rules—both before and during the contest. The athlete must observe the rules of the particular competition in which he takes part: he must not cheat in any way. This applies in any contest, amateur or professional. If Paul were here thinking of the professional athlete, as he probably was, he had in mind the strenuous effort required during the contest itself and before the contest. The professional had to undergo severe training for nearly a year before a major event. Timothy must not shirk effort, hardship and endurance.

Timothy had to train himself in godliness (see discussion on 1 Tim. 4:7). In his ministerial "effort" he must have a true aim; he must run to win, and must box to knock his opponent out. Half-heartedness would not be good enough. It would mean guarding the deposit of Christian truth and preaching and teaching it without fear or favor. It would mean the pastoral care of the church and of individuals even at the cost of his own inconvenience. It would require the maintenance of his own spiritual life of private prayer and study of the Scriptures, and giving an example of a high moral standard. He must manifest personal holiness. He must walk with God and at the same time not lose the common touch. In fact he must do everything laid down by the apostle in these epistles!

The *athlete* knows in advance what is demanded, if he is to be *crowned,* i.e., win the prize. Timothy must understand this.

Verse 6: It is the hard-working farmer who ought to have the first share of the crops: Not merely the farmer. The point is that the hard work has the first claim. The possible "results" of Christian work are now becoming prominent. The athlete's prize has become the fruits of the earth. Only toil can be productive. The *crops* would be the conversions which would take place as a result of faithful ministry, conversions which could only take place as a consequence of God's owning and blessing the ministerial labors; and to a somewhat lesser degree the "support" given by the church (cf. 1 Tim. 5: 17 f.). The Greek verb for *hard-working* is the same as that for "labor" in preaching and teaching, and we still speak of "ministerial labors." The corresponding noun is used in 1 Thessalonians 1:3, "labor of love." Faith would inspire work and love would inspire toil and labor.

If Timothy had been one of those "who labor and are heavy laden" (Matt. 11:28) and had come to Jesus, we can discern an analogy between his experience and that of Paul. Paul had changed his jailer (see on 2 Tim. 1:8); Timothy had changed his labor. In the one case the imprisonment continued; in the other the labor and toil continued; but what a difference was made by Christ!

The three illustrations suggest: no distractions—concentration; no half-heartedness—exertion; no cessation—persistence. Good watchwords for the minister!

Verse 7: Think over what I say, for the Lord will grant you understanding in everything—because the staying power in suffering is derived from understanding. There is a right way in which to endure and a wrong way. Some men summon up all their resources and determine to go through with the business and get it over. They steel themselves in the spirit of the Stoic. They have no vision of God to aid them. The world, and nothing more than the world, is before their eyes. Their spirit, admirable and praiseworthy and even moving at times, is akin to that of the British people at the height of the bombing. A slogan passed from lip to lip: "We can take it." In defiance they make light of their troubles.

Others just collapse. If they have any thought of God they accuse him of unkindness and pity themselves. They have no idea of his loving purposes or of the fact that their sufferings may be allowed by him for reasons beyond their wildest dreams. They forget his wisdom.

The true secret of endurance is to use the intelligence and to *understand.* Timothy should realize the force of Paul's three illustrations (vv. 4–6). His very work involves suffering but power is available to him (see on 2:1). He should therefore enter more deeply into the meaning of Paul's words, letting it sink in. The final reward would be great. In the meanwhile, and as a reason for emphasizing thought, Paul was sure of the Lord's gift of intelligence (cf. Prov. 3:11; Heb. 12:5).

In his certainty that *the Lord will grant* intelligence to Timothy, Paul did not press the matter or elaborate. It would hardly be necessary. With continued reflection and with the Lord's gift, Timothy would grasp the point in this and *in everything.*

4. Power Exhibited (2:8–10)

The power available to Timothy may be seen in two mighty facts. Jesus was raised from the dead, never to die again; and though preachers may be imprisoned, the Word of God ranges far and wide. If Paul can endure, Timothy can—with eternal results.

Verse 8: Remember Jesus Christ, risen from the dead, descended from David, as preached in my gospel: A real death and a real resurrection of one who was really known and really offered to men when preached. Timothy must keep this fact in mind always, for the disciple is as the Master. Suffering is followed by resurrection. Some scholars think that Paul was here quoting two brief articles from some form of primitive creed already known to Timothy. Its Jewish Christian origin is betrayed by its second article, *descended from David,* and it is not unlike similar material in Romans 1:3 f. In the present context the reference to Davidic descent is irrelevant.

Timothy might indeed have recognized a quotation from the formulated content of Christian belief and proclamation, but no part is really irrelevant. *Descended from David* points to the fact that Jesus was indeed the Messiah (cf. 2 Sam. 7:12; Ps. 89:3 f.; 132:11; Acts 2:29–32 is instructive); and that the incarnation was real. The Son of God really did become man and really did suffer. If it is argued that this was already known to Timothy, it may be similarly asserted that the resurrection of Jesus was known also.

He who really died is really *risen from the dead.* The tense of the verb (perfect) is significant. It implies that he who "has been raised" has a present characterization: "he is now 'up' " and is permanently so (cf. Rom. 6:9). This is in line with *my gospel* (cf. Rom 2:16; 16:25; 1 Thess. 1:5). He who really died and is really risen was really known by the apostle (see on 1:12) and was really offered to men for them to receive when he was *preached,* for Paul knew what it was to preach in the power of the Spirit and see men converted (cf. Col. 2:6).

The continued remembrance of the resurrection of Jesus Christ will have practical importance ("No cross, no crown") in proportion as it is understood in its fullness. In brief: it is the final proof of the deity of Christ (Rom. 1:4) and of the fact that God has accepted his sacrifice for the sin of men (Rom. 4:25). It is the pledge of the future resurrection of believers, for Christ is the first fruits of those who have fallen asleep (1 Cor. 15:20). It is the moral type of Christian experience and the call to live in newness of life (Rom. 6:4, 11; Col. 3:1). These facts are vital for Christian proclamation and for Christian life, both of minister and people.

Verse 9: The gospel for which I am suffering and wearing fetters like a criminal. But the word of God is not fettered: The test of Paul's convictions.

It is one thing to have a theory; how far will a man go in its dissemination? The intensity with which he feels its truth and the value which he sets upon it may be measured by what he is willing to suffer and the lengths to which he will go. Paul was absorbed in the gospel—the life blood of his existence as a believer and the air which he breathed as a preacher. It involved a theory, for it had a meaning and could be stated in words; but it was far from being a mere theory; it was the living Christ in the fullness of his meaning.

That Paul was *suffering* goes without question, and it was suffering with indignity (Acts 9:25; 2 Cor. 11:33). Just as his Master had been obedient to the length of death (Phil. 2:8), so Paul suffered to the length of bonds. Just as the Lord was numbered with criminals (Luke 23:32 f., 39), so Paul was treated *like a criminal*. It is an unsavory and ominous word. *But the word of God is not fettered.* It does not lie in chains like the man who had spent his days in preaching it. This is not a mere upsurge of an optimistic spirit. Paul believed in the living Christ and in the activity of the Holy Spirit. "The Word of God is living and active . . ." (Heb. 4:12). The man was in chains but his tongue was free. Would not the guards hear the Word from the prisoner? Would not the church be emboldened to renewed evangelistic effort? (Cf. Phil. 1:12–14.) Timothy was still at Ephesus, and if he followed the apostle's instructions he would teach other faithful men the contents of the Word so that they in turn might teach others (see on 2:2). Over a wide area of the Roman Empire there were men at work in the spreading of the good news. History records that their proclamation did not fail. In the mercy of God the Word is still with us, and in the sovereignty and providence of God the Word needs preachers (Rom. 10:14–17). In a time of persecution their work may be impeded or threatened, and evangelism becomes an "underground movement." (Cf. 1 Kings 18:4, 13.) But the pressure of the Word continues and there are not wanting men to make it known. For the Word of God is not fettered and God raises up men to preach it. Necessity to preach presses hard upon them. They cannot but speak of what they have seen and heard (Acts 4:20; 1 Cor. 9:16).

The verse reveals Paul as an example to Timothy. His unbroken spirit, the depth of his insight and his unshaken faith could well be emulated by the timid young man at Ephesus. For the success—or, better, the achievement— of preaching the gospel does not depend on a man's natural endowments—on a tenacity which may be no more than a disguised obstinacy or an aggressiveness which may be no more than unregenerated pugnacity. It depends on the gift of God, a spirit of power (1:7). That gift shines forth from the apostle's prison.

Verse 10: Therefore I endure everything for the sake of the elect, that they also may obtain the salvation which in Christ Jesus goes with eternal glory: The doctrine of election has very practical consequences. It provides the motive power for the apostle to *endure everything:* to *endure* it all in his present circumstances as he has endured *everything* throughout his ministry. The endurance is not wasted because the Word of God is not in chains. Paul was able to endure because of the consequences. It was all *for the sake of the elect*. At one stage in the life of each one of them they were *elect* and so destined for *salvation* but it had not yet fallen to them to *obtain* it. This would happen when they heard the Word and believed. Paul had spent long years in spreading the Word and had seen men receive it. He had seen men change from elect men to elect and saved men and he was still willing to endure for the encouragement of those who were engaged in preaching the Word.

The text implies that it is not the bare fact of election which saves men. The gospel of Christ crucified has to be preached even to the elect in order that they may believe and be saved (Acts 16:31). God ensures that it is preached to them, and through the ministry of the Holy Spirit they freely yield themselves to him. It should be clearly observed that in the cross our Lord redeemed all men and thus made *salvation* available, but they do not *obtain* it until they repent of their sins and put their trust in the Savior.

The elect . . . obtain . . . salvation when they believe, and they do not believe until they have heard God's call which comes when the Holy Spirit applies the preached Word to their hearts. In the discussion on 1 Timothy 6:12 further references are listed to texts concerned with "call." These should be consulted. The "order of events" is given in Romans 8:29 f. God's purpose unfolds in foreknowledge, predestination, calling, justification, glorification. It is only an outline, though a valuable one. It does not claim to be exhaustive. With justification, for example, should be associated regeneration and adoption. They take place at the time of justification but are to be distinguished from it. Glorification is yet to come.

The salvation which is *in Christ Jesus* has already been considered. (See 1 Thess. 5:8 f.; 2 Tim. 1:9 f. with its added references.) See on 1:1 for *in Christ Jesus*. To say that salvation goes *with eternal glory* gives the impression that *glory* is prior. This is not so. Believers have salvation now but must await the glory. Once they were not within sight of it; now they are (Rom. 3:23; 5:2). Paul's purpose was that the elect might *obtain the salvation which* is *in Christ Jesus* through response to the proclamation, *with eternal glory* in heaven. For *glory* see on 1 Timothy 3:16; for *eternal* see on 1 Timothy 6:12. God's manifested presence in his Son will be enjoyed by his people for all eternity and for them the experience will be ever new.

5. Principles to Inspire (2:11–13)

From death will come life—with Christ. If Christians endure they will share his kingdom. To deny him is to repudiate the only Mediator. If faith falters he is ever the same and loyal to his people.

Verse 11: The saying is sure: If we have died with him, we shall also live with him: Everything depends on the company we keep. *With him* is the crucial phrase. The introductory sentence recalls 1 Timothy 1:15 (see discussion; cf. Titus 3:8) and we have to ask whether *the saying* looks backwards or forwards. Scholarship has been divided. Some think that it looks back, especially to verse 8. The distance separating the two verses is against this view, though it is balanced by the fact that in the Greek we should render literally "For *(gar)* if we died with him . . ." The obstacle is not insuperable however. The way in which the RSV has set out verses 11–13 reflects a widely held theory that Paul was here quoting from a hymn. He has given us four "lines," each of two members (e.g., "If we . . . , we . . ."), and it just happens that the first line which he quoted begins with "For." If this theory is true we can ignore the "for." It is not impossible that the hymn may have been composed by Paul himself. The present verse seems to reecho Romans 6:1–11, especially verse 8.

When did we die with Christ? Our Lord speaks of taking up one's cross daily and of carrying it (Luke 9:23; 14:27) after one has first denied oneself. The picture points not to crucifixion but to a readiness to be crucified. This death of self took place when we first yielded to Christ in repentance and faith. On the Damascus road the strong-willed Saul sought to know the Lord's will, not his own (Acts 22:10), and he later pictured it as if he had been one of the criminals who had been crucified with Christ (cf. Gal. 2:20 with John 19:32; the same compound Greek verb is used in both verses). The inner attitude of self-renunciation is brought out into the open in baptism: "We know that our old self was crucified with him . . ." (Rom. 6:6; cf. Gal. 5:24). This crucifixion of self has to take place daily. "Consider yourselves dead to sin . . ." (Rom. 6:11). If you do not so "consider" you will find yourself alive in the wrong sense.

This has its bearing on suffering and endurance and has its lesson for Timothy. Naturally timid, he shrank from hardship of both body and mind: he was to take his share of suffering and not be ashamed. If he declined to do this it would be because the old self was asserting itself. It had been crucified once; it should be crucified every time he was tempted to take the line of least resistance. Christ was not absent when he first yielded his heart to him; he was not absent from the service of baptism; he is not absent now. You died once, Timothy; therefore put to death what is earthly in you (cf. Col. 3:3, 5). You are with Christ crucified when you thus die; you will *also live with him*. For "because I live, you will live also" (John 14:19).

Verse 12: If we endure, we shall also reign with him; if we deny him, he also will deny us: Positive and negative encouragement. In the first "line" the previous pattern is maintained. We know that Jesus was able to *endure,* and he is now "seated at the right hand of the throne of God" (Heb. 12:2 f.). Endurance is the same as steadfastness (see on 1 Tim. 6:11). The result of endurance is blessedness (Jas. 1:12; cf. 5:11). Paul looked even further ahead and said that *we shall . . . reign with him.* Endurance carries with it a guarantee of participation in the royal government, the kingdom, of Jesus. (Cf. Luke 22:28–30; Rom. 8:17; 1 Cor. 6:2; Rev. 3:21; 22:5.)

And *if we* do not *endure?* It is dangerous to "deny the antecedent," as the logicians say, and to assume that the consequent must also be denied. If men who are Christians fail to *endure,* or suffer a momentary or even a long lapse, they can humbly remember that the Lord deals gently (cf. Heb. 5:2) with his people because he himself has experience of their trials (Heb. 4:14 f.) and makes intercession for them (Heb. 7:25). (Cf. Rom. 8:34; 1 John 2:1.) In Romans 2:8 Paul did not say "those who do not endure" or "show patience" (v. 7). Such have failed to catch the vision of being able to *reign with him* but they "will be saved, but only as through fire" (1 Cor. 3:15).

Dying and living with Christ (v. 11) recalls the resurrection of verse 8. Similarly to *reign with him* implies that he is "descended from David" (also v. 8)—a king.

The second "line" seems extraordinarily severe, and it should be said at once that it states a principle rather than refers to an episode. It is a grievous matter to *deny him* and at first sight we are inclined to say that *he also will deny us.* Yet there was once a man who denied the Lord almost to his very face over a period of time and did it with vigor; and yet the Lord did not deny him. On the contrary after his resurrection he purposed to meet him, for he was included by name in the angelic message: ". . . go, tell his disciples and Peter that he is going before you to Galilee; there you will see him, as he told you" (Luke 22:54–62; Mark 16:7). And see him they did. Peter was there, was told to "follow me," and was commissioned for the apostolate (John 21:1–22). The inference is that *if we deny him,* and it is but an episode in a life of discipleship, we may be forgiven. By "episode" it must not be thought that we are making light of a denial. The word is used to bring out the fact that we are thinking of a temporary lapse, not a permanent attitude.

For Paul was stating a principle, the principle of mediation. Christ is the one Mediator between God and men. See on 1 Timothy 2:5 and the Introduction to 1 Timothy. No man can draw near to the unapproachable God except through him. Through him we have access, reconciliation, peace, salvation, sonship, confidence. Through him worship is offered to God and with it thanksgiving. Victory is given to us through Christ. Through him God will execute judgment.

Now we have seen in the "episode" of Peter that *if we deny him, he . . . will* not *deny us.* But there are people whom *he will deny* and it will close the door into God's presence. They deny that Jesus is the Christ; and the repudiation of Christ carries with it the repudiation of the Father. Denial is the opposite of confession and is the refusal to believe in Jesus. Such men are characterized by the terms "liar" and "antichrist" (cf. 1 John 2:22 f.). The stern words of Peter to the Jews when he told them that they had "denied the Holy and Righteous One" (Acts 3:14), i.e., the Christ, reminded them that "his own people received him not" (John 1:11). The gospel was still offered to them (Acts 3:19). Until they receive it they have no access to the Father. The principle of mediation stands fast. "There is salvation in no one else . . ." (Acts 4:12; cf. 2 Pet. 2:1).

Our Lord's own words are often quoted in this connection (Luke 12:9). They reflect the same principle, and it is seen even more clearly a few verses earlier (Luke 12:4 f.). "I tell you, my friends, . . . fear him who, after he has killed, has authority to cast into Gehenna." He who has such authority is God. On the one hand we have Jesus, calling men his friends (*philoi*); and on the other, God who is to be feared. Jesus is the Mediator, the friend of sinners, "for the Father himself admits you to the circle of his friendship (*philei*), because you have loved me and have believed that I came from the Father" (John 16:27). Access to God is determined by men's attitude to his Son. *If we deny him,* the Father has no place for us. This principle is absolute. (Cf. Matt. 10:33; Mark 8:38; Luke 9:26.)

It is assumed that faith is expressed in confession (Rom. 10:9 f.). To *reign with him* is rather different from that envisaged as sitting on either side of the Lord in his kingdom (Matt. 20:21; cf. Mark 10:37).

Verse 13: If we are faithless, he remains faithful—for he cannot deny

himself: Human disloyalty, divine loyalty. It seems more in accordance with
the spirit of the passage to take *faithless* in the sense of "lacking in loyalty"
or "wavering in faith," "weak in faith" (cf. Rom. 4:20) rather than the
decisive "without faith" or even "unbelieving." The attitude is that of the cry,
"I believe; help my unbelief!" (Mark 9:24). In the face of this the Lord
remains faithful. Even if our trust grows weak, he *remains* trustworthy. (Cf.
1 Cor. 1:8 f.; 1 Thess. 5:23 f.; 2 Thess. 3:2 f.) He is loyal to his pledged
word (Heb. 10:23; 11:11). The thought of the covenant is not far away. God
is faithful to his covenant with his people in spite of their conduct. "My
steadfast love I will keep for him for ever, and my covenant will stand firm
for him" (Ps. 89:28). Though transgression be committed God will not
violate his covenant, even though he punish (cf. vv. 30–34). (See on 1
Tim. 1:2, mercy and *ḥesed.*)

The tenses (present) are appropriate to this interpretation, whereas the
note of warning is sounded in the previous verse: "If we shall deny him, he
also will deny us."

The concluding clause, *for he cannot deny himself,* may be an addition
by the apostle to the quotation. It rounds off the hymn and explains why
he remains faithful. The explanation is not out of place, because if the
reader has been carried along by the rhythm he may have expected something like "if we are faithless, he will prove faithless"—an impossible
statement. His surprise is removed by the final affirmation: *he cannot* repudiate *himself. He cannot* do what sinful men are called to do (Luke 9:23).
The picture is one of a man about to follow Jesus. He looks at his "other
self," as it were, and says to him: "No! I disown you. Your ideals are not my
ideals; your hopes are not my hopes; your character I reject." If God were
faithless it would mean that he looked at his "former self," the God who
established the covenant, "the faithful God who keeps covenant and steadfast love" (Deut. 7:9), and said: "You are nothing to do with me. I am
totally different from you. I will not honor obligations undertaken by you.
Your promises I will not keep. The objects of your love mean nothing to
me. I am going my own way." God *cannot* act like this. He changes not.
With him there is no variation (Jas. 1:17). His faithfulness endures to all
generations (Ps. 100:5). He remains eternally loyal. (Cf. Rom. 3:3 f.)

V. TASKS AND CHARACTERISTICS OF A MINISTER (2:14–26)

The members of the church are to be warned against battle about words, for serious consequences may result. The minister should be a conscientious expositor whom God can use, avoiding the chatter of false teachers. Such chatter increases ungodliness, as known examples illustrate, distorts the truth and topples the faith of some believers. Even so God's truth is itself unshaken. The great qualification for service is to be cleansed by abstinence and pursuit. The characteristics of the Lord's servant are listed and his influence shown.

1. Ministerial Tasks (2:14–19)

The minister is to charge his people solemnly to avoid argumentation, for its effects may be ruinous. His own sterling character should be manifest to God and especially as a faithful expositor of his Word. Godless chatter spreads and leads to further godlessness and the crash of faith. This is borne out by known facts. But God's truth stands fast.

Verse 14: Remind them of this, and charge them before the Lord to avoid disputing about words, which does no good, but only ruins the hearers: Contending for the faith must rise above the mere quibble. *This* refers particularly to the contents of verses 11–13 and in a general way to verse 2. There is no means of identifying *them* and in any case it does not appear in the Greek. In consequence of this we can render the present tense by "Keep giving reminders of *this*," or ". . . of these truths." *Charge* is strong language, with its implication of the giving of orders. (Cf. 1 Tim. 5:21 and discussion; 2 Tim. 4:1.) The seriousness with which Paul viewed the matter is indicated by the manner in which Timothy was to *charge them.* It was to be *before the Lord,* in his presence and with his authority. See on 1 Timothy 6:13. In one sense everything we do is in the sight of God, but Paul seems to have had something special in mind. He might have been thinking of the solemn moment during the sermon when the congregation is hushed before the felt presence of God. In such an opportunity which has gradually grown during the worship Timothy could well tell his listeners that they must abandon *disputing about words.* Paul was very sensitive to the damage done by false teachers and troublemakers. (Cf. 1 Tim. 1:3; 4:1; 6:3 and their contexts; Titus 1:10 f.; 3:9–11.)

This raises the whole question of religious controversy. On the one hand the deposit of Christian truth is to be guarded (see on 1:12–14; 2:2) and we must "contend for the faith which was once for all delivered to the saints" (Jude 3) because there are opponents in the field who must be conquered (1 Cor. 9:24 f.). On the other hand strife about mere words *does no good* and can be actually harmful. Whether or not we are to engage in *disputing* depends on the issues at stake. It may at times turn on the presence or absence of a single letter. A theological battle was fought in the Nicene Age to decide whether the Son of God is *homoousios* or *homoiousios* with the Father: whether he is of one substance with the Father or only of like substance. Paul was not advocating peace at any price: his attack at times could be far from irenic (cf. 1 Tim. 6:4). He was not unconcerned about words, because they can nourish or infect (1 Tim. 4:6; 6:3; 2 Tim. 1:13). In the heat of controversy, however, men may lose sight of the great principles for which they have been contending. It is right to insist on a correct definition of redemption, for example, partly to witness to its truth and partly to ensure that Christian and non-Christian (or just "mistaken") protagonists are disputing about the same subject. But if tempers are roused, merely verbal points loom larger than they deserve. *Disputing about* principles descends to *disputing about* mere *words*. It is not a long step from this to offensive personal remarks and their repudiation. In the end *disputing about words* seeks not the victory of truth but the victory of the speaker. Instead of quietly reasoning with his opponent, he blusters and is belligerent. The Christian should thus always ask himself if the subject actually under discussion is worth a fight or a martyrdom. Otherwise he may learn that it *does no good;* on the contrary it *only ruins the hearers.* It does not lead to their edification. When he should be building them up he is doing precisely the reverse: he is tearing them down, acting "for their ruin." The picture is seen in Acts 15:16, "I will rebuild its *ruins.*" The disciple, like the apostle, should act "for building up and not for tearing down" (2 Cor. 13:10; cf. 10:8).

Verse 15: Do your best to present yourself to God as one approved, a workman who has no need to be ashamed, rightly handling the word of truth: The right policy to maintain in the face of false teachers looking for an argument. *Do your best* combines the ideas of speed, eagerness and seriousness (cf. 2 Tim. 1:17). If Timothy had not yet begun he should start at once. Men do not drift into conscientious ministry: he must be enthusiastic about it. And he must give it the weighty attention which so serious a matter ought to have. Much depends on how he acts.

Paul did not secularize the ministry. He did not seek a highly trained and successful efficiency with no questions asked. Timothy must be *approved* indeed. He must have passed the test and so become qualified. Paul himself knew what this meant (cf. 1 Thess. 2:4; 5:21; 1 Tim. 3:10). But it must be the test in which God himself is the examiner. And it must not be thought by Timothy that once he had passed the test he was qualified forever; he must at all times maintain the standard because he is always under God's eye. Paul expressed this by telling him *to present* himself as a qualified man, *as one approved,* approved already, *to God,* conscious of work well done. It is a high, if not a frightening, ideal to set before a young minister. *Present yourself* recalls Romans 6:13 ("yield"). After qualifying, Timothy must be ready for yet more service.

By this time Paul could bring himself freely to use the word *workman* (*ergatēs*) without the innuendo that such a person was a "work man" and not a "faith man" (cf. Phil. 3:2). At one time he had to deal with "bad workmen." He was not here afraid that Timothy would be accused of preaching justification by works. The term goes back to Jesus, the "laborers" of Luke 10:2.

If Timothy followed the apostle's lead and achieved his ideal, he would have *no need to be ashamed.* His work would stand examination and he would have no need to be ashamed of it. It is a big "if." The exhortation is sound, but it is an exhortation; and it raises the question whether ministerial achievement is ever really complete. When everything commanded has been done (if it has been done!), the minister is to say, with his fellow ministers, "We are unworthy servants; we have only done what was our duty" (Luke 17:10). This is a fitting attitude for disciples. They must hope and strive that their Master will say, "Well done, good and faithful servant," seeing the faithfulness if not complete success (Matt. 25:21, 23).

To pass the test practically and so to be *approved* and to avoid being *ashamed,* Timothy must devote himself to *rightly handling the word of truth.* The general meaning is plain though the actual figure is uncertain. The picture may be that of a mason "squaring" his bricks; a plowman cutting a straight furrow; or a man making a road straight to its destination. The thought is suggested that in the preaching of Christ in any one given sermon it is not great slabs of truth which should be passed on, rough-hewn from the quarry of the gospel. The preacher should give one brick at a time, rightly proportioned and fitting in easily with the bricks which have already been given. Or he should move confidently over the territory of gospel truth, not turning to the right or to the left away from the gospel into vain speculation or myth. A series of sermons should be understandable in language, coherent in themes, and should have an aim.

The practice of positively setting forth the truth is more effective than constantly having arguments with false teachers.

Verse 16: Avoid such godless chatter, for it will lead people into more and more ungodliness: This is not cowardice but strategy. The *godless* has no religious value; it is often rendered by the word "profane" (see discussion on 1 Tim. 6:20). The *ungodliness* is a different Greek word (*asebeia*) and is the opposite of "godliness" or piety, man's duty to God. (See discussion on 1 Tim. 6:11 and on other passages there given.) *Ungodliness* is the religious condition of the heathen (Rom. 1:18; cf. Deut. 9:4 f., LXX). It was for the ungodly that Christ died (Rom. 5:6). If those who indulge in the *chatter* are members of the church, they should realize what they are doing and where they are leading their fellow members.

It will lead people is an attempt to deal with an awkward piece of Greek. Literally we should say, "they will advance," for metaphorically "they are cutting their way forward." The picture is that of pioneers making their way forward through virgin forest, cutting down trees and branches and making a trail. The "chatterers" or false teachers are making progress and are advancing *more and more*—into *ungodliness!* It is possible to advance on a wrong road, as many a motorist will wryly agree.

It is sometimes said that "advanced" thinkers have made their progress and should thus lead the church forward. It should be remembered that speculation, for the Christian, should always be under the control of the truth. Guard the deposit! Its function is at times to guard Christians themselves from a false progress.

The place of reason in theological thinking may be compared with that of a constitutional monarchy. In her official acts the Queen of Canada does not strike out on her own but always responds to the "advice" of the Prime Minister. In like manner Christian thought, the exercise of reason, should not oppose the truth in any way but should follow it. The false teachers were not contributing to Timothy's spiritual progress (1 Tim. 4:15) or to that of others, and certainly not to the progress or advance of the gospel (cf. Phil. 1:12, 25. See also 2 Tim. 3:9, 13).

The *godless chatter,* as Paul severely calls it, must not be compared with the buzzing conversation of social butterflies or the idle talk of men gathered in a tavern. Paul was thinking of false doctrine. A mistake here is not just an error for which a seminarian would lose marks in an examination but which is otherwise of no particular consequence. The consequences of theological error are practical, not merely theoretical. False teaching can rend the church into rival camps, divide households, inspire bitterness and lead to terrible deeds. In short it leads to *ungodliness.* It was the doctrine of the *Herrenvolk,* of the master race, that led Hitler into his enormities.

Verse 17: And their talk will eat its way like gangrene. Among them are Hymenaeus and Philetus: An illustration of "progress" or advance. *Eat its way* is an excellent rendering of the Greek "will have pasture" (cf. John 10:9). The picture is that of a flock which enters a field through a gate and from there spreads out all over the field ("advance"). Each sheep can *eat its way* forward. The emphasis in the text is not on the sheep but on the devouring. A house on fire is "pasture" to the devouring flames. Paul's simile is *gangrene,* which has been described as the first stage of the mortification of the living flesh. False doctrine is deadly. Paul did not say who would be affected thus by *their talk.* In leaving this to the imagination he heightened the effect of his words. The danger is near to everyone who listens.

At times Paul could quote names (cf. 1:15). *Hymenaeus* has been encountered before (1 Tim. 1:19 f.). He had rejected conscience, had shipwrecked his faith, and had been excommunicated. The hope had been that the "shipwrecked mariner" would eventually be picked up (see discussion) but there is no sign of it in the present verse. *Hymenaeus* is an example of persistence in sin. Persistence is not always a Christian virtue. He may possibly be one of the casualties caused by "disputing about words, which . . . only ruins the hearers" (v. 14). In the passion of argument someone may have gone too far, and it did not edify. He may have been confirmed in a natural obstinacy and have advanced "into more and more ungodliness" (v. 16). At any rate we find that he was still on the scene and causing trouble. The "upsetting [of] the faith of some" (v. 18) repeats in another idiom the *talk* which *will eat its way like gangrene.* One of the surprising facts about some such men is that they may have the reputation of being sincere yet they can contemplate leading men into ungodliness with equanimity. With the rejection of conscience and the shipwreck of faith we may expect spiritual insensitiveness (cf. Phil. 1:9).

Philetus is not otherwise known. He and *Hymenaeus* illustrate one of the problems with which Timothy probably had to deal. A persistent heretic with a long start is a formidable opponent for a young and timid minister. Much would depend on how Timothy handled the situation—and the men.

Verse 18: Who have swerved from the truth by holding that the resurrection is past already. They are upsetting the faith of some—because they were not rightly handling the word of truth (v. 15). Neither their furrow nor their path was straight. The Greek verb (*astocheō*) is rendered by "swerving" in 1 Timothy 1:6 and by "missed the mark" in 1 Timothy 6:21 (see discussions). At some time their aim faltered.

The surprising doctrine *that the resurrection is past already* teaches that "it has already happened." It is not over and done with, for its effect remains. At first we might think that any unsophisticated Christian could have refuted it by the blunt remark that "I am not dead yet, nor buried either; how can I have been resurrected?" If we put it like this we find it hard to imagine how any one could have been led astray by such an obvious absurdity. But the doctrine is not so simple. It is a form of Paul's own doctrine, with false deductions drawn. In his teaching about baptism he saw the death and resurrection of the believer (Rom. 6:4; Col. 2:12; 3:1; cf. Eph. 2:6 and possibly 5:14). The false teachers had materialized a spiritual experience and had spiritualized the resurrection of the body. Once a man had been baptized and had been "resurrected" it could be said that he had already received immortality and would never die.

The false teachers were wrong because it was a wrong interpretation of Paul's doctrine, because the future resurrection is one of the foundation truths of the Christian faith (1 Cor. 15:1–58), and because justice was not done to the Christian doctrine of the body. According to the biblical teaching, man is an animated body and his body is part of the human personality. ("Animated" here includes "rational" and "spiritual.") It was the Greeks who held that man is a soul imprisoned in a body and that at death the tumbledown shack completely collapses, leaving the soul free. Scripture teaches the unity of body and soul.

The false teaching was obviously congenial to the Greek mind, which looked upon resurrection with distaste. The door was opened to abuses also. Man could save himself by his rigorous treatment of the body (cf. 1 Tim. 4:3 and discussion); or he could despise his body and indulge in all kinds of licentiousness, forgetting that the body is not meant for immorality but for the Lord, for it is a member of Christ and a temple of the Holy Spirit (cf. 1 Cor. 6:13–20).

This verse is outstanding as indicating what the false teachers really taught. It points to an incipient Gnosticism, which flowered in the second century.

The manner of the *upsetting* of *the faith of some* is seen in the story of the cleansing of the Temple. Our Lord upset or "overturned" the tables of the money-changers (John 2:15). It is a vivid picture. Pillars are not thus easily upset (cf. 1 Tim. 3:15). It would seem that *the faith of some* was rickety and without a firm foundation. They were not "standing firm" or "standing fast" (cf. 2 Thess. 2:15). We have to face the fact that even in the believing church there are those with weak rather than strong faith. One of the problems of the ministry is to prepare Christians to meet false teaching, and yet another problem is to deal with those whose faith has been "upset." It may be that sufficient attention has not been given by weaker members to all the means of grace. To neglect Bible study, prayer and public worship is to ask for trouble, and such people do become upset in faith (cf. Titus 1:11). But these weaker members may have been neglected, as perhaps the *some* were. It is remarkable that Paul told the Romans to carry out a duty so appropriate to the present context. "As for the man who is weak in faith, welcome him, but not for disputes over opinions" (Rom. 14:1). The weaker brother should be surrounded by warm fellowship, and by skillful strategy the mature and strong Christians should keep him from hearing doctrinal arguments. Perhaps the *some* of whom Paul spoke had heard too much. They should have been encouraged by loving fellows to be "rooted and grounded" (Eph. 3:17): grounded in a strong and deep foundation but also rooted in an organic connection with the living Lord (cf. Col. 2:7). "I am the vine, you are the branches" (John 15:5). Human faith may be upset, but such a thought of instability led Paul on to think of God's firm foundation which stands fast.

Verse 19: But God's firm foundation stands, bearing this seal: "The Lord knows those who are his," and, "Let every one who names the name of the Lord depart from iniquity." But! There is tremendous force in this word *but (mentoi)* as Paul gave the other part of the story. The faith of some Christians is being overturned but *God's firm foundation* cannot be overturned and it still *stands* and always will. *Firm* means "solid" as opposed to liquid (cf. Heb. 5:12, 14). The faith which was being overturned resembles the hovercraft which rests on an air cushion. Such "believers" were not characteristic of "the churches (which) were being con-solid-ated in the faith" (Acts 16:5; the Greek verb is cognate).

We have to ask what is meant by *God's . . . foundation*. Much scholarly opinion takes the view that the church at Ephesus was in the mind of Paul. Some of its members may have been upset in faith but the main body would continue. However true this may be it does not seem to do justice to the thought. The theory is made more tenable if the church at Ephesus is regarded as sharing the indestructibility of the universal church or if the whole church is understood to be present in the Ephesian church. This interpretation accords with Paul's words elsewhere. He told the Corinthians that he had laid a *foundation* and another man might build on it (1 Cor. 3:10, 12). He was speaking of the founding of a congregation, as Arndt and Gingrich tell us (*Lexicon*, p. 356; cf. Rom. 15:20). Yet in between these two verses he could say that any foundation other than Jesus Christ is impossible (1 Cor. 3:11). The use of *foundation* for both the congregation and the Lord reveals in an unstudied way that though the Lord is always to be distinguished from his church he is not separated from it. This is parallel to the description of the church as the bride of Christ: always distinct but never separate. Apostles and prophets are part of the foundation, as they are the human means through which Christ is made known. But he himself is not absent: he is the cornerstone (Eph. 2:20).

These facts should make us hesitate to think of the *foundation* of God as the church in Ephesus. Jesus Christ himself is not absent. Now *mentoi (but)* is a strongly adversative particle, and we might find a clue in the comparison which Paul was making. Is the contrast between the few who had been "upset" and the majority who would remain firm? Or is it between a faith poorly grounded, rickety, unstable and the objective fact which cannot be overturned, *God's firm foundation,* the Christian faith in which men should persist and from which they should not shift (cf. Col. 1:23; and discussion on 1 Tim. 3:9; 6:10)? The latter is more worthy and *this* dual *seal* expresses the objectivity of the status and duty of those who have not "shifted."

It was the custom in very ancient times for temples to bear an inscription recording their purpose. Paul may be here making an allusion to this, though he may have done it unconsciously. More important is the content of the inscription, *this seal* as he calls it. The first part is a quotation from the Septuagint version of the Book of Numbers (Num. 16:5, LXX), with *the Lord* instead of "God." In one sense everybody on earth may be counted among *those who are his* but the meaning here is narrower and deeper. Paul had in mind the true believers, who belong to God not only by creation but also by redemption. "You are not your own; you were bought with a price" (1 Cor. 6:19 f.; cf. 7:23). They belong to him also by conversion and are members of, or rather, constitute his own people, his prized possession (Titus 2:14; cf. 1 Pet. 2:9). (Cf. Exod. 19:5.)

God not only *knows* the identity of his people and could give their names as it were. He—or perhaps we should say rather *the Lord*—knows them in the intimacy of fellowship. He loves them and protects them. In the biblical sense he has known them a long time. He elected them (see on 1:9; 2:10), predestinated them, and called them into his own kingdom and glory. He thus distinguishes believers from unbelievers and he will keep his own (1 Thess. 5:23 f.). *God's firm foundation* implies eternal security for *those who are his.* The teaching of the Fourth Gospel is here recalled (John 10:3–5, 27–30). The knowledge which God has is illustrated on earth by our Lord's knowledge of Nathanael (John 1:47 f.).

The second part of *this seal* is a loose amalgam, reechoing with varying degrees of clarity some Septuagintal notes. (Cf. Lev. 24:16; Josh. 23:7; Ps. 6:8 [9]—see Matt. 7:23; Luke 13:27—Isa. 26:13; 52:11; and perhaps Num. 16:26 f., all in LXX). It expresses Christian duty. The way to avoid hearing the divine sentence, "Depart from me," is to *depart from iniquity.* But it is more than an expression of duty; it is a means of identifying true believers. They have departed from iniquity: they neither give nor receive false doctrine.

Hymenaeus and Philetus are each in his way the Korah of the New Testament (see Num. 16). If this epistle and its contents ever came to their knowledge they should recognize its challenge to them. They *depart from* their *iniquity* or else eventually *depart from* the Lord. The thrust of the word *depart* is as individual and personal as the knowledge whereby *the Lord knows those who are his.*

2. Ministerial Characteristics (2:20–26)

If the minister cleanses himself he can be used by God in the noble duties of ministry. Some activities should be completely avoided; others should be the object of his concentration in the company of likeminded associates. Silly controversies must be left severely alone so that peace may characterize every aspect of the minister's work. By this means even opponents may be won.

Verse 20: In a great house there are not only vessels of gold and silver but also of wood and earthenware, and some for noble use, some for ignoble: A simple illustration to account for the presence of false teachers in the church. The *great house,* as opposed to a mean shack, stands for the church. The emphasis falls on the building, though it is not an empty one but inhabited, and the idea of "household" creeps in (cf. 1 Tim. 3:5, 15). It is easy to imagine an illustrious family displaying and using *silver* goblets on some high festal occasion. The *vessels of . . . silver* are honored by the *use* to which they are put. The same family will use *vessels . . . of wood and earthenware* but they will not display them, for they are not honored by their use. They are kept in the background—as we should say, wastepaper baskets, trash cans, pails for dirty water after the washing of the floor or receptacles for rubbish. The head of the house knows of the differences of value and of use, and the providence of God has permitted "all sorts and conditions of men" to exist in the visible church. This accounts for the presence of those who are far from being "pure gold." Even those with heretical views can be used by God to throw into high relief the true believers whose views are sound (cf. 1 Cor. 11:19). Some would trace back behind providence to the order of creation itself (cf. Rom. 9:21). *Some for noble use, some for ignoble* brings out the force of the more literal "some for honor, some for dishonor."

A vessel is not like a machine. It does not work by itself. It cannot be set running and then left, like an engine. Its value, apart from its intrinsic value which is determined by its *gold* or *silver, wood* or *earthenware,* lies in the fact that it can be used. The choice of such a word prepares the way for the teaching in the next verse. Christians who witness to the gospel, church workers generally and the whole ministry, including apostles, however devoted their lives, do not really "do" anything. They are "used" by God because they are *vessels.* That is why the glory belongs to God and not to them.

Vessels are containers. The obvious examples *in a great house* are saucepans, basins, pitchers and jugs. These are not only kitchen utensils (i.e., they may be used) but they hold water, milk or cream. So the Christian "contains" the grace of God within him (see on 1 Tim. 6:6, "contentment") and by suitable speech can offer it to others for their acceptance. A man does not have to be a minister to do this (Eph. 4:29), though it is the work of ministry. Paul was "a chosen instrument [vessel, the same word, *skeuos*] of mine to carry my name before the Gentiles and kings . . ." (Acts 9:15). The value of the contents of the vessel is inestimable, though the vessel itself may be broken at any time. That is the point of his remark that "we have this treasure in earthen vessels" (2 Cor. 4:7). The treasure is the gospel, and by the containers he meant himself and his colleagues. They were themselves subject to the hazards of life. "Earthen" here is not used in the pejorative sense. Paul and his friends were indeed being put to *noble use.*

Verse 21: If any one purifies himself from what is ignoble, then he will be a vessel for noble use, consecrated and useful to the master of the house, ready for any good work: It is not what we are made of but how clean we are, which counts. The verse combines in a curious way the literal and the meta-phorical, the theme of the illustration of the previous verse and that of the Christian who is cleansed and holy, one whom God can "use." The beginning is plain enough. *If any* person (not "vessel") *purifies himself* . . . . (See on 1 Tim. 1:5, "pure.") In the deepest sense of purification—that which makes a man fit to approach God—the only agencies are the Word and faith (John 15:3; Acts 15:9). Now "faith" means "a man believing": he is doing some-thing, though it is not counted as a meritorious service. The human spirit is thus not quiescent even in the moment when he is first accepted by God. In the growing Christian life it is not quiescent either and there are times when a man *purifies himself*. Paul himself did so by declaring the whole counsel of God. "I am 'pure' of the blood of all of you" (Acts 20:26 f.). After preaching to the blasphemous and resisting Jews at Corinth he turned away from them to the Gentiles. "Your blood be upon your heads! I am 'pure' " (Acts 18:6). (Cf. 2 Cor. 7:1.) We can purify ourselves by avoiding wrong associations, and by not doing certain deeds (cf. Jas. 4:8).

Paul had in mind a separation from the false teachers.

From what is ignoble is literally "from these (things)" and the reference is to "some for ignoble" (use), literally "some for dishonor" (v. 20). At this point the illustration comes back, only to recede. The primary thought is of "vessels for dishonor," but the dominant thought is of the men thus illustrated. Keep away from the false teachers! *If any one* does that and so *purifies him-self, then he will be a vessel*. He will be a "container." He will possess the pure gospel; he will have a knowledge of the truth. He will also be a "utensil." He will be capable of being used by God. This is the force of the illustration, as far as it is retained. *He will be a vessel* for honor, that is, *for noble use*. Even if his natural quality is "wood and earthenware" (v. 20; cf. 2 Cor. 4:7) he has the same function as the "gold and silver."

From this point on, the illustration is dropped, apart from the faint trace of it in *the master*. The Greek word is *despotēs,* which can have a divine reference (cf. Luke 2:29; Acts 4:24). The Sovereign Lord who made the universe is more than an owner of slaves or a householder. It was no doubt because the translators of the RSV thought that the illustration was sustained that they added *of the house.* "And we are his house" (Heb. 3:6). The man who *purifies himself* will be *consecrated . . . useful . . . ready.*

He who has been sanctified or *consecrated* (perfect tense) is now holy. (See on 1 Tim. 2:15 for "holiness.") *Useful* suggests that a sanctified man will not engage in "disputing about words" because it "does no good," that is, it is "useful for nothing" (v. 14). He is *useful* because he can be "used" by *the master,* and it is because he is holy that he can be so used. It will be part of the expression of his holiness that he will seek to help rather than to hinder others; to make their way easier and not harder; to encourage instead of criticizing; to lead rather than to bludgeon; to set an example of the attrac-tiveness of faith rather than give it a bad name by boorishness. He will bear in mind that what may be safe for a mature Christian may be dangerous for a babe in Christ. He will walk with God and do his will. He will be faithful in his preaching, and loving in his behavior. He will not tone down the message to suit the convenience of unspiritual men, and he will not let his heart cool towards those who are unsympathetic to his message. He will not bully the

church nor will he be spineless when he contends for the faith once delivered
to the saints. He will rejoice with those who rejoice and weep with those who
weep, and at the same time give the impression of the versatility and sympathy of a man of faith and not the fickleness of the world's chameleon. He
will be catholic in his approach to all the varieties of human personality and
at the same time a man of one driving purpose—to know nothing save Jesus
Christ and him crucified. He will vary his utterances but he will have one
theme. His one purpose is to know and glorify Christ.

He will be *ready for any* and every *good work.* The second perfect participle
in the verse, "having been made ready," justifies the simple "(now) *ready.*"
Readiness implies both willingness ("I am ready . . . to die," Acts 21:13)
and preparedness (like that of soldiers: Acts 23:23). It is one of the marks
of the *consecrated* Christian that he is *ready* to obey the Lord, sometimes
against his natural inclination or what he is tempted to think is his better
judgment. Preparedness implies some sort of "equipment." Holiness in itself
does not give men a technical preparedness. For example, it does not teach a
man how to read. But it does give a man the motive power to learn. The great
Phillips Brooks never forgot his first experience of the theological seminary.
The prayer meeting was a new world to him and the devotion and piety of
the men left him puzzled and ashamed. The following day he discovered that
these selfsame men had not learnt their Greek and that they never did.
Holiness will not give a man a knowledge of the language, but if he is
consecrated and really believes in the Word written, he should be able to
harness the motive power of holiness to the technical task of mastering "the
language of the Holy Spirit."

The separateness which is involved in holiness should mean that the
sanctified man is free from much of the baggage which impedes other men.
The way will be clear for him to tackle *any good work.* The holy man will not
lose touch with God, and when he is led by God into new ventures and has to
trust when he cannot see, he will know that God is not improvising. He has
thought about the matter beforehand—like the apostle, I speak after the
manner of men—and the tasks which challenge are the "good works, which
God prepared beforehand, that we should walk in them" (Eph. 2:10). In a
real sense the duties match the man and the man matches the duties.
"There's a *work* for Jesus only you can do." It is the possession of holiness
which qualifies "you" to do it.

*Verse 22: So shun youthful passions and aim at righteousness, faith, love,
and peace, along with those who call upon the Lord from a pure heart:*
Negative and positive aspects of the program of Christians, to be constantly
carried out. See on 1 Timothy 6:11 for *righteousness, faith* and *love;* on 1
Timothy 1:2 for *peace;* and on 1 Timothy 1:5 for *love* and *pure heart.*

The *youthful passions* or desires which Timothy was to *shun* not once but
always are varied. They may include sensuality but are by no means limited
to sexual matters. Timothy's age has been considered already (1 Tim. 4:12
and discussion). The age in which we now live and the expressions of student
power ought to aid the interpreter here. There are desires which though not
absent from older men, even elderly men, are characteristic of the younger
generation. Until a person has matured he may manifest a desire for self-
assertion which issues in intolerance. Timothy must not minimize the gospel

and must assert it; but he need not always assert himself. He must not tolerate false doctrine but he should go a long way to tolerate people. He should not fly at their throats at the first mention of heresy. Heresy is at times 10 percent theological error and 90 percent stubborn self-will. Intolerance of the person may merely confirm him in his stubbornness.

It has been said that "none of us are omniscient, even the youngest." In their ardor to put the world right, some young people are tempted to claim a great deal of knowledge—and some of them may have it; but inevitably they lack experience. So a young minister, in his certainty of the truth of the gospel, may tend to think of himself as an oracle. The result is that he "knows that he is right," not only about the gospel but about the policy of the local church. The result is an impatience with those who are slow to understand and to follow his lead in, say, desiring to tear down the church building and erect another.

Hotheads love disputes for their own sake; demonstrations and fights can become ends in themselves. Some may think that even in the church meeting there must always be an opposition, like a political party which is not in power. Novelties can always attract those who are impatient with "the old paths," and a youth devoid of ambition is not always a healthy sight.

All this kind of thing Timothy was to *shun*—to keep on shunning. It is not a question of putting an old head onto a young shoulder, but of working out holiness in the pastorate.

Two interpretations are possible of the expression *along with those* . . . . Some take it closely with *peace*. The thought is then that Timothy must do nothing to break the unity of the church. His permanent pursuit must be *peace . . . with* his fellow Christians. He must not be on one side of the fence and they on the other. This anticipates verse 24, and reflects the teaching of Romans 12:18 and Hebrews 12:14. This view, however, is really thinking of the peace of the local church as a whole, and if this were Paul's aim we should have expected *"peace* among those who . . . ." A better interpretation is therefore to take the meaning thus: *"aim at . . . love, and peace,* in company with *those who* . . . ." A sanctified Christian can certainly make these his private aim, and he can refresh his spirit for the effort to attain them by entering into his own room for private prayer. But in the fellowship of like-minded men he can find a buoyancy for his purpose. Together, with mutual encouragement, they can make progress. If it takes the united contribution of all the saints to grasp what is the breadth and length and height and depth of the love of Christ (cf. Eph. 3:18), because grace is many-sided (1 Pet. 4:10), and men's experiences of it differ, then it is not surprising that Timothy is urged to pursue *righteousness, faith, love, and peace* in company with other Christians.

The Christians are described by reference to the characteristic activity of genuine believers, *those who call upon the Lord*. They invoke the Most High —and his Son Jesus. (Cf. Acts 2:21 [Joel 2:32]; 7:59, kjv; 9:14, 21; Rom. 10:12 f.) Paul's greeting to the Corinthians speaks of those who "call on the name of our Lord Jesus Christ" (1 Cor. 1:2). This suggests that in 2 Timothy 2:22 *the Lord* means Jesus.

Verse 23: Have nothing to do with stupid, senseless controversies; you know that they breed quarrels: Common sense, strategy and pastoral care combined. Dying Christians will not receive the best ministry from a man who is redolent of strife. The text recalls verse 16. (See on 1 Tim. 4:7; 5:11.) The *controversies* are *stupid* because Christians ought to know better what the consequences will be: no good achievement, quarrels, and the ruin, not the edification, of the hearers (cf. v. 14). As Christians they are committed to seek the glory of God and the godliness of men. Controversies result in the opposite. They are *senseless* as being "uninstructed" or "uneducated." The participants have not been adequately instructed in Christian doctrine or trained in Christian behavior, nor do they know from experience the Lord's discipline. It is bad enough to have a spiritually uneducated man in the pulpit; it is worse when ignorance passionately plies its wares in hostile groups. Uninformed men rejoice in a verbal victory and angels weep at the damage done to the witness of the church. *Controversies* are prolific, spawning *quarrels* and fights to the third and fourth generation. (See on 1 Tim. 6:4 f., "which produce.")

Verse 24: And the Lord's servant must not be quarrelsome but kindly to every one, an apt teacher, forbearing: The aggressive teacher may defeat his own purposes. This is not only a question of tactics. *The Lord's servant* must be as his Master, a picture of whom is given in the Servant Songs of Isaiah (Isa. 42:1–4, 5–7?; 49:1–6; 50:4–9; 52:13–53:12). "A bruised reed he will not break, and a dimly burning wick he will not quench" (Isa. 42:3). Timothy must remember that he, too, "came not to be served but to serve" (Mark 10:45). He represented a King whose kingdom is not of this world, and he did not need to fight to preserve either the King himself, or the kingdom, or the message (cf. John 18:36). The "quarrels" of the previous verse is literally "fights," and the thought is continued in verse 24, *the Lord's servant must not* fight. Timothy was indeed to be a "good soldier of Christ Jesus" (v. 3), but he was to fight evil, not persons. "For we are not contending against flesh and blood, but against the principalities . . ." (Eph. 6:12).

He *must . . . be . . . kindly to every one. Kindly (ēpios)* occurs in a difficult passage (1 Thess. 2:7) with the meaning "gentle." It points to an essential quality in a man who is to be *an apt teacher,* that is, skillful in teaching. (See on 1 Tim. 3:2.) He will of course use all the resources available to him, such as his knowledge of the subject and the choice of suitable illustrations—think of our Lord's use of parables. But kindliness implies much more. Given the fact that a Christian *teacher* is inflexible in his convictions; given the fact that he will not minimize the truth in any way; given the fact that he will at all times "guard the deposit"; even so in the practical work of teaching he can show a considerable measure of elasticity. Sometimes when faced with opponents he can only give a flat denial of what they say. But often in dealing with their theories he can begin by saying something like this: "There is an element of value in what you say. You do recognize that . . . . But I should like to add . . . ." Suppose today we were seeking to "teach" and win a Roman Catholic and that the subject at issue was the infallibility of the pope. We could either sweep it aside as historically without foundation and unscriptural, or we could adopt another policy. We could deal with the matter thus: "We Protestants do not say that you are a hundred percent wrong. We believe in the prophetic voice of the church. But we do not concentrate it in one person as you do." Similarly if Timothy were face-to-face with the false teachers and they were speculating in the field of Old Testament interpretation, he could say that he recognized the rightful place given to Scripture, but would they consider his view of Christ as the fulfillment of all the Old Testament "shadows" (cf. Heb. 10:1)? (See on 1 Tim. 1:4.)

Such a *kindly . . . teacher* will not use sarcasm or so parade his learning that he shows up his listeners as ignoramuses. He will not bully or bludgeon and will be patient with those who are slow to understand. In this way he may disarm the opposition and create a receptiveness for the Word. In some cases he will give preliminary study to what is in the back of their minds, to find out the presuppositions which make them think as they do. Some modern ministers have found that they have not been rejected out of hand, because they had remarked that "I see you have been reading So-and-so." The listeners realized that empathy had been established.

All this concerns the *teacher* rather than the preacher. The teacher may at times listen; the preacher proclaims. He will certainly begin with what the ancients called the *captatio benevolentiae,* the capturing of the goodwill of his listeners. Why start by antagonizing them? But he will be a messenger bursting with good news more than a teacher maneuvering for position. (See on 1:11; cf. 1 Tim. 2:7 and discussion.) It is a moot point how far some ministers, including the Apostle Paul, could teach without preaching!

Even when the teacher makes a kindly approach, he may meet with no response and no answering warmth. On the contrary his hearers may be surly, rude and critical. When this happens he has to be *forbearing.* This means that he puts up with the wrong done to him and the pain occasioned and does so without resentment. The listeners may be positively sinful in the violence of their reaction. The forbearing man does not at once rebuke them for their sin against him.

Verse 25: Correcting his opponents with gentleness. God may perhaps grant that they will repent and come to know the truth: Education as a form of pastoral care and evangelism. Long ago men spoke of "the converting power of edifying preaching," and this will now have to be broadened to include teaching. *Correcting* stands for a Greek word which means "to educate" (cf. Acts 7:22, "instructed") and reechoes the "uneducated" ("senseless") of verse 23. The teacher educates believing men by informing them of the basic truths of their faith, and in a receptive spirit they receive them. He educates his opponents by *correcting* them, but he must do it *with gentleness.* This word, which differs from the "kindly" of the previous verse, means restrained strength. A feeble old lady holds a baby feebly, not gently: that word is reserved for the strong arms of the father, which do not crush the little child. So Timothy was not to hurl corrections at his hearers or shatter them with his verbal brilliance. He must correct them by the exercise of a virtue which is a fruit of the Spirit (Gal. 5:23). In this he is an example which the spiritually minded should follow in their attempts to restore a brother who has sinned (Gal. 6:1). The implication is that Timothy must guard his own devotional life. The doctrinal corrections of a prayerless man may be formally correct but will they carry spiritual authority?

Timothy must act in this spirit whatever happens. But he should be encouraged by the hope that something may result. *God may perhaps grant to them repentance leading to knowledge of the truth. Perhaps,* which arises from the syntax and is not a translation of a separate word, does not imply doubt but that the possibility is open. If *they . . . repent* it will be the gift of God, not Timothy's work. Yet without him (or someone in his place) they would not have repented. Timothy will have been "used." He will have proved "useful to the master" (v. 21). Repentance, as is well known, means a change of mind, and its primary meaning here is the change of views on the part of the false teachers. They abandon their wrong theories in favor of Christian doctrines. But the change is not purely academic. Repentance has a strongly religious flavor. The false teachers have been sinning by holding and advocating their ideas and now they repent. This is confirmed by the outcome of their repentance. It leads them to "knowledge of the truth." This phrase (two words in Greek) appears in 1 Timothy 2:4 (see discussion); 2 Timothy 3:7; Titus 1:1; (cf. 1 Timothy 4:3). Its religious overtone implies that they come, or come back, as the case may be, to Christ. They now give credence to Christian doctrine; they give themselves in trust to Christ; they find that in faith they actually know him. He is the truth.

Such is the outcome, Timothy should hope, of correction given in *gentleness*. It is not hard to imagine what might have resulted if Timothy had spurned Paul's advice. Controversies would have left him with a fight on his hands (v. 23)—just as unhappily we see in some quarters today. It is right to witness to, and contend for, the faith with vigor, and even at times to give public rebuke and public refutation to those within the visible church who have publicly denied the faith. But it does not help the cause of our Lord as a matter of both policy and pleasure, constantly to attack individuals, to show them up and humiliate them. Some faithful brethren have been harassed and bullied by ignorant men who will talk too much (1 Pet. 2:15). Bystanders and supporters enjoy it all, and the result is a section of the professing Christian community known for nothing more than their quarrelsomeness—even among themselves.

There is a better way: to be tolerant in spirit but not tolerant in mind.[1] Controversy should be approached with reluctance, and all who engage in it should maintain a true Christian dignity, with courtesy and fairness. Brawling in public with zest does not ensure "that the ministry be not blamed" (2 Cor. 6:3, KJV). Great influence can be exercised by those for whom controversy is the exception and not the rule. To illustrate the point, I tell a story privately given to me by the late Bishop of Rochester (Dr. C. M. Chavasse) about his father, also a bishop in the Church of England. It was at a time when feeling was running very high about certain proposals which greatly offended evangelical and Protestant susceptibilities. At a meeting of the bishops, the senior Dr. Chavasse said something like this: "I am a man of peace. Dissension is abhorrent to me. But if these proposals are carried through, I shall fight." The proposals were dropped. It is quite possible that they would not have been abandoned if it had not been known that the speaker was indeed what he said—a man of peace. The value of resistance may sometimes lie in its rarity.

---

1. Cf. John R. W. Stott, *Christ the Controversialist* (London; Downers Grove, Ill.: Inter-Varsity Press, 1973). p. 17.

The implications of this verse are very relevant today. There is a good deal of "reinterpretation" of the Christian faith and much seems to be lost in the process. In addition men are not afraid to stand before their fellows and state quite calmly that "today we cannot believe that . . . ." By the air in which it is done and the inconsequential manner in which the words are spoken, an observer might imagine that only trifles were being considered. Paul did not look at it like this. To hold false doctrine is sin.

It is sin for a number of reasons. To begin with, it is disbelieving God as he has revealed himself. Christ is the revelation of God, the ultimate truth of God expressed in event and act, the very presence of God on earth as Man. But he is not a person about whom nothing can be said. He is, as it were, clothed in doctrine. He is known through the benefits which he brings and which indeed he is. He saves men because he is the Savior. To deny this or so reinterpret it that it becomes unrecognizable is sin.

This is not just a mistake of simple believing men who trust in Christ for their salvation but are unskilled in doctrine. When it is the considered opinion of theologians and their deliberate choice, it departs from the realm of honest ignorance. It detracts from the glory of God. If such views are stubbornly held, the sin is apparent when men are stiff-necked.

The heat which may be engendered and the controversies aroused are not edifying. Brotherly love can be entirely forgotten. The picture of a representative of the church denying the faith of the church which he is pledged (and paid) to proclaim and defend disturbs even the elect, is a stumbling block to the world, and causes blasphemers to exult. This cannot be right and it is not. Paul regards it as sin. *God may perhaps grant that they will repent and come to know the truth.*

Verse 26: And they may escape from the snare of the devil, after being captured by him to do his will: The hope of the previous verse is continued. The origin of false teaching is traced to *the devil.* (See on 1 Tim. 3:6–7; and for Satan, 1 Tim. 1:20; 5:15.) "We are not ignorant of his designs" (2 Cor. 2:11), long term and short. In Paul's day, when there were gods many and lords many, it was no disadvantage to the devil to show his hand. Today, in a scientific civilization, to reveal the existence of a spiritual (even though evil) world would give too great an advantage to the church. He therefore works in secret, persuading the sophisticated that he does not exist. It is significant that in the darkest places of primitive ignorance, if not savagery, he need not follow this policy. Missionaries have found that some places are reeking of evil. When secularism banishes the devil, he merely infiltrates.

Such, at any rate, is part of the truth. But by a paradox, even in our scientific civilization, there has been a widespread growth of interest in the occult. Horoscopes, spiritualism, witchcraft, and satanism fascinate millions. Even the film industry can turn areas of the occult to profit. According to Anne C. Long, the growing appetite for the psychic, occult, and demonic is the logical outcome of dispensing with God.[1] Bereft of him in a materialistic environment, unsatisfied souls fumble for meaning beyond it in the supernatural. "They have sown the wind, and they shall reap the whirlwind" (Hosea

---

1. See J. Stafford Wright, *Christianity and the Occult* (London: Scripture Union, 1972), introduction by Anne C. Long, pp. 9–16.

8:7, KJV; cf. Gal. 6:7 f.). It is an opportunity for the church. God still offers salvation and the church must faithfully proclaim the truth.

Escape gives us one part of the so-called "pregnant construction." Literally we should render, "sober up *from the snare of the devil*," that is, "regain their senses and *escape from* . . . ." The pictures are vivid. The false teachers are "drunk" and trapped. The *snare* is already familiar (1 Tim. 3:7; 6:9 and discussions). The metaphors may be mixed, but only faintly so. The drunkenness suggests that the perception of the teachers has been dulled and confused —they cannot sort out the evidence properly. Their conscience has become insensitive—they do not realize what they are doing. Their wills have no power—they did not and do not resist the allurements of falsity. *The snare* has them in its coils and from this they cannot *escape,* certainly not by their own efforts. That is why the hope is expressed that "God may perhaps grant that . . . they may escape. . . ."

After being captured renders a Greek word which means "to take alive" (as a prisoner, instead of killing). Thus Herodotus (1. 86) tells how the Persians captured the city of Sardis, took King Croesus alive and brought him to Cyrus. The verb is used in Luke 5:10 of "catching men" (alive), not fish. When Simon the fisherman became Peter the disciple and apostle he would "catch" men; and they, when converted, could be described by the verb in the present verse, *captured*.

This verb has here a double significance. It is a perfect participle, and the perfect tense expresses the abiding result of a past act. "Having been captured" means "being now captive in his power." It repeats the thought of *the snare,* or rather it shows us the captives actually in the net—alive, drunk as well, and with no possibility of *escape.* Yet "God may perhaps grant . . . ."

The second significant feature lies in the fact that Peter will capture men and the devil captures men. The same vocabulary is used for both conversion and "anti-conversion." The false teachers are false converts of a false king. We may observe the use of the Christian vocabulary to describe the activities of Satan, the great imitator, in the establishment of his unholy fellowship in 2 Thessalonians 2:3, 9.

The last words, *by him to do his will,* have puzzled scholars because of the use of two different pronouns, *autos* and *ekeinos* (*by him* and "with a view to" *his will*). The possibilities are: both refer to the devil; or both refer to God; or one refers to the devil and one to God. The RSV is surely right in taking both pronouns as referring to the devil and understanding the use of *ekeinos* as anaphoric—referring back to the devil.

VI. THE LAST DAYS (3:1–9)

In the last days there will be times of stress owing to the character of men at that time. They are described in detail and should be avoided. Typical among them are the insidious people who captivate sinful and impressionable women. Such men oppose the truth and lack faith; but everyone will see through their folly.

1. The Character of Men in the Last Days (3:1–5)

The mere form of religion without its essential power gives rise to selfishness, pride and all manner of evil. The long list of evil types shows that when the root of religion is cut the foliage of morality withers. Men of this kind are to be avoided.

Verse 1: But understand this, that in the last days there will come times of stress: Timothy is not to be surprised at his problems. The passage beginning with 1 Timothy 4:1 is recalled (see discussion). Paul was giving a reminder rather than new information. *The last days* are those immediately prior to the Parousia. *Times of stress* are times which are difficult to endure, difficult to get through, and difficult to deal with. Paul wrote *will come* but he was not saying: "note the tense: they *will come;* they are not here yet." He was rather alluding to the early Christian belief—and perhaps his own earlier teaching— that grievous times would come before the End. The Christian teacher especially finds them *times of stress* because he is working against the spirit of the age. In one sense this is nothing new: the Acts of the Apostles does not give us a picture of apostles and evangelists going out into an "easy" world. With the approach of the Parousia, however, the difficulties are intensified.

Certain problems have here to be faced. It is sometimes said that the early church expected an imminent return of Christ, and as he did not come they were mistaken. If Paul saw in the moral collapse around him an indication that the coming of the Lord was at hand (cf. Jas. 5:8), then in company with the rest of the church he was wrong.

It is important to notice where the "mistake" lies. If we lay stress on the fact that the church expected the Lord "now" or "tomorrow" or possibly "next week," then obviously they were wrong. But this mistake is made by everyone in the world who is expecting anything. For example: a man calls at a house in order to see the owner who lives there. He says, "I must see him; it is urgent." The lady of the house invites him to come in and tells him,

[186]

"My husband will not be long; he has just gone up the street; I am expecting him at any moment." Now in actual fact the husband has encountered a business acquaintance and has gone downtown. Such is the importance of the matter that the caller waits, and waits for some hours. As he frets and fumes he says to the wife (in his own idiom!), "Where is the promise of his coming?" (2 Pet. 3:4). She replies, with considerable justification, that her husband had said that "I shall not be long." Note carefully the situation. From the time that he left she has been expecting him. From that time, every minute during the waiting period she has been expecting him, and every minute she has been wrong. He has not come. She was wrong in her timing but she was not wrong in having a spirit of expectation. In expecting his return at any moment she was only doing what he had told her to do. This "mistake" in timing is made by everybody who is expecting anything, and the "mistake" is repeated time and time again until the actual expectation is fulfilled.

There is therefore nothing wrong about the "mistake" in the timing of the early church—or, come to that, of the medieval or the modern church. And no mistake was made in expecting the Parousia. Early Christians were just being obedient.

There is a further point. The view has been expressed that moral collapse, apostasy, and rebellion against God are characteristics of ages of violence, of times immediately after great wars and revolutions. Why see in them signs of *the last days?* The answer is that in any period of history they may not be "the" signs but just signs. In other words the spirit of the age may have an eschatological flavor without necessarily being the herald of the actual End. The stimulus to the believing and expecting church is plain. (Cf. 2 Pet. 3:8 f.)

Verse 2: For men will be lovers of self, lovers of money, proud, arrogant, abusive, disobedient to their parents, ungrateful, unholy: Every characteristic makes it harder for the minister and evangelist. *Lovers of self* are so intent on their own interests that they are often reluctant even to listen to the minister; and even if they do listen, their attitude to his message is, "What do I get out of this?" They can "get" a good deal, but they are only interested in "godliness" if it can be proved that it is "a means of gain" (cf. 1 Tim. 6:5). For many of them are *lovers of money* (cf. 1 Tim. 6:9 f.). Such men, especially if they possess it, think that money can do anything and in this they are *proud.* They are "boastful" and claim more than is justified by the facts of the case (cf. TDNT 1:226 f.). (Cf. Jas. 4:16; 1 John 2:16.) They think that they have the future in their hands and can determine everything. Why bother about salvation? Hence they prove *arrogant* and haughty when the minister approaches them. He is a humble man; their purpose is to "keep him down," and they show it by their manner—and lack of manners. So they become *abusive,* railing at him and blasphemously at the God whom he serves. Such conduct would make their parents turn in their graves but they care nothing for this. They have been emancipated from the apron strings of an older generation, and long before their death they were *disobedient to their parents.* They believe that they owe them nothing for a godly upbringing and have long been *ungrateful* to them and to everyone else. They are self-made men, and if they worship at all, they worship their creator. For they are essentially *unholy* (cf. 1 Thess. 2:10; 1 Tim. 2:8).

We have followed the theme of the *men* and the minister, but it all applies to *men* in general, *mutatis mutandis.*

Verse 3: Inhuman, implacable, slanderers, profligates, fierce, haters of good: The list continues. *Inhuman* implies the lack of love, whether family affection or social benevolence. *Implacable* men will never make a truce and will never be reconciled to enemies. *Slanderers* play the role of the devil, the accuser or calumniator; and even of some feline women—which no doubt would injure their pride. (Cf. 1 Tim. 3:11.) The *profligates* are utterly without self-control. They have no rein to their temper, no limit to their passions. Even when, apart from the heat of the moment, they coolly plan some outrage, no consideration of any kind restrains them. They have no "better nature" to hold them back. The *fierce* are as untamed and brutal as any savage. *Haters of good* have no love for good men, who are a standing even if silent rebuke to them, for they hate even the reflected light of the light of the world (Matt. 5:14; John 3:19 f.; 17:14). They may not hate what is good in the instrumental sense, good as a means to an end, like a "good" fountain pen; but they are not drawn to the intrinsically good which may be present in things as opposed to persons. "Whatever is true, whatever is honorable . . ." leaves them cold (Phil. 4:8).

Verse 4: Treacherous, reckless, swollen with conceit, lovers of pleasure rather than lovers of God: Moving towards the climax. No wonder the apostle spoke of "times of stress" (v. 1)! We wonder if the list will ever end. Each of the *treacherous* could prove to be a Judas (Luke 6:16) or a member of a wider group which would see the highest and betray it (Acts 7:52). The *reckless* throw caution to the winds, no matter what disaster or punishment they may bring upon their fellow citizens (cf. Acts 19:36, 40). Those who are *swollen with conceit* need to be cut down to size (see on 1 Tim. 3:6; 6:4). From all the characteristics so far described they have derived some pleasure or other; for they are *lovers of pleasure.* This does not necessarily mean "dance halls" and "the world." It does mean that in everything, business deals, social relations or even in the family circle, if they have one, they please themselves. Paul used the comparison of intensity to bring out their enormity. They are *lovers of pleasure rather than lovers of God.* This exhibits a figure of speech known as meiosis or understatement. In literal fact they always please themselves and they do not love God at all.

Verse 5: Holding the form of religion but denying the power of it. Avoid such people: The outer act and the inner Pharisee. *Religion* is the "godliness" of 1 Timothy 6:11 (see discussion and references there given). For the true "external" in religion, see James 1:26 f. The denial is practical as well as verbal (Titus 1:16). If these men are the false teachers, it is a remarkable example of the kind of character which can be joined to "religion." The dangers of the rejection or distortion of Christian doctrine are manifest. It is not surprising that Timothy was told to *avoid such people.* (See on 2:16, 23.)

The negative implications of the apostle's attitude are significant. *Avoid* and "have nothing to do with" are too frequent to be ignored. (Cf. also 1 Tim. 4:7; 5:11; Titus 3:9 f.) The changes are rung on three different Greek verbs, with the underlying ideas of turning away from, making a detour around and perhaps even to beg off from, to make excuses so as to avoid (cf.

Luke 14:18 f.). Christians are to "abstain from" certain activities (1 Thess. 4:3; 5:22).

It should be said at once that Christianity is not merely negative. But it has its negative side, which men ignore at their peril. Sin in every form is to be utterly avoided. Those who after every appeal persist in their sin take their color from their sin and are likewise to be avoided. This raises the whole question of separatism, a subject which is repugnant to some, partly because of a laudable desire to "get out into the world and evangelize" and partly because of a dislike of the extremes to which some separatists have gone.

A distinction should be made between the particular attitude which is pastoral and the attitude of Christians in general. Timothy—and pastors generally—should *avoid* certain people when it is clear that they are set in their obstinacy. This is not because hope has been abandoned but because of the practical necessity of avoiding further controversies and even "fights" and the positive need to deal with those who are receptive to teaching and pastoral care.

The Christian who is not a minister may not meet the problem with all the sharpness with which the pastor encounters it. But sooner or later he will have to make a decision: in what sense is he to be "separate"?

The teaching and example of our Lord provide illumination. He did not pray for his disciples to be taken out of the world; on the contrary he sent them into it, though they did not belong to it. He prayed that they would be kept from the evil one (John 17:15–18). He himself is "separated from sinners" because he is now "exalted above the heavens" (Heb. 7:26); and he was so separated when on earth. But it was not the separation of quarantine but a separateness of spirit, a freedom from contagion or infection. The goal is set before his followers. With a certain type of man, "let him be to you as a Gentile and a tax collector" (Matt. 18:17). The striking fact is that the Lord received such people and ate with them (Luke 15:1 f.). Their aims, ideals and activities are not to be shared, but as persons they are to be won. (Cf. 1 Cor. 5:9–13; 2 Thess. 3:14 f.) Separatism is an inner attitude, not of the holier-than-thou type, but of a commitment to the Lord and a resolution to be obedient to him. If thus a Christian is "in the world" he must ask himself whether he is in it merely to take his place in it and to enjoy it, or whether, in fidelity to his Master, he takes his standards at all times from the Lord and is not colored by his present company. "Lead us not into temptation" (Matt. 6:13) is the true separatism.

2. A Typical Example (3:6–9)

It is from a group of this nature that there come the smooth-tongued rascals to do further damage to credulous, unstable and sinful women. They are corrupt in mind and their faith does not ring true. They oppose the truth. Final success eludes them for their folly is evident to all.

Verse 6: For among them are those who make their way into households and capture weak women, burdened with sins and swayed by various impulses: The silly and sinful are an obvious target for plausible rogues. In Romans 1:28–32 Paul was looking out on the heathen empire of his day. Here, however, though he began with men in the last days, the stage before his eyes became increasingly peopled with the false teachers. They were an unscrupulous yet plausible crowd when they turned to salesmanship. *Among them are those who* know where to find a ready soil for their labors. The men folk are away at work, leaving the women at home. No doubt with an engaging smile and a soft, sympathetic question, they insidiously *make their way* inside. Arndt and Gingrich excellently bring out the spirit of their entry by the rendering "worm their way" in. There is no need to storm the place, because they have "cased" it already. They do not spend long on the house of a Priscilla (cf. Acts 18:26). They seek—and find—the gullible, and before very long they *capture* them. They sweep them off their feet so that they are "carried away," enslaved by a velvet tongue.

How can we account for their success? It is because the object of their veiled attack was "bits of women." The RSV *weak women* and the KJV "silly women" are attempts to bring out the meaning of a word which is so simple that translation eludes us. It is a single word in the Greek, a diminutive of the noun for "woman" or "wife" *(gunaikarion, gunē)*. In a derogatory sense it can imply weakness, silliness, empty-headedness—very much the weaker vessel in mind as well as body (cf. 1 Pet. 3:7). We prefer to render "bits of women" and leave the rest to the imagination.

These are not women of robust faith. On the contrary they have a past. So have all Christians. But the past of genuine believers is forgiven, put away, forgotten; and the greater the degree of Christian maturity, the greater the Christian certainty. These women are *burdened with sins*. The *sins* are "heaped up" upon them (cf. Rom. 12:20). They may or may not realize it, but they have problems. Idle housewives who will not face the gifts or the demands of the gospel are fruit waiting to be plucked by a "nice man" with a novelty.

They are in addition *swayed by various impulses*. To be *swayed* implies that they are easily led. Already, before the caller "worms his way in," they are frequently led by their own desires. When a novel carrot is placed under their nose, it is the most natural thing in the world for them to want it. The caller offers the carrot of his doctrine and they eagerly seize it.

The *impulses* or desires are *various*. It is significant that trials likewise are *various,* and trials merge into temptations (Jas. 1:2, 12 f.). If only the *weak women* had recognized the man with the smooth tongue for the temptation that he was and had refused to admit him (2 John 10 f.)! They need not have been *weak* if they really had a faith in Christ, for grace is varied to meet the *various* temptations which befall us (1 Pet. 1:6; 4:10). There is one grace with which to meet bereavement and another grace to aid a young man going to college for the first time; and yet another to aid *weak women* to show "unholy" (v. 2) men to the door. God aids his people in their varied experiences for he exercises *various* powers (cf. Heb. 2:4).

The underlying idea of *various* is "many-colored," "dappled," and a modern example would be shot silk: from one side it looks one color and from another side another. As a climax we have the "iridescent" wisdom of God (Eph. 3:10).

Verse 7: Who will listen to anybody and can never arrive at a knowledge of the truth: Obviously! "This is my beloved Son; listen to him" (Mark 9:7). *Who will listen to anybody* is a vigorous paraphrase of the literal "always learning." We must not think of the women as being always at their books. The point is that they are always "taking in information," whatever the source. Hence is derived the force of the impact of *who will listen to anybody*.

For *arrive at a knowledge of the truth* see discussion on 2:25 and the references there given. The women in question *can never* reach this *knowledge* for two main reasons. First, it is because they are always receiving new information and, as academic people say, they are receiving it uncritically. Everything goes into the hodgepodge of their minds. All the items which come are treated alike. They are not weighed. They are not sifted and tested (cf. 1 Thess. 5:21). They have not the sense or the confidence to consult their husbands (1 Cor. 14:35). Paul's words to the Corinthians strikingly contain the very Greek word "learn" *(manthanō)* rendered "listen" in the verse under discussion. "If there is anything they desire to learn . . . ."

Secondly, they are now listening to false teachers who resist *the truth* (v. 8.). They are not likely to *arrive at a knowledge of* it under their ministry, and in fact *can never* do so. When the blind attempt to lead the blind the consequences must be disastrous (Matt. 15:14).

There is a place, and a rightful place, for a broad as well as a deep culture; for a catholicity of interest and a sympathetic understanding of all the affairs of human life. But even this in a secular form is not necessarily without a sense of perspective and a scale of values. These "weak women" seem to be devoid of both. The test of education is not what we know but what we love. The impressionable women did not joyously "think on these things" (Phil. 4:8, KJV).

Verse 8: As Jannes and Jambres opposed Moses, so these men also oppose the truth, men of corrupt mind and counterfeit faith: An old tale reenacted. The allusion is to Exodus 7:11, 22 though the names *Jannes and Jambres* do not appear in the Old Testament. They are mentioned in the so-called Targum of Jonathan. (A targum, originally oral, was an Aramaic paraphrase of the Old Testament with interpretative comment. Targums came into being when Hebrew was no longer the ordinary medium of Jewish social intercourse.) They are also named by some pagan authors and figure in some Christian apocryphal writings. Paul may have drawn on his knowledge of legends about *Jannes and Jambres* in order to emphasize the danger of being associated with the false teachers. If they want to dabble in Jewish myths (cf. 1 Tim. 1:4) they should remember the fate of the Egyptian magicians (Exod. 9:11). Note how the Old Testament events were "typical" as well as actual and "were written down for our instruction" (1 Cor. 10:11).

Paul was making a comparison: *as . . . so . . . .* Apart from the consequences, two points of similarity should be observed. The Egyptian magicians acted with evil motives; so do the false teachers, for they *oppose the truth*. Paul would find it hard to conceive of a more heinous sin (cf. 1 Thess. 2:15 f.). Their method of approach was that of imitation. The magicians of Egypt "did the same" as Aaron did. So the false teachers professed to be doing what Christian apostles and evangelists did and probably claimed to be doing it better. The method is still used. There are men who claim that it is not their intention to abandon the gospel, which they say they believe, but to express it in such a way that modern man can understand it and believe it. They may be quite sincere, but the melancholy fact remains that the "interpretation" sometimes bears little likeness to the original. It is not that the gospel was understandable in the first century and is obscure in the twentieth. It was obscure from the beginning; it was folly to the perishing and beyond the reach of the unspiritual man—apart from the illumination of the Holy Spirit (cf. 1 Cor. 1:18, 23; 2:14). The modern problem of "communication" is not new; and it is no problem to the Holy Spirit.

It is a fact which needs no elaboration or proof that the modern age is steeped in the thoughts and pictures of crime, of the chase by the police and the final appearance in the criminal court. Whodunit stories abound and television shows us the rest. All this mass of material could be used by the preacher and teacher to illustrate his message, and it would certainly be talking in the thought forms of the people. The difficulty is that many have given up anything like a forensic interpretation of the gospel and then complain of the problem of communication. At heart modern man is as dull—and as promising—as ancient man. The gospel should be interpreted to men; then it need not be reinterpreted.

It has been suggested that the false teachers indulged in magical practices. Ephesus would be a good field for this (cf. Acts 19:19), though it is not necessary to bring the false teachers within this activity. Superstition is bad enough. They were *men of corrupt mind* (see on 1 Tim. 6:5) *and counterfeit faith.*

The last phrase cleverly recalls 1 Thessalonians 5:21 f. The Greek means "rejects in regard to the faith." A "reject" means that the examiner in the test is not satisfied with a coin which does not ring true. He rejects it and it joins the pile of "rejects." (In illustration: certain manufacturers keep their best products for export. Goods with a flaw may still be sold as second-class material but not exported. They are "export rejects.") When it comes to the Christian faith the false teachers do not ring true.

The attitude of the apostle should not be unnoticed. He was contending for the faith and guarding the deposit. There are people who object to the clear-cut distinction between black and white. Paul would overrule their objections. He could recognize false doctrine and was sensitive to unbelief.

Verse 9: But they will not get very far, for their folly will be plain to all, as was that of those two men: Magna est veritas et praevalebit (truth is great and it will prevail). They will not advance, will not make progress, further or *very far.* See on 2:16 f. and discussion where they do, and do not "advance."

Paul had in mind either the church at Ephesus or the universal church. If the local church loomed large in his imagination he felt that the rank and file could be trusted to distinguish between truth and error. The church did not consist entirely of the "bits of women" who appear in verse 6! And the work of Timothy would have its effect also. As for the universal church, it is "the pillar and bulwark of the truth" (1 Tim. 3:15). "The church of the living God" will be kept by him. Whatever advance is made by false teachers, God's church will continue and his truth will not fail.

The *folly* arises from the "corrupt mind" (v. 8) and is not mere stupidity. The word is used in Luke 6:11 ("fury") to express the pathological state of men who oppose the truth in thought and act and are frustrated by their own failure to get the better of Jesus. The false teachers are clearly running their heads against a brick wall. They are moved by bias and animus, cranks every one of them. They are too blind to see what will be the consequences of their deeds, for others and for themselves.

Their folly will be plain to all. It was plain enough in the days of Moses and Aaron, the "opposite numbers" of Jannes and Jambres. The Exodus must have been *plain to all.* It was *folly* then to oppose the God of the Hebrews and his servants. It was still *folly* to oppose the same God revealed now in his Son; *folly* to oppose his truth and *folly* to oppose his ministers. *Their* manifest *folly* is the reason why *they will not get very far.* They will convince some; but the good sense of believing men leads them to suspect the crank. And when he rings with falsity, lacking both doctrinal truth and personal faith, to say nothing of love of the brethren, he is dismissed with one word which sums up the moral and spiritual verdict: "crazy!" (Cf. Acts 20:29 f.; Rev. 2:2 f.) Paul would agree that doctrinal purity should always be accompanied by love to God and men—godliness. "Crazy!" must be a spiritual verdict and not just a term of abuse.

VII. APOSTOLIC STIMULUS (3:10–17)

The details of Paul's experience have been observed by Timothy: his teaching and conduct generally; his inner life and the external blows and persecutions. The Lord delivered him from them all. True godliness always involves persecution, and evil and error spread and develop. In contrast, Timothy should continue in his certainties, assured of the authority of his teachers and of Holy Scripture. The nature of Scripture is described.

1. Paul's Known Experience (3:10–11)

Timothy is well aware of the content of the apostle's teaching, of his moral behavior and of the spirit which inspired it. He knows of the persecutions suffered in various places and of their nature, and how the Lord brought deliverance.

Verse 10: Now you have observed my teaching, my conduct, my aim in life, my faith, my patience, my love, my steadfastness: Evidence of a Christian life. This is for the encouragement of Timothy. *Now* is not temporal ("at this particular moment") but transitional or resumptive. The Greek (*su de*) can be taken in a different way, "But *you* (in contrast to the false teachers) . . . ." This makes good sense. From the time that he had joined forces with the apostle Timothy had *observed*, not as a bystander but as a willing learner. He had seen, understood and "followed" (see on 1 Tim. 4:6—the Greek verb is the same). He had adopted the *teaching* to his own soul's good, and had taught and preached it to others. He had imitated the *conduct* (cf. 2 Thess. 3:7, 9) of his mentor and had come to share his *aim in life*, his purpose—the dual purpose of discipleship (cf. Acts 11:23) and evangelism. Discipleship demands drive, not drift. (Cf. also 1 Cor. 9:16; Phil. 3:8–10.) The *faith* had been taught to Timothy when he *observed* the *teaching* and he had seen it constantly exercised. He had noted situations which in other men would have aroused impatience and had learnt the lesson from the great apostle of biding his time (see 1 Thess. 5:14; 1 Tim. 1:16). He had seen the great teaching on *love* (1 Cor. 13:1–13) embodied in the life of Paul, had been inspired by it and had imitated it. The fruit of love is *steadfastness*, for "love . . . endures all things," and Timothy had seen and shared the apostle's *steadfastness*. For *love* and *steadfastness* see on 1 Timothy 1:5; 6:11.

Some underlying implications must now be brought out. It is said that Gandhi was once asked when he would become a Christian. "When I see

[194]

one," he snapped. We may ignore the severity of the judgment: the church is not devoid of saints. The question is, if Gandhi had ever met a true Christian would he have recognized him? An unbeliever may rightly be said to have *observed . . . teaching . . . conduct . . . patience* and *steadfastness.* But how far can he "observe" an *aim in life, faith* and *love?* Yet Paul betrays no fear that Timothy has not so *observed.* The solution to this problem may be found in a consideration of an analogous problem, that of the nature of the church.

There is much stress laid today on the visible church. If it is asked what is seen when a man looks at the visible church the answer is not easy. He sees buildings, people, people on their knees or singing hymns. He understands that they are praying, but can he really see men praying if true prayer is foreign to him? Can he observe *faith?* To say that after all the church is invisible raises further problems. It has been well remarked that it would be difficult to operate a church the members of which were known only to God. Sometimes reference is made to the visible mark of baptism, the indelible seal. But if two men are walking down the street it would be hard to distinguish which one was baptized and which one not. The "indelible seal" is not a tattoo.

The answer lies in the fact that the church is visible but visible only to faith (cf. "looking to Jesus," Heb. 12:2). The life of the church, like that of the individual believer, is a hidden life (cf. Col. 3:3). Yet the members recognize one another in the interplay of faith (cf. Rom. 1:12). It was like this in particular with Paul and Timothy. Timothy could observe the apostle's *faith* because he shared it. They both approached the same throne of grace and both trusted and served the same Savior. The ethical life of the believer is to some extent visible to all. The good works should be manifest (Matt. 5:16) and should prompt inquiry into their spiritual source. Even if it had been possible for Gandhi to see a Christian, it does not follow that he would automatically have become one himself. He might not have approved of what he saw. The cross is always a stumbling block; the Lord himself was crucified. But the evidence could not fail and did not fail to leave its impress on Timothy; for he also was "in Christ." (Cf. 1 Cor. 4:16 f.)

Verse 11: My persecutions, my sufferings, what befell me at Antioch, at Iconium, and at Lystra, what persecutions I endured; yet from them all the Lord rescued me: Evidence of the Lord's faithfulness. After speaking in general terms Paul went on to give particular examples. These could not fail to stir Timothy, because they were on his home ground. The details are recorded in Acts 13:14, 45, 50; 14:1–7, 19–22. The *Antioch* is Antioch of Pisidia. It was situated in Asia Minor, the Turkey of today, and its ruins are near to Yalovach.

The *sufferings* are a comment on the *persecutions* and reveal their inner story. Even after the elapse of years the memory seems to have stirred the apostle's emotions. This is suggested by the repetition and the detail and the fact that only a selection was being made: "(experiences such) as *befell me at Antioch . . . .";* as well as by the fact that the language is that of an exclamation. *"What* manner of *persecutions I endured!"* Note the exclamation mark.

But *the Lord rescued* him out of (*ek*) *them all.* He had indeed been "in" them, which illustrates the following verse. The rescue, both then and now, is determined by the Lord's love and wisdom, and by his purpose. Paul finally died as a martyr. He would not dissent from the view that *the Lord* had still *rescued* him, though in a different way. Even death cannot separate us from the love of God in Christ Jesus our Lord (Rom. 8:38 f.).

2. Inevitable Opposition (3:12–13)

To be forewarned is to be forearmed. Persecution will always fall upon those who aspire to a life of godliness in Christ. Timothy must be ready. Evil and deluded deceivers will grow worse. Timothy must not be surprised.

Verse 12: Indeed all who desire to live a godly life in Christ Jesus will be persecuted: A spiritual law with a variety of applications. The persecution is not necessarily working in full force all the time. It may be quiescent but at any time may be stirred into activity. Nor is the persecution always political. The attitude of government may be neutral or even friendly. But social groups or even individuals may be antagonized by Christian witness, and it is not always the fault of the Christians. There are men for whom the word "sin" is as a red rag to a bull; men who resent the quality of life of the authentic Christian; men whose evil deeds are exposed by the contrast of Christian lives. They not only will not come to the light but will do everything they can to extinguish the light. For much of the time the hostility of the world slumbers. Even the world gets tired. It may, however, be stirred when it feels its interests threatened; a single act of witness may be a spark to set gunpowder ablaze. (Cf. John 3:19 f.; 15:18–25.)

Those *who desire to live a godly life* are in marked contrast to those who hold the form of religion but deny its power (v. 5). To *live* does not here mean merely to exist or to dwell ("He lives in New York"). It is the verb cognate with the *life* of "eternal life." *All who desire . . .* find a relish, a zeal, for *life* in godliness (see on 1 Tim. 6:11). They love the life under the eyes of the Lord (cf. 1 Pet. 3:10-12). This recalls "the life which is in Christ Jesus" (see on 1:1). It should be noticed that *a godly life* is not visualized as mechanical or automatic. It is truly lived in the power of the Spirit by those *who desire* it.

This is not the first time we have found Paul speaking in this vein. His words about "affliction" cannot fail to be recalled (see 1 Thess. 3:3 f.).

Verse 13: While evil men and impostors will go on from bad to worse, deceivers and deceived: Timothy must know the worst. This makes explicit what was implicit in the thought of fighting the good fight of faith (1 Tim. 6:12), and of being a good soldier of Christ Jesus (2 Tim. 2:3). Christianity is not wildly (and wrongly) optimistic; nor is it pessimistic; it is realistic. For evil, in the person of *evil men*, does not stagnate. Its very malignancy drives it to activity. *Evil men . . . will go on from bad to worse*. Literally we should say, *"will* advance to the *worse"* (see on 2:16; 3:9). This is retrogression, but the paradoxical thought of "progress" backwards may reflect the determined purpose of the *evil men*. In any case it is a continuation, perhaps intensified and accelerated, of what has been going on through the centuries. As men's knowledge and abilities increase, the area of possible temptation is enlarged. New knowledge may mean new industries; and these in turn give birth to new sins. No doubt they can be brought under an earlier general description, but the tools of sin are increased and refined. Murder is murder however it is committed; but to hide a bomb in a passenger airplane or to introduce a poison under cover of intravenous feeding is a fairly recent possibility. The same sins have new outlets. It would be safe to prophesy that if men ever do land on the moon and establish themselves there, new sins will arise. Apart from a vulgar international scramble for any available precious metals, to consign a group of men to a perpetual lunar orbit through a regrettable "mistake" or failure would be a more refined form of a medieval dungeon. If new metals were discovered, they could be used to minister to the pride of the few in the manufacture and sale of "moon-metal" jewelry.

"Advance to the worse" may include new heresies, new methods of fostering unbelief, new tools and outlets for old sins, new hypocrisies and wider propaganda. In our own day we have seen the rise of radio followed by that of television. Is it always pure truth that is broadcast?

The *impostors* are sorcerers, wizards or jugglers. Perhaps the word "manipulators" conveys the right nuance. Their main object is not the unvarnished truth, though some may think that it is. They are *deceivers* but may even be sincere, for they themselves are *deceived*.

The false teachers at Ephesus will not get very far (v. 9) but others will arise and will be more widespread.

3. The Authority of Teachers and of Scripture (3:14–17)

Knowing this, Timothy must stand firm in his convictions. He can rest on the authority of his teachers; on the fact that Scripture has stood the test of time and can mediate salvation; and on its divine origin. Its various uses show what the man of God can do with it: it is a weapon in the good fight of faith and an instrument in the production of every good work.

Verse 14: But as for you, continue in what you have learned and have firmly believed, knowing from whom you learned it: Christian convictions are supported by the character of those "through whom you believed" (1 Cor. 3:5 f.). *But as for you (su de)* is the same Greek as the beginning of verse 10 (see discussion). It would hardly have been wrong if Paul had told Timothy to "keep in mind" what he had *learned*. Memory is not without significance in the Christian life. But his choice of words is even more significant. *Continue* expresses more than mere continuity. It represents the same Greek word as the Johannine "abide." It is true that Timothy should never forget *what you have learned* and should keep it *in* his mind. But Paul put it the other way round. Timothy must be *in*, must abide *in*, *what* he had *learned*. This recalls our Lord's words about abiding "in my word" (John 8:31). The corresponding Greek noun is used of the "many mansions" (John 14:2), many "abiding places." (The RSV "rooms" is not quite so effective as the "mansions" of KJV.) The Christian looks forward to heaven with its many mansions. In the meantime he has the mansion of *what you have learned* and of "the sacred writings" (v. 15) of Holy Scripture. Let him abide in them!

The same thought was suggested by Paul in Romans 6:17, "the standard of teaching to which you were committed." This RSV rendering is a little obscure. It reminds us of "commitment," of "committed" Christians, complete consecration and the like. But "committed" is a "tradition" word (see 1 Cor. 15:3; 2 Thess. 2:15). Paul knew that his readers had received the tradition which had been delivered, had been handed over, to them. But again he put it the other way round. They had been handed over to the doctrine. They were not only "committed" to it; they were in its grip; they lived in it. The implication for Timothy was that though the doctrine had been entrusted to him and he should "guard the deposit," he was not in control of it or master of it. He must not alter it. He must remain *in* it.

Have firmly believed means "have become convinced of." Timothy had not only "ideas" but convictions. They must direct and inspire his life, not because they are his but because they are the Word of God made his. Conviction by itself is not enough; it must be the right conviction. Timothy could be encouraged if he reflected on this by remembering *from whom you learned it.* The authority of Scripture is final, but this should not lead any man to minimize the authority of the teacher. Timothy should ask himself: Did my teachers give me the Word of God? What was the character of my teachers? Some men can teach Scripture in a secular way. In some parts of the world schoolboys have groaned under the deadening effects of men who under the system had to teach a subject in which they did not believe. Timothy was surely in the position of *knowing* that his teachers had themselves tried and proved the message which they were giving and were themselves solid evidence of its effect. Saul the persecutor is outstanding here (cf. 1 Tim. 1:16).

Verse 15: And how from childhood you have been acquainted with the sacred writings which are able to instruct you for salvation through faith in Christ Jesus: Timothy's spiritual roots were deep. The scenes *from childhood* which would come back to Timothy would bring renewed warmth to his faith. Unlike new, and especially Gentile, converts, he would not have much to unlearn. (Cf. 1 Thess. 1:9.) He had started at an early age. Jewish parents were under obligation to teach their children the Scripture. "At five years the age is reached for the study of the scripture" (*Pirqē Aboth* 5:27). This quotation is made from a set of aphorisms preserved in the Jewish Mishnah ("instruction"), the authoritative collection of the Jewish Oral Law. *Pirqē Aboth*, or "Sayings of the Fathers," are still used in the modern Jewish prayer book.

The sacred writings here mean the Old Testament, the Bible of the early church. Timothy may have read it first with purely Jewish eyes; but after conversion he must have found in due course "Christ in all the scriptures." The quotations in the New Testament reveal both prophecy and pattern (cf. 1 Cor. 10:11); and Paul could find the principle of grace even in the law (cf. Rom. 4:23 f.).

Paul's treatment of Scripture is eminently sound and sane. The Scriptures *are able*, he says. They must be read or taught or preached before they begin to "operate," and even then they require the response of *faith in Christ Jesus*. They do not work mechanically or automatically. It is not enough to possess a Bible or to hold it in the hand.

The Scriptures are *sacred* in contrast to the profane character of false teaching (see on 1 Tim. 1:9; 4:7; 2 Tim. 2:16). They *are able to instruct*, to "make wise," when others indulge in "godless chatter." They have the permanence of what is written, whereas chatter, though repeated and as dangerous as rumor, may change. They make wise with a view to *salvation* because they embody the revelation of God, in contrast to mere speculation (cf. 1 Tim. 1:4) which is of human origin and cannot save. They make wise when the activities of false teachers are marked by folly (cf. 3:9). For *salvation* see on 2:10 with its further references.

Instruct . . . for salvation contains a dual idea. The Scriptures will *instruct* a man with a view to his *salvation*. The thought here is of salvation accepted, or conversion. But the Scriptures will continue to *instruct* him in *salvation*. Either the Greek preposition (*eis*) "into" is to be taken, as often, in the sense of "in" (*en*) or, more probably, we must think of "with a view to (future) *salvation*." This accords with Pauline doctrine. Justified men will be saved (Rom. 5:9). The thought is then of salvation expected. The Scriptures show a seeker what he must do in order to be saved (Acts 16:31); they show him further how he is to enjoy salvation here and now, how he is to behave in accordance with his salvation, and what he is to expect in heaven.

This double sense of *salvation* accords with the directions to Timothy to abide in what he had learned (v. 14). He would not need to study constantly the means to his own conversion; and even if he had to study such means in order to preach evangelistic sermons correctly, his duties were wider than, though they included, evangelism. His preaching was to be pastoral, that is, was to be addressed to those who were already Christians. The various uses of Scripture in pastoral work are given in verse 16.

Instruct (*sophizō*) here means to "make wise." It is not the wisdom (*sophia*) of this world which is in view (1 Cor. 1:17–2:5) but the wisdom whereby a man can understand the preached Word and accept it. There is a wisdom for those who have already received salvation, a wisdom which looks forward to that future salvation which Paul called glory (1 Cor. 2:6 f.).

Through faith in Christ Jesus seems at first to go closely with *salvation*. (Cf. Eph. 2:8.) It seems better, however, to construe thus: the Scriptures *are able to instruct you through faith in Christ Jesus*—with a view to *salvation*. The point then is that it is *faith in Christ Jesus* which is the key to the Old Testament. It is sometimes said—rightly—that the Old Testament is needed in order to explain the New. The opposite is also true: the New Testament is necessary in order to penetrate the deepest meaning of the Old. Without the New, the Old Testament is left unfulfilled. It requires completion, that is, *faith in Christ Jesus*. Through this the door is unlocked.

An obvious grouping would take *faith-in-Christ-Jesus* together, and it would not be wrong though perhaps inadequate. The structure of the Greek resembles that of 1 Timothy 3:13 (see discussion) and is analogous to that of 2 Timothy 1:1 (see discussion). The Scriptures are able to make "wise" enough for salvation through a certain instrumentality. It is by means of *faith*. Such *faith* has two characteristics. It is certainly *faith in Christ Jesus*. But it is *faith* in him exercised by a man who in virtue of his faith becomes *in Christ Jesus*. The latter interpretation is richer because it includes the former. This is once more the "mystical union" of the believer with Christ.

Verse 16: All scripture is inspired by God and profitable for teaching, for reproof, for correction, and for training in righteousness: A comprehensive description of origin and use. *All scripture* has been interpreted in two ways, because of the absence of the Greek definite article. It may mean "the whole of scripture" or "every scriptural text," "whatever is scripture," "any text you like to pick out." The difference is between Scripture as a whole and Scripture in any of its parts. In the end the result is the same: add up all the separate texts and the "answer" to the "sum" is Scripture in its totality. But what is Scripture? In the present context it must be at least the Old Testament. Spicq (p. 377) would include also what was written by or approved by the apostles, and gives as an example the Gospel according to St. Luke. (Cf. 1 Tim. 5:18 and discussion.) If the statement that *all scripture is inspired by God* is a principle, then it can be interpreted as covering the New Testament as well as the Old. The rendering, "every inspired scripture is also profitable . . . ," is unlikely to be correct. The construction is parallel to that in 1 Timothy 4:4, "everything created by God is good" (note the "is"). And would the apostle even hint that some Scripture might not be inspired?

Inspired stands for the Greek *theopneustos.* This is a rare word and means "God-breathed" or even "God-blown." The last two syllables are cognate with a verb meaning "to breathe out (something)" or "to blow" (used of the wind: John 3:8; 6:18), and with a noun (*pneuma*) meaning both "wind" and "spirit" (hence the verb "inspire"). The breath of God suggests the quiet and unseen influences in inspiration; the wind, especially the "mighty wind" (cf. Acts 2:2), points to the compulsive powers of the Spirit. In the voyage recorded in the Acts a tempestuous wind struck down, the ship was caught, and "we . . . were driven" (Acts 27:15, 17). In like manner men were "driven" by the Holy Wind (Spirit) and spoke from God (cf. 2 Pet. 1:21). (The Greek word for "driven" is the same, *pheromai.*) The "drive" behind prophecy did not come from the will or impulse of man at any time. We can never "see" the processes of inspiration at work in a man, and no man ever could see the inbreathing activity of God. But the result is manifest—the Scripture. The nearest approach we can make to the compulsive influence of the Holy Spirit and to the experience of being "driven" is the mind of the true preacher. Try to silence him; offer him huge sums of money to quit his pulpit; reward him with high (and lucrative) office in ecclesiastical administration or with a distinguished professorial chair in a great university, on condition that his Sundays are days of rest and his preaching over. The result is agony. He must preach. The inner pressure cannot relax. A fire burns within him and the preacher is weary with holding it in—and he cannot (cf. Jer. 20:9). It need hardly be added that this does not turn a man into a machine. He is driven indeed; but he lets his ship speed before the wind, consenting to be thus swiftly borne along.

All scripture is . . . profitable because it can be used. If it is not used it is of no value. It is thus a potentiality, a fact which is illustrated by Paul's earlier statement that the Scriptures "are able to instruct you" (v. 15). We say that a man is able to write. But does he do it? The Scriptures can be used. Are they used? They are *profitable for teaching* as a sourcebook of doctrine both religious and ethical, as a record of the power of God in the lives of men, and as a stimulus to deeper discipleship. They are useful *for reproof.* This is not quite the same as rebuke. *Reproof* exposes false doctrine and shows it to be false by refuting it; it unmasks the false teacher and shows where he is wrong. It is somewhat negative.

Teaching and *reproof* are concerned with the mind. *Correction* has to do with the practical life. "Reformation" conveys something of the idea. It is the correction of the man rather than of his thoughts and speech. It is the restoration of the man who has strayed so that he returns to the right path. Correction lifts up those who have fallen so that they stand fast and firm (see 1 Thess. 3:8; 2 Thess. 2:15). *Training* means "education" (2:25 and discussion) or "discipline," even "chastening." The subject matter in which training is to be received is *righteousness.* Paul here seems to echo his own words. See on 1 Timothy 6:11 for *righteousness* and "man of God" (next verse). Educational experts will perceive the relation between the success of *training in righteousness* and "aiming at righteousness." In all education the sluggish student is at a disadvantage.

Who does the *training?* If, as seems certain, Timothy was to give the *teaching, reproof* and *correction,* it is likely that he himself was to give the *training in righteousness*. It is a solemn thought for any minister. This is indeed a practical aspect of the ministry of which we have heard so much in recent years. Some parts of the modern church need to be reminded that for a practical ministry the Scriptures are still the best instrument. It is true that there are other "educational aids." Most *profitable* are the Scriptures, which can be used as a stimulus or as a consolation (Rom. 15:4).

Verse 17: That the man of God may be complete, equipped for every good work: Ready for anything! In 1 Timothy 6:11 (see discussion), the *man of God* is Timothy himself. In the present verse the reference is wider. A principle has been stated and it is continued here. Scripture is inspired and profitable, so *that the man of God,* whoever he may be in any given instance, *may be complete.* The principle applies to Timothy and to every other *man of God.* From *complete* we may infer not his own individual perfection but that he need not lack any particular qualification for ministry. The purpose is that he may be adapted to the duty set before him. He is not likely to be a philosophic square peg in a religious round hole if he has steeped himself in the Scriptures. Thus he will be *equipped;* there will be a "finish" on him. He will be not only ready (see on 2:21) but able.

There is a subtle point about *every good work* which ought to be observed. Paul did not mean comprehensiveness, as if the minister should actually do everything. His thought was of versatility or adaptability. *The man of God* should have the tools to deal with (not every individual task but) any *good work* which may challenge him. *Every* here means "any" task which may arise and clamor to be done.

Who is sufficient for these things? It can only be the *man of God* who abides in what he has learned (cf. v. 14 and discussion). And what has he learned? It is doctrine, to be sure; but it is more than doctrine. It was his joy to "learn Christ" (Eph. 4:20).

VIII. THE FAREWELL GLORY (4:1–18)

Urgent and solemn exhortations are given to Timothy to fulfill his evangelistic and pastoral ministry. The present opportunity must be seized because the time will come when men will not tolerate sound teaching. The appeal is all the more moving because the apostle has fulfilled his own ministry and is about to depart to his reward. Requests are made for sundry personal favors and Timothy is warned against a man who had resisted Paul and had done him damage. At the preliminary hearing Paul had stood alone in court but the Lord was with him. In the confidence that the Lord will bring him safely to his heavenly kingdom, Paul utters a short doxology.

1. Summary Exhortations (4:1–5)

Deeply aware of standing in the divine presence and of the Lord's coming and his kingdom, Paul bids Timothy to take and make every opportunity for bringing the Word to bear on a variety of situations. This has special importance: doors—and ears—will be closed to the truth of sound doctrine and men will provide themselves with their own teachers to tickle their fancy. In the meantime Timothy must fulfill his ministry at any cost.

Verse 1: I charge you in the presence of God and of Christ Jesus who is to judge the living and the dead, and by his appearing and his kingdom: Divine certainties are brought in to invest the commands with intense solemnity. Notice the divine existence, presence, manifestation and authoritative rule.

I charge you in the presence of God repeats the Greek of 2:14, where the RSV says "before" instead of *in the presence of.* (See discussion and further references.) It might be thought that Paul would have been satisfied by speaking of *God* and of *Christ Jesus.* He was carried on by his emotion and the elaboration intensifies the solemnity and heightens the effect. Christ Jesus *is to judge the living and the dead.* In some pagan philosophies this could express iron fate, for *is to* can have an ominous ring. But no mechanical destiny is meant, no predetermined program of judgment in which the Judge has not been consulted. Christ Jesus is not a pawn in the hands of destiny. *Is to* expresses a certainty with regard to the future, for it is by divine decree that Christ will judge. The Father has committed judgment to the Son and the Son has accepted the commission. The Greek verb (*mellō*) can imply not only a bare futurity but also an intention. We may therefore translate *is to* (which is quite correct) by "who intends to" judge. Nobody will escape the net. Just as both living and dead Christians will enjoy the blessings of the Parousia (1 Thess. 4:15), so *the living and the dead* will be judged—Christian and non-Christian alike, though in a different mode. The judgment of unbelievers will be concerned with the question of their final destiny. The judgment of believers will not be concerned with whether they go to heaven or hell but will be a judgment of awards and of their place in the heaven which they have been promised. (Cf. 1 Cor. 3:13–15; 2 Cor. 5:10, ". . . that each one may get back his bodily conduct, good or bad, in proportion to his deeds.")

The language passes on to that which is appropriate to the oath. (This does not mean obscene or blasphemous language. Cf. 1 Thess. 5:27, "I adjure you by the Lord.") In writing to Timothy, however, Paul charged him *by his appearing and his kingdom*. These abstract terms really mean "by Christ manifest" and "by Christ finally ruling." *Appearing* or "epiphany" here means the Second Advent. (See discussion and references on 1:10.) *Kingdom* implies its final consummation, when it will no longer be appropriate to pray, "Thy kingdom come," because it will have come. The *appearing* and the *kingdom* are certainties as solid and immutable as deity itself. The oath or adjuration *by his appearing* is uttered *by* that which is certain and unchanging. It is a sad commentary on human sin that it can be regarded as immutable as God himself. "The Lord God has sworn by his holiness . . . by himself . . . by the pride of Jacob" (Amos 4:2; 6:8; 8:7). (Cf. perhaps Heb. 6:17.)

His kingdom: The subject of the kingdom of God has been the aim of much research and the literature is immense.[1] The following points should be kept in mind. *Kingdom* does not mean a place, a realm ruled by a king, but an activity; God's royal rule or sovereignty. The kingdom of God existed in the Old Testament. "Thy kingdom is an everlasting kingdom, and thy dominion endures throughout all generations" (Ps. 145:13; cf. Ps. 103:19). But when Jesus preached the kingdom of God he was not merely reiterating the Old Testament teaching. The *kingdom,* the royal rule, "has drawn near" and therefore "is at hand" (Mark 1:15). God is no longer ruling, as it were, at a distance. (This does not mean deism. It does mean that God was inaccessible to men who would oppose him. In Christ the metaphysically distant God who rules everything entered history.) "The kingdom of God is among (*entos*) you" (Luke 17:21). There stood Christ in their midst, the embodiment of the *kingdom,* of God ruling. After the cross, resurrection and ascension, and the outpouring of the Holy Spirit, the kingdom was within believing men, for Christ dwells in their hearts through faith (cf. Eph. 3:17). God is over all in his providential rule. He was among men in the days of the ministry of Jesus, and he is in believers. He is still "over" all, only we now know that it is in Christ (Col 1:13–18); and he is "in" all believers in Christ through the Holy Spirit.

The kingdom is present (Matt. 12:28; Luke 11:20). It is "righteousness

---

1. For excellent surveys and bibliographies see George Eldon Ladd, *Jesus and the Kingdom: The Eschatology of Biblical Realism* (New York: Harper & Row, 1964; reprint ed., Waco, Tex.: Word Books; London: S.P.C.K., 1966); and Gösta Lundström, *The Kingdom of God in the Teaching of Jesus: A History of Interpretation from the Last Decades of the Nineteenth Century to the Present Day* (Edinburgh and London: Oliver and Boyd, 1963).

and peace and joy in the Holy Spirit" (Rom. 14:17). "Thine is the kingdom
. . ." (Matt. 6:13, RSV footnote). The manuscript authority for this last por-
tion of the Lord's Prayer is not good, and it is often regarded as an ecclesiastical addition. But recent Semitic scholarship has shown the unlikelihood of
a prayer ending without a doxology. The manuscripts may just assume it. And
if the church added it, why is there no normal Christian ending like "for
Jesus Christ's sake"? [1]

The kingdom is also future. All attempts to limit it to the present (realized
eschatology) break down in the face of one piece of evidence: "Thy kingdom
come."

The New Testament speaks of entering the kingdom (Matt. 23:13; cf.
7:21; 18:3). It means consciously putting oneself under God's royal rule in
Christ ("Jesus is Lord," cf. Rom. 10:9), and this involves conversion. It is a
striking fact that we read of a man "discipled to the *kingdom*" (Matt. 13:52,
literal), and of one "discipled to Jesus" (Matt. 27:57, literal). In fact it
amounts to the same thing whether we inherit eternal life, follow Jesus, enter
the kingdom, or are saved (Mark 10:17–26), as it is all one experience.
Paul's great aim of testifying to the gospel of the grace of God was fulfilled
when he went about preaching the kingdom (Acts 20:24–25).

Providentially and invisibly God still in Christ rules nature and history.
Invisibly in Christ he rules in the hearts of believers. In the final consummation of all things he will in Christ rule openly: all things, all people, and
especially his own believing people. Christ is already Lord of nature and
history ("at the right hand of God"). He is King in the realms of nature,
history, and grace. At the end he will be known of all as Creator and Sustainer
of the universe and Head of the Church. And his people will continue to
rejoice to be under the rule of him who is Lord, and to say "that there is
another king, Jesus" (Acts 17:7).

The judgment is a particular aspect of the royal rule or *kingdom*. It is not
arbitrary but is God's final implementation of human choice. Judgment is
already operative in this life, because it means a sifting, a making of distinctions, a separation. John sees in judgment the division of men into two main
classes, those who come to the light and those who do not (John 3:19–21).
At the Last Judgment the judicial sentence is the final gift to men of what
they have sought in their lives, God's retributory "amen" to their secular
prayers. Those who consistently refused to come to the light go into outer
darkness. Those who "have loved his appearing" (cf. v. 8) go into eternal
splendor and glory. (Loving *his appearing,* even before he appears, is not of
course a "secular prayer.")

In a sense, men judge themselves. But this is not the last word. God's
final judgment is his, in Christ, and it is related to men's lives. There is a
preview of the final judgment in Romans 1:24, 26, 28. It should not be
thought that God redeems in love and judges in righteousness. He always
acts in the totality of his attributes. Both redemption and judgment come from
the one God who is both love and righteousness always. For God is present,
and judges, in Christ. It may be that men feel the "impact" of one more than

---

1. W. D. Davies, *The Setting of the Sermon on the Mount* (Cambridge: The University Press, 1964), Appendix VIII, pp. 451–53.

the other at different times in their lives. A man under conviction of sin may dwell on the righteousness of God; and in the first flush of his conversion he may think of nothing but the love of God. But God in Christ is always both righteousness and love.

Verse 2: Preach the word, be urgent in season and out of season, convince, rebuke, and exhort, be unfailing in patience and in teaching: The spearhead of Timothy's ministry. Other duties follow but these constitute the "point." It is striking that when the apostle was on the point of handing over to Timothy (cf. v. 6), his main concern was with preaching, not sacraments.

The verbs in the series are aorists. The Greek aorist tense makes a bare mention of an act, bringing its scattered parts into a focus. It has been called "punctiliar" because it views even a sustained action as a "point." The whole moral and spiritual life of our Lord is summed up in a "pinpoint"—Christians are to keep on walking as "he walked" (1 John 2:6). (See my *Hidden Meaning*, pp. 14–23.)

Preach the word has thus a certain decisiveness, and it sums up the whole ministerial life of Timothy. This is to be his one comprehensive duty. It is to fill his whole horizon and absorb his whole intellect. It is to be the dominant purpose of all his days and the one emotion which includes all emotions. Everything that follows in the verse is to be related to the supreme task, *preach the word*.

Timothy must *be urgent in season and out of season. Urgent* does not necessarily here mean putting pressure on men or racing against time. (He must always "be unfailing in patience.") The Greek verb, the translation of which is not easy, has the idea of standing by or near, though the "standing" part tends to become metaphorical. Thus sudden destruction comes upon men (cf. 1 Thess. 5:3) and "that day" may "come upon" men suddenly, if they do not take heed (Luke 21:34). The time of Paul's departure "has come" (v. 6). It is neither the literal coming of a journey nor the literal standing of a man.

The best rendering of *be urgent* is the expression used metaphorically in an army, "stand by." If an officer comes into a room and barks out, "What do you mean by it, wasting time and doing nothing?" the soldier may reply, "I am standing by, sir; we are waiting for an important telephone call, and as soon as it comes I have to report it." He may or may not be "standing," but he is there, ready, on the alert for action *in season.* This last phrase means "opportunely," "at the right moment." In other words Timothy is to be "on the spot" when the opportunity comes, and is to take the opportunity to *preach the word.*

It is conceivable that the soldier who was "standing by," knowing the issues at stake, grew alarmed at the delay and decided to wait no longer. He therefore himself tried to call the people from whom he was expecting a message. Here he was acting *out of season.* He did not take the opportunity, because there was none. But he made the opportunity. In short Timothy was ever to be on the alert to take or make the opportunity to *preach the word.* There is no "open" or "closed" season for the preaching of the gospel, not at least in the sense that in the "closed" season it must not be preached. Preachers are not shooting ducks or deer; they are telling men the words of life. If the season seems "closed" because of lack of opportunity, then "open" it. There is still room for Timothy and every other preacher to exercise wisdom in making the opportunity.

Convince is the verb cognate with the "reproof" of 3:16. It savors of "unmask," "expose." Things are "exposed by the light" (Eph. 5:13). Men who sin by partiality are exposed by the law as transgressors (cf. Jas. 2:9). The exposure need not be in public. ". . . go and tell him his fault [expose him] between you and him alone" (Matt. 18:15). Timothy need not make startling revelations about men's personal lives or teachings. *Preach the word:* that in itself will expose and *convince.*

To *rebuke,* according to E. Stauffer, belongs to God and to Christ (cf. TDNT 2:625 f.). There can therefore be only one way in which it can be done by Timothy. He must not do it in his own name. Once more he must *preach the word.* For *exhort* see discussion on 1 Timothy 1:3 with its further references. It means to "persuade with authority." If Timothy were to persuade with the sole influence of his own personality, it would be possible for some other person, perhaps one of the false teachers, to come along and persuade in the opposite direction. The persuasion must be backed by authority. Hence again he must *preach the word.* The Word, coming through his lips, will persuade men just as it will expose or *convince* them and *rebuke* them.

In all these different aspects of preaching the Word the preacher must *be unfailing in patience and in teaching.* For *patience* see discussion on 1 Timothy 1:16. As the Lord showed all patience with Saul of Tarsus, so Timothy was to show all patience with his people. The message itself has urgency, but in dealing with men Timothy must learn to give them time—without letting them waste it. The word is one but its impact may be varied. All *teaching* must be given, though not necessarily in one sermon or one invitation or interview. The message must not be out of proportion. In an extended ministry due balance should be preserved. There is the call to conversion and the call to edification; the call to godliness and the call to righteousness; the call to spiritual life and the call to moral behavior.

The word is a brief and comprehensive expression for the Word of God, the word of the Lord, the gospel, the gospel of God, or the gospel of Christ. When men *preach the word* they preach Christ—wisdom, righteousness, sanctification, redemption (cf. 1 Cor. 1:30).

Verse 3: For the time is coming when people will not endure sound teaching, but having itching ears they will accumulate for themselves teachers to suit their own likings: Strike while the iron is hot. In time Timothy may not be able to strike at all, because *people will not endure* it. *For* introduces the explanation either of the need to preach the word (v. 2) or of a suppressed sentence. The thought would then be: "Preach the word . . . . (This is important and there is no time to be lost.) *For the time is coming . . . ."*

Endure here is not the same as the endurance of steadfastness as in 3:10 (see discussion; and cf. on 1 Tim. 6:11). It means rather "to bear with," "to put up with." It is remarkable that *people* who have themselves been endured by God will not *endure* the *teaching* about him. Our Lord put up with a faithless generation (Mark 9:19), and God did and does the same. Paul spoke of "the riches of his . . . forbearance" (Rom. 2:4; cf. 3:25).

God stays his hand and does not inflict punishment at once. The Fall of Jerusalem (A.D. 70) was a generation after the crucifixion. *People* on the other hand react at once, adversely. The fact that they *will not endure* means that they will not go on listening. They have not even a little of God's "riches" of forbearance. More was expected from the readers of the Epistle to the Hebrews (13:22). The *people* who have been endured but will not themselves *endure* are like those who have been forgiven but will not themselves forgive (Matt. 6:12–15; 18:21–35).

Sound means "healthy" (see on 1:13). What *people* want is obviously going to be bad for their spiritual health (cf. 3 John 2). Their taste ranges from pure poison to inferior food and a polluted atmosphere. If told that the *sound teaching* of the Christian preacher will build or edify them, they reply that they could not care less for his teaching as they have a better. If asked if they desire health (cf. John 5:6) they bluntly decline it—by the methods of the Christian preacher. They are thus deluded.

In fact they are suffering from a "new" disease, *having itching ears*. Their *ears* need to be scratched or massaged and this is done not by the hands but by the words of their new *teachers*. It is not always a compliment to say that a man can "get the crowd." As the older commentators used to say, they may go "to get their ears tickled." The "itch" is relieved by novelties (cf. Acts 17:21), scraps of spicy talk, ingenious or sensational addresses, even "smooth things" (cf. Isa. 30:10). Much modern talk about what is "relevant" may come under this head. The preacher should study needs rather than wants.

The *people* accordingly *accumulate for themselves teachers*. They "pile them up," a fact which suggests their insatiable appetite and a preoccupation with novelties. Nothing satisfies and they are always bent on listening to "the next man." *For themselves* implies their utter spiritual selfishness. They know what they want and they intend to have it. Not all *teachers* qualify. They must be men who *suit their own likings*. The *teachers* match the congregation.

A distinction should be drawn between *people* of this nature who act "according to their own desires" and obtain teachers in abundance to tickle their fancy, and an authentic church of believers who know and do the truth and look for a minister to preach the Word. Superficially the two groups may resemble each other: both seek *teachers to suit their own likings*. But there is a vast difference between them. The *people* want to be pleasantly entertained; the church which really believes wants teachers who will minister the Word. Everything depends on whether they "are of God." If they are, they delight in his Word and those who preach it *suit their . . . likings*. For they too "are of God. Whoever knows God listens to us, and he who is not of God does not listen to us. By this we know the spirit of truth and the spirit of error" (1 John 4:6). This prepares the way for the verdict decisively given in the next verse.

Verse 4: And will turn away from listening to the truth and wander into myths: To soothe the itch rather than to slake the thirst (Ps. 42:1 f.). Paul had spoken earlier (1:15) of men who had turned away from him, the representative of *the truth*. Now he thinks of those who *will turn away* not only from *the truth* itself but even from *listening to it*. They must not be regarded as listless or no longer feeling the attraction of *the truth*. They must not be compared with the people in whom the pulse of religion throbs but feebly and therefore they stay away from church services instead of eagerly seeking to be present. They must be pictured as unwilling to listen and therefore refusing to listen. There is a large element of deliberate choice. They should more fittingly be compared with men who have turned on their radio and found themselves listening to a preacher of the gospel, and who mutter to themselves, "I can't stand this," and tune in to another station.

For when they *wander* they do not do so unconsciously. It is not the pathetic "we have erred and strayed from thy ways like lost sheep." Paul used the same Greek word when he vigorously told Timothy to "avoid the godless chatter and contradictions of what is falsely called knowledge" (1 Tim. 6:20). He did not mean him dreamily to wander away from godless chatter. Avoid it! So these people will "take evasive action" *into myths*. *Wander* is thus deliberate and has an ominous ring. Men may move into "vain discussion" and even "after Satan" (1 Tim. 1:6 f.; 5:15). For *myths* see on 1 Timothy 1:4. To prefer *myths* to *the truth* is not only to accept false doctrine in place of true, which could be a purely intellectual matter. It is to leave the historic Jesus and the exalted Lord. And what divine object of praise and worship can fill the vacuum? A man's doctrine reveals itself when he is on his knees in private, and it is very probable that those who *wander into myths* abandon the life of devotion. See also on 1 Timothy 4:7. Godliness requires a religious experience rooted in the historical Jesus, and will therefore not be inspired by *myths*.

Verse 5: As for you, always be steady, endure suffering, do the work of an evangelist, fulfill your ministry—In contrast to false teachers and false listeners. *As for you:* cf. 3:10, 14 and discussions. Whatever other people do, whether false teachers or their dupes, Timothy must "go on being sober in everything." Some scholars take this to mean that Timothy should avoid the potent drink of the new doctrines. But was he ever in danger of adopting them? It is more natural to think of an exhortation to "keep his head" in all circumstances; even if he sees the church flooded with error; even if the time comes when the congregation refuses to listen to him any more. Do not panic; do not go to extremes; do not make wild decisions; do not take offense and act in anger. This seems to be the spirit of the apostle's words. There is a corresponding thought in his call to the Thessalonians, "let us be sober" (1 Thess. 5:6, 8). Similarly both "a bishop" and "the women" should be "temperate" (see on 1 Tim. 3:2, 11).

The letter now proceeds to three sharp, staccato commands which sum up the life of Timothy as it should be: *endure—do—fulfill.* Paul was in a strong position from which to tell Timothy to *endure suffering,* because he himself was doing so (see on 2:9). There is perhaps no *suffering* so painful as that which comes to a man when his own congregation turns against him, especially if he has been a faithful preacher and minister of the Word and his people are rejecting both it and him. Timothy must brace himself for this and indeed for any eventuality. It had not yet happened, though already there were causes of suffering. One of the minister's hardest tasks is to deal with self-opinionated men who wish to instruct the church in their false and sometimes foolish doctrines. Controversies breed quarrels

(2:23), and the minister must not be quarrelsome (2:24). The attitude which he adopts often means a drain on his spiritual energies, and this in turn brings suffering. For the sake of the gospel he must *endure* it (1:8; 2:3 and discussions), forewarned by the knowledge that all who desire to live a godly life in Christ Jesus will be persecuted (3:12 and discussion). In telling Timothy at this point to *endure suffering* Paul did not think it necessary to repeat himself and dwell again on the means by which he might so endure. It may be assumed that some people need no reminder of the power of God as their aid (1:7 f. and discussion), if already told.

In the meantime, even if the time had not yet come when people would not endure sound teaching, Timothy was to endure suffering and *do the work of an evangelist*. In passing, it should be noticed that the church which rejected the teaching and the gospel was really rejecting the gift of Christ. The ascended Lord gave evangelists and teachers to his church. They are, strictly speaking, the gifts of Christ and not the hired employees of the church. The teacher teaches the teaching or the doctrine of Christ; the *evangelist* preaches the evangel, the gospel, in order that men may receive it and believe. This Timothy was to do. (Cf. Eph. 4:11.)

Some people seem to think that all an *evangelist* does is to talk. In one sense this may be true, though it is not mere chatter. The gift of speech is from above, and the New Testament sometimes uses the word "utterance." ". . . the Spirit gave them utterance." "Peter . . . lifted up his voice and 'uttered' to them." "But Paul said, '. . . I am "uttering" the sober truth' " (Acts 2:4, 14; 26:25). Paul however when exhorting Timothy did not emphasize speech. To preach the gospel is *work*. This should arrest those who cynically say that the minister merely "talks." Just as the deeds of Jesus were words in action (they had a message) and his words had the effects of deeds, so the words of the *evangelist* have mighty power (cf. 1 Thess. 1:5) and accomplish much. His words are *work*. The activity of visitation and counseling is not ruled out, but we have only to imagine what would happen if a dumb evangelist came to a city to realize the importance of speech. The preacher's uttered sermon is *work*.

In all his pastoral care; in all his concern to guard the flock from the poison of heresy and from the controversies which are the very reverse of edification; in all the responsibility of teaching and appointing other men to the work of teaching in order that the deposit may be guarded and the message be spread more widely; in all this Timothy was not to forget the necessity of giving the Word to those who had never heard it, that they too might enter the kingdom and enjoy the salvation which is in Christ. The combination of pastoral care and evangelistic outreach suggests both the uniqueness of Timothy's position and the fluidity of the distinction between teacher and evangelist. And in spite of his uniqueness, in some respects Timothy is very like the minister of today. He shepherds the flock and he seeks to bring the wanderer home. There is a wholesomeness about the dual task: new converts are not left untended and the church is not shut off from the world in a secret corner.

A clue to the meaning of *fulfill your ministry* is afforded by thinking of an unfulfilled ministry. It raises pictures of tasks undone, unattempted, even unimagined. Timothy must do everything which, as a minister of Christ, he is called to do. It requires gifts of character, spirituality and conscientiousness. He must be loyal to the truth and must declare the whole counsel of God. His own character and life must commend the gospel which he preaches and teaches. He must maintain the spiritual glow of his own inner life. He should exercise his imagination to discern both needs and remedies. He may be something of an individualist and yet should be able to work with other men. His ideal and aim is to be able to say to the Lord "at that day" that "what you commanded has been done" (Luke 14:22).

2. The Threshold of Glory (4:6–8)

Paul looks back over his own part in the common fight of faith and forward to the reward which will be shared by those who have longed for the Lord's coming. The luster of glory is thrown back onto the exhortations and forward onto the next sections.

Verse 6: For I am already on the point of being sacrificed; the time of my departure has come: Death is an act of worship. This is implied in the apostle's choice of metaphor. The verse begins with a contrast. Timothy was contrasted with false teachers and false listeners (v. 5); in the present verse it is the two different situations which come to the fore. The pronoun *I* is emphatic, and both contrast and emphasis can be brought out thus: "As for you, . . . fulfill your ministry. As for me, (do what I say) *for I am already* . . ."

The reference to *being sacrificed* needs to be clarified. It is not the businessman's "giving up" ("goods sold at sacrifice"), nor is it the ambitious man's policy of scorning delights and living laborious days. It is quite impossible for Paul to be alluding to the Jewish belief that the death of a martyr had atoning value. (Evidence for the belief is to be found in 4 Maccabees 6:27–30; 17:20–22.) Paul's actual words are, "I am already being poured out as a libation, a drink-offering." Part of the preliminary ritual of certain sacrifices was the pouring out of wine at the altar (cf. Exod. 29:40; Num. 28:7). On the other hand, at the Feast of Tabernacles water was poured out on the altar after the morning sacrifice on each of the first seven days of the festival (see the Jewish tractate, Sukkah IV 1, 9). The apostle has not written with precision. He emphasized the "pouring out," no more, and it is part of worship. If we dwell on the preliminary aspect, then death is to be regarded as the real beginning of worship. (Cf. Rev. 4:10; 22:3–5.) If we think of the libation as coming after the sacrifice, then death is the climax of earthly worship. Philippians 2:17 points in this direction, but it should not be pressed. A preacher's illustration repeated after a matter of years need not be an exact repetition.

It is plain that the end was near. *Already* Paul was being poured out and *the time of my departure* is "standing by" (see on v. 2). His head was not actually on the block but it soon would be. The metaphors for death are of pastoral value. The world sees merely the end of life, even a gallows or execution by beheading. When Stephen was violently stoned, Luke saw it as the experience of being put to sleep (Acts 7:60). Who put him to sleep? The ingressive aorist tense and the passive voice suggest that it can only be one—Jesus. *Departure (analusis—*cf. *analuō,* Phil. 1:23) may be used of a ship which weighs anchor or casts off, or of men who "strike camp" by taking down their tents and continuing their journey. The ship reminds us of the other shore; the tents, even those of the vacationists, tell us of the temporary nature of our life. The best is yet to be!

Verse 7: I have fought the good fight, I have finished the race, I have kept the faith: The backward look of confidence, not pomposity. The operative word is *the.* "I have fought a good fight," the rendering of KJV, has done harm to the apostle's reputation, giving rise to accusations of self-esteem, conceit and complacency, even of pomposity. He meant that he had taken his part in the fight which is common to all Christians (see on 1 Tim. 6:12) and that his "fighting days" were now over, not because of retirement but because of imminent death. He merely varied the metaphor when he added that *I have finished the race.* A man does not go on running when he has breasted the tape. The implication is that Paul had now finished what Timothy was still doing.

There is a sense in which a Christian can make even *the good fight,* the common fight, his own. Years earlier Paul had said that he did not set any value on his own life, his purpose being that "I may accomplish my course and the ministry which I received from the Lord Jesus . . ." (Acts 20:24). His purpose was now fulfilled and "my course," "my race," is identified as *the race* which all Christians run. (The Greek word, *dromos,* is the same in both texts.)

The three Greek verbs in verse 7 are all in the perfect tense and may be reinterpreted in the present. The meaning is thus: *"The good fight* is over —for me. (I have memories of the Lord's mercy and faithfulness. I know the power of his Word and Spirit.) *The race* is over—for me." Paul is at the end; he has not fallen by the wayside because he had not run "aimlessly" but had kept his body in subjection; he is not "disqualified" (cf. 1 Cor. 9:26 f.). Timothy would surely feel the challenge and the inspiration of the veteran's words. He surely heard the call afresh as an echo: "fulfill your ministry" (v. 5). Keep fighting; keep on running!

This is relatively clear. Not so obvious is the reinterpretation of *I have kept the faith.* It seems to mean that *the faith* is intact in my hands. It has not been lost through carelessness, abandoned through frivolity, neglected through underestimation. The deposit has been guarded and is still safe. If Timothy were to draw the inferences he would tell himself that all that Paul had ever told him about *the faith* still held good. No amendment was to be made. He would know further that *the faith* wore well. It had suffered many stresses during the apostle's arduous and dangerous life. It had not failed him. And Paul was still believing. He has *kept the faith* up to the very moment of writing. It will see him through his last painful adventure, fortify him as he faces what is unknown to men apart from *the faith* and prepare him and sustain him for meeting his Master. Indeed it will encourage him, as the next verse shows.

Paul's personality was a strong one and his determination was great. But the ultimate secret of his ability to *have kept the faith* did not lie in his own mental and spiritual resources. He kept it because he himself was kept (John 17:11–15; 1 Thess. 5:23). Timothy was "taking over," and many were the duties to be done. But he had a testimony to encourage him: *the faith* had been tried and proved and he himself still possessed it in its wholeness. It would see him through.

Verse 8: Henceforth there is laid up for me the crown of righteousness, which the Lord, the righteous judge, will award to me on that Day, and not only to me but also to all who have loved his appearing: Individual, personal religion and confidence in a context of fellowship. This is not the presumption of an individual who has a high estimate of himself but the eager and believing anticipation of the climax of grace. *There is laid up* is the language of storage. In a storehouse or barn ample goods may be *laid up* (cf. Luke 12:19). Better than "goods" is "the hope laid up for you in heaven" (Col 1:5) which the Colossians had heard about when the gospel was preached to them. The apostle was feeding on the bread of life which he had given to others. He himself lived by the faith which he preached. If we say that something is laid up or is "in store," it is a natural question to ask who did in fact store it away. A similar question can be asked about "the kingdom prepared for you from the foundation of the world" (Matt. 25:34). Who prepared it? There can be but one answer. God prepared it, the entrance to it is Christ, and the right to stay in it is Christ, for he is both our mediator and our hope (1 Tim. 1:1; 2:5).

In particular *the crown of righteousness* is in store. The allusion is to the victor's *crown* at the games (cf. 1 Tim. 4:7 f. and 2 Tim. 2:5 and discussions), but it is only an illustrative allusion. Paul was not thinking of the crown of athletics but of *the crown of righteousness*. (For the last word see on 1 Tim. 6:11.) *The crown* is the final recognition of the *righteousness* of the believer. It recognizes it as imputed, that is, after death the justified sinner remains justified. And it recognizes it as achieved; it recognizes effort. Even this is not the sole work of the believer. He has to fight and strive indeed, but he knows that his labor is not in vain and that thanksgiving is due to God who keeps on giving us the victory through our Lord Jesus Christ (cf. 1 Cor. 15:57 f.). The reward is thus of grace and it comes from the Lord, from Jesus. This is proved by the reference to *his appearing* (cf. 1:10; 4:1 and discussions). *The righteous judge* will make no mistakes with regard to either fact or value. He knows all the circumstances of every life and even the secrets of men's hearts. He "is to judge the living and the dead" (4:1) *on that Day* (see on 1:12, 18). He is *righteous* and can recognize *righteousness* when he sees it, both imputed and inspired or "achieved."

Paul was not thinking of a special apostolic reward and still less of a special reward for himself from which others would be excluded. It is for *all who have loved his appearing.* This expression does not refer to those who have ardently speculated about the date of the Second Advent but to those who with steady faith have looked forward with joy to meeting the absent object of their faith and love. ". . . we would rather be away from the body and at home with the Lord" (2 Cor. 5:8). The preference ("rather") corresponds to the love of his *appearing*. The perfect tense of *who have loved* suggests a steadily burning flame which has continued from its original outburst up to the present moment. Contrast verse 10.

His appearing can be *loved* only by those who believe in him. Their love is an expression of their authentic faith. It is clear that when they receive their final *award* the purpose of election will have been achieved. God did not elect and carry out his purpose mechanically; nor did he elect and allow himself to be frustrated. He elected; redeemed; called and justified; and will glorify. See discussion on 2:10.

3. Several Requests (4:9-13)

Paul asks Timothy to come quickly, bringing Mark with him. Only Luke is with him now. He asks for the cloak, the books and especially the parchments, all of which Timothy would have no difficulty in identifying.

Verse 9: Do your best to come to me soon: The heart of the apostle is laid bare. He could stand alone, if need be, and die alone; but he craved companionship, which is no discredit to him. In Gethsemane our Lord desired his disciples to watch "with me" (Matt. 26:38, 40). Apart from the natural desire of any man in such a situation not to be alone, Paul was longing to see his son in the faith (1:4; see the discussion there for the fellowship between the older and the younger man). The longing is now no longer merely mentioned. *Do your best to come* is a command, though not quite like one of the directives in these epistles. It is an urgent personal request, repeated in verse 21.

It would take a few months for the letter to reach Timothy and for him to reach the apostle. It would seem therefore that the directives in the epistle are long term: the young man has a long ministry before him at Ephesus. The situation there envisaged is not so serious that he must remain on the spot. Even in "difficult" churches the minister is able to take a vacation. Timothy could visit Paul and risk absence from Ephesus. The "faithful men" (2:2) there could hold the fort until his return. And Paul might not have been so close to death that Timothy's journey would prove fruitless. The "first defense" (v. 16) was over and legal proceedings could still continue.

Do your best implies that Timothy should lose no time. Delay must be avoided: he should leave at once and travel with speed. He should spare no pains: inconveniences, difficulties and hardships should be overcome because of the seriousness of the matter. Though he would, and no doubt should, remember the church left behind for the time being, for the moment the journey should be his dominant interest. He should be eager to cover the ground and *to come to me soon.* See further on 2:15. We may perhaps see in *do your best* a call to a particular act of ministry and an example of the pursuit of righteousness and love (cf. 1 Tim. 6:11).

Verse 10: For Demas, in love with this present world, has deserted me and gone to Thessalonica; Crescens has gone to Galatia, Titus to Dalmatia: A double tragedy. A Christian was dazzled by the glitter of *this present world* and an apostle was *deserted.* The thought is that *Demas* fell *in love with this present world.* He may have been working up to it, may have felt the allure; but as Paul expressed it there was a moment of decision. Any resistance came to an end and off he went *to Thessalonica.* The separation was the outcome of the "falling in love."

Demas can hardly be regarded as a prominent member of the group "who have loved his appearing" (v. 8). He had been caught by the transient and was forgetting the abiding; he had paid more attention to the seen than to the unseen (2 Cor. 4:18). It would be an instructive exercise for the student to attempt to assign Demas to his position in the Parable of the Sower (Matt. 13:18–23; Mark 4:14–20; Luke 8:11–15). Did he flee from affliction or did he seek the pleasant illusion of wealth? Had the Word been sown upon rocky ground or among thorns? Was he manifesting the wisdom of the sons of this world? (Cf. Luke 16:8.) With such wisdom Paul would never have seen the inside of a prison.

This present world is "this age" (*aiōn;* see discussions on 1 Tim. 1:17; 6:12, 17). The contrast is between "this age" and "the age to come." Through preoccupation with *this present world* Demas had *deserted* Paul. He had forsaken him, left him in the lurch—something which God never does (cf. 2 Cor. 4:9; Heb. 13:5). Demas was not guilty of apostasy but of failure in discipleship. His "downward path" may be traced or expounded by an arrangement of texts. 1. Demas, a fellow worker of Paul, sends greetings (Philem. 24). 2. Demas (just the name—no "fellow worker") sends greetings (Col. 4:14). 3. Demas . . . *has deserted me.* It is possible to wonder if jealousy moved him by the presence of "Luke the beloved physician." The later careers (after Col. 4:14) of the two men, Luke and Demas, invite comparison. Each Christian worker showed such promise. It is not possible to tell why it was to Thessalonica that Demas went. It may have corresponded to the modern "call to a better church" and to a more congenial setting. for ministry. Or it may have been sheer worldliness, the desire for more amenities and more money in a secular trade. In either case the fault lay not in going to the "better church" or to the "business promotion" but in doing it when he did. A bigger man would have waited until Paul's case had been settled. The sting lies in the word *deserted.* It was because of his keen feeling that he had been left in the lurch that Paul appealed so urgently to Timothy *to come to me soon. For* the fellow worker on whom he relied had failed him.

*Crescen*s enters the New Testament in this verse and at the same time leaves it. Little is known of him. The name as printed is Latin and is not frequent in Greek. His absence is regretted by the apostle, so it seems, because it heightens his isolation; but he does not seem to blame him. He is not in the same category as Demas. *Galatia* is well attested though a few good manuscripts read "Gallia," Gaul. Such a variant reading supports the view that *Galatia* here indeed means Gaul. It was so used until well into the Christian era, and from the beginning commentators have understood *Galatia* as Gaul (France—cf. Theodor Zahn, *Introduction to the New Testament* 2: 25, n8). The other Galatia was more fully described by such an addition as "in Asia." The church was spreading towards the West.

Titus had been recalled from Crete (Titus 1:5; 3:12) and had gone *to Dalmatia,* the southern part of the Roman province of Illyricum (cf. Rom. 15:19), the modern Yugoslavia. The leader is in prison; a worker defects; but the work is of God and must go on. And it does go on: the Word of God is not bound (2:9).

Verse 11: Luke alone is with me. Get Mark and bring him with you; for he is very useful in serving me: Two tributes. *Luke* is the beloved physician and Paul's fellow worker (Col 4:14; Philem. 24). He wrote the Third Gospel and the Acts of the Apostles and was an intimate companion of the apostle. A study of the "we-sections" of the Acts is recommended. (They are listed in the discussion on 1 Tim. 5:18.) He was an educated Greek with a flair for his

own language: he could write good Greek and also "Septuagint" Greek; and
he was a skilled historian (Luke 1:1-4). He must be one of the most self-
effacing Christians on record. There are only three entries under his name in
Moulton and Geden's *Concordance to the Greek Testament* (p. 606). And
yet, to the sympathetic reader, he is a real person. Part of the explanation for
his being the beloved physician lies in his self-effacing loyalty. He *alone is
with me*. The presence of Timothy would bring added refreshment to Paul;
and a third man would relieve *Luke* of some duties.

Mark must have been under religious influences from comparatively early
days, for a prayer meeting took place in his home (Acts 12:12; cf. 2 Tim.
1:5; 3:15). He may have been the young man in the linen cloth (Mark 14:51
f.). He joined Barnabas and Saul (Acts 12:25) and went with them on Paul's
first missionary journey (Acts 13:5) either to make himself generally useful
or as a sort of "junior clergyman" and "minister of the word" (Luke 1:2).
He left them before the journey had been completed (Acts 13:13) and
returned to Jerusalem, presumably to his mother's home. In the eyes of Paul
he was accordingly in disgrace, and when Paul refused to take the risk of his
presence on the second journey, he went off with Barnabas (Acts 15:36-41).

Reconciliation followed: Paul told the Colossians to receive Mark (Col.
4:10), and he conveyed his greetings to them. He also called him his fellow
worker (Philem. 24). His association with Barnabas is well known: they were
cousins. It is not so often remembered, though the reader who has looked up
the references may have noticed it, that Mark and Luke were associated. It is
fascinating—and frustrating—to speculate whether the two authors of Gospels
ever discussed their work.

Paul's words imply a tribute to Luke for loyalty and to Mark (a repentant
Demas?) for being *very useful in serving me*. The service may include
"ministry." The assumption that Mark would be willing to come may well be
a tribute to his courage. He was called "my son" by Peter (1 Pet. 5:13) and
is traditionally his interpreter, embodying his reminiscences in his Gospel
(cf. Eusebius 3. 39. 15).

This was not the age of the automobile, but the spirit of *Get Mark* is
brought out by our everyday remark, "I'll pick you up on my way to the
station." Timothy must first "pick up" Mark and then *bring him with you*.
The same Greek verb is used in the Septuagint version of Genesis 45:27.
"When Jacob saw the wagons which Joseph had sent to pick him up . . . ."
Similarly the soldiers picked up Paul and brought him . . . (Acts 23:23
f., 31). It is not of course suggested that Timothy had a vehicle. To this very
day a man can say, "I'll pick you up at the entrance and take you up to the
dining room."

Verse 12: Tychicus I have sent to Ephesus—to replace Timothy. This
seems to be a reasonable assumption. The verb may be an epistolary aorist.
Greek views such cases from the standpoint of the receiver of the letter. We,
on the contrary, think of the present moment when we are writing. The correct
translation would therefore be "I am sending *Tychicus*." He probably carried
the letter to Timothy with him. If he were to replace Timothy he would no
doubt have the supervision of the "faithful men" to whom reference has been
made (v. 9).

Tychicus had traveled with Paul, probably as a delegate of his church bearing their contribution to Jerusalem (Acts 20:4–6; cf. 1 Cor. 16:3 f.). He was an Asian Christian and knew Timothy as they were both accompanying Paul. In some sense he was the apostle's representative and probably his letter carrier to the Ephesians and the Colossians (Eph. 6:21 f.; Col. 4:7 f.). He is described as a beloved brother, faithful minister and fellow servant. He had the gift of *paraklēsis,* of "persuasion with authority" (see discussion on 1 Tim. 1:3 and further references). He might have been sent to Crete to replace Titus (Titus 3:12). He was clearly a trusted lieutenant.

We might wonder why Paul did not keep Tychicus with him and let Mark go to Ephesus. Apart from the desirability of new fellowship with the rehabilitated Mark, to say nothing of the joy and the witness, Tychicus was more suitable. As an Asian he would be on his home ground and could assess the local situation better. A Jew, like Mark, who hailed from Jerusalem might bring problems as well as solve them. Is a Texan the best person to handle Texans? In any case Tychicus would not be coming as a stranger if he had previously taken a letter to Ephesus and had encouraged the Christians there. There may be more in this Pauline move than meets the eye. The apostle may have known of a warm welcome awaiting his emissary and may have had the prospect of a fruitful ministry.

Verse 13: When you come, bring the cloak that I left with Carpus at Troas, also the books, and above all the parchments: An indication of Timothy's route. From Ephesus he would go northwards to *Troas* and from there take ship to Macedonia (cf. Acts 16:8–12). He could cross Macedonia by the Via Egnatia and then sail to Brundisium (Brindisi) in Italy. It was at Troas that Paul had had the vision of the man of Macedonia and Timothy was there at the time. Timothy may even have taken a small part in the discussions following the vision. It was Paul who had seen the vision, but it was "we" who at once sought to go on into Macedonia (cf. Acts 16:3, 10). We can only guess at Timothy's thoughts at the prospect of retracing an earlier route. The first time he was a member of a team whose purpose was to preach Christ. Now he would be alone and he would serve Christ by ministering to the Lord's aged servant in his need.

Timothy was again with Paul in Troas (Acts 20:4–6) when Eutychus fell down from the third story. The energy of the apostle was remarkable. Paul prolonged his speech until midnight, was interrupted by the death and restoration of Eutychus, resumed his talk and continued until daybreak "and so departed" (Acts 20:7, 11). Now he was languishing in prison and likely to feel the cold. (Cf. also 2 Cor. 2:12 f.) Timothy could still serve Christ by aiding the Lord's servant, but now the nature of his service would be changed. He would minister to him in his weakness rather than in his strength.

Paul's arrest or departure under arrest may have taken him by surprise or at any rate prevented him from settling all his affairs. This may explain the property *left with Carpus.* He is otherwise unknown. A kindly deed has brought him the immortality of a place in the New Testament.

The *cloak* was in shape rather like an ecclesiastical surplice. Its material was heavy and thick, a good protection from cold and rain. Winter was on its way (v. 21). The request is touching, especially when we remember that it had to be brought from such a distance. Were there no Roman friends to care for him (cf. v. 16)?

The books may be interpreted in two ways. The singular (*biblion*) is
used of "the book of the prophet Isaiah" (Luke 4:17) which Jesus "closed"
(ptuxas) after reading (v. 20). It was thus a scroll which he rolled up. Paul
may therefore have been asking for some Old Testament Scriptures which he
had left behind. On the other hand the term *biblion* can describe "a certif-
icate" of divorce (Matt. 19:7; Mark 10:4; cf. Deut. 24:1, LXX). This means
a document rather than a book and Paul may have been thinking of private
correspondence, letters to him from various churches, or some papers needed
for his defense. On the whole, the meaning of *the books* seems best covered
by the expression "books, etc." A person who sends for his possessions
(which can be carried by one man on a journey) may easily ask for "that
small box of books and things."

Above all, "especially," is used by Paul of a group which is part of a larger
group. Thus God is the Savior of all men, especially (within the group of
"all") of those who believe (1 Tim. 4:10; cf. 5:8, 17; Titus 1:10). Paul
thus wanted the "books, etc." and if a selection had to be made from them,
the priority must be given to *the parchments.*

The latter term probably means a codex or book, the pages of which consisted of animal skin or vellum. Paul might well have cherished as a treasure
certain parts of the Old Testament. If this were his residuary estate it was
little enough; it reminds us of the few silver spoons left by John Wesley. Some
think *the parchments* consisted of Paul's stock of blank "pages," and that he
planned further writing. When he could not preach to people he would write
to them and for them. It is a suggestive and moving thought. But how was
he able to write to Timothy? Had his stock run out now? We do not know.
The theory is not so convincing as the view that he treasured a book or two
of the Old Testament. It is a fair inference that this invincible man, if it came
to it, preferred the Old Testament Scriptures to bodily warmth.

4. A Warning (4:14–15)

Timothy is told to beware of a certain Alexander who had given great
resistance to Paul's message. No trace of vindictiveness is to be seen in the
apostle's attitude.

*Verse 14: Alexander the coppersmith did me great harm; the Lord will
requite him for his deeds:* Two objective statements of fact. The first concerns
the past: he *did me great harm.* No details are given, but *Alexander* seems to
have acted from motives of personal hostility. The same Greek expression is
used in Genesis 50:15, LXX, for the evil actions of Joseph's brothers against
him. It is significant that a few verses later (v. 20) Joseph told his brothers
that they had meant evil "against me." This must be hostility.

Alexander was a common name, and identification, by us at any rate, is
precarious, though he was obviously well known to Timothy. Some see in him
the Jew of the same name mentioned in Acts 19:33 f. This is attractive, but
solely because it shows an *Alexander* in Ephesus. He might have nursed a
grievance against Paul for years. Others turn their attention to the man who
had rejected conscience, had made shipwreck of his faith, and had been dis-
ciplined by Paul (1 Tim. 1:19 f.). This is more convincing though the
identification cannot be proved. The *great harm* might have been done to

Paul at the time of the excommunication or afterwards as an act of revenge. The two references can refer to one and the same man only if we assume that the Jew was converted and later had the relapse. Whoever he was, he was a dangerous opponent to a preacher (v. 15).

The second statement of fact looks to the future: *the Lord will requite him.* The rendering of the KJV, "the Lord reward him," is based on an inferior Greek text (optative mode instead of indicative) and is unfortunate. It makes Paul's words the expression of a wish, and he can be accused accordingly of vindictiveness. This is not the spirit in which he wrote. He was stating what in fact would happen. It is important to notice two ways in which even future fact could be stated. A man could say, *"the Lord will requite him.* Good! That will teach him!" This is as vindictive as a wish, perhaps even more so, because it is certain that the wish will be fulfilled. On the other hand the apostle meant this: *"The Lord will requite him.* It is not for me to seek revenge for personal injury. The matter may be safely left in the Lord's hands. I will repay no one *harm* for *harm* (cf. Rom. 12:17. *Harm* and 'evil' both render the Greek *kakos*). It is *the Lord* alone who can say, 'I will repay' " (Rom. 12:19). This is both personally and theologically consistent. The forgiven sinner has no right to appoint himself judge (cf. 1 Tim. 1:13).

This was not the first time Paul had spoken like this. He had told the Romans that God would reward a man according to his works or *deeds* (Rom. 2:6). This is virtually a quotation from Psalm 61:13, LXX; Proverbs 24:12, LXX. (The reference in RSV is Ps. 62:12.) Our Lord knew the Old Testament teaching and his words approximate it (Matt. 16:27).

The Greek verb rendered by *requite* in the verse under discussion, by "repay" in Matthew 16:27, and by "award" in 2 Timothy 4:8, conveys the idea of "giving back." For some it means the crown of righteousness; for some, punishment or a scantier reward. The uses in verses 8 and 14 represent two sides of the same coin. The Father will "reward" (same Greek) good deeds (Matt. 6:4, 6, 18). Cf. Romans 2:6–8, where God will "render" (same Greek) eternal life or wrath and fury.

Verse 15: Beware of him yourself, for he strongly opposed our message: No vindictiveness does not mean no warning. Paul had summed up the many evils done to him by Alexander the coppersmith in an aorist tense, "did." Now he told Timothy to "keep on being on your guard against" him. He also (*yourself*) must do this, as well as Paul. Paul might be able to handle him; Timothy might find himself out of his depth. Be forewarned! This again is not vindictiveness but is written in the interests of the kingdom of God. It reveals the apostle not only as a man with a memory but as a judge of character. What Alexander had already done he could attempt to do again. If therefore Timothy hears of his approach it might be best to avoid him. If an encounter takes place he must be ready for anything. Even to know that Alexander is in the district should put him on the alert.

This raises the whole question of judging. Christians have been told to "judge not, that you be not judged" (Matt. 7:1). Could Paul be accused of judging Alexander? The answer is that he did not set himself up as a judge and was not acting censoriously. As we saw in considering the previous verse, he left him in the hands of the Lord. On the other hand he could not deny the evidence of his own eyes. He had suffered much harm at the hands of Alexander, and he ascribed it to him not because some gossip had told him that Alexander was at the bottom of all his troubles but because *he . . . opposed our message.*

There can be no doubt that the problem was a serious one. Alexander had done great harm, "many evils." *Strongly* implies a very high degree of intensity. His opposition was a deliberate policy, not a momentary flash of anger. It was consistent and continued, not sporadic or spasmodic. It was implacable and not half-hearted. Any evangelist or preacher who ran into trouble like this, whether he was engaged in an itinerant ministry or was a local pastor, would be justified in warning his fellow preachers of the difficulties they would be likely to meet.

There is precedent for this "judging," if judging it is. Our Lord told his disciples to beware of the leaven of the Pharisees and of Herod; he taught his hearers to beware of the scribes (Mark 8:15; 12:38–40) and of the leaven of the Sadducees (Matt. 16:6). Pharisees and scribes stand for hypocrisy and ostentation (cf. Luke 12:1), a religion which is all show with a concentration on detail and a forgetfulness of weighty principles (Matt. 23:23). The Sadducees are the representatives of materialism (Acts 23:8), what we should call the religion of rationalism. Herod is a mixture of second-hand religion (Matt. 2:8) and no religion (Matt. 2:16). Of all such men and their permeating influence beware! And beware also of false prophets with their deceptive harmlessness (Matt. 7:15 f.) and indeed of men generally (Matt. 10:17). Paul did not "judge" but knew Alexander the coppersmith from his fruits.

Alexander's strong opposition was directed against *our message,* "our words." This is not a silent rejection of the gospel but an active contradiction both of its content and its proclamation. It may cover personal "heckling," incitement to violence, false information given to authorities, or some action leading to the apostle's arrest or his continued detention. Anything which impedes the preacher is ultimately opposition to the *message. Our* may refer to Paul himself or he may be associating others with him. Paul the preacher was the spearhead. The enormity of the offense of opposing the gospel recalls 1 Thessalonians 2:16.

5. Alone But Not Alone (4:16–18)

When Paul was first brought before the court he had no advocate and no one came to support him with his presence. But the Lord stood by him and enabled him thus to set forth fully the gospel message at the center of the world. On that occasion Paul was delivered from the immediate danger. The same Lord will deliver him from all evil in the salvation of the heavenly kingdom. Eternal glory is ascribed to the Lord.

Verse 16: At my first defense no one took my part; all deserted me. May it not be charged against them: Isolation without bitterness. The *first defense* is not the defense which must have been given at the time of the first imprisonment (Acts 28:30 f.). The occasion was the opening part of the trial during the second imprisonment. This was a preliminary investigation which was adjourned; Paul was facing a future appearance in court, and proceedings might drag on for some time.

At the first appearance Paul had been alone. *No one* turned up from the church in Rome to give him support, either as advocate or as witness. This is one of the mysteries of early Christianity. There were those who did not look with favor on the apostle (Phil. 1:15, 17). Apart from such people, were the rest diffident or afraid? They may have been pessimistic and unwilling to make their own position even more dangerous. It is a sad episode in the life of the church to which Paul had sent his great epistle.

All deserted me: They did what Demas had done (v. 10). Paul did not say that they had fallen in love with this present world, but what he did say reveals his spirit. He felt their absence keenly but he did not say that every member was a Demas. On the contrary he prayed that their neglect would *not be charged against them.* He here used the same Greek verb as he had earlier used when he said that "God was . . . not counting their trespasses against them" (2 Cor. 5:19). His prayer follows that of Jesus (Luke 23:34) and of Stephen (Acts 7:60). He obviously regarded the Roman omission as a sin. In his thinking the matter had not yet been closed. It had not yet been *charged against them.* It is a testimony not only to the character of Paul but to the nature of God. The Lord is slow to anger. To use popular language, Paul was hoping that the Recording Angel would not put pen to paper—he had not yet started to write.

The prayer of Jesus for the forgiveness of those who were crucifying him stands alone. It sums up in speech what he was doing in action on the cross. Stephen and Paul were not dying for the sins of the world, but apart from that crucial difference they were following in Jesus' steps (1 Pet. 2:21). And yet there was a difference between them. Stephen was forgiving his enemies; Paul was forgiving his friends. The persecutors of Stephen were in no sense in fellowship with him, certainly not in any deep sense. They were human beings indeed and Jews by birth and nominal religion, but they shared no common life and faith with him (Acts 6:11–14). The Roman Christians and Paul were disciples of the same Lord. Therein lies the poignancy. The bitterest of wars are civil wars, with citizen fighting against citizen, comrade against comrade, though both should be together in a common allegiance. The Roman Christians failed their own fellow believer—and he forgave them.

If any man had any doubt about the spirit in which Paul wrote verse 14, he should be reassured from the present verse.

Verse 17: But the Lord stood by me and gave me strength to proclaim the word fully, that all the Gentiles might hear it. So I was rescued from the lion's mouth: Human absence, divine presence. When the Roman Christians failed to appear, *the Lord stood by* his servant. In a sense, as J. Jeremias sees, *the Lord* was his "legal adviser" (p. 59). This is unexpected. Paul might have hoped for an advocate, a defending attorney. Instead he had no one to speak for him but he did have one who spoke to him. A legal adviser advises, and the promise given by Jesus was fulfilled: "And when they bring you to trial and deliver you up, do not be anxious beforehand what you are to say; but say whatever is given to you in that hour, for it is not you who speak, but the Holy Spirit" (Mark 13:11; cf. Matt. 10:19 f.). The Lord *gave* him *strength* so that he was able to conduct his own defense. This was more than physical strength or intellectual acumen. It was spiritual power. The Greek verb (*endunamoō*) is used also in Acts 9:22; Philippians 4:13; 1 Timothy 1:12;

2 Timothy 2:1, and it recalls the power with which Paul had preached at Thessalonica (1 Thess. 1:5).

Paul was absorbed in his message. Any legal minutiae, even though relevant, took second place in his thinking. The Lord had empowered him for one purpose, that "through me the proclamation might be completed and *all the Gentiles . . . hear it.*" This was the climax of Paul's ministry (Acts 9:15; 23:11; 27:24). He turned his speech of defense into a sermon, the dock in which he stood into a pulpit. In the best sense of the word he was an opportunist. He was both "in season and out of season" (v. 2). In the crowd which attended the trial we may see the representatives of *all the Gentiles.* Both at the time and in the subsequent gossip the gospel was made known to men. The Word had come to the capital. Not only were there saints in Caesar's household (Phil. 4:22); the Word was preached in his court.

There is an illustration of Paul's opportunism from modern secular life. A generation ago certain political trials took place in Europe, and a defendant in the dock fearlessly made known his political doctrines and thus found a platform from which he could address all Europe. So today in the United Nations a speaker can reach the whole world, however his words may be chosen. They may be quite irrelevant to the subject under discussion, but he still has his platform. (Cf. Luke 16:8.) Within narrower limits, some Christians who were prisoners of war in Germany in World War II were denied the privilege of preaching but obtained permission to hold "meetings for discussion." They were delighted at the opportunity—which they took— of preaching Christ.

The lion's mouth from which Paul *was rescued* reminds us of the Roman amphitheater and the fate of persecuted Christians. But as a Roman citizen he would be beheaded. The phrase is a stock expression for great peril (cf. Ps. 22:21). As a result of the Lord's aid whereby he preached with power, his case was adjourned and he *was rescued* from immediate execution.

Verse 18: The Lord will rescue me from every evil and save me for his heavenly kingdom. To him be the glory for ever and ever. Amen: Eternal praise for an eternal rescue. The apostle had been delivered once, by the mercy of God. He had not yet been condemned in the earthly court. But when his case came on again he had little doubt about its outcome (cf. vv. 6–8). With the prospect of men doing their worst he lifted his eyes to the eternal salvation which he had in Christ. *The Lord will* indeed *rescue* him. He will be delivered *from every evil* which man can do to him. *Every evil* plan or device and *every evil* deed which may be its expression will leave his soul intact. *The Lord . . . will save* him and bring him into *his heavenly kingdom.* Paul was already a member of the kingdom but he looked towards its final consummation. His position in it corresponds to "the crown of righteousness" which is "laid up" for him (v. 8).

Notice that the apostle is already saved and still will be saved. See the discussion on 1:9 and from there trace the further references and discussions. For *kingdom* see discussion on 2 Timothy 4:1. Black though the immediate earthly prospect is, the nearness of *his heavenly kingdom* moves Paul to his depths. From his heart arises the doxology, *to him be the glory . . . . Glory* belongs to God. The Greek has no verb and we may say "*to him* is *the glory*" as well as *be the glory.* If we emphasize the *be,* we should say that the apostle calls on men to ascribe *glory* to God; to ascribe to him his being, his character, his majesty and his might. (See discussion on 1 Tim. 1:11.) Two other doxologies are given in the Pastoral Epistles, a shorter one (1 Tim. 1:17) and an apparently short one which in spirit is much longer (1 Tim. 6:15 f.). The discussions should be consulted.

IX. GREETINGS AND FAREWELL (4:19–22)

Greetings are sent from Paul and others to Timothy and others expressing personal interest and association. There is a small item of news and a request for Timothy to come before winter. The epistle ends characteristically with grace.

Verse 19: Greet Prisca and Aquila, and the household of Onesiphorus: With danger around him and heaven before him, he can yet remember friends. *Prisca* or Priscilla *and Aquila* are frequently mentioned in this order. The wife may have been of higher rank than her husband or of a more thrustful personality. *Aquila* was a Jew who hailed from Pontus on the Black Sea (cf. 1 Pet. 1:1). They seem to have been very mobile—Rome, Corinth, Ephesus, Rome again and finally Ephesus. A good deal of information about them is compressed into a few verses (Acts 18:1–3, 18 f., 26; 1 Cor. 16:19; Rom. 16:3–5). (The last chapter of the Epistle to the Romans is thought by some to be addressed to Ephesus as an addition to a copy of the Roman letter. The theory is not conclusively proved. If it is true, it brings Prisca and Aquila to Ephesus earlier and perhaps bypasses Rome.) For *Onesiphorus* see on 1:16–18.

Verse 20: Erastus remained at Corinth; Trophimus I left ill at Miletus: Former comrades of Timothy. *Erastus* was the treasurer of the city of *Corinth,* where he naturally *remained.* Both he and Timothy sent greetings to the church at Rome (Rom. 16:21, 23). The name is a common one but there is just the possibility that he was the man who appears with Timothy in Paul's helpful retinue (Acts 19:22).

Trophimus was an Asian who, with Timothy and others, accompanied the apostle (Acts 20:4). He is also described as an Ephesian (Acts 21:29). He is of some importance today because he was *left ill at Miletus.* (Cf. Acts 20:17.) It is sometimes said by advocates of faith healing that "it is not the will of God for you to be ill." If the universal statement that illness is contrary to God's will is pressed, it is necessary to explain the apostle's ignorance—or his apparent ignorance—of the fact, and why, if he did indeed possess any kind of miraculous power, he did not heal Trophimus. He may have had very good reasons. It implies at least that great caution should be exercised when describing the divine attitude to illness. (Cf. 2 Cor. 12:9; Gal. 4:13.)

Verse 21: Do your best to come before winter. Eubulus sends greetings to you, as do Pudens and Linus and Claudia and all the brethren: Cold prospect and warm greetings. For *do your best* see on verse 9. It might have been an example of "now or never." The seas were not open all the year round, and if Timothy lost the last boat *before winter*, he might never see the apostle again. The date implied is late summer or early fall. *Eubulus* is a Greek name; the other three are Latin, a slight indication that Paul was writing from Rome. *Pudens* is quite unknown, like *Eubulus. Linus,* according to tradition (e.g., Eusebius 3. 4. 8), succeeded Peter as bishop of Rome. Eusebius obviously refers to the verse under discussion and confirms Irenaeus. (Cf. Eusebius 3. 2. 1; 5. 6. 1.) None of the four seem outstanding, though the presence of a woman is to be noticed. Is *Claudia* in any sense to be compared with the women at the cross and at the tomb?

It is doubtful if there is any serious contradiction with verses 11 and 16. They were not, like Luke, part of Paul's inner circle; and, like many simple, faithful members of a church today, would not think of "taking it upon themselves" to appear in court in the role of defender. It was the leaders and prominent members of the church of Rome, and any men of influence, who failed the apostle. In any case it is not necessary to assume that the four people mentioned were in close association with Paul. *All the brethren* could hardly have seen him frequently. What is more likely is that Luke suggested to Paul that he might send the greetings of the Roman Christians, after he had met with them. What could be more natural than for Roman believers, hearing from Luke that Paul was writing to Timothy, to say, "Tell him to 'say hello' to Timothy for us"?

Verse 22: The Lord be with your spirit. Grace be with you: A message for Timothy (*your spirit*) and for the church (*you* is plural). (See on 1 Tim. 6:21; 2 Tim. 1:2.) There is no verb in either sentence in the Greek.

Titus

INTRODUCTION

Titus

DATE

There is little to add by way of formal introduction to what has already been written in the introductions to the other Pastoral Epistles. They have been treated together, as they deserve, and they stand or fall together. The Second Epistle to Timothy is the latest of the three and was composed shortly before the apostle's death. The First Epistle is somewhat earlier, and the Epistle to Titus must be dated at about the same time. Beyond that it is hardly possible to go. We have to allow time for Paul's varied activities after his release from his first imprisonment. These seem to include a mission in Crete (1:5), though he had left the island when he wrote to Titus. We do not know the place from which he wrote. He had not yet arrived at Nicopolis (3:12). As he had decided to spend the winter there (not "here"), it is likely that he was writing in the late summer or early fall.

The absence of greater detail is disappointing, but it does not detract from the value of the epistle. In fact it almost orders us to concentrate on its subject matter, and to this we now turn. We must try to unravel its leading theological ideas.

THEOLOGY

The letter begins in the conventional form, though it is heavily weighted with doctrine. Paul is "a servant of God and an apostle of Jesus Christ" and has been entrusted with a message. This can only be the gospel, but our question is, how is it to be formulated?

The Gospel

It can be formulated. It is not a vague benevolence. Certain matters must not be taught and men have no right to teach them (1:11). Any man who persists in his obstinacy is to be admonished and left severely alone (3:10). The language of the teacher must be such as befits sound doctrine and must itself be sound (2:1, 8). It must surely be the Word of God (cf. 2:5).

In seeking a starting point for our formulation we may begin with a number of questions. The epistle speaks of the "knowledge of the truth." Is it important to know it? Do all men know it already, simply by being men? Reference is made to the "hope of eternal life." Do all men have it? If they do not, what is the reason? There are men who "reject the truth" (1:14). Are they wise

[227]

in doing so? What makes them reject it? We read of "God our Savior." Do we need one? The minds and consciences of some men are corrupted (1:15). Is something wrong?

Something is indeed wrong and Paul described it in some detail, out of his own experience and that of his fellow Christians. "We ourselves were once foolish, disobedient, led astray, slaves to various passions and pleasures, passing our days in malice and envy, hated by men and hating one another" (3:3). The education which grace gives trains us "to renounce irreligion and worldly passions" and suggests that we have lived the opposite of "sober, upright, and godly lives" (2:12). Paul summed it up in the term "iniquity," or "lawlessness." We were impure and far from being "zealous for good deeds" (2:14). We were "disobedient" to God and obedient, as slaves, to our own desires. We had failed to obey the first and great commandment, that we should love the Lord our God; and we had failed to obey the second, that we should love our neighbor as ourselves. We had fallen far short in godliness or piety; we had shown no deep and abiding righteousness.

Now God is the living God. He knows all that goes on and all the thoughts and secrets, motives and intentions of the human heart. He sees the deeds and he reads the heart. What he sees does not please him, for he has an attitude to men. Such people—and we Christians know it most clearly—are sinners (cf. 3:11) and as such are not only disobedient but also "unfit for any good deed." They are therefore "detestable" (1:16).

This concept of "abomination" is deeply embedded in the Old Testament, where it manifests a consistent pattern. When God thus "detests" he keeps the object of his detestation at a distance; his wrath and hatred are raised against it and he is indeed opposed to it; he is moved to destroy it. But God has also another attitude to men, even to sinful men. Paul speaks in the epistle of "the grace of God, remedial for all men" (2:11). He begins and ends the letter with grace (1:4; 3:15). He makes prominent the goodness and loving kindness of God our Savior (3:4) and expounds it by reference to his mercy (3:5). God's attitude is twofold.

It is expressed in his action, and his action was—Christ. The grace of God "appeared" and there can be no question about what is implied. Paul was thinking of the incarnation. When Christ "appeared" on the human scene it was the appearance of the grace of God. Thus God is Savior (1:3; 2:10; 3:4) and Christ is Savior (1:4; 2:13; 3:6). Christ gave himself for us (2:14). This can only refer to the cross. His purpose was to redeem and to purify. On the cross he accomplished what he had set out to do.

How does this affect sinful men? As a result of what our Lord did on the cross, a benefit awaits them. They have to be told about it, which is the reason why Paul was an apostle. He did not choose himself for this task and he did not invent his message. He was entrusted with it by command of God our Savior (1:3). Even if there were no other evidence in the epistle, we could infer from this verse that God is the living God. He did not leave orders behind him, to be carried out after his death. Men have not only to be told about the benefit; they have to be offered it; they have to be told the conditions on which it may be received; and they have to receive it.

The reception of the benefit, our salvation, did not and does not originate in our deeds in the sphere of righteousness. God saved us (3:5) when we responded to the offer of the benefit. He saved us by means of the washing which consists of regeneration and the renewal created by the Holy Spirit. The washing and renewal took place when we exercised faith, when we first believed.

Faith is prominent in the epistle. When Paul was pressing the need of good deeds on the members of the Cretan church he described them as "those who have believed in God" (3:8). Faith is not for a small proportion of highly mature "saints" in the church. It is required of all. It is "a common faith" (1:4), common to all who are in Christ. Weakness or unhealthiness in faith is bad; men should be healthy, "sound in faith" (2:2). The importance of faith is indicated by the characteristic description of "the faith" (cf. 1:13). The children of elders should be believers (1:6). Unbelief is a disaster (1:15). Even the elect must have faith (1:1). Cf. 3:15.

The use of the verb "justified" in 3:7 should not be missed. This is its only appearance in the Pastoral Epistles, apart from the special sense in 1 Timothy 3:16. It completes a triple Pauline description of what God has done for men in Christ. In Romans 3:23–25 "justified" points to the law court and acquittal; "redemption" takes us to the slave market where a man is bought and set free; "blood" reminds us of sacrificial religion and cleansing. These three pictures appear as one in the verses in question. In the Epistle to Titus they are separated. Two of them come together and one on its own. "Justified" occurs in 3:7. In the law court we are given the verdict and with it the inheritance. In 2:14 we read that Christ "gave himself for us to redeem us . . . and to purify. . . ." "Redeem" involves slavery and emancipation. "Purify" suggests the sacrificial blood. The verses in Romans are not copied or quoted, and if the Epistle to Titus was not written by Paul we may observe that its author has cleverly and subtly done this part of his work. In view of all the evidence, however, it is more satisfactory to think of three favorite pictures used by Paul the preacher and spontaneously coming into his mind at different stages of the letter to Titus.

The "benefit" having been received, the believer becomes an heir of eternal life (3:7; cf. 1:2; 2:13). He has infinite prospects to add to his present experience. Even in this world the Christian "lives" (2:12). The renunciation of irreligion and worldly passions, here mentioned, covers what is elsewhere called "repentance," the first step of faith.

The close association of "God our Savior" and "Christ Jesus our Savior" is to be noted. God's gift of the Holy Spirit through Jesus Christ our Savior (3:6) points to the doctrine of the Trinity but does not elaborate it.

The Life of the Christian

We must now speak of the life of the Christian. The word "boldness" (*parrēsia*, Eph. 3:12) is not used in the epistle, but it might have been. In regard to the past, believers are elect (1:1); in regard to the future they have hope; at the present moment they are "those who have believed in God" (3:8). The perfect tense is significant. It means the abiding result of a past act. Those who have believed "are now believers." It was their "first faith" which made them acceptable to God. Their present faith still does. Paul's expression suggests that justification by faith not only marks the beginning of the life of the Christian but sets up a permanent relationship between him and God. In Christ in whom he believes he "is acceptable"—not "was acceptable" but "was and is and always will be." (To believe in Christ is to believe in God.) The unbelieving may profess to know God, but the authentic Christian in the exercise of his faith knows him (1:16). He was justified by grace through faith, and grace continues to come: grace is "to you" and "with you" (1:4; 3:15).

The Christian is called to do good works (2:7, 14; 3:8; 3:14), and to manifest a certain Christian character (2:2–10; 3:1–2). The church is not specifically mentioned but it is present in "a people of his own" (2:14). It is implied in expressions which in some way suggest what is common to all believers: the common faith; the elect; heirs; the steward of the "estate"; and the Holy Spirit richly poured out on "us." The use of the word "we" and similar expressions in the Pauline literature is worthy of study. He gave himself for "us." He is Christ Jesus "our" Savior. He saved "us."

Provision is made for believers to receive pastoral supervision and to be cared for by the ministry. Presbyters or elders were to be appointed by Titus in every town, hardly to be distinguished from bishops. Their desirable characters are described. They have to teach and exhort the faithful and defend them from false teachers (1:5–9).

There may be a hint at the Christian doctrine of creation in 1:15.

The theological ideas of the Epistle to Titus exhibit a pattern which is very much like the plan of salvation. Once more this is not an Epistle to the Romans, either in length or in thought. What is there, explicitly stated or in allusion, is enough for us to see the thought and life, the faith and the experience of the Apostle to the Gentiles still shining brightly. It is the same preacher and the same religion; the same devoted servant of Christ our Savior, but seen and heard under different conditions.

OUTLINE

Titus

COMMENTARY

Titus

I. GREETING (1:1–4)

The conventional form is followed once more: writer, recipient, and blessing. It is the longest greeting in the Pastoral Epistles, being filled out with weighty, theological phrases. The technical terms and the words generally are strongly reminiscent of the language which we have already noticed in the other two espistles.

Verse 1: Paul, a servant of God and an apostle of Jesus Christ, to further the faith of God's elect and their knowledge of the truth which accords with godliness: An immediate plunge into the depths. This cannot be compared with "a simple sermon on the popular level." For *Paul . . . an apostle* see discussions on 1 Timothy 1:1; 2 Timothy 1:1. He delighted to call himself *a servant* (see on 2 Tim. 2:24). The word means literally "a slave." All that Paul ever taught about obedience to God is summed up in the word. Our Lord said that he did not call his disciples servants (John 15:15) but friends. There is no real contradiction. Even though *servant* is correlative to "Lord," the Lord's attitude is one of grace and Paul's is that of discipleship. This is an instance where piety is not wrong in making a distinction between what the Lord calls his people and what they call themselves. We must not think of the apostle here disobeying his Master. He was kneeling at his feet.

To further the faith of God's elect . . . seems to imply that the work of Paul as an apostle was to lead the *elect* ever deeper into *the faith:* in fact to enlarge their belief and to deepen their trust. We hear of conventions, like the famous Keswick Convention, "for the deepening of the spiritual life." The phrase almost suggests that Paul was an itinerant "convention speaker." Now he did care for his converts, as the Epistles to the Thessalonians testify. His pastoral heart yearned over them. In his obviously prolonged absences others had to take his place and he appointed elders or presbyters to tend the flock. But his primary work was evangelism. The expression might possibly mean that he was an apostle whose task was, under God, to create faith in the elect, so that they passed from being "elect" to "elect and saved." This interpretation would save his evangelistic priority but it is not the natural interpretation.

This view is really a cul-de-sac, a dead end street. We must go back to the Greek. *To further* is an attempt, not in itself illegitimate,[1] to bring out the force of the preposition *kata* governing the accusative case. The translators

---

1. See R. A. Ward, *Hidden Meaning in the New Testament* (Old Tappan, N.J.: Fleming H. Revell Company, 1969), pp. 79 f.

might have given as an alternative "toward the faith," "with my eye on the faith" (Phil. 3:14), and might have derived support from Paul's endurance for the sake of the elect, that they also may obtain salvation (see on 2 Tim. 2:10). But a more natural treatment is possible. *Kata* with the accusative case is often rendered by "according to," and "according to godliness" has been rendered in the present verse by a relative clause, *which accords with godliness*. *Kata* in this sense is used when some sort of standard is in mind. Now the apostle should not be regarded as checking his doctrine by that of others, even the *elect*. But he is saying that his apostleship tallied with *the faith of God's elect*. What did he mean?

When Paul preached the gospel the *elect* heard the call of God through him. In their response in *faith* they knew that he was the bearer of the Word of God and that he had been sent, i.e., that he was *an apostle* who had been divinely commissioned. Paul was not thinking of his original call on the Damascus road but of his continuing work as an apostle which resulted from the call. He preached—and was "recognized." This corresponds roughly to the practice of some Christian churches today: after a new minister has been inducted into his local charge he is "recognized" in a Service of Recognition. "Whoever knows God listens to us, and he who is not of God does not listen to us. By this we know the spirit of truth and the spirit of error" (1 John 4:6). *God's elect* thus continue to "recognize" the apostle as he travels far and wide in the work of evangelism. As believers they can recognize a believing preacher when they see one, and in particular, whether converted under his ministry or otherwise, they can "recognize" *an apostle of Jesus Christ*.

For *elect* see further on 2 Timothy 2:10 and the references there given.

We may similarly translate "(according to) *their knowledge of the truth*." The elect knew the truth, and when Paul preached they heard the truth from his lips. The authenticity of his apostleship was confirmed by what he said, by his message. The elect realized this and Paul was therefore *an apostle* "according to" their *knowledge*. Paul was certain of his message and of his apostolic authority; but without doubt he was inspired by the attitude of the elect and was fortified by their prayers and other support.

Notice the close association of *faith* and *knowledge* and see discussion on 2 Timothy 2:25 with its further references.

The truth which accords with godliness must be kept together, for this is how the words should be grouped. The expression may at first occasion some surprise. Does not all *truth* accord with *godliness*? No doubt in a sense it does: all truth is God's truth. But within the broad field of truth are some elements to which the godly pay special attention. The truths of mathematics, for example, ultimately derive from him who is the truth, the eternal Word. The truths or laws of nature owe their origin to him who "invented" and constituted them; but they are not so immediately relevant to godliness as the fact and meaning of Christ. The crucial word here is "immediately." All truth is ultimately related to Christ, for "in him all things were created . . . all things were created through him and for him . . . and in him all things hold together" (Col. 1:16 f.). To adopt a metaphor from geography, however, Paul was thinking of *truth which* is in the latitude of *godliness*. *God's elect* knew *the truth* which was the inspiration of their walk with God, and Paul's apostleship, whether at any given time he was addressing them or not, "spoke to their condition." Thus as believing men and as men who knew the truth in its impact on their piety they "recognized" in *Paul . . . an apostle of Jesus Christ.*

For piety or *godliness* see on 1 Timothy 6:11; 2 Timothy 3:5. It is the fulfillment of man's duty to God. If men know *the truth which accords with godliness* it is because they have been taught properly: they have received "the teaching which accords with godliness" (1 Tim. 6:3). Paul was writing to Titus but he was looking beyond him to the false teachers (vv. 10–16). Hence his mention of his apostleship and by implication his authority. The letter would not be kept private but would be used in support of Titus. The farewell was not limited to him (3:15).

Verse 2: In hope of eternal life which God, who never lies, promised ages ago: A sure hope, already tested and proved. (See 1 Tim. 1:16; 4:8; 6:12, 19; 2 Tim. 1:1; 1:9 f.; Titus 3:7 and discussions.) We might ask to whom God *promised.* A first answer might be "the prophets" (cf. Heb. 11:17)—a tenable theory. But *ages ago* seems to look even further back into the past. The expression is used in 2 Timothy 1:9 and the parallel is remarkable. God promised eternal life *ages ago* and he gave his grace to us in Christ Jesus *ages ago.* He could not have given his grace to us directly. We were not there. We did not even exist. The grace is "in Christ Jesus," and even now it is given to us only in him. The inference is that he received the grace from God on our behalf. If we follow the parallel we can say that God promised to us in him. Again, we were not there. Therefore God made the promise to Christ Jesus who received it on our behalf.

This promise has been kept. *God . . . never lies.* He cannot lie, because to do so would involve a contradiction in his very nature. God is light and in him is no darkness at all (1 John 1:5, 10; 5:10). He cannot lie and he will not, because he is faithful (Heb. 11:11; cf. 6:18). Paul was prepared to take his stand on the faithfulness of God against all the world (Rom. 3:3 f.). The manner in which the promise has been kept is shown in the next verse. In the meantime it must be said that the *hope of eternal life* is made sure by the fact that already eternal life has been received by believers. It has been brought to light through the gospel. Those who have received the gospel have received the life and in eternity they will enter into it more deeply and enjoy it ever more fully. For they have already received Christ—our hope (1 Tim. 1:1).

Verse 3: And at the proper time manifested in his word through the preaching with which I have been entrusted by command of God our Savior: What was promised was actually given, visibly. When Christ came, the promise was fulfilled. In him God broke—not his silence but—his invisibility. God had spoken in his prophets. He had brought about the great events in Old Testament history. But he had acted, not with remote control, but from the unseen. Now the promised life is visible.

It is important to notice how the life was manifested. What actually appeared was Christ (2 Tim. 1:10; cf. Titus 2:11; 3:4). But we can still think of the appearance of life, because it is true to say not only that life is in Christ but that he himself is the life. "I am . . . the life" (John 14:6). John boldly says that the life was seen and he says it in a context of seeing, hearing and handling (1 John 1:1 f.). Life is not abstract, a sort of glow of well-being which is given to men in Christ in such a way that they can go on to enjoy it in itself, apart from Christ. Men have life only and as long as they remain in Christ.

The manifestation of the life was *at the proper time.* The expression has already been used by the apostle. God's invisibility ended when he thought fit; and we can now see its wisdom. The earthly scene had been prepared by God's providence. (See further on 1 Tim. 2:6; 6:14 f.)

It looks as if Paul had intended to write thus: "life which God ... promised ... and manifested ...." Here the relative pronoun "which" is the direct object of both "promised" and "manifested." This is plainly what he meant. But he actually wrote: "which God ... promised ... , and manifested his word. ...." *His word* takes the place of the expected "which" (=life). How did he get from "life" to *his word?*

He was thinking of his apostleship and its thrilling work of preaching Christ. He offered life to men when he preached Christ to them and he had seen them receive it. In an abundant number of examples he had seen "life from the dead." So the first step is easy and natural, from preaching life in Christ to preaching Christ (cf. Col. 3:4). But preaching Christ is preaching the Word of God. Paul had told Timothy to "preach the word" (2 Tim. 4:2). With his mind full of his apostleship Paul understandably wrote *his word,* which after all is what Jesus Christ is. There is a true sense in which "life" is *manifested* whenever *his word* is faithfully preached, but this meaning is secondary here. This no doubt explains why the RSV has inserted *in,* thereby enabling the "which" to be continued in thought as the object of *manifested.* The life was *manifested* in the incarnation of Jesus Christ and in a secondary sense is still manifested (in another way) in the sermon. What was originally *manifested* in the flesh of Jesus (cf. Rom. 8:3) is in preaching *manifested* through the Holy Spirit.

The next part of the verse is somewhat condensed. The manifestation is *through the preaching. Through* seems to have been chosen by the RSV because *in* had already been inserted before *his word.* The Greek preposition *(en)* is very elastic, but it may be doubted if *through* is its best rendering in the present phrase. Paul meant: "(God) manifested his word (as contained—cf. Eph. 2:15, KJV—in the message with which I was entrusted ...." This interpretation of the Greek text saves Paul from limiting the manifestation to his own sermons. God *manifested ... his word* and that very *word,* Jesus, was the subject of Paul's preaching and was contained in *the preaching.* Notice the two uses of the word *preaching.* When we wrote of "Paul's preaching" we were thinking of his verbal activity and other movements such as gesture. But *the preaching with which I have been entrusted* means "the preached message," "the proclamation." Some scholars indeed take the word here to indicate the preaching office, but we prefer the above interpretation. The message was more than the preacher. The same noun *(kērugma)* is used in 2 Timothy 4:17; "preacher" *(kērux)* appears in 1 Timothy 2:7; 2 Timothy 1:11; and the verb "to preach" *(kērussō)* in 1 Thessalonians 2:9; 1 Timothy 3:16; 2 Timothy 4:2. Paul was very conscious that he had been *entrusted* with the gospel (1 Thess. 2:4; 1 Tim. 1:11 f.). He was not only "allowed to preach"; the gospel was in his hands *by command of God our Savior* (cf. 1 Tim. 1:1; and perhaps Rom. 16:26).

Verse 4: To Titus, my true child in a common faith: Grace and peace from God the Father and Christ Jesus our Savior: The weighty introduction leads into warm, personal greeting. Like Timothy, *Titus* was the apostle's *true child* (see on 1 Tim. 1:2). Paul must have been the means of his conversion. A subtle distinction of expression should be noticed. Timothy was not the apostle's child by a blood relationship but by a spiritual one. He was a true "child-in-the-faith" and would always remain so. *Titus* became—and remained—the apostle's *true child* "in virtue of" (*kata* here, not *en*) a *common faith*. From the moment that Titus believed, trusted, he had *faith*. But this is precisely what the apostle himself had. They both therefore had the same faith from the time of the conversion of Titus, and if they had the same faith, it was common to both of them, a *common faith*. The response of faith given by Titus to the apostle's preaching or teaching forged a spiritual link between them. Not all Christians are children of Paul in this intimate sense, but all share with him a *common faith*. This is a simple example of what the New Testament calls fellowship or communion, the heart of which is that which is *common*. Titus had come the same way as Timothy, but Paul explicitly drew attention to what created the special relationship. Timothy was already a "child-in-the-faith" and Titus had become so "in virtue of" *a common faith*. Jude similarly speaks of a "common salvation" (Jude 3). Unlike money (Acts 2:44; 4:32), these are shared but not shared out.

For *grace and peace* see on 1 Timothy 1:2. There is significance in the easy way in which the apostle alternates between "God our Savior" (v. 3) and *Christ Jesus our Savior*. This does not "prove" the doctrine of the Trinity, but it is part of the data which are to be used in the formulation of the doctrine. It is a highly valuable pointer because it unobtrusively arises from the deep religious life of Paul. He was not theorizing or inventing a doctrine.

Titus is not named in the Acts of the Apostles, possibly because he was a relative of Luke. He was a Gentile, an uncircumcised Greek, who accompanied Paul and Barnabas into the heart of "enemy" territory, Jerusalem (Gal. 2:1, 3; cf. 2:12). He seems to have earned the apostle's respect and to have been entrusted with a number of commissions. He figures especially in the Second Epistle to the Corinthians (2:13; 7:6 f., 13–15; 8:6, 16–18, 23; 12:18). He may have traveled with the apostle, who certainly left him in Crete (Titus 1:5) and later summoned him from there to Nicopolis (Titus 3:12). Later still he went to Dalmatia (2 Tim. 4:10), probably in agony at having to leave Paul. In addition to being a *true child* he was "brother," "partner" and "fellow worker." "Partner" (2 Cor. 8:23) is a pleasing word. *Common* in Greek is *koinos* and "partner" is *koinōnos*. In the Christian *comm*unity, in the *comm*union of the Holy Spirit (2 Cor. 13:14), the man who held with Paul the *common faith* was a "*comm*oner" in the *koinōnia* or fellowship.

II. ELDERS AS THE SOLUTION TO A PROBLEM (1:5-9)

Titus had been left in Crete because all was not well in the island. He was to appoint elders in every town if he could find men with the necessary qualifications. The reason given for their choice is that a bishop must be blameless. The relationship between elder and bishop is thus implied. The characteristics of a bishop, both positive and negative, to fit him for office, are listed.

Verse 5: This is why I left you in Crete, that you might amend what was defective, and appoint elders in every town as I directed you: An existing commission reaffirmed. If Titus had already started this work and had run into opposition, the letter from the apostle would add to his authority. He was not acting on his own initiative and he would now have written evidence to prove it. Possibly the best men were reluctant to assume office or unsuitable men were ambitious and pressing Titus to appoint them. Here were directions for the guidance of all.

Crete is the island in the Mediterranean Sea, south of the Aegean Sea, which lies between Greece and Asia Minor (Turkey). Paul had clearly visited it and had probably had a mission there, but later than the references in the Acts of the Apostles (Acts 27:7 f., 12, 21).

This looks forward, the effect being thus: *This is why . . . ,* (namely) *that you might amend . . . .* The Christian community in Crete had reached a certain stage of growth, and so far so good. But there were certain deficiencies. Titus was to remain in Crete so that he might attend to what remained to be done. *Amend* almost means "mend." It was a work of correction, of putting right, and is in the spirit of what we call "reformation." It was to be the correction of a situation, at any rate as a beginning, rather than the correction of wrong ideas, though this follows. It corresponds to the "correction" of a man, for which "all scripture is . . . profitable" (see on 2 Tim. 3:16). What was right could be left as it was; what was wrong had to be put right.

Titus could deal with this situation by the appointment of elders. The force of Paul's words is: *"that you might amend . . . , and* (in particular) *appoint . . . ." In every town* does not imply "whether there are Christians in it or not." The absence of Christians would call for an evangelist rather than an elder. Paul wanted the Christian community *in every town* to have at least one elder. In this he was consistent. At Lystra, Iconium, and Antioch of Pisidia he and Barnabas "had appointed elders for them in every church" (Acts 14:23). (Cf. 1 Tim. 5:17, 19 f. and discussion.)

Paul was giving both directions and support. His *I* is emphatic: *as I,* the apostle, *directed you.* The Christians in the island seem to have been disorganized. The church there may have been started as a lay movement connected with Cretans who had been in Jerusalem on the day of Pentecost (Acts 2:5, 11). There was an obvious need for pastoral care.

The appointment of elders raises the question of the importance of the ministry to the church. It sometimes happens today that a minister leaves his charge and the appointment of his successor is delayed. The pastorate is vacant; there is no elder or presbyter to supervise. When concern is expressed, the comment is occasionally made that this particular church can safely be left on its own. It is a tribute to its spiritual vigor and maturity. It should be observed, however, that this should not be taken as a rule to guide the churches generally. The church in question may invite ministers from other churches to come and conduct their services and to preach; or

they may produce their own members for this purpose. They clearly need
ministry and some of their own people may be thinly disguised ministers!

The sturdy independence and vigor is a value which should not be thoughtlessly thrown away. But it should not be forgotten that this thriving church
has been built up through the years by the devoted labor of a minister.
It is one thing to leave them alone for a few months because they can be
trusted. It is quite another for a troubled and indeed misled community like
the Christians in Crete to be allowed to work out their own salvation in
isolation. They need the ministry for the promotion of righteousness and
godliness (see on v. 1). The ministry is not a dispensable luxury. It is the
gift of Christ (Eph. 4:11 f.) and it ought not to be refused.

*Verse 6: If any man is blameless, the husband of one wife, and his
children are believers and not open to the charge of being profligate or
insubordinate:* The qualifications of the elders. The thought is:"appoint as
elders whoever is blameless . . . ." *Blameless* is a relative term; see discussion
on 1 Timothy 3:10. The necessary qualifications should be compared with
those required of a bishop (1 Tim. 3:2–5), and the relevant discussions
consulted. An interpretation has already been suggested there for *the husband
of one wife. Children* who are not *believers* are a living, permanent contradiction of an elder's message and may—but not always and not necessarily—
point to his own failure. In any case they "cramp his style." Every time
he offered a rebuke or made an appeal he would be open to the charge,
"What about your own children?" Notice how appropriate here is the word
"charge." An elder is to be one who cannot be "charged" because he has
given no grounds for accusation.

Being profligate or profligacy is translated by "debauchery" in a context
of drunkenness (Eph. 5:18). It is wider in meaning than drunkenness (cf.
1 Pet. 4:4). The corresponding adverb is used of the Prodigal Son who
squandered his property "in loose living" (Luke 15:13). The Greek adverb
means "unsavingly," and so the prodigal lived. The thought is of excess in
the spending of money, and this includes spending it on liquor. He scattered
his money as a farmer scatters seed, and he reaped a dreadful harvest (cf.
Gal. 6:7 f.). It would be unedifying and indeed a stumbling block for an
elder to be taken to see his children's harvest.

More encouragement is to be derived from the positive side. If *his children
are believers* he has the support and the prayers of his family, and the
world has the witness of a Christian home.

The requirement that an elder's *children* are not to be *insubordinate* is
not discriminating against children. Our Lord was subordinate to his earthly
parents (Luke 2:51). The Greek verb translated "was obedient" is cognate
with *insubordinate.* (The reference to "parents" is not a denial of the Virgin
Birth.) Cf. Luke 2:41, 43. Wives should be subordinate to their husbands
and all Christians subordinate to one another, the whole church being subordinate to Christ. There will be no "bullying" if husbands love their wives
as Christ loved the church, and if fathers do not provoke their children to
anger but bring them up in the Lord's education and instruction. All should
be subordinate to the secular authorities. (Cf. Rom. 13:1; Eph. 5:21–25;
6:4.) Paul went on to speak of these matters later in the epistle (Titus 2:4 f.,
9; 3:1), including love of wives for husbands and the subordination of slaves.

In the love of a Christian home, believing *children* would be safe. If the *children are* not *believers* they are not under grace but under law. For "the law is . . . laid down . . . for the lawless and disobedient" (1 Tim. 1:9—same Greek word). Strange company! (Titus 1:10).

Verse 7: For a bishop, as God's steward, must be blameless; he must not be arrogant or quick-tempered or a drunkard or violent or greedy for gain: Typical examples of what can be blamed. *Blameless* is repeated from the previous verse and is the same Greek word, different from the "above reproach" of 1 Timothy 3:2. The *steward* is not the owner of the estate but the "manager," what in Scotland they call "the factor" (see on 1 Tim. 1:4b). None of the characteristics listed are suitable in a *steward.* If he is *arrogant* he is "self-willed"; and the steward must serve his master's interests, not his own. The *quick-tempered* man is not the true representative of his master: if he himself is "testy," by contrast the Lord is slow to wrath. Such a man prejudges the issue and does not give the matter his mature consideration. He does not give himself time to deal with a situation and to win over a difficult man (cf. Matt. 18:15). Anger has already shown impatience and it clouds the judgment. A *drunkard* is not in a fit condition to administer his master's estate and to deal with men on his behalf. A *bishop* who is a *drunkard* undermines his own message, for he tells the world in act if not in word that he will not inherit the kingdom of God (cf. 1 Cor. 6:9–11; Gal. 5:19–21). How can he extol the grace of God by saying that "such were some of you"? How can he care for the flock of God? The *violent* man, who is pugnacious and a bully in word and deed, misrepresents his master (cf. Matt. 11:29) and may block the road to repentance (cf. 2 Tim. 2:24 f.).

If a steward is *greedy for gain* he will not be too scrupulous about the method of gaining it. He will thus be untrustworthy; and "it is required of stewards that they be found trustworthy" (1 Cor. 4:2). A bishop with such a character will make spiritual decisions for economic motives: he will be concerned with his own financial advantage rather than the moral and spiritual welfare of others. (Cf. 1 Pet. 5:2.) The flock must be fed, not "milked." A bishop, like any minister, is to give rather than get. He is concerned with the free gift of grace (cf. Rom. 3:24; 5:15).

It should be noticed that the qualities which Paul had in mind are not merely desirable. They are a *must.*

The introductory words, *for a bishop,* are highly significant. The apostle has just given directions with regard to the appointment of elders or presbyters. He justifies his requirements for presbyters by listing what is necessary in a *bishop.* It is obvious that a presbyter is a bishop. A *bishop* is a generic term and refers to all bishops. When we say that "a soldier must be brave" we mean "all soldiers."

The verse is relevant to much contemporary discussion. The union of churches is in the air and episcopacy is being advocated and repudiated. If any union is to have a biblical base it is important to know what a *bishop* really is. Some men insist on episcopacy; others, equally passionately, refuse it.

It would seem that all Christians, with perhaps a tiny proportion of dissentients, agree that the church should not be without pastoral care and supervision. A local church which is lacking in oversight is a prey to false teachers of every kind, moral and religious. There is nobody to lead it ever further in an exploration of the unsearchable riches of Christ (Eph. 3:8); and nobody to seek and find and bring back the wanderer. To that extent the advocates of episcopacy are right. The opponents of episcopacy, however, are not opposed to pastoral care but to the second-century monarchical bishop and his successor in the medieval prelate. In other words, there is no disagreement worth mention about the need of oversight. The question at issue is, who is to do it. It would clarify much discussion if it were realized that *episcopē* means "oversight" and an *episcopos* or bishop is "one who exercises oversight." Problems arise when two or more men claim the oversight over the same group of Christians, a question which is out of place here.

Deacons are not mentioned (cf. 1 Tim. 3:8–13). The specific qualities required in presbyters and bishops are examples of "the sort of man" who is acceptable. They are not exhaustive. After giving the negative side Paul goes on to give the positive (vv. 8 f.).

Verse 8: But hospitable, a lover of goodness, master of himself, upright, holy, and self-controlled: Pedestrian virtues against temptation (v. 7) are supplemented by others for positive ministry. For *hospitable* see on 1 Timothy 3:2. *Lover of goodness* may be taken as including the idea of loving good people. It may be contrasted with "lovers of self" and "lovers of money" (2 Tim. 3:2). A man who exercises pastoral oversight needs to love his flock. At times there may be a clash of personalities. A bishop will do well to remember that even here he is probably dealing with good people. Whatever his feelings he must love them in action. He must love unbelievers also, though there is a difference. He should love believers because they are in Christ as much as he is; he should love unbelievers for the sake of Christ.

Master of himself (sōphrōn) is rendered in 1 Timothy 3:2 by "sensible." It means something like "in his right mind" (cf. Mark 5:15; Luke 8:35; 2 Cor. 5:13) and so "level-headed." Such a man is not easily thrown off his balance by sudden emergency and is sometimes a rock on which others can lean. *Upright (dikaios)* is often translated "righteous." Now every Christian, as the Puritan Edward Elton pointed out, is as righteous as Christ is, but not "in the same manner." The Lord's righteousness is inherent; the Christian is righteous by imputation. In Christ he is related to the Father as a son. Paul could not here be thinking of "righteous" in this sense. If he were, every Christian—as far as righteousness is concerned—would qualify as a bishop. Paul was thinking of the righteousness of faith which is expressed in righteousness of life. The man who is thus righteous is *upright*: he performs his moral duties. But his morality has not been secularized. His duty to God is godliness; his duty to man is righteousness, but it is a duty imposed by God. (See on 1 Tim. 6:11.)

Holy is a word appropriate to the religious cultus. A man who is *holy* is welcome and at home with God. The supreme example is our Lord (Acts 2:27; 13:35). The word is a cultic counterpart to the forensic "righteous." The *holy* man can draw near to God in worship; the righteous man is under no condemnation. This distinction corresponds roughly to that between the Epistle to the Hebrews and the Epistle to the Romans. If he is *holy* the bishop is well on the road to "godliness." (See further on 1 Tim. 2:8.)

The *self-controlled* are the opposite of the "profligates" of 2 Timothy 3:3.

There may be an analogy between *lover of goodness* and *self-controlled* on the one hand and "haters of good" and "profligates" on the other. (See on 2 Tim. 3:3.) Self-control means the mastery of the self by the self—by the new self. This is the contrast between "the old man" and "the new man" (cf. Eph. 4:22–24; Col. 3:9 f., both KJV). It is not merely a question of a strong will. The secret is the presence of the Holy Spirit. "The fruit of the Spirit is . . . self-control" (Gal. 5:22 f.).

Verse 9: He must hold firm to the sure word as taught, so that he may be able to give instruction in sound doctrine and also to confute those who contradict it: Offense and defense. The *word* is *sure* because it is trustworthy, credible; it is to be believed. It is the Word of God. The bishop is to be as devoted to it as a slave to one master (cf. Matt. 6:24). There is only one Word of God. It is not said by whom the *word* was *taught*. Paul might have been thinking of the doctrine taught generally in the apostolic churches, especially those founded by himself. In that case the bishop was to "guard the deposit" (1 Tim. 6:20 and discussion). But he might have been recalling the fact that even a bishop was once taught by somebody. He was then subtly recalling the subsidiary authority of the teacher. Like Timothy, the newly appointed bishop should "continue in what you have learned . . . , knowing from whom you learned it" (2 Tim. 3:14 and discussion).

There is a purpose in the required tenacity which goes beyond the care of the bishops's own soul. He is to *hold firm* in order that he may be qualified for a double duty. He must *be able* because it is his task to *give instruction*. This is more than merely passing on information. It includes exhortation and encouragement, "persuasion with authority." (See discussions referred to at 1 Tim. 1:3.) The "state of the congregation" will often determine the line of approach. The teacher, with the same doctrine, sometimes encourages and sometimes challenges, and at times will comfort. For *sound* see on 2 Timothy 1:13. Not all *doctrine* imparts spiritual health. The specter of the false teacher is rising.

There will be those who *contradict* the message. They flatly deny the truth. It will be the bishop's further task to deal with such men. It is not enough to denounce them. He must *be able . . . to confute* them. *Confute* is rendered by "convince" in 2 Timothy 4:2 (see discussion). Men who speak against the faith are to be exposed for the errorists that they are. If the Word is deeply in the heart of the bishop; if he clings to it, meditates on it and dwells in it; then he will have a spiritual vitality and liveliness whereby he *may be able* to deal with the opponent. With growing sensitiveness he will observe not only the points of doctrine where the antagonist is wrong but also the motives which lie behind his contradiction. He will answer those who *contradict* in word and those who "deny . . . by their deeds" (v. 16).

The Apostle Paul is himself one of the best illustrations of a man who can *confute* or expose. When he was in the island of Cyprus he unmasked the false prophet, Elymas, with devastating invective. "You son of the devil, you enemy of all righteousness, full of all deceit and villainy, will you not stop making crooked the straight paths of the Lord?" This is exposure *par excellence*. Elymas had "withstood them, seeking to turn away the proconsul from the faith." Paul was not guilty of vulgar vilification. He showed the man up for what he was. Luke is careful to say that Paul was "filled with the Holy Spirit" (Acts 13:6–10). The proconsul gained the benefit.

III. THE MEN WHO CONSTITUTE THE PROBLEM (1:10–16)

The reason why elders were needed in every town was the widespread existence of false teachers, especially men of the circumcision party devoted to Jewish myths. Because of the damage they were doing they were to be refuted and silenced. Their teaching was associated with men of defiled mind and conscience whose deeds contradicted their profession of faith and showed them up for what they really were.

Verse 10: For there are many insubordinate men, empty talkers and deceivers, especially the circumcision party: The reason why elders must be appointed. The significance of *for* should not be lost. One false teacher can do a lot of damage: the effect of leaven must not be judged by its quantity. When the numbers are *many,* the church itself is in danger and the situation demands emergency measures. This does not mean that elders are to be chosen merely to deal with an emergency. They are a permanent feature of the church (see on v. 5). The emergency calls attention to the fact that the Christians in Crete were as sheep without a shepherd. The measures which we called emergency measures do not consist in the appointment of elders but in the speed with which they must be appointed. There was no time to be lost. Much damage had already been done by the *many.* The elders had to repair the damage, undo the work of the false teachers, unite the church in the truth, and make sure that every member was well grounded in the faith.

The *many* had taken the bit between their teeth, for they are described as *insubordinate* (see on v. 6). This is not the free-lance activity of youthful enthusiasts who forge ahead in evangelism without consulting the authorities of the church and bring some confusion into current arrangements—a forgivable piece of work! These men are *empty talkers.* Paul's Greek (*mataiologos*) would raise our hopes high (*logos* means "the word") if it were not for the preliminary adjective, *mataios.* Their "word" is not "the Word." From the point of view of the apostle it is barren of results. It is "in vain." They have their purpose indeed, when they speak; but it does not impress anyone with a love of the gospel. Their many words lack the one saving Word. No doubt the *talkers* achieved something of their own purpose, but it was of no benefit to the church. It was "futile" (3:9; cf. 1 Tim. 1:6 and discussion).

Whether they set out to be *deceivers* is an open question. They certainly succeeded and were guilty of misleading many in the church. The chief offenders were those of *the circumcision party.* This was a sore point with the apostle, who could not forget his earlier battles (cf. Gal. 2:12). But the battleground had changed. It was now a matter of myths and genealogies (see on 1 Tim. 1:4; 4:7), to which Paul returned (Titus 3:9), rather than the method of justification. "Those of the circumcision" is a description of Jews, no doubt professing the Christian faith (vv. 13 f.), but in need of correction. They may not have emphasized circumcision as such but are described by their distinctive mark.

Verse 11: They must be silenced, since they are upsetting whole families by teaching for base gain what they have no right to teach: In the church they have no "democratic" rights. There are some people who think that because they are members of the church they have the right to express themselves in any way they think fit. They have not. If the church were a democracy, each member might possibly have the right to advocate whatever he liked. But the church is not a society in which government is government by the people for the people. It exists for the sake of Christ and for his glory—not theirs. And "the government will be upon his shoulder" (Isa. 9:6; cf. Luke 1:32 f.)—not upon theirs.

There is only one remedy. Such people *must be silenced.* They must be told to be quiet ("rebuke them sharply" v. 13). Their false doctrine must be exposed and answered. A man can sometimes *be silenced* by a demonstration of the falsity of his views and even of their silliness (1 Tim. 4:7). Train the church in the truth in such a way that each member holds it fast, and nobody will listen to the purveyor of silly myths; he will thus be *silenced.*

It all seems highly autocratic, but great issues are at stake. These false teachers *are upsetting whole families* (cf. 2 Tim. 2:18). Their faith was being overturned. In the discussion on 2 Timothy 2:18 attention was drawn to the undesirability of letting a weak believer hear arguments about doctrine. In the present passage Paul wants false doctrine to be suppressed entirely. This raises the whole question of what might be termed censorship in the church. Is it fitting that men in Christ should not be allowed to hear and test for themselves? Is not censorship an attack on Christian freedom?

It is a preliminary answer to say that freedom must not be used as an opportunity for the flesh (cf. Gal. 5:1, 13). Of even more importance is the degree of maturity reached by the Christian in question. Strong believers who have been in Christ for many years may be trusted to "read anything, hear anything," because it is as good as certain that they will reject the false and hold fast that which is good. They can help their weaker brethren by telling them that they have already examined the teaching and that it falls below the Christian standard, and can advise them to steer clear of it. This is all to the good: strong Christians do not need a censorship. But weak Christians, especially those in weak and disorganized churches and lacking experience of a fellowship which is "the pillar and bulwark of the truth" (1 Tim. 3:15), need to be protected. Hence, for their sake false teachers *must be silenced.* In any case *they have no right* to teach false doctrine. The size of the fee demanded may be an index. "Censorship" is no problem if ministers are respected and loved (cf. 1 Thess. 5:12 f., 21).

The fact that *whole families* were being affected suggests that the false teachers penetrated separate houses rather than addressed the Christian congregation when gathered together for worship (see on 2 Tim. 3:6). We may surmise either that the "bits of women" were the first to be impressed or, the state of the church in Crete being what it was, every member of the household resembled their women folk in the weakness of their grasp of the faith. The teachers were turning religion to their own financial advantage and making it a means of gain; but it was *base gain.* It is godliness with contentment which brings the true gain and it is great (cf. 1 Tim. 6:5 f. and discussion). The ministry should always realize this. The "wages" in themselves are honorable; the motive of ministry should save them from being *base* (cf. 1 Tim. 5:17 f.; 1 Pet. 5:2).

Verse 12: One of themselves, a prophet of their own, said, "Cretans are always liars, evil beasts, lazy gluttons": A pagan "prophet" quoted to support an apostle. It must not be thought that Paul could not have found ample scriptural—and other—arguments if he had wanted to do so; but it was a sound move to quote a Cretan against Cretans. The implication is: Cretans cannot reject what I say just because I am not one of themselves. I am merely reminding them of a Cretan opinion. The quoted line, a hexameter in the Greek, has been attributed to Epimenides (first half of the 6th cent. B.C.), and in the spirit of a proverb sums up the Cretan character. If the false teachers were natives of the island, beware of them! They will prove to be *liars.* (Paul would not have the patience to consider the fallacy involved, even if he had thought of it. If a Cretan made the statement, then it was not to be believed! Paul's point was sufficiently clear.) The *evil beasts,* as wild animals, would not spare the flock (cf. Acts 20:29 f.) if they could derive "base gain" from it. *Lazy gluttons* do not love work. If they can find gullible people to listen to them, and to pay them into the bargain, they will gladly be "deceivers" and will defy the church. "Insubordinate men" will take the money and lead their listeners astray.

Paul was not placing a pagan prophet on the same level as that of an Old Testament or Christian prophet. If his word must be justified it is enough to refer to the "prophecy" of Caiaphas (John 11:49–51). Epimenides had some reputation as a prophet.

Was Paul being tactless? Perhaps he was. But the situation called for strong treatment and he was not the man to mince matters. A spade is a spade even if some "nice" people prefer to call it an agricultural implement. We must not secularize the apostle. He walked with God and was possessed of the Holy Spirit. It would be rash to say that his inspiration failed him here. For all we know it might be these very "tactless" words which the Holy Spirit could use to bring back the deluded to their senses and to their faith.

Verse 13: This testimony is true. Therefore rebuke them sharply, that they may be sound in the faith: Paul's purpose is practical, not literary. He could make use of allusions to pagan authors when he wanted to do so. "In him we live and move and have our being" is also traced to Epimenides. "For we are indeed his offspring" comes from the *Phainomena* of Aratus, a Greek from Cilicia (born about 315 B.C.), with a side glance at the *Hymn to Zeus* of Cleanthes (c. 330–c. 231 B.C.), who succeeded Zeno in the leadership of the Stoic school. These two quotations were made in the speech before the Council of the Areopagus (Acts 17:22, 28). "Bad company ruins good morals" (1 Cor. 15:33) appears in the *Thais* of Menander (c. 342–292 B.C.), the famous dramatist of the New Comedy. It is of some significance that in both the Acts and the Pastorals Paul could refer to the same context of Epimenides.

Even so, Paul was not quoting in order to tickle itching ears (cf. 2 Tim. 4:3 and discussion). He was driving home his point by quoting a Cretan against Cretans; by beating them on their own ground. The Christian faith does not depend on the utterances of unbelievers, but their utterances can sometimes be used very effectively. If the preacher quotes the (unbelieving) "idol of the masses" in support of his theme, he has got under the masses' protective armor. Paul did not set out to entertain; rather he selected a rapier from Epimenides in order to "stab their souls awake."

In view of the evidence thus afforded, the *testimony,* and the fact that it *is true,* Paul prescribes his remedy: *rebuke them sharply. Rebuke* has already appeared in the chapter as "confute" (v. 9 and discussion). Titus should "expose," should "unmask," the false teachers and should do it "severely." Paul had himself faced the possibility of having to be severe (2 Cor. 13:10). More is meant than sharpness or abruptness in speech. Titus must not be content if the false teachers merely soft-pedal their doctrines. They must completely abandon them. There must be a clean cut, a severance. We have spoken of Paul's remedy. It involved something like a surgical operation. The gangrenous limb must be severed (cf. 2 Tim. 2:17).

The motive is of the highest, *that they may be sound in the faith.* If the purpose is fulfilled, the remedy will be effective and the teachers will be healthy *in the faith.* For *sound* cf. v. 9; 2 Timothy 1:13 and discussion. The apostle did not say "*sound* in doctrine," though he might have done. He traced the error further back. Unsound doctrine comes from men who are of unsound faith. *The faith* means "the Christian religion" (see discussion on 1 Tim. 3:9; 6:10). It imposes standards and requires effort and it should be kept. It may be missed, denied or abandoned: men may rebel against it or wander away from it. "Unhealthiness" is caused by living in a polluted atmosphere. It is only as men live *in the faith* that they are in pure air. Paul might here have written "in Christ."

Verse 14: Instead of giving heed to Jewish myths or to commands of men who reject the truth: The particular fashion and the permanent danger. For *myths* see on 1 Timothy 1:4; 4:7; 2 Timothy 4:4. *Giving heed to,* paying attention to, suggests the attractiveness and fascination of *myths* and human systems. It is sometimes said that "Christianity has failed to attract the mass of the population . . . " and the speaker gives the impression that there is something wrong with the faith. In actual fact he is damning most of society: what are they *giving heed to?* The *commands of men* may proceed from constitutional authority (Rom. 13:1–7); these should be obeyed. Other commands come from a power which is in a position to persecute and which makes demands in excess of its authority. It may have a legal authority: we learn from lawyers that Hitler's position was constitutional as he had been given full powers; but it lacks moral authority and divine authority. "We must obey God rather than men" (Acts 5:29). In other cases the commands issue from a man who has made himself the head of a prevailing fashion in doctrine and who rules his followers ruthlessly. He may have no power of physical violence and yet men obey him. Such may be the power of the crank or the pervert. A false tradition may likewise cast its spell. Our Lord denounced those who left the commandment of God and taught as doctrine the precepts of men (Mark 7:6–8). The false teachers worshiped in vain, and their talk (v. 10 and discussion) resembled their worship.

The tenses of the verbs in this and the previous verse bear examination. "Keep on exposing them severely, in order that they may continue healthy in the faith, not giving their attention to Jewish myths . . . ." These words would allow for a "visitation" of the island. Titus would go to city after city, and in each one he would unmask the false teachers. The exposure would therefore be repeated, a fact suggested by the present tense. It would seem that so far the false teachers are in danger but not yet ruined. Even the men whose *commands* are mentioned "are rejecting," "are turning away from" *the truth*. Paul did not here say that they had completed the action, as he did when reporting on "all who are in Asia" (2 Tim. 1:15). These "turned away" from him: they left him, repudiated him, rejected him. Paul did not go so far as this in speaking of the "men of the *commands*." They had not yet "turned away" from *the truth*. ("Turn away from" and *reject* render the same Greek verb.) As they are still "turning away" there may be hope for them—if they repent. But Paul saw the danger from men who had actually turned away and he went on to picture a darker scene.

Verse 15: To the pure all things are pure, but to the corrupt and unbelieving nothing is pure; their very minds and consciences are corrupted: A question of attitudes. The primary reference is to the ascetic requirements of the false teachers (cf. 1 Tim. 4:1–5 and its discussion and references). Christians no longer need to draw distinctions between clean and unclean foods. To the pure in heart, to those who have been made clean by the Word received in faith (Matt. 5:8; John 15:3; Acts 15:9), all foods are clean (Mark 7:19). God is their Creator and all that he made is good. *The corrupt,* the defiled, religiously (John 18:28) as well as morally, because they are *unbelieving,* cannot take this attitude. As unbelievers they cannot say that Jesus has declared all foods clean. In practice they themselves may "eat anything," but they have not a Christian doctrine to justify their action. They do not believe Christian doctrine. In consequence to them *nothing is pure.*

Their attitude is not merely the absence of a doctrine. Because they are unbelievers and have not been cleansed by the Word, even *their . . . minds and consciences* are unclean and defiled. To them *nothing* in the world *is pure;* not even themselves. They have no doctrine to justify it and no experience to prove it. They are still in their sins. For *minds* see discussions on 1 Timothy 6:5; 2 Timothy 3:8. For *consciences* references are given in the discussion on 2 Timothy 1:3. The plurals are used because each man has one mind and one conscience; "they" therefore have *minds and consciences.* (Cf. also Luke 11:41.)

The first part of the verse sounds like a popular maxim, and it is so used today. What it certainly does not mean is that everything, good and bad, can be bundled together into one parcel and labeled *pure* without distinction by *the pure.* If this were the meaning it would be dangerous doctrine. The author remembers a visit paid to a circus in his boyhood. In the fairground were a number of sideshows where for a small price of admission patrons could see various "wonders." Inside, the showman quoted our proverb, *to the pure all things are pure,* and then after an appropriate little homily he told us that we were to see Eve, the first woman. The curtain was raised and revealed a scantily dressed woman. The reason for quoting the text was now obvious; but the exegesis was wrong. Even *the pure* do not make the new morality right.

Verse 16: They profess to know God, but they deny him by their deeds; they are detestable, disobedient, unfit for any good deed: Profession, practice and evaluation. Paul has passed on from the false teachers who may be won back (v. 13) to the extremists whose *deeds* belie their words. *Profess* is a word of confession: see on 1 Timothy 6:12 f. They were confessing with their lips but not believing in their heart (Rom. 10:9 f.). God is known in Christ and having faith in Christ is the same as knowing him. John indeed can link faith and knowledge very closely. "We have believed, and have come to know, that you are the Holy One of God" (John 6:69); "we know and believe the love God has for us" (1 John 4:16). The variation in the order of faith and knowledge corresponds to the different "moods" of the spiritual life. *To know God* is not a characteristic of the heathen. (See further 1 Thess. 4:5; 2 Thess. 1:8; 2 Tim. 1:12.) It is through faith that Christ dwells in our hearts, and he gives to his believing people the power to know the love of Christ which surpasses knowledge (Eph. 3:17–19).

When the extremists *deny him* they repudiate him as God and reject him from their lives; and they *deny* their claim *to know God*. This they do *by their deeds*. Words and *deeds* conflict. They have "disowned the faith" (cf. 1 Tim. 5:8 and discussion). It is clear from the rest of the verse that in Paul's view they had passed the point of no return. Their denial was not an episode in their lives; they had erected it into a principle (see on 2 Tim. 2:12 f.). Our Lord has provided for the "episode": "every one who speaks a word against the Son of man will be forgiven" (Luke 12:10). The principle of their practical denial reflected "minds and consciences" (v. 15) finally closed to the gospel, the ultimate unforgivable blasphemy against the Holy Spirit. For *they are detestable.*

Detestable is an adjective, the noun of which is often translated "abomination" (cf. Luke 16:15). If we trace the meaning back to its origin we find some such idea as "loathing and disgust in the presence of a bad smell." Shakespeare caught the sense in *Hamlet:* "my offence is rank, it smells to heaven" (act 3, scene 3). The background of the word is the Old Testament, where the concept of abomination manifests a fairly uniform pattern. God's abomination of anything—or anybody—involves his distance, anger, hatred, opposition and destruction. The extremists among the false teachers clearly stand under judgment.[1]

They are *detestable* because they are *disobedient:* they are not only "insubordinate" (v. 10) to men but *disobedient* to God. Paul knew from experience what this meant (3:3), but he had not spurned the grace of God (3:4–7; cf. 1 Tim. 1:12–16). He had not been disobedient to the heavenly vision (Acts 26:19). These false teachers were probably disobeying the law; they were certainly *disobedient* to the gospel, for the gospel is to be obeyed as well as believed (cf. Rom. 10:16; 2 Thess. 1:8; 1 Pet. 4:17). In consequence they were *unfit for any good deed.*

Unfit (*adokimos*) might have been used in 2 Timothy 3:8 (see discussion) to render the same Greek adjective, "unfit in regard to the faith." The extremists were "rejects" when it came to choosing any one *for any good deed.* By their disobedience they were "disqualified." Each one of them was in marked contrast to "a vessel for noble use, consecrated . . . , ready for any good work" (2 Tim. 2:21). Consecration is impossible without obedience.

---

1. For detailed examination of "abomination" see R. A. Ward, *Royal Theology: Our Lord's Teaching about God* (London and Edinburgh: Marshall, Morgan & Scott, 1964), pp. 75–87.

IV. THE CHARACTERISTICS OF DIFFERENT CHRISTIAN GROUPS (2:1–10)

As befits sound teaching, Titus was to call for Christian virtues appropriate to the age or status of the various groups. Senior citizens should be sober and serious, manifesting sanity and health in faith and life, the women living out their faith in fitting demeanor and language and temperance. They should train their younger fellow Christians to be good wives and mothers, exemplars in a Christian home in their service of the Word of God. Titus was to inspire the younger men to self-control by his words and deeds. He himself should be a model Christian; nothing should mar his teaching or his speech. This would undermine an opponent's criticisms of the ministry even before they were uttered. Slaves should add luster to doctrine by their submissive loyalty to their masters, their honesty and trustworthiness.

Verse 1: But as for you, teach what befits sound doctrine: A medical lecturer should not spread germs, even verbal ones. Christian *doctrine* is healthy and wholesome. As long as Titus continues to *teach,* the substance of his words must not contain anything which would infect his hearers. The false teachers were already doing that, for they were themselves not "healthy in the faith" (1:13, literal). On the contrary Titus must bring health to his listeners by the purity of his words.

There is a strong contrast here between Titus and the men he has to oppose. *But as for you (su de)* recalls 1 Timothy 6:11; 2 Timothy 3:10; 3:14 (see discussion); 4:5. The preacher should not be afraid to be "different." He should stand out in vivid contrast to others, especially errorists, deceivers and those who merely give the people what they want.

Titus will succeed in carrying out the apostle's exhortation if he not only holds fast to *sound doctrine,* keeps it and guards it, but also abides in it, dwells in it. The "many mansions" of Christian doctrine are not the insalubrious tenements which characterize a slum. They are the clean and wholesome home in which every Christian, and especially every minister, should dwell.

Titus must not merely "visit" the many mansions when he needs a sermon! Nor should he be regarded as one who discharges his obligation if he takes a single opportunity to *teach* and thus gets his evidence on the record. Nor is it enough for him to give a course of lectures or sermons which will *teach* what is necessary. He may do this. But the apostle was looking out into the future, at least until the time when he sent for Titus (3:12). Until then Titus must "keep on" with his speaking and teaching.

The *sound doctrine* is the doctrine of Christ (cf. John 7:16 and 2 John 9). Charles Wesley caught the spirit of the "health" which it brings.

> Jesus! the name that charms our fears,
>   That bids our sorrows cease;
> 'Tis music in the sinner's ears,
>   'Tis life and *health,* and peace.

It is plain that the work of Titus was not to be purely academic. There is a place for academic instruction, for theology is such a discipline. But the work of Titus was to be pastoral.

Verse 2: Bid the older men be temperate, serious, sensible, sound in faith, in love, and in steadfastness: Detail in moral and religious instruction. *Temperate* appears also in 1 Timothy 3:2, 11 (see discussions). In the present verse the literal meaning is prominent, without necessarily rejecting the idea of being "temperate in all things" (cf. 2 Tim. 4:5 and discussion). The Cretans, it will be remembered, were "lazy gluttons" (1:12) and *the older men* would be open to temptation from both unbelieving fellow citizens and "the old man" within them. The exhortation may seem pedestrian in the church, and it may be thought that no Christian needs to be told not to get drunk. The counsel is far more applicable than some people suppose. When older men are converted they have more sins in their experience than younger men, and the pressure of their past is all the stronger. It is a striking fact that when our Lord told the sinless to take the lead in stoning the woman taken in adultery, it was the eldest who went away first (John 8:7–9). They had more sins on their conscience as they had lived longer. *The older men* are indeed in Christ. But no man should presume. It is dangerous even for a mature Christian to adopt the attitude that "I am above that kind of temptation now." It may be true; it should never be taken for granted; and it is safer always to be on guard. In any case we do not know that the older men in Crete were mature. Some of them may have grown rapidly in the spiritual life; but age in itself does not always imply maturity.

Serious corresponds to the "respectful" of 1 Timothy 2:2; 3:4, and to the "gravity" of Titus 2:7. It is used in reference to deacons and women in 1 Timothy 3:8, 11. A full discussion is given on the elusive meaning of the word in the comments on 1 Timothy 2:2. Perhaps the spirit of the word may be given by a contrast. An elderly "playboy" is not an edifying spectacle, but the laughter of an old man does not in itself detract from the fundamental seriousness of his continuing faith and godliness. The empty-headed chattering of a social butterfly may reveal nothing but shallowness, whereas the joy of a beautiful woman may well arise from a deep Christian faith. "The fruit of the Spirit is . . . joy" (Gal. 5:22). The joy of the Christian is not shallow and does not depend on outward circumstances, because it is at heart *serious*.

The older men should resemble a bishop in being *sensible*. The same Greek word (*sōphrōn*) is used to describe a desirable quality in a bishop (see on 1:8) and is translated "master of himself." Such men are not overwhelmed by sudden wild alarms but remain level-headed. In a situation of this nature a bishop can give leadership to his flock, and *the older men*, though not in office as elders but as "ordinary" church members, can themselves exercise a steadying influence on the rest. The rocklike qualities are of additional value when they are spread over the church and not limited to the ministry; though it does not help the church to have a weak minister.

Sound continues the metaphor of health (see on 1:13). It is possible to be an unhealthy Christian, "weak (or 'sick') in faith" (Rom. 14:1 f.; cf. 1 Tim. 6:4 and discussion). We sometimes say that a man is *sound* or "fit" in head, heart and lungs, thus specifying the points in which he has a clean bill of health. So *the older men* are to be healthy *in faith, in love, and in steadfastness.* Soundness in "the" faith (1:13) was appropriate to men who had been teaching. Soundness in personal faith was sought in the group under review. Just as "soundness in lungs" means that a man goes on breathing vigorously and well both in rest and in activity, even when the activity is strenuous; so soundness *in faith* means that *the older men* go on exercising their faith, go on believing and trusting, in both the normal life of the church (cf. 1 Tim. 2:2) and in its strenuous endeavors and emergencies.

So it is with *love* and *steadfastness.* The Christian who is healthy in these virtues will go on loving both God and man. This corresponds to "godliness," and "righteousness," our duty to God and man. See discussion and references on 1:1, 8. And he will go on doing so, whatever the cost. He will stand his ground, for this is the meaning of *steadfastness.*

Faith, love and *steadfastness* are closely associated in 2 Timothy 3:10 (see discussion). The men described in this verse come into the church as liquid concrete. When they "set," they reinforce it and hold it together—all "humanly speaking."

Verse 3: Bid the older women likewise to be reverent in behavior, not to be slanderers or slaves to drink; they are to teach what is good: The same call to holiness—in a woman's dress. There is a certain fittingness which should be the mark of *older* Christian *women's behavior.* By *reverent* Paul did not mean that they should behave at home exactly as they did "in church." General talk about family matters, the weather or the latest news is not inappropriate in the home; but when it takes place in the congregation gathered for worship it rather suggests an absence of purpose and of concentration. He sought rather a behavior on the part of those who were presumably mature in the faith which would reflect in the home their behavior "in church." In everything they said and did they should be "like" people who had gathered with the Christian community for worship. Church life and home life should cohere. All their conduct, though not mechanically repeating their conduct at worship, should fit it. It should never be possible for a critic to say that "you are a Christian; you believe, and you worship with your fellow Christians; your present conduct, your behavior just now, does not 'suit' you." The apostle's meaning is given more fully in his expression, "as befits women who profess religion" (see discussion on 1 Tim. 2:10). The *behavior,* both in church and at home, should express the presence of the faith in the heart; should silently tell the story of the Christ within (cf. 1 Pet. 3:1 f.). This applies whether husbands are Christians or not.

It has been said that gossip is the perennial temptation of women. Paul knew this well (1 Tim. 5:13). *The older women* might have more time and opportunity for it, because their children would be off their hands. Some gossip is quite innocuous and is indeed no more than the kindly interest in others. But sometimes it spreads tales which are untrue, either thoughtlessly or even maliciously. Pride comes in. The unconscious thought is that "I do not do this sort of thing; but you may have heard that . . . ?" This kind of talk is little different from making an accusation, and a false accusation is slander. *The older women* are to guard against such *behavior.* They should make it a subject of prayer *not to be slanderers.*

Once more, they may have time on their hands and may suffer from boredom. They should avoid the steps which lead to their being *slaves to drink*. Far better would it be for them to be *slaves* of righteousness and *slaves* of God (Rom. 6:18, 22). A healthy fear would not be out of place. Drunkenness is no laughing matter. Drunkards will not inherit the kingdom of God (1 Cor. 6:10). Such women probably represent the more wealthy members of the church (cf. 1 Cor. 11:21). It is at first strange to notice that Paul used stronger language with regard to the women than he did with regard to the men, who were to be "temperate" (v. 2 and discussion). It may be that drunkenness in a woman is a more distressing sight; and that, though *older women,* age had not brought Christian maturity (cf. Heb. 5:12–14).

Though *the older women* are to *teach what is good* they are not teachers in the church; they are not permitted to teach (1 Tim. 2:11 f. and discussions). Paul was thinking, not of the teaching office, but of what we should today be inclined to call "influence." There is influence exercised in silence, the testimony of a godly life; and there is such influence with the addition of the speech of social intercourse. By both deeds and words the more senior members of the community can influence the younger. They can set an example, start or support a fashion, or by advice and persuasion lead the younger members into the right course. Paul seems to have had the latter in mind, to judge by what he went on to say in the next verse.

Verse 4: And so train the young women to love their husbands and children: The training is not formal. The life and words of the older women are to be consciously adapted to the purpose of bringing *the young women* to the sensible practice of loving *their husbands and children*. We have deliberately written "bringing to the sensible practice" because the verb means "to bring someone to his senses." It is *sōphronizō,* cognate with *sōphrōn* (see on 1:8; 2:2). Paul did not mean that the young wives were out of their mind. He did mean that the love of husband and children was not only a duty but also sound sense. The woman who is devoid of domestic love can disrupt the home, a result which is far from sensible. With love in her heart for husband and children she can be steadying influence.

The "stay at home" wife may not be the obvious person to call rocklike. But if she loves her husband she will support him, not oppose him. She will aid him in his work and witness, even if he does not hold office in the church, and not wear him out with an unloving obstructiveness. She will encourage him in his private life of prayer and devotion and not divert him with incessant domestic troubles and worries. If he is tempted to be slack it is she who will take the lead and suggest that it is time to get ready to go to church. If she loves her children she will protect them and guide them, steering them firmly and lovingly and not leaving them entirely to their own choice and devices. In regard to her husband she will be a "helpmeet." In regard to her children she may well prove to be another Eunice (cf. 2 Tim. 1:5; 3:15). As a matter of fact the older women who *train* the younger ones do so, not by being or attempting to be teachers in the church, but by adopting the role of Lois, the grandmother of Timothy. A wise woman can *train,* in Paul's meaning of the word, without teaching!

We are inclined to assume that *young women* love their husbands and children automatically. They no doubt "fell in love" at some time, and there

is such a thing as the maternal instinct. But love does not always flow
out of a person, even a wife and mother, as from a mountain spring. Love
in the family requires thoughtfulness and the mother has to work at it. Paul
recognized this, and the older women could inspire the younger.

*Verse 5: To be sensible, chaste, domestic, kind, and submissive to their
husbands, that the word of God may not be discredited:* The detailed outworking of their family love. *Sensible* is *sōphrōn* again: see discussion on the
previous verse. We should distinguish this from the language of a person who
is trying to persuade, even to tempt: "Now do be sensible . . ." In actual
fact what they suggest may be the opposite of what is truly sensible. The
level-headed wife is a prize for any man, and he should value her.

Chaste (*hagnos*), pure or holy, is a cultic word and may be used of God
or Christ (cf. 1 John 3:3). The RSV has, however, done rightly in preferring
the word which is relevant to sex. Paul used the same Greek word in 2 Corinthians 11:2, " . . . I betrothed you to Christ to present you as a pure
bride to her one husband." Timothy was told: "keep yourself pure" (1
Tim. 5:22). In the context of the "training" of the previous verse, to be
chaste is not only a moral duty; it is a form of being sensible. All the
qualities in the present verse are to be the results of the "training." Each of
them is to be the result of "being brought to the sensible practice," because
the construction continues.

Domestic means "working at home," almost "domesticated." They not
merely should stay at home, as opposed to flitting round from house to house,
but should find in the life of the home the outlet for their energies. There
is work to be done, work which their husbands cannot do; they should do it.
This again is sensible. If wives and mothers do not work at home the result
is chaos.

To be *kind* is the natural expression of love for husband and children.
If kindness fills the house, complaint will rarely be heard. It cares for the
children and makes the due preparations for the husband's return from work.
It is a thoughtful activity, though not a bare calculation, because it springs
from love. But it is indeed sensible; its absence could disturb the peace of the
home.

In bidding wives to be *submissive to their husbands* Paul was striking a
familiar note in the ancient world, though with an addition. It was not
merely domestic morality which he had in view. It was all "in the Lord."
(See discussion on 1:6.) *Submissive* means "subordinate," "subject to" (Col.
3:18).

The ultimate purpose of the behavior of the wife and mother is *that the
word of God may not be discredited.* For *the word of God* see the discussion on
2 Timothy 4:2 and its further references. It will be *discredited* if the behavior
is bad. Failure at any point will reflect on *the word.* If "the young women"
do not love their husbands and children they can be charged with disobedience: the word is not working in their lives. They have received love,
the love of God in Christ—so it may be said; but they are not giving love,
as the Lord commands. "Thou shalt love the Lord thy God . . . and thy
neighbor . . ." (Matt. 22:37-39, KJV). Who is a closer "neighbor" than
the members of one's own home and family? Perhaps the most relevant comment here is to quote 1 Thessalonians 4:9, ". . . you yourselves have been

taught by God to love one another." What is taught by God must be *the word of God.* If it is disobeyed the world criticizes the Word rather than the disobedient.

If the women lose their heads and are not *sensible,* they have gained no profit from the education which the grace of God brings and are not "sober" (see on v. 12); and it is *the word of God* which has told them of the grace of God. The same applies if they are not *chaste.* If they (Christians!) are not *domestic* and *kind,* the blame will be laid on *the word* for failing to inspire the right sort of homemaker. If they refuse to be *submissive* they will break the peace and create strife in the home, a product of the flesh which will be attributed to *the word* (cf. Gal. 5:19 f.).

Discredited is literally "blasphemed." It is significant that both *the word of God* and "the name of God," as well as "the teaching," may be blasphemed (see 1 Tim. 6:1 and discussion). When men attribute the failures of Christians to the teaching which they have received and not to their own weaknesses, the Word of God and the name of God are blasphemed.

It is noteworthy that Paul has inserted a good deal of the life required from the young women by including it in the training which the older women should give. The latter look very much like deaconesses (see on 1 Tim. 3:11). When they are "reverent in behavior" (v. 3) they are "serious."

Verse 6: Likewise urge the younger men to control themselves: Sōphrōn again! (See on 1:8; 2:2, 4 f.) The verb is *sōphroneō.* If *the younger men* are level-headed they will *control themselves.* This is appropriate advice to those who have not yet attained to Christian maturity, in whom the tides of sex are flowing strongly, and who have a background of heathenism. The Cretans were hardly likely to have a lofty code of sexual morality. A wider reference to the wildness of Cretan youth is not ruled out. They should think of themselves with sober judgment (cf. Rom. 12:3).

Urge means "persuade with authority" (see on 1 Timothy 1:3 and its further references). Paul here displays great tact. When a minister is dealing with young men, especially Cretan young men, the soft approach of mere suggestion will probably fall on deaf ears. Simply to order them about will probably antagonize them. To attempt to persuade, with all the authority of the Word of God, is the wisest course.

In spite of differences of duties appropriate to older men, older women, younger women, and younger men, there is a certain similarity. *Likewise* (cf. v. 3) suggests that Titus has the initiative. The various groups presumably do not come to him and ask for detailed instructions in their Christian duty. In any case it is part of his work of "amendment" (1:5). The appointment of elders would do much to set right what was defective, but Paul did not mean to suggest that they could do it all.

Verse 7: Show yourself in all respects a model of good deeds, and in your teaching show integrity, gravity: "Like people, like priest" (Hos. 4:9), i.e., the people will be like the priest. The bad side of the relationship is seen in the Book of Hosea. Without diminishing in the slightest the power of a man of God to rise to greater spiritual heights than those attained by his minister, we can still say that to a large degree the tone of a congregation is set by the minister. If he is utterly dedicated to Christ, his object is to lead his people into ever deeper knowledge of him—and he does not fail completely. If he is skilled in doctrine, he will teach them "the deep things of God," God's profundities (cf. 1 Cor. 2:10). If he has not grown in grace himself, and does not grow, he will leave his people as immature as he found them. If he is himself something of a saint, in the popular sense of the term, it is likely that their spiritual life may grow in "godliness" and they may advance in sanctification.

So in his *good deeds* Titus was to show himself *a model.* Obviously he was to be an example to the church and to that extent was an example to be copied. But the thought seems to be that if any one asked what a real Christian was, it would be enough to point to Titus and say: look at him. His faith comes out in his works. He is a "work man" who has no need to be ashamed, for his faith rightly "works" through love (cf. Gal. 5:6; 2 Tim. 2:15). Note the *motif* of "work." *Deeds* are "works."

Timothy was similarly to be an example of what a Christian is (cf. 1 Tim. 4:12 and discussion). Paul specified the details to him: he was to be *a model* "in speech and conduct, in love, in faith, in purity." With Titus, Paul was content to say *in all respects.* This we may regard as Paul's call to Titus as a Christian. Every Christian ought to be a model, though the duty is pressed home hard on a minister. But Titus had other work which was not open to every member of the church. He was a teacher and *in* his *teaching* he was to *show integrity.* The last word does not mean that Titus was to be "intellectually honest." Paul would want him to be, but that is not the present meaning. *Integrity (aphthoria)* is literally "incorruption." Nothing was to "spoil" the teaching which Titus gave. The Christian message must be given in its entirety and be rightly proportioned and balanced, without distortion. It should not suffer the disadvantage of being given for the sake of private gain. The *teaching* must be right and the motives must be right.

Gravity is the quality of "seriousness" (see on 2:2). In dealing with the younger men it would be important not to misunderstand its import—and its importance. It would not help if Titus never even smiled because he was always trying to show *gravity.* It would be on the right lines if Titus always remembered (without saying so) that he was a minister of Christ; if he guarded against saying and doing anything which he would regret; and if prayer with anyone would not be an embarrassment.

Verse 8: And sound speech that cannot be censured, so that an opponent may be put to shame, having nothing evil to say of us: Denying him ammunition! *Sound speech* is healthy speech. (Cf. 1:9, 13; 2:1, and discussion on 2 Tim. 1:13.) Doctrine can be healthy and without infection. A man's faith can be healthy and uncontaminated by the efforts of false teachers. A minister ought to be healthy in both faith and doctrine, but even this does not exhaust his obligations. It is possible, certainly it is possible in theory, for a man to be *sound* in faith and doctrine and yet spoil the impact of his preached message by unhealthy *speech.* It might set forth the truth of God in Christ with faithfulness and yet be redolent of bad spirit and jealousy. A preacher might not be unmindful of the pattern of sound words and yet through his speech show that even in preaching Christ he was trying to outdo his less gifted brethren. Paul had found this in his own experience. "Some indeed preach Christ from envy and rivalry . . ." (Phil. 1:15–18). To glorify oneself when engaged in preaching Christ is to divert attention from the Savior to the preacher; and if successful in gaining a personal following it confirms people in their spiritual immaturity (cf. 1 Cor. 3:1–4).

When the preacher or teacher uses *sound* language it *cannot be censured* in the sense that in actual fact it contains no defect. There is nothing unhealthy about it, nothing from which a listener can "catch a disease." This does not mean that some people will not try to censure it! *An opponent* is ever on the alert, and one of the motives in using sound speech is to disarm him. He is waiting to criticize, but if the speech is sound he will have no opportunity. He has *nothing evil to say of us.* Paul is realistic here. Logically, if the language were at fault, it would be the *speech* which should be under attack. The *opponent* would have something *evil to say* of "it," not *of us.* But Paul knew—as many a minister knows—that when the language is not up to standard and is not *sound,* it is the preacher who receives the missiles, not the *speech.* Further, the apostle said *of us,* not "of you, Titus." He knew the irrationality of sinful men. Let one preacher disgrace himself one day in the pulpit and the critics will be yelping about "you preachers." In addition, in saying *of us,* Paul was identifying himself with Titus. They were engaged in the same struggle. This would encourage Titus.

The *opponent* is not further defined. The term could cover the critical pagan or, as we should say today, "the outsider," and even "the theological watchdog" in the congregation or any person with a grievance. Being *put to shame* seems slightly ambiguous. It may mean really making the opponent feel ashamed of himself, an experience which might be a step towards his conversion or sanctification. This is in the spirit of 1 Corinthians 4:14; 6:5; 15:34. The meaning might, however, savor of *so that an opponent may be* "embarrassed" by *having nothing evil to say of us.* That, if anything, will silence him (cf. 1:11). *Evil* means "to our discredit."

It should be noticed that Titus must combine excellence of personal life and of teaching. The reminder of the dual obligation is relevant today. People say that "it is the life which counts," and indeed it does. Some are fond of saying that "it was not your sermon which influenced me but the Christian character of my neighbor." If this kind of remark calls the church, minister and people alike, to a life of holiness, it is all to the good. But the impression is given that the sermons are of no consequence. Some may not be; but the attack is not only on individual sermons but on preaching as such. This attitude is to be resisted. Preaching and teaching the Christian faith are as necessary as the Christian life truly lived. The life reinforces the preached word; the word explains the quality of the life. An unpreached Christianity is a failure in witness just as much as faith without works is a failure. "You shall be my witnesses . . . make disciples . . . teaching them . . . wherever the gospel is preached" (Matt. 28:19 f.; Mark 14:9; Acts 1:8).

Verse 9: Bid slaves to be submissive to their masters and to give satisfaction in every respect; they are not to be refractory: A long-term policy. For *submissive* see on 1:6; 2:5. A detailed discussion of *slaves* will be found in the section on 1 Timothy 6:1 f. *Submissive* means that they do not attempt to "get above themselves." *To give satisfaction* implies that *their masters* are pleased with their work. If *they are not . . . refractory* they will not refuse their masters; will not contradict them; will not speak against them either to their face or to others; will not oppose them; and certainly will not "answer back." In seeking *to give satisfaction,* i.e., to be pleasing, slaves who are Christians have the inspiration of knowing that "Christ did not please himself" (Rom. 15:3).

There is an all but insoluble problem of punctuation with regard to *in every respect.* The phrase can be taken with *submissive* or with *give satisfaction.* It is not of great moment because either interpretation will carry the other. (Cf. Eph. 6:5–8; Col. 3:22–25.) The thought is prompted, from a comparison with these other passages, that *slaves* should please men but not merely please men: their work is ultimately only the means of pleasing the Lord.

Verse 10: Nor to pilfer, but to show entire and true fidelity, so that in everything they may adorn the doctrine of God our Savior: The comprehensive motive. *Pilfer* is the word used of Ananias and Sapphira who "kept back some of the proceeds" of the sale of a piece of property (Acts 5:2 f.) for themselves. It is sometimes on the scale of petty theft and sometimes even bigger. Those who work in large establishments frequently have opportunities to turn public property, or the property of the firm or the hotel, to their own use. It is almost impossible to check small items without searching clothes and rooms—and even stomachs! Slaves without property of their own would be especially susceptible to such temptations. The trend continues. In societies which have emerged from slavery, the lower rungs of the social ladder are still marked by much pilfering.

Christian slaves, by contrast, are to show that they are completely to be trusted. Nothing which belongs to their masters is to be found at any time in their own pockets. This in itself would mark out the Christian slave, because he would be an outstanding exception. If the master ever inquired of his slave the reason why he never took anything; if he ever said, "Why is it that I never catch you doing this sort of thing?" it would be an opportunity to preach Jesus.

An untrustworthy slave would hardly be a rarity. But if he were known as a Christian the church would come in for a share of the blame and the Name of God would be blasphemed (cf. 1 Tim. 6:1). Paul now put this thought positively. The motive of the Christian slave must be *in everything* to *adorn the doctrine.*

This is a lovely expression, and it may be taken as the apex of Paul's vision for the slave. In spite of the conditions of his work, sometimes fearful, sometimes tolerable, sometimes almost enjoyable in a good family, the slave is really serving the Lord Christ and will not lose his reward. Slave though he is, he is really a benefactor. This is an ambitious description of a slave, for it was given as a title to princes and other rulers (Luke 22:25). The name of Ptolemy Euergetes springs to the mind, one of the kings of Egypt (246–221 B.C.) after the empire of Alexander the Great had been carved up. (Euergetes = benefactor.) Paul spoke in 1 Timothy 6:2 of the *euergesia* rendered by a slave.

Yet now Paul looked higher still. In one sense *the doctrine* is to be left alone. No one must tamper with it, even to embellish it. Christian truth stands alone in its solitary grandeur. But the slave could *adorn* it with the quality of his life. Two leading ideas are suggested. He could bring out its grandeur by the unfailing (*in everything*) witness of the life he leads. He could make *the doctrine* like the temple, "adorned with noble stones and offerings" (Luke

21:5). And he could make it attractive to those who made inquiries of its content. When a bride is "adorned for her husband" (Rev. 21:2) her object is not to repel. The slave's submissiveness and *fidelity,* with all the traits of character of which Paul had spoken, would clothe *the doctrine* with beauty. Years ago the present writer was told by an aged missionary that Japanese bankers were always glad to employ Chinese Christians because of their eminent trustworthiness. They did indeed *adorn the doctrine.* This would be a high privilege for slaves, and the thought of it should encourage them to continue a faithful and unfailing discipleship. The modern hired hand, though far from being a slave, could well get the message.

For *God our Savior* see discussion on 1 Timothy 1:1 and the further references; cf. Titus 1:3 f. The alternation previously noted, of God our Savior and Christ our Savior, prepares the way for verse 13.

V. THE JUSTIFICATION OF THE PRECEDING EXHORTATION (2:11–15)

The grace of God, which appeared with its offer of salvation for all men, educates Christians in particular in their obligations. All groups should repudiate impiety and worldly desires and live now for God and for others, while their eyes should look to the future. They should eagerly await the coming of the Savior who redeemed them from all that they should repudiate and made them his own people, eager to do his will while they wait for him. This is the substance of what Titus should say to his congregations. He was not to be disregarded.

Verse 11: For the grace of God has appeared for the salvation of all men: A theological reason for ethical behavior. The significant word "for" (*gar*) corresponds to the causal *hoti* ("because") in the First Epistle of Peter where "it introduces the theological ground of an ethical injunction." [1] Examples are 1 Peter 2:21; 3:18. Christian life grows out of Christian faith, and faith is directed towards Christ crucified. His death for us substantiates the claim of his example to us.

If a novelist in his descriptive narrative suddenly said that "love" had *appeared,* we should expect some reference to the hero or heroine. There can be no love without some person who loves. Love has no existence by itself. So it is with *grace.* Paul meant that it was possible to point to some appearance and say, "that is God being gracious." A prophet or a preacher may tell "about" *the grace of God.* But however true and moving their words may be, they cannot rise to the heights implied by the word *appeared.* The aorist tense implies a decisive act, almost a sudden act, and the expression refers to the incarnation of Christ. The "appearance" began at the nativity, but Paul had in mind the whole life of Christ on earth. At a precise point in history (cf. Luke 3:1 f.), not merely "in the ancient world before the middle ages," God intervened. The day of *grace* dawned "to give light to those who sit in darkness and in the shadow of death" (Luke 1:79).

---

1. E. G. Selwyn, *The First Epistle of St. Peter,* 2nd ed. (London: Macmillan & Co., 1952), p. 217.

When *the grace of God . . . appeared,* Christ *appeared;* or rather, when Christ *appeared* it was *the grace of God* which *appeared.* Jesus is the embodiment of *grace.* The thought is the same as that of 2 Timothy 1:10 (see discussion). The verb *appeared* is cognate with the noun "epiphany." Christians stand between the first and the second epiphany, the First Advent and the Second. The verb is repeated in 3:4. For *grace* see further on 1 Timothy 1:2.

For the salvation of all men is not easy to elucidate. Paul did not teach universalism though he offered the gospel universally. The "salvation" word is an adjective and its spirit would be shown by rendering thus: *"the grace of God . . . appeared,* remedial for *all men."* Consult further the discussions on 1 Timothy 1:15; 2:4; 4:10.

Verse 12: Training us to renounce irreligion and worldly passions, and to live sober, upright, and godly lives in this world: Grace redeemed once, and once for all, saves everyone who believes, and educates everyone who will listen. *Training* is a word which belongs to education, not to sport. A man may be trained for a running or swimming race, but in the larger business of life he needs the training which is education. A. B. Bruce once wrote a book entitled *The Training of the Twelve* and it reminds us that Jesus was—and is—the supreme educator. He was the teacher and the Twelve were the disciples, and he still teaches us. The disciples were men who received information, observers who saw their Master embody his lessons in his own life, and apprentices who learned by doing, keeping their eyes on the Master.

Renounce is our Lord's word "deny" (Luke 9:23; cf. Matt. 16:24; Mark 8:34). Any man who thus refuses to "repudiate himself" is guilty of *irreligion.* Both "self" and *irreligion* the disciple must *renounce.* They amount to the same thing: thou shalt love the Lord thy God. *Passions* are "desires" and they are *worldly* when limited to the present world and characteristic of it: the world hates the disciples, Jesus and God (John 15:18–24), and therefore goes its own disobedient way. Our Lord's words about looking at a woman lustfully, "to desire her" (Matt. 5:28), show that he was *training* his men *to renounce . . . worldly passions.* The *passions* or desires may not always be concerned with sex. The Prodigal Son "was desiring" to eat the swine's food, when his father's hired servants had ample food and a banquet awaited him in his father's home. The "far country" does not inspire the best desires (cf. Luke 15:16–23).

The *training* which Jesus gave was "the grace of God . . . , *training us."* Its lessons are given afresh in Scripture, which is "profitable for . . . training . . ." (see on 2 Tim. 3:16). The lessons which were given in act are not of course repeated; but the record is there, to be used by the preacher or teacher; and the Holy Spirit illumines.

So much for the negative side. Timothy was told to "shun youthful passions" (2 Tim. 2:22 f.; cf. 3:5; and discussions). Positively our education teaches us the kind of life we should lead in Christ *in this world,* in this present age (see on 2 Tim. 4:10). *Sober* largely concerns ourselves and has been considered already as "sensible" (see on 2:4 f., *sōphrōn*). *Upright* is "righteous" and means doing our duty to our fellowmen (see on 1:8). The *godly* life, or godliness, piety, appears as "our religion" in 1 Timothy 3:16. It recognizes and performs man's duty to God. (See on 1 Tim. 6:11.)

The grace of God, embodied in the historic Jesus, gave *training* in living *sober, upright, and godly lives. Sober* is illustrated in the restoration of the demoniac to "his right mind"—"sitting at the feet of Jesus" (Luke 8:35); and in the Lord's command not to be anxious (Matt. 6:31). *Upright* or "righteous" is a necessary quality in which the disciples must surpass the scribes and Pharisees (Matt. 5:20). Prayer forms a considerable part of godliness and it was included in our Lord's teaching (e.g., Matt. 6:5–15).

Verse 13: Awaiting our blessed hope, the appearing of the glory of our great God and Savior Jesus Christ: Ethical behavior is inspired by a theological hope. *Awaiting* implies more than merely letting time pass. A condemned criminal lies in his prison, *awaiting* his execution. This is far from the meaning here. The Greek verb is used of receiving, of welcoming people: Jesus welcomes sinners (Luke 15:2; cf. Rom. 16:1 f.; Phil. 2:29). When the welcome is directed towards an event, the verb has the idea of "I am already welcoming," if the event is still in the future. Hence comes the meaning, "I am eagerly awaiting." When the forty Jews plotted to assassinate Paul and to entangle the Roman tribune in their plan, they were eagerly waiting for his consent (Acts 23:21). In the same spirit Christians should be looking forward with glad anticipation to the Second Advent.

In one sense, if men are hopeful they do not wait for a hope, as they already have it. "I am hoping" means that "I now have hope." In the present verse *hope* therefore means "the object of hope," "what is hoped for." Paul wrote elsewhere of "Christ Jesus our hope" (1 Tim. 1:1 and discussion). This *hope* is *blessed.* The term is applied to God (1 Tim. 1:11; 6:15 and discussions). In his inherent nature he is above the labors, the sufferings and the corruptibility of human life. As applied to Christ our *hope,* it must mean that he also shares these attributes. He, too, is *blessed.* This involves no denial of his toil and suffering on earth in the days of his flesh. We are thinking of the attributes of deity rather than the experiences of humanity. There is an underlying thought that when the *hope* is realized and *the appearing* occurs, the labors and sufferings, the temptations and the corruptibility will belong to the past. By grace—not by right or by their own inherent nature—the people of God will be *blessed.* "Come, ye blessed of my Father . . ." (Matt. 25:34; the different Greek verb hardly affects our statement).

"The blessed hope and appearing," with only one definite article, is a single idea, brought out by the apposition of *blessed hope, the appearing. Appearing* is "epiphany," for which see discussion on 1 Timothy 6:14. Inasmuch as our *hope* is Christ, *the appearing* means "Christ being manifest." But Paul did not put it exactly like this. He spoke of *the appearing of the glory.* For *glory* see discussions on 1 Timothy 1:11, 17; 3:16. Christ is himself *the glory* of God: in him we see revealed the being, the character, the majesty and the might of God; in him is the "radiance" of God, "the glory of God in the face of Christ" (2 Cor. 4:6). It would hardly have been surprising if the apostle had spoken of *the appearing of the glory* of God and he would not have been wrong. As it is he wrote of the glory of Christ. Christ has his own glory, as Paul's earlier language suggests: "the body of his glory" (Phil. 3:21, RV). It is in no sense in competition with the glory of God, which is Christ himself. The term is very appropriate in the context. At present Christ is hidden, though known to believers through the Holy Spirit. In his *appearing* will be revealed the now hidden Christ: his being, his character, his majesty and his might, in all the splendor of that magnificent day. Men will then know that he exists—his being; they will realize his holy and righteous character when those who have finally spurned his love in the gospel are dealt with by him; they will gaze in wonder at his majesty when he is glorified in his saints and marveled at in all who have believed; and they will shrink at the sight of the angels of his power and the glory of his might. (2 Thess. 1:7–10; 2:8 hereby takes on new meaning.) Christ has his own glory; and because *the appearing of the glory* is *the appearing* of Christ, he is (as well as has) his own glory. Thus Christ is the glory of God and is the glory of himself. Perhaps we ought to have realized this earlier: "I and the Father are one" (John 10:30).

The one who will thus be present in his *appearing* is described by the apostle as *our great God and Savior Jesus Christ.* There can be little doubt that this is the correct translation. Some indeed prefer the RSV footnote, "the great God and our Savior," largely because of the reserve shown by the New Testament in simply calling Jesus God. There certainly is reserve, perhaps because of a healthy instinct which hesitated even to seem to place him among the "many gods" (1 Cor. 8:5). Even here, however, we have to remember that the church did not falter at the name of "Lord"—though there were "many lords."

If the word "mediator" had been used by the apostle instead of *God,* it is doubtful if any questions would have been raised. The one (Greek) definite article would lead naturally and smoothly into "*great* mediator *and Savior.*" (In translation we should, of course, have to bring forward the Greek possessive pronoun and say *our great* ...) The argument from the one article is not determinative but it is weighty.[1] *God and Savior* is an expression used in the period in view, especially of Roman emperors. Paul might well be stating the truth of the matter. *Appearing* or "epiphany" is appropriate to the Second Advent; we are concerned with the coming of Christ. It is pointed out that God is not called *great* elsewhere in the New Testament. But Jesus is: "He will be *great*" (Luke 1:32). He is the *great God* in contrast to both the emperor and heathen deities. Cf. Acts 19:27 f., "Great is Artemis of the Ephesians!" (see TDNT 4:538–40).

(Texts for further study are: John 1:1, 18—RSV note b; 20:28; Romans 9:5—RSV note n; Phil. 2:6; Col. 2:9; 2 Thess. 1:12; Heb. 1:8 f.; 2 Pet. 1:1; 1 John 5:20. See TDNT 3:104–6. Oscar Cullman regards it as probable that in Titus 2:13 *God* refers to *Christ.*)

Further points deserve some emphasis. Paul was using theological language but he was not writing with the cold precision of a textbook, even a textbook of orthodox theology. He did not set out to include everything. His words are the words of faith and worship. If Jesus is not God we ought not to worship him. Every time prayer is addressed to Jesus we are saying in deed if not in word that Jesus is God (cf. Acts 7:59). Error would enter if, when saying that he is God, we insisted that this is the whole story. We say that he is man, and nobody objects: there is more to be said. We say that he is God: let nobody object. There is more to be said. He is the eternal Son of God, coequal with

---

1. See Nigel Turner, *A Grammar of New Testament Greek* 3:181; and his *Grammatical Insights into the New Testament,* pp. 15 f. C. F. D. Moule (*An Idiom Book of New Testament Greek,* p. 110) thinks the correct omission of the second article is probable.

the Father and the Holy Spirit, and for us men and our salvation he became man without ceasing to be God. He has, and is, his own glory, as well as being the glory of God. He will come "in his glory and the glory of the Father ..." (Luke 9:26). Verses 12 and 13 give the purpose and the content of the "training." We should "renounce" decisively, live a life of "sobriety . . . ," all the while *awaiting.*

Verse 14: Who gave himself for us to redeem us from all iniquity and to purify for himself a people of his own who are zealous for good deeds: This explains the blessedness of the hope. He who is eagerly awaited is none other than the Redeemer. It is not necessary to ask to whom he *gave himself.* The expression points to the death of Christ: he *gave* "his life" (Mark 10:45). He did not fight to avoid death and then lose. He did not merely submit because he could not avoid it. He did not die, protesting all the time. He freely *gave himself* and voluntarily died. It was his Messianic task: he "must" (Mark 8:31; 9:31; 10:32–34); and yet he gladly did (Heb. 12:2). This is the "second stage" of the giving, in which the Son continued what his Father had begun. "God so loved the world that he gave his only Son . . ." (John 3:16). (Cf. John 10:17 f.)

It was not a meaningless death. He did not throw away his life. His death was *for us.* Some people tell us that they are more interested in the fact of the atonement and know little or nothing about its theory. To emphasize the fact is excellent; to deny knowledge of its theory is unnecessary. It has a meaning, indicated by its purpose. He died *to redeem us.*

Redemption is a means of deliverance from captivity, from slavery, or from punishment (cf. Exod. 21:28–30) by the payment of a ransom. The picture is a vivid one, but its details must not be pressed with regard to the atonement. Thus we should not ask to whom the ransom was paid. For nearly a thousand years Christian thought was dominated by the idea of the payment of the ransom to Satan, until a corrective was administered by Anselm (A.D. 1033–1109) in his *Cur Deus Homo?* (Why did God become Man?). It is legitimate to look into the question of the price of the ransom, in view of Peter's statement. ". . . you were redeemed [same Greek verb] . . . not with perishable things such as silver or gold, but with the precious blood of Christ, like that of a lamb without blemish or spot" (1 Pet. 1:18 f.). The crude "price" of commercial transaction is here rejected, but the cost or effort is retained. Redemption did not just "happen." It was not due to a divine fiat. The Savior *gave himself,* his life. The language of "blood" is sacrificial, with the result that two concepts are brought together, redemption and sacrifice. (See discussion on 1 Tim. 2:6; and cf. Eph. 1:7, " . . . we have redemption through his blood." See also Rom. 3:24 f.; 5:9.)

Paul did not here say *to redeem us from* captivity, slavery or punishment. He said *from all iniquity.* This term (*anomia*) means "lawlessness," and it refers to a frame of mind or a lawless deed. "Sin is lawlessness" (1 John 3:4). Lawlessness is thus a captivity, a slavery (John 8:34), and is deserving of punishment. The Redeemer *gave himself* in order that he might *redeem us from* it *all.* This part of the verse recalls Psalm 130:8 (Ps. 129:8, LXX; cf. Ezekiel 37:23, LXX).

A second aspect of his purpose is *to purify.* Paul could hardly have been thinking of a merely ceremonial purity. The question to be decided is therefore whether he was thinking of a formed character or whether he was looking further back. Did he think of men with clear consciences or of something in addition? His teaching here seems to overlap that of the Epistle to the Hebrews. This indeed is suggested by his allusion to *a people of his own* (*laos periousios*) in Exodus 19:5, LXX. The passage goes on to speak of the *people* as a priesthood (Hebrew: "kingdom of priests"), and a priest is one who can draw near to God (cf. Exod. 19:22; Ezek. 44:13). This is a privilege which, according to the Epistle to the Hebrews, is thrown open to all God's people. All may draw near, provided they have been purified. If the sprinkling of the blood of animals led to the purification of the flesh, "how much more shall the blood of Christ . . . purify your conscience from dead works to serve [sacerdotal term: cf. Heb. 8:5] the living God" (Heb. 9:13 f.). The blood qualifies a man to approach God and offers him access to God. ". . . we have confidence to enter the sanctuary by the blood of Jesus . . ." (Heb. 10:19).

There are two aspects to be kept in mind. Without the blood men may not draw near to God. The way has been "opened" (v. 20) which before was closed to men. By means of his sacrifice Jesus has "put away" sin (Heb 9:26). But further, "without the shedding of blood there is no forgiveness of sins" (Heb. 9:22). This introduces a new factor: not all men have been forgiven. The blood makes forgiveness possible but it has to be received. It would be inadequate for an unbelieving man to refuse to "draw near" on the ground that everything had been done. The Epistle combines the shed blood with the human response. "Let us draw near with a true heart in full assurance of faith, with our hearts sprinkled clean from an evil conscience and . . ." (Heb. 10:22). Priests were sprinkled with blood as a "qualification" for their priestly duties. It was hardly done without their consent. So men must "let themselves be sprinkled": they must trust the one who died for them.

We have seen above that redemption was associated with sacrifice. In the Epistle to the Hebrews sacrifice was associated with redemption (9:12, 15). Redemption cuts the bonds of sin's liability and offers deliverance. Sacrifice offers access to God; and it does so because purification for sins was made (Heb. 1:3). See further on 1 Timothy 1:5.

Those who receive the benefit of the purification by drawing near to God in faith are called *a people of his own*. The context of this allusion is illuminating (Exod. 19:5). "You shall be my own possession [*sequllah*] among all peoples; for all the earth is mine." God not only makes a distinction within his own property; he makes an evaluation. His people are his prized possession. He chose them (cf. Deut. 14:2) and loves them (Deut. 7:6–9) and is their covenant God. This is no reason for ecclesiastical complacency but is a call to holiness. The "possession" is a "treasure" (1 Chron. 29:3), which may be likened to a king's "privy purse" in contrast to "crown property" which he holds in trust for public and state purposes. On a humbler plane we may think of a boy's special treasure, a toy or other object which he prizes above all others.

This has practical consequences for the Christian. The present writer as a boy once heard a preacher call attention to a section of the hymn book entitled "the privileges of believers." There was no section of a similar nature for unbelievers. All God's mercies are open to the unbeliever who will cease to be an unbeliever. When he puts his trust in Christ he joins the *people* who are

God's very *own*. All others are his too; but not in the same, intimate sense. (Cf. Acts 20:28; 1 Pet. 2:9.)

A further practical consequence is the nature of the life which God's people should lead. They—strictly "it," to describe *a people,* like "a nation"—are called to be enthusiasts *for good deeds.* All the ardor shown by the Jewish zealot in his struggle against the occupying power of Rome (cf. Luke 6:15; Acts 1:13) or by the modern "demonstrator" should be manifested by the whole church.

The *people of his own* corresponds to the church as the bride of Christ. God is a jealous God, and as the husband of his people he says to all false gods and all who would lay hands on the church: "She is my wife, not yours; she is my *own.*" Society in general admits this attitude as a general principle and cannot logically criticize the divine concentration. All may join.

Verse 15: Declare these things; exhort and reprove with all authority. Let no one disregard you: A word to Titus and to the church. *Declare (lalei)* picks up the "teach" of verse 1. The contents of this whole chapter are to be the substance of the constant teaching of Titus: "keep on saying these things." *Exhort* means "keep on persuading with authority." (See on 1 Tim. 1:3 with its further references; and on Titus 1:9; 2:6.) *Reprove* is the "confute" of 1:9 and the "rebuke" of 1:13 (see discussions). As with *declare* and *exhort* the present imperative means "keep on doing it." On some subjects it is not enough for a minister to say that "I have already preached on that." With all the variety at his command he must consider the ministry of repetition.

Authority usually represents the Greek *exousia,* which in its verbal forms means "I have the right to." The word in the present verse is *epitagē,* translated in 1 Timothy 1:1 and Titus 1:3 by "command." Its meaning seems to be something like "commandingness," well brought out by the rendering of Arndt and Gingrich (p. 302), "with all impressiveness." Perhaps "mastery" would suit. The phrase goes with *reprove.* Paul meant that when it was necessary for Titus to unmask people he should not merely "bring it to their attention." He should "tell" them.

Nobody was to *disregard* Titus. (See on 1 Tim. 4:12.) It was not here a question of the age of Titus. Paul was telling the Cretans to recognize the ministerial status of Titus.

VI. GENERAL ATTITUDE TO SECULAR AUTHORITIES AND TO OTHERS (3:1-2)

The Christians were to be reminded to give submission and obedience to earthly rulers; to be ready for every good work; and to make it plain to all that they were "easy to live with."

Verse 1: Remind them to be submissive to rulers and authorities, to be obedient, to be ready for any honest work: Promptitude enriches submissiveness and obedience. *To be submissive:* "to be subordinate, to be subject to" (see on 1:6). This is not the abject submission of the church to the state, the so-called Erastianism in which the civil authorities have an ascendancy over the church, even in church affairs, and legislate accordingly. There comes a time when the church has to say that "we must obey God rather than men."

The point which Paul was making is that Christians should be good and loyal citizens. The state has its function, given to it by God, and the church must recognize it. It would not help the cause of the kingdom of God if the suspicion arose that the church was a revolutionary body. There is a sense in which the whole message of the gospel can revolutionize society. Leaven so "revolutionizes" dough. But this is not political revolution. Christians are members of the secular society, "the world," as well as of the church. They are "under" the regularly constituted authorities. They must be willing to stay "under," partly because this is God's purpose for the ordering of the world and partly to allay possible suspicion. The preaching of "another king, Jesus" (Acts 17:7) inevitably leads to heathen misunderstanding until the authorities learn that the aim of the church is not the overthrow of the state. Until the authorities realize this, why stoke the fires of their suspicions? Some scholars have thought that one of Luke's purposes in writing the Acts of the Apostles was to show the political harmlessness of Christianity (cf. Acts 26:30–32). (See also Rom. 13:1–7; 1 Pet. 2:13–17.) If Christians are *obedient,* they will not resist the authorities and so will not resist "what God has appointed."

Rulers and authorities are not merely synonyms. The *rulers* means those who are actually ruling; *authorities* tells us that they have the right to do so. The turbulent Cretans already know their duty of submissiveness, but they need Titus constantly to *remind them.*

The prayers of Christians (cf. 1 Tim. 2:1 f.) should overflow in the performance of civic duty. The members of the church should not be sluggish in responding to the call of the state. If they were asked to commit murder, it would not be an *honest work;* but if they were urgently summoned to help in putting out a fire, they should act with alacrity; for Christians should *be ready.* This is one of the practical consequences of sanctification. If they are purified and consecrated they will be *ready.* Holiness will not teach them the best way of dealing with a house on fire; but it will supply a motive power (cf. 2 Tim. 2:21 and discussion).

Verse 2: To speak evil of no one, to avoid quarreling, to be gentle, and to show perfect courtesy toward all men: High ideals for a rough community! If people *speak evil,* they slanderously charge others in their malicious gossip, as Paul had found (cf. Rom. 3:8), or they "denounce" them (cf. 1 Cor. 10:30). We see the very opposite of this in Jesus. When he might have commented on John the Baptist and discussed the possibility of his impatience, depression, misunderstanding or even failure of faith, he spoke highly of him behind his back. John was a prophet, and more than a prophet (Luke 7:18–30). Paul knew from experience also of men who would *speak evil* to his face. The Jews in jealousy contradicted and "reviled him"; they opposed and "reviled him" (Acts 13:45; 18:6). The Christians were to be entirely innocent of this sort of thing. Cretans though they were and constitutionally given to telling lies (1:12), they had a magnificent opportunity for Christian witness. Let them engage in the un-Cretan activity of not telling lies about people! (The preacher could illustrate by reference to un-American activities.) Let them stand out from the general populace by the kindness of all their conversation.

They should not only *avoid* actual *quarreling:* even a quarrelsome person can do that at times. Like the bishop, they should not be quarrelsome (1

Tim. 3:3). They must not be pugnacious, always spoiling for a fight. Once more they were to be un-Cretan and not be "beastly" (1:12).

Like the bishop, the Cretan Christians were *to be gentle* (see discussion on 1 Tim. 3:3). This is a quality which might show itself differently in church members who do not have the supervision of the community. Whereas the bishop should be less rigid in his oversight, the members were to be less rigid in their association with one another and with non-Christians. Without departing from Christian principle the Christians were to be "right" without their rightness hurting people. They should restrain themselves in word and deed. Their "case" may be right but how do they present it? Their claims may be right, but in what spirit do they exercise them? We sometimes hear of well-meaning people whose views are correct and whose motives are above suspicion and yet they do damage by asking for too much, too soon. They cannot unbend. This does not mean that Christians can tamper with the gospel or with the law of God. They must "guard the deposit" at all costs and not water down the faith or God's claims on his people. Godliness and righteousness are still the program. It does mean that there should be a largeness of approach, a winsomeness rather than a threatening, the search for a point of contact rather than a head-on collision. It will have become manifest that there is a "roominess" about this word *gentle* (*epieikēs*) and the concept of "equity" is a helpful start in its interpretation. The Christian should not be so "regularly regular," with his bristles perfectly straight, that he ruins his message of love!

The *perfect courtesy toward all men* has two main features. It avoids all discrimination, because it is exercised *toward all men* and not only toward those who reciprocate. And in any dealings with one particular man, whoever he may be, it does not lapse or falter. It is "all" *courtesy,* not some *courtesy;* and it is toward everybody, *all men* without exception. As "gentleness" it is the fruit of the Spirit (Gal. 5:23). It is not greatly concerned with the external forms of social politeness, like raising one's hat to a lady or standing back to let her go first. It describes the spirit and manner in which actions are done. A man who has been detected in doing wrong is to be restored or "mended" in "a spirit of gentleness" (Gal. 6:1). Opponents are to be corrected "with gentleness" (see discussion on 2 Tim. 2:25) and in the same spirit a defense is to be made of the hope within us (1 Pet. 3:15). When *courtesy* is present, the bully is absent, even the spiritual bully, there is no sign of "superiority," and speech is not heated. All this requires a deep devotional life, godliness as Paul called it. *Courtesy* in the present sense can be hard work and Christians need the aid of the Holy Spirit. It is through him that their actions manifest "warmth" ("his heart warmed towards him") without "heat."

VII. A SIMILAR JUSTIFICATION OF THE PRECEDING REMINDER
(3:3–7)

The earlier reminder was reasonable. For Christians were once as the pagans to whom they now had to witness in their lives, bereft of sense, obedience, direction and mastery, hating and hated. But God in his manifest kindness and goodness saved them, renewing them in their rebirth and giving them the Holy Spirit and making them heirs of eternal life.

Verse 3: For we ourselves were once foolish, disobedient, led astray, slaves to various passions and pleasures, passing our days in malice and envy, hated by men and hating one another: The Christians themselves once needed to be tolerated. From the previous verses in this chapter we can gather the kind of reaction which pagan behavior created: insubordination, laziness, pugnacity in word and deed, and toughness generally. Pagan conduct was answered by pagan conduct. Christians by contrast should answer it by Christian conduct. They knew from their own pre-Christian lives that the normal behavior of pagans needed to be tolerated or sweetly parried, or trouble would result and the social attitudes soured. Paul's exhortations were therefore reasonable. *For* Christians once shared the pagan vices.

This seems to be the force of the explanatory *for*. It explains, not the exhortations themselves but the reasonableness of the exhortations. The thought is: remind them to act in a Christian way towards pagan society, which obviously needs a kindly environment. (They will understand the reasonableness of ·this.) *For we ourselves were once foolish . . . For* thus gives the reason which explains the suppressed sentence. This is a not uncommon Greek idiom which we have met before. (See the discussion on 2 Tim. 4:3.)

There is a tact and a humility in *we ourselves*. Paul did not say "you Cretans." He meant "us Christians" and could include himself—a sure sign that the work of grace had gone deeply into the heart of the former proud Pharisee. He, with others, had been "slow . . . to believe" (Luke 24:25). When he was still "in the flesh" (cf. Rom. 7:5; cf. Eph. 2:3; see on 1 Tim. 3:16) he was quite confident that he himself could do all things needful to enable him to bear God's scrutiny (Phil. 3:4–6), like the *foolish* Galatians in their retrogression (Gal. 3:1–5). He too had known *foolish* desires (cf. 1 Tim. 6:9; cf. Rom. 6:12; 7:8) just as *we ourselves had*. The folly is mainly that of spiritual unintelligence and blindness. *We* had not yet "the mind of Christ" (1 Cor. 2:16).

Disobedient means primarily disobedience to God, with an undertone of restiveness under duly constituted civil authority. *We* wanted to go our own way and so were *led astray*. And we did not always have to be *led;* we went astray (Matt. 18:12). "All we like sheep have gone astray; we have turned every one to his own way" (Isa. 53:6). Each of us so "turned."

Men who were *slaves to various* desires *and pleasures* perforce "obeyed" them (cf. Rom. 6:12). Obedience is precisely what *slaves* have to render. Such unwilling service is vividly pictured in Romans 7:14–25. The universality of sin is implied by the term *various*. When we are thinking of all sorts and conditions of men /we have to remember that one man's meat is another man's poison. The desires or *passions* of one man are not the same as those of another. We do not all enjoy the same *pleasures*. For the meaning of *various* see discussion on 2 Timothy 3:6. Some people, ever bored and restive, are always looking for different kinds of pleasure.

At the heart of the characters already described is selfishness. It is therefore small wonder that they are summed up as *passing our days* or "spending their lives" *in malice and envy*. *Passing* is not meant to suggest that they are always seeking new pastimes, something to make the time pass away. Such people will not "lead a quiet and peaceable life" (1 Tim. 2:2). *Malice* desires and plans evil for others. It looks upon any good which they may have, wishes they did not have it, and wants it. It thus manifests itself as *envy. Malice and envy* do not always deign to hide themselves. Feelings come out in word and deed. Those who speak and act with *malice and envy* find themselves *hated by men* because they are indeed "odious." Their own desire for evil to befall others grows into hatred for them and it is fed when they find themselves the objects of hatred. Thus we find men *hating one another.* Hatred is mutual.

This is hardly the picture of the unbelieving man who is yet deemed to be "a good citizen," respected by neighbors and of some consequence in the community because of his character. Paul's language may have been colored by the general unpleasantness of unconverted Cretans. But there is a deeper reason. The "good citizen" is living on inherited spiritual capital, fast running out. And quite apart from that, civilization itself is a veneer, a thin lid which barely covers a savagery below. In the explosive times and seasons of history, the lid cannot stand the pressure from below and the result is hatred, violence and dissolution. Paul was describing the essential heart of man. The Victorians covered it up. Today it all comes out, in word and deed. One of the best comments on the present verse would be to refer to the newspapers, the radio, and television. Evidence in abundance is supplied. It is an elaboration, through the media of sound and sight, of the one theme, "all have sinned" (Rom. 3:23). Paul included himself in the *we ourselves.* Was he exposing the inner life of the man who cast his vote against the Christians (Acts 26:9–11)?

Verse 4: But when the goodness and loving kindness of God our Savior appeared: A contrast to human badness and hatred. The voice of experience continues, though the proof of this does not appear until the next verse. We were once—living like Cretans! But that has been changed now. As a vital step to this we read of the action of God. The grace of God appeared (2:11); *the goodness* and the *loving kindness of God* appeared. The verb is the same in both verses (see on 2:11) and it would be remarkable if Paul did not have the same event in mind. Whereas in the earlier part he made reference to salvation and then went on to speak of the life which grace "trains" Christians to lead, here he lingered on the subject of salvation before insisting on good works.

Goodness and loving kindness are not easy to distinguish and they are perhaps best interpreted as contrasts to the "malice and envy" of the previous verse. Sinful men desire evil and plan evil for others. God desires them to have nothing but good and he planned accordingly. His desire for their good, his own *goodness, appeared* in Jesus Christ. Sinful men do not want their fellows to have what is good and desire it for themselves. God is not envious of men and does not even need anything which they have (Acts 17:25). On the contrary he has love for all men and this *loving kindness appeared* in Jesus Christ.

If we translate Paul's two Greek words consistently we find grace and *goodness* associated. He spoke of "the immeasurable riches of his grace in goodness toward us in Christ Jesus" (Eph. 2:7). God's *grace,* God's *goodness* toward us, appeared—in Christ Jesus. When he appeared, God's grace appeared; God's goodness toward us appeared. It is contrasted with his severity in Romans 11:22. It gives men gentle pushes towards repentance (cf. Rom. 2:4). God is "good" to the ungrateful (Luke 6:35). The spirit of

God's goodness is illustrated by the remark that "my employer has been good to me."

The Greek of *loving kindness* is *philanthrōpia,* which has become the English "philanthropy" in its restricted meaning. God's philanthropy is his universal love for men. The word, or its cognate, occurs in only two other places in the New Testament and in both instances action is suggested. At Sidon the centurion Julius "dealt kindly" with Paul, not merely "courteously" (Acts 27:3, KJV). He showed not the outer shell of a formal politeness but took the responsibility of giving him "shore leave" to visit his friends. It might have had serious consequences for Julius if anything had gone wrong. Again, the natives of Malta showed "no ordinary philanthropy" to the shipwrecked men, kindling a fire and welcoming them in the cold and rain (Acts 28:2). *Loving kindness* means action, and action took place. It *appeared*—a deceptively simple expression which covers the whole life of Christ on earth.

God our Savior anticipates the verb of the following verse. See discussion on 2:10.

Verse 5: He saved us, not because of deeds done by us in righteousness, but in virtue of his own mercy, by the washing of regeneration and renewal in the Holy Spirit: The decisive act of God in which he received us as his forever. (See discussion on 2 Tim. 1:9.) Two aspects of salvation should be kept in mind. There is the work of Christ, accomplished once and for all on the cross; and there is the human response. The sins of men have been erased, wiped out, obliterated, in two corresponding senses. They have been blotted out—for God (cf. Col. 2:14). They can be blotted out—for men. "Repent therefore, and turn again, that your sins may be blotted out" (Acts 3:19).

The act in which God *saved us* is not incidental to his goodness and loving kindness (v. 4); nor does it go beyond them; it expresses them. His goodness appeared; and what men saw was Christ, and in particular Christ crucified. His loving kindness appeared; and what men saw was Christ crucified for all men. The salvation of men expresses the goodness and loving kindness of God; and the goodness and loving kindness of God express his eternal grace (2 Tim. 1:9). The origin of salvation lies in the grace of God.

There might have been a subsidiary origin, though Paul rejected it. It is conceivable that God might have decided that if men performed a certain number of *deeds* he would save them. It is conceivable, because Paul conceived it. If God had so decided, the ultimate origin of salvation would have been his grace (if the deeds were not too many and too hard!) and the nearer origin would have been the *deeds done by us in righteousness.* Paul repudiated this thought. In no sense does salvation arise out of our deeds. It comes from God's grace.

The grouping of the words is of some importance. We ought not to say *deeds done by us in righteousness.* The phrase *in righteousness* is in the Greek securely tied to *deeds.* Paul meant *"deeds in* the sphere of *righteousness* which we did." *Righteousness* is that whole realm of duty, imposed by God, towards our fellowmen. (See discussion on 1 Tim. 6:11; cf. 2 Tim. 2:22; 3:16.) This is broader than legalistic "works of law" (Rom. 3:28). Salvation does not spring, even in a secondary sense, "out of works, in order that no one should boast," should take the credit to himself (Eph. 2:9 f.). Works do not originate; they are originated. They are not a ground of salvation but a path in which saved men should walk.

Paul felt the contrast deeply, as we can see from his emphases. He came down heavily thus: "not by *us* but in virtue of *his own* mercy." *In virtue of* gives the cause of salvation in a picturesque way. The phrase means "in line with." The salvation of men "squares with" the *mercy* of God. *Mercy* set the standard, and salvation did not fall below the standard. Paul had himself received mercy (1 Tim. 1:13, 16).

The apostle now went on to consider the work of God in us, as opposed to the anterior work of God for us. This involves the human response. God *saved us . . . by* means of *the washing of regeneration and renewal in the Holy Spirit.* These words must not be taken in isolation from what has already been said about the Savior who gave himself for us to redeem and to purify us (cf. 2:14). When the gospel is preached and received, when in response men repent of their sin and give themselves in trust to Christ, then certain events take place in their own experience. Paul called them *washing* and *renewal.* In the cross God provided salvation for men; it is now effective in men; at the final appearing (2:13) it will be brought in its fullness to men, the fullness of what is already theirs in principle.

The means through which salvation is made effective in men is *the washing* which consists *of regeneration and* the *renewal* which *the Holy Spirit* creates. *The washing* corresponds to the second part of purification by the blood of Jesus (see discussion on 2:14). Through the blood, sins are "put away" in the objective atonement; and through the blood, sins are forgiven. We have already commented on sin's being blotted out both in God's sight and in the experience of men.

Now when a man puts his faith in Jesus he is given a start in the Christian life. Notice the word "life." Before his "first faith" he was dead in trespasses and sins. Now he is alive in Christ. But he was already alive in one sense. An inanimate block of wood does not exercise faith. The first life continues, and he who lived it and still lives it has also a new life in Christ, a second life. He has already been born once in the process of nature. He has now been born through the activity of grace. If we choose to count, he has been born a second time. This is precisely the meaning of *regeneration.* His conscience is clean because his sin has been both put away and forgiven. He has been justified (v. 7) and has started to be sanctified (see discussion on 2 Tim. 2:21). He is clean in "status" before God, and in his experience of faith in Christ he has been cleansed. His encounter with the living Christ through the Holy Spirit has been a *washing* of his personality, a *washing* which consists *of regeneration.*

It will be objected that *washing* implies water, not blood. The text which speaks of Jesus Christ as the one who "washed us from our sins in his own blood" (Rev. 1:5, KJV) is based on inferior manuscript authority. So much can depend on a single letter (*lusanti* and *lousanti*)! H. B. Swete finds it "not so easy to decide" between the two readings, though he thinks that "washed" gives good sense and a more usual metaphor.[1] The manuscript

---

1. H. B. Swete, *The Apocalypse of St. John* (London: Macmillan & Co., New York: The Macmillan Company, 1906), p. 7.

evidence must decide the issue, though Swete's opinion has weight.

The implication of water leads many scholars to see a reference to baptism in *the washing of regeneration*. This view need not be accepted solely on the ground that it is water which washes, not blood. "They have washed [*eplunan*] their robes and made them white in the blood of the Lamb" (Rev. 7:14). Even so water is mentioned: " . . . our bodies washed with pure water" (Heb. 10:22); "Christ cleansed her [the church] by the washing of water with the word" (Eph. 5:26). There may be an allusion to baptism, though Hebrews 10:22 might be thinking of Christians exercising the priestly privilege of drawing near, duly qualified by blood and water (Exod. 29:4, 21; 30:20; 40:30; Lev. 8:30). The apostle might have a picture in his mind's eye, in which baptism crystallizes and makes visible the experience of faith. But would he have said that God *saved us* by means of *the washing of regeneration,* and meant thereby that baptism effects *regeneration?*

This is a widely held theory. It is modified to some extent by the view that Paul was glorifying the mercy and grace of God and did not need to mention faith at this point; but the modification is limited if it dwells on the effects of baptism and not its conditions.

The "effects" of baptism can only mean *regeneration.* In consequence Paul's gospel of salvation depends on faith and baptism, and it is baptism which regenerates. If this theory is accepted, though it is gravely open to doubt, its proponents have to give satisfactory answers to certain objections. Why did Paul fight so passionately for justification by faith? Why not justification by faith and baptism? If so much depended on baptism—*regeneration* —how could he be so vague about those whom he had baptized at Corinth? How could he get himself into the position of saying that "Christ did not send me to baptize but to preach the gospel" (1 Cor. 1:14–17)? Why when he was alone in Athens did he preach? If the response had been great, many would have had to wait to be baptized and to be regenerated (Acts 17:16–18, 30). Can any person receive the Holy Spirit without being regenerated? Unbaptized people received the Holy Spirit (Acts 10:47). Can baptized and therefore regenerated people be without the Holy Spirit? It happened in Samaria (Acts 8:14–16). Can it be said of a baptized and therefore regenerated person that "you have neither part nor lot in this matter" (Acts 8:13, 21)? Was the penitent though unbaptized thief saved though not regenerate (Luke 23:39–43)? Hitherto he has been regarded by many as a superb illustration of justification by faith.

To these questions which involve biblical interpretation can be added others of a more practical nature. Some of the bloodiest dictators and some of the most wicked of men have been baptized people. Were they regenerated as the effect of their baptism? It seems that we have here a dilemma: either they were not regenerated at all or if they were, they received something, regeneration, which is not worth having. As a matter of fact baptism is never to be interpreted mechanically; and in New Testament times the situation was fluid. Then, as now, *regeneration* may take place before, at or after baptism. Baptism is "necessary," as it is one of the commands of our Lord— like many other things. And in the New Testament it was for converts.

There are people, some of them intimately known to the writer, with whom there was a long lapse of time between "first faith" and baptism. It is one thing for scholars to say that faith plus baptism represents an indivisible unit and that in New Testament times baptism followed immediately on profession of faith. Even then there is the question of the content of Paul's preaching. Today the position is not quite the same. Some men and women are unquestionably of devout Christian faith. They believed and they lived the Christian life for some years before being baptized; and some are not yet baptized. Are they regenerate or are they not? Were those who had become relatively mature in the faith before their baptism regenerated in their baptism? It may be said that the New Testament does not raise these problems and that the people in question "ought" to have followed the New Testament pattern and ought to have been baptized. Perhaps so; but the questions still need an answer.

It would facilitate discussion if it could be settled once and for all whether *regeneration* marks a deep spiritual experience. If it does, it is not necessarily linked with baptism; if it does not, what is it?

Those who assert that baptism "effects" *regeneration* have rendered at least one service. Baptism, when it is Christian baptism, is not repeated. Attention is thereby drawn to the fact that regeneration occurs once and once only. The spiritual experience is described further in the verse. God *saved us . . . by* means of . . . the *renewal* of *the Holy Spirit,* i.e., the *renewal* brought about by *the Holy Spirit.* This is a change of figure. Through the ministry of *the Holy Spirit* in his heart, interpreting and applying the Word, a man who sets his faith in Christ is made new. He retains his identity and his memory. Saul renewed is still Saul; but he is also Paul. Christ lives in him; that is the "newness" (Gal. 2:20); and "he" goes on living, in the flesh and in faith in the Son of God who loved him and delivered himself up for him.

The *renewal* takes place at the time of *regeneration* but it may be repeated and grow. A man is either regenerate or not but his "newness" may fluctuate. At "first faith" he becomes a new creature (2 Cor. 5:17). He looks out with new eyes onto the glories of God's creation. "This is my Father's world." And he dwells in the realm of grace, with its new joys and victories and hopes (cf. Rom. 5:1–5). The old legalisms are gone (Gal. 6:15). Death may be at work in his battered body but he does not lose heart: his inner nature is being renewed every day (cf. 2 Cor. 4:12, 16). Challenged, even attracted, by the fashion of the world, he is constantly to be transformed by the *renewal* of his mind (cf. Rom. 12:2). He is a member of the new covenant, and his God is faithful; he belongs to God's treasured people (2:14). He is called to a moral and spiritual "walk" which is on the plane of resurrection (cf. Rom. 6:4; 7:6). The Holy Spirit who renewed him in his "first faith" does not desert him but aids him in his prayers when feelings are too deep for words (Rom. 8:26). (Cf. also Eph. 2:15; 4:20–24; Col. 3:10.)

God then *saved us:* his Son died for us and the impact of the cross on the believing heart results in *washing* and *renewal.* In the cross salvation is achieved; in the preaching it is offered to men; the *washing* and the *renewal* are the signs that it has been accepted.

Verse 6: Which he poured out upon us richly through Jesus Christ our Savior: The *which* should be rendered by "whom." The reference is to the Holy Spirit—a "he" and not an "it." The Holy Spirit is more than a force or an influence; he is a person. The RSV no longer says, "Our Father which art in heaven," but rightly uses "who" (Matt. 6:9). Admittedly the Greek word for "Spirit" *(pneuma)* is neuter. To rely on such a principle, however, would land us in difficulties. To be consistent we should speak of "the truth who accords with godliness" (1:1), because "truth" *(alētheia)* is feminine. The personality of the Spirit is clearly recognized in the RSV rendering of John 15:26. "But when the Counselor [masculine] comes, whom I shall send to you from the Father, even the Spirit [neuter] of truth, who [not 'which,' in spite of the neuter *ho*] proceeds from the Father, he [*ekeinos, masculine*] will bear witness to me."

The "pouring out" of the Holy Spirit is a strong contrast to the pouring out of God's wrath in the Old Testament. The figure of rain is suggested. "If the clouds are full of rain, they empty themselves ['pour out,' LXX] on the earth" (Eccles. 11:3). The same figure is retained in the well-known text in Malachi 3:10, "(The Lord of hosts) . . . will . . . open the windows of heaven for you and pour down for you an overflowing blessing." The Apostle Paul's immediate allusion was to the prophecy of Joel, quoted by Peter on the Day of Pentecost, and the thought of rain is not entirely absent. "He has poured down for you abundant rain . . . I will pour out my spirit on all flesh" (Joel 2:23, 28). Peter's words, in the Greek, keep to the LXX version in saying "I will pour out [some] of my Spirit" (Acts 2:17–18, KJV). This is a partitive expression. The RSV has boldly dropped it in favor of "I will pour out my Spirit," and not without justification. God *poured out . . . richly.*

The Holy Spirit is God's supernatural gift to sustain the life of his people. They do not have to subsist on natural religion. They have the "rain" from heaven, not the inundation of the land as in Egypt (cf. Deut. 11:10–12). After the ascension of Jesus they were "parched" until the Holy Spirit came.

The teaching of our verse is reflected in the Acts of the Apostles. Paul said that "God *poured out . . . through Jesus Christ.*" Peter said: "This Jesus . . . exalted at the right hand of God, and having received from the Father the promise which consists of the Holy Spirit, he has poured out this which you see and hear" (Acts 2:32 f.). The promised Spirit was received by Jesus from the Father and then *poured out.*

The imagery of rain must fade but the theological importance should not be overlooked. The gift of the Holy Spirit does not come straight from the Father, as it were. If there were no relation whatsoever to Jesus, the character of the Holy Spirit might be completely unknown. But he is the Spirit of Jesus (Acts 16:7). His character is that of Jesus. He interprets the work of Jesus and "applies" it to human hearts. He glorifies Jesus. Apart from this relationship to Jesus we should be in the dark about the nature of his ministry. As it is he has been described as God's method of the presence of Jesus.

Paul likewise reflects the teaching of the Gospel of John. The Father gives the Spirit in response to the prayer of Jesus (John 14:16). The Father sends the Spirit in the name of Jesus (John 14:26). Jesus himself sends the Spirit, but he sends him from the Father (John 15:26). Jesus himself sends the Spirit (John 16:7).

Richly may imply that the people of God have all that the disciples had in the historic Jesus, and more. This must be expressed very carefully, because the Holy Spirit does not depart from the message of Jesus nor does he go beyond it. But he gives reminders of it and interprets it; and he is present in the heart of each believer in a way which could not happen when the Lord was on earth. "It is to your advantage that I go away . . . ." It is through the Holy Spirit that the living Christ is present, and not a mere memory, to believers. The Spirit is given in order "to be with you for ever. . . . I will not leave you desolate [literally, 'orphans']; I will come to you" (John 14:16, 18). The Spirit comes; Jesus comes. John was not "confounding the Persons." The presence of the Spirit is the presence of Jesus in power. Herein lies the deepest fulfillment of the Messianic prophecy, ". . . his name will be called . . . Everlasting Father . . ." (Isa. 9:6). Jesus is not the Father; but he is aptly so described, because by the Spirit he is forever with those who would otherwise be "orphans."

The "pouring out" is the gift of God (Acts 10:45), and its "richness" is known in the experience of men. It is through the gift that we are made aware of the love of God. A man may sincerely believe that God loves him and yet the fact may not register. It may not sink in. Through the Holy Spirit he really knows, and it is in such a knowlege that he can and does face the changes and chances of human life. "God's love has been poured into our hearts through the Holy Spirit [who] has been given to us" (Rom. 5:5). The context should be studied. The man who stands in grace rejoices in sufferings (in them, not because of them), because he knows of the "production line" of Christian experience. From suffering is produced endurance, character (the veteran does not lose his head and panic), hope, a hope which is not illusory. Through the Holy Spirit he is deeply aware of God's love for him and what it has done in him. God will not fail him now. Through the Holy Spirit he constantly hears the living Christ saying to him, "I will never leave thee nor forsake thee." He will not let him go nor let him down (cf. Heb. 13:5; see on 2 Tim. 4:10, 16). He still has a future for him, and the believer is sure of this. His living hope is due to the Holy Spirit. Part of the "richness" of the gift lies in the fact that it is never exhausted. The Holy Spirit is himself an *arrabōn,* a first installment, down payment or pledge (2 Cor. 1:22; 5:5; Eph. 1:14). The term is used in modern Greek, we are told, for an engagement ring.

Verse 7: So that we might be justified by his grace and become heirs in hope of eternal life: The final purpose but one. In its full meaning *so that* means "in order that" and much depends on which verb is the one to introduce it. Are we to say "God *saved us* . . . in order *that we might be justified . . . and become heirs . . .";* or *"he poured out* (the Holy Spirit) . . . in order *that we might be justified . . ."*?

As Paul's words stand thus rendered in English we have no option but to reject the first grouping. Paul would never have said that men were saved in order to be justified. It could be argued that God gave the Holy Spirit to work in men's hearts and create the faith by which they are justified. This points to the second grouping, though even this has difficulties: the verb *poured out* does not suggest the secret influences of the Holy Spirit at work upon or in an unbeliever. It may include this activity as a beginning, but the "richly" looks rather to something in the nature of Pentecost.

Now from the point of view of formal linguistics, the translation is accurate, though it is not the only possible rendering. In many cases the alternatives do not matter either way. It does not matter very much whether we say: "He had breakfast and went to the garage" or "Having had breakfast he went to the garage." But consider the following sentence: "We reminded him of his appointments, in order that having had breakfast he might go to the garage." The meaning might be that it was getting late and that two things remained to be done. He must have breakfast and then get away to the garage. On the other hand it might still mean that it was getting late. He had had breakfast. Why the further delay? He must leave for the garage.

The latter is analogous to Paul's meaning in the present verse. *Justified* is subordinate to the verb *become* and prior to it, not only in its position in the clause but also logically if not chronologically. We might therefore translate: "God *saved us* . . . in order *that,* having been *justified by his grace, we might become* heirs . . . ." This accords with Pauline doctrine. The wages of a man who "works" are not calculated by reference to grace (*kata charin*) but come to him as his due (Rom. 4:4). Justification is based on grace and is in no sense man's "due." We are "justified by his grace as a gift" (Rom. 3:24).

Justification takes place when a man puts his faith in Christ. It thus marks the beginning of the Christian life, the time when he passed from death to life, from the state of being lost to the state of being "safe." "By grace you have been saved through faith" (Eph. 2:8) and are therefore now "safe." The perfect tense of the verb is warrant for this statement. Justification sets up a relationship between the believer and God which persists. In Christ he is forever acceptable to God, and it is forever by grace and through faith. Justification is thus the mainspring of salvation.

Justification takes place in the mind of God. He "justifies him who has faith in Jesus" (Rom. 3:26); he "justifies the ungodly" (Rom. 4:5) The faith of the man who trusts is reckoned to him as righteousness. Who "reckons" it? It can only be God. The term expresses what goes on in the divine mind. It is vividly illustrated from a secular usage. Complaining of the effect of Paul's preaching in Ephesus the silversmith Demetrius said that "there is danger . . . that the temple of the great goddess Artemis may count [literally, 'be reckoned'] for nothing . . . " (Acts 19:27). The temple was solid enough. It was one of the wonders of the world. Solid though it was, it was likely to be reckoned as nothing in human minds—and still remain as it was. Demetrius was obviously thinking of what would go on in men's minds. And when Paul spoke of righteousness as being "reckoned" to a man, he was thinking of the divine mind.

God acts on his thoughts, and accepts and welcomes the man who trusts in Christ. In his experience the man who is justified receives the washing which consists of regeneration and the renewal created by the Holy Spirit. These are concomitants of justification, but are in thought to be distinguished from it. (See the discussion on "righteousness," 1 Tim. 6:11, and the further references there given.) "Justify" means "to deem righteous." Clarity is easier if the link between verb and noun is remembered. Justification is eschatological. The Day of Judgment is advanced to the moment when a man believes. Then he is acquitted.

God's purpose, then, in our salvation, is that, *justified by his grace* as we have been, we should *become heirs*. We are to repeat the experience of the Jews with Canaan (cf. Deut. 9:4–6). The thought of inheritance repeats the thought of *grace*. *Heirs* have riches left to them. The wealth is not usually due to them. If it were we should speak more of the recovery of what is one's own rather than of inheritance.

The thought of the rich outpouring of the Holy Spirit also lies in the background. We are *heirs* because we are children of God, and we know that we are his children because we have received the spirit of adoption. The Spirit himself bears witness with our spirit that we are children of God (Rom. 8:14–17).

Heirs are people who, merely by being *heirs,* have *hope.* They expect that one day certain properties will be theirs. We need not therefore group the words in such a way that we say: "heirs of eternal life—in hope." This would be saying the same thing twice. God's purpose is that we may *become heirs;* this in accordance with the *hope of eternal life.* Our *hope* is Christ Jesus (1 Tim. 1:1) and in him we have *hope of eternal life* (see on Titus 1:2). If the hope is real—and it is as real as Christ Jesus—then we are indeed heirs, people with great expectations, people to whom something is coming. But unlike heirs in ordinary life they have received the inheritance already! *Eternal life* is theirs already in Christ. They have already tasted of its blessedness. Its fullness is to come.

What we have called "the final purpose but one" is to be in the dual position of being *heirs* and yet at the same time of possessing *eternal life.* Such life is in direct contrast to the death which is the wages of sin: we were dead in trespasses and sins. We were "far off" in our separation from God. Now we have been brought near, and we are alive in Christ. The *life* which we have in him is real; it is not the semblance of life and it is not merely a life which is coming into existence. It is the life which is life indeed. We have been born into it by spiritual regeneration and are called to live in newness of life. Eternal life is the gift of God and is received by faith. Paul's words about knowledge of the truth recall the Johannine idiom. "This is eternal life, that they know thee the only true God, and Jesus Christ whom thou hast sent" (John 17:3). Father and Son are united in the work of men's salvation. Both salvation and *eternal life* are *by* God's *grace* and "through Jesus Christ our Savior" (v. 6). (See discussion on the references given in the comment on Titus 1:2.) It should be observed that *eternal life* may be described in more ways than one. *Life* is inherited; Jesus is followed; the kingdom of God is entered; men are saved (cf. Mark 10:17–31). It may mean exhilaration, but it must not be identified with feelings. It may bring a largeness of fellowship—and persecutions. Paul knew of sorrow and tears as well as mounting up to paradise. There is an inner core of subjective experience, based on the objective reality of Christ.

VIII. GOOD WORKS, NOT SPECULATION (3:8–11)

In consequence Titus was to be insistent: believers must give themselves to good works. This would be both good and beneficial. Speculation about genealogies and points of law and the quarrels thereby raised should be avoided because of their lack of value and their failure to achieve anything. A heretic after two warnings was to be left alone in his sin, self-condemned.

Verse 8: The saying is sure. I desire you to insist on these things:

Salvation by grace is not an incidental. The first sentence is already familiar to us. (See discussions 1 Tim. 1:15; 3:1; 4:9; 2 Tim. 2:11.) The reference here is backwards. No precise *saying* can be identified. It is thought by some that verses 3–7, or parts of the section, are quoted from a hymn or baptismal service. The *saying* might recall to the readers or hearers what they knew fairly well. On the other hand Paul might mean that "the language, the message, is to be believed." All that he had just written is summed up in the word *logos,* which is far from being merely a single "word" in meaning. Thus the bishop "must hold firm to the sure word as taught" (1:9). If *the saying* may indeed be traced to some Christian hymn in regular use, it has passed through the apostle's mind and bears his stamp. It is not precisely "in quotes." The same sort of thing happens when a preacher in his sermon makes use of a stanza of a hymn and adds or amends according to his theme.

When he said *I desire,* Paul was speaking as an apostle. It was not merely his personal preference or a matter of taste. There is authority present. "It is my wish." (See discussions on 1 Tim. 2:8; 5:14; 6:9.) Titus was to *insist,* so that Christians who have received salvation by grace may manifest behavior by works. There may be a further reason. The false teachers may lurk in the background, as we shall shortly see in the next verses. At Ephesus Timothy was faced with men who *insist,* who "make assertions" (the same Greek word, 1 Tim. 1:7), and Titus probably had the same sort of problem on his hands. When they "insisted" he was to counter them: he was to *insist* also. Apart from the "thrust" which rises within the true preacher, he had the apostle's authority. It is one aspect of "guarding the deposit."

So that those who have believed in God may be careful to apply themselves to good deeds: Salvation offered, received and outworked. The stimulus of *good deeds* is the gratitude of believers for all that God has done for them in Christ. Grace prompts *good deeds,* not inactivity or sin. Paul dealt with this distortion earlier (Rom. 6:1–4). *Careful* does not mean anxiety or laboriousness. Paul designed the Christians to give concentrated thought to the matter and to be intent on it. The *good deeds* should not occur casually. They should arise as the result of deliberate thoughtfulness all the time, and "taking pains." The Christians should "see to it that. . . ."

Those who have believed in God are people who at some time in the past "first believed" (cf. Rom. 13:11). They have continued to do so up to the time of writing. They have persisted in the faith. They "are now believers still." They are to "busy" themselves with *good deeds.* It is to be their "business." Like the disciples in Antioch they were to be trading as Christians (cf. Acts 11:26). Their "line" was *good deeds*—with no shoddy manufacture and prices ridiculously low!

This is part of the education which grace gives (2:12). The active mind which plans *good deeds* is in contrast with the (literally) "idle stomachs" of unregenerated Cretans.

These are excellent and profitable to men: Value and utility together. *These* are the *good deeds* already mentioned. They are the opposite of the controversies and quarrels of the next verse.

Verse 9: But avoid stupid controversies, genealogies, dissensions, and quarrels over the law, for they are unprofitable and futile: They do not build but overturn. They achieve nothing but disaster. (See discussions on 1 Tim.

1:4; 6:4; 2 Tim. 2:23; Titus 1:10–16.) For the apostle this was a well-worn theme. For "avoidance" see discussion on 2 Timothy 3:5.

Paul did not say what was to be done if the insubordinate men refused to be silenced. Presumably Titus would "steer" the talk in informal meetings and himself concentrate on the positives. If he gained the general support of the church by his positive teaching, the insubordinate men could be silenced by losing their audience. The man in the next verse seems to be an exception.

Verse 10: As for a man who is factious, after admonishing him once or twice, have nothing more to do with him: The time comes for a complete break. (Cf. 2 Tim. 3:5 and discussion.) The *factious* man has chosen his own doctrine and form of religion and persists in his course. He tries to gather adherents and the tendency is to divide the church. He will not respond to pastoral guidance, which includes doctrinal guidance, and is a stubborn rebel. To persist, from the minister's side, in admonition is to invite quarrels, and these are unseemly in both minister and people (2 Tim. 2:24; Titus 3:2 and discussion). In *admonishing him* on two solemn occasions the pastor has given him his opportunity (2 Tim. 2:25) and fulfilled the spirit of Matthew 18:15–17. The church undoubtedly knows all about it by this time. And in any case it is not a private disagreement between two men. The faith of the church is at stake. The example of the minister in such an extreme case may save some members from becoming infected. Certainly the weaker members need such an example. (Cf. Rom. 16:17–20; 1 Tim. 1:20.) This does not rule out a "rescue operation" when the heretic falls on evil days. A man in hospital with a serious illness or after an accident is often more willing to listen to the minister than he was on the golf course. (See Rom. 12:20.)

Verse 11: Knowing that such a person is perverted and sinful; he is self-condemned: He has been turned aside and is therefore on the wrong road. *He is sinful:* he goes on sinning by remaining on the wrong road. He is *self-condemned* in that he has rejected conscience, made shipwreck of his own faith and is willing to overturn the faith of others (cf. 1 Tim. 1:19; 2 Tim. 2:18) without a thought or a care for the welfare of the church or its members. What do such people care if they have taken from a poor widow the only consolation she knows? To diminish or distort the faith is not always a purely intellectual matter discussed in academic circles. It gets out into the marketplace and into homes. Those who are responsible are prepared to defend their position to the length of controversy and quarrel; and to laugh at the damage they do. They are *self-condemned* if after warning they choose to propagate their teachings among any followers they can get; for they are sinning against the very light which has been pointed out to them. (Cf. Mark 9:42; John 3:18–20.) Their position is perhaps summed up by a remark made by an official of the British Foreign Office. After some very difficult negotiations with an obstructive power he gave it as his opinion that "X has sold himself to the devil, and I fancy he knows it."

IX. SUNDRY DIRECTIONS TO TITUS (3:12–14)

Titus was to join the apostle and meanwhile send off two visitors well equipped for their journey. Christians must learn the lesson of helpful good works and thus be fruitful.

Verse 12: When I send Artemas or Tychicus to you, do your best to come to me at Nicopolis, for I have decided to spend the winter there: Weighty doctrine or heresy notwithstanding, life goes on. Paul's head was not in the theological clouds. His life was hid with Christ in God (Col. 3:3), but his feet were firmly on the earth. *Artemas* is not otherwise mentioned in the New Testament. For *Tychicus* see discussion on 2 Timothy 4:12. One or other of them was to replace Titus, though it had not yet been decided which of the two was to go, or when. For comment on *do your best* see discussion on 2 Timothy 4:9 and further references. *Nicopolis,* the city of victory ("Victoriaville"), is probably the city of that name in Epirus. It lay on the western shore of Greece, south of the island of Corcyra, the modern Corfu, and was founded by Augustus Caesar in 31 B.C. to celebrate his victory over Antony and Cleopatra at the Battle of Actium. Paul would *spend the winter there* until such time as the seas were open again (cf. Acts 27:12; 28:11). He had not yet arrived *there* or he would have written "here."

Verse 13: Do your best to speed Zenas the lawyer and Apollos on their way; see that they lack nothing: Kindly thought for others and full reliance on Titus. *Zenas* is not otherwise known. *Apollos* had ministered in Ephesus and Corinth (Acts 18:24–19:1). He combined biblical knowledge with a glowing spirit and eloquence and made a deep impression on at least a section of the church at Corinth (cf. 1 Cor. 1:12; 3:4–6; 4:6; 16:12). He supplemented Paul's work there. Far from being the "owner" of a partisan group, Apollos was himself "owned" by the whole church of the Corinthians (1 Cor. 3:22), in common with Paul and Peter and even the world itself.

Notice Paul's thought and care for his assistants, and the hospitality which looked after traveling Christians.

Verse 14: And let our people learn to apply themselves to good deeds, so as to help cases of urgent need, and not to be unfruitful: A third person imperative, to be passed on by Titus. To *apply themselves* . . . recalls verse 8 (see discussion). The *cases of urgent need* might include at some time the "factious" man of verse 10. To be *unfruitful* would surely resist the Holy Spirit. "The fruit of the Spirit is . . . kindness" (Gal. 5:22). Perhaps the "rough diamonds" of converted Cretans were more willing to give hospitality to traveling Christians than to local "hard cases."

X. FAREWELL (3:15)

Greetings are sent and are to be passed on. Blessing.

All who are with me send greetings to you. Greet those who love us in the faith. Grace be with you all: Greetings from group to group, including Titus. *In the faith* might well be "in Christ." The letter starts "to Titus" (1:4) and ends with *grace* for *all.* (See discussion on 2 Tim. 4:22.) Zenas and Apollos were probably the letter carriers.

ANNOTATED BIBLIOGRAPHY

LEXICONS

Arndt, W. F. and Gingrich, F. W. *A Greek-English Lexicon of the New Testament.* Chicago: University of Chicago Press; Cambridge: University Press, 1957. Covers early Christian literature outside the New Testament. Based on Walter Bauer's *Griechisch-Deutsches Wörterbuch* and takes account of scholarly work up to 1954. A gold mine for preachers who will take the trouble to dig into it.

Liddell, H. G. and Scott, R. *A Greek-English Lexicon.* 2 vols. 9th ed., revised by Sir Henry Stuart Jones and Roderick McKenzie. Oxford: Clarendon Press, 1940. Liddell and Scott has long been the standard dictionary for ancient Greek.

Moulton, James H. and Milligan, George. *The Vocabulary of the Greek Testament.* London: Hodder and Stoughton, 1929. Grand Rapids, Mich.: Wm. B. Eerdmans. Light is shed on Greek usage by extensive quotations from the papyri and other nonliterary sources.

Souter, Alexander. *A Pocket Lexicon to the Greek New Testament.* Oxford and New York: Oxford University Press, 1916. Makes unobtrusive use of new knowledge derived from the papyri. Invaluable for the traveling preacher's briefcase.

SEPTUAGINT

Rahlfs, Alfred. *Septuaginta.* 3rd ed. Stuttgart: Privilegierte Württembergische Bibelanstalt, 1949. This is the standard edition.

GRAMMARS

Blass, F.; Debrunner, A.; and Funk, R. W. *A Greek Grammar of the New Testament.* Chicago: University of Chicago Press, 1961. Highly technical but rewarding.

Goodwin, W. W. *A Greek Grammar,* 2nd ed. London: Macmillan; New York: St. Martin's Press, 1894.

————. *Syntax of the Moods and Tenses of the Greek Verb.* London: Macmillan; New York: St. Martin's Press, 1875. Both books are on the advanced level. The beginner should try something much simpler.

Moulton, James H.; Howard, Wilbert F.; and Turner, N. *A Grammar of New Testament Greek.* 3 vols. Edinburgh: T. & T. Clark; Naperville, Ill.: 1908, 1929, 1963. Full and even minute attention to detail by a succession of masters in the field.

Robertson, A. T. *A Grammar of the Greek New Testament in the Light of Historical Research.* New York: Hodder & Stoughton and George H. Doran, 1923. Reprint. Nashville: Broadman Press, 1947. Over fourteen hundred pages of fascinating reading written by an eminent grammarian and devout believer. Full enjoyment depends on the degree of competence in Greek.

Turner, Nigel. *Grammatical Insights into the New Testament.* Edinburgh: T. & T. Clark; Naperville, Ill.: Allenson, 1965. Exciting discussions for the general reader as well as for the scholar.

WORD STUDIES

Hatch, E. and Redpath, H. A. *A Concordance to the Septuagint.* 2 vols. Graz, Austria: Akademische Druck-u. Verlagsanstalt, 1954. Hatch and Redpath is indispensable for the discovery of Old Testament (Greek) background of a New Testament text.

Moule, C. F. D. *An Idiom Book of New Testament Greek.* 2nd ed. Cambridge and New York: Cambridge University Press, 1959. A careful discussion of many passages helps the reader to come to his own conclusions when right interpretation depends on syntax.

Moulton, W. F. and Geden, A. S. *A Concordance to the Greek Testament.* Edinburgh: T. & T. Clark; Grand Rapids, Mich.: Kregel Publications, 1957. A standard work.

Ward, R. A. *Hidden Meaning in the New Testament.* Old Tappan, N.J.: Fleming H. Revell; London: Marshall, Morgan & Scott, 1969. Pictures and movements suggested by the language stimulate ideas and illustrations for preachers and teachers.

NEW TESTAMENT INTRODUCTIONS

Guthrie, Donald. *New Testament Introduction. The Pauline Epistles.* London: Tyndale Press; Chicago: Inter-Varsity Press, 1961. Exhaustive treatment by a well-known conservative scholar. Two other volumes (*The Gospels and Acts,* and *Hebrews to Revelation*) complete the series.

Harrison, Everett F. *Introduction to the New Testament.* Grand Rapids, Mich.: Wm. B. Eerdmans, 1964. A sound work prepared primarily for students, after teaching the subject in the classroom for a quarter of a century.

Kümmel, W. G. *Introduction to the New Testament.* London: SCM Press, 1966. Not so conservative. Very full discussion, including such matters as text and canon.

THEOLOGY

Bultmann, Rudolf. *Theology of the New Testament.* 2 vols. London: SCM Press, 1965. New York: Chas. Scribner's Sons, 1970. Radical and to be used with care. More for those who want to know what is going on in New Testament studies and what is being criticized than for the pure expositor.

Cullmann, Oscar. *The Christology of the New Testament.* London: SCM Press, 1959. Rev. ed. Philadelphia: Westminster Press, 1964. An antidote to Bultmann. A significant examination of the titles of Christ.

Ellis, E. Earle. *Paul's Use of the Old Testament.* Edinburgh and London: Oliver and Boyd, 1957. The value of this profound study is increased by the lists of Old Testament quotations and allusions.

Kittel, Gerhard and Friedrich, Gerhard, eds. *Theological Dictionary of the New Testament.* 8 vols. Translated by Geoffrey W. Bromiley. Grand Rapids, Mich. and London: Wm. B. Eerdmans; 1964–1972. This monumental work is a translation of Kittel's famous *Theologisches Wörterbuch* and is indispensable for the advanced student. Patience and application will yield rich rewards even to those who have only a working knowledge of Greek.

Richardson, Alan. *An Introduction to the Theology of the New Testament.* London: SCM Press, 1958; New York: Harper & Row, 1959. This study combines the wide sweep of a comprehensive view with consideration of many individual texts.

Stauffer, Ethelbert. *New Testament Theology.* London: SCM Press, 1955. New York: Harper & Row. Profound scholarship and stimulating language. There are extensive bibliographies.

Tasker, R. V. G. *The Old Testament in the New Testament.* Grand Rapids, Mich.: Wm. B. Eerdmans, 1963. A survey of New Testament usage.

THE PASTORALS—GENERAL

Ellis, E. Earle. *Paul and His Recent Interpreters.* Grand Rapids, Mich.: Wm. B. Eerdmans, 1961. A survey of the discussion of authorship is included.

Guthrie, Donald. *The Pastoral Epistles and the Mind of Paul.* London: Tyndale Press, 1956. A Tyndale Lecture which acutely faces the problems involved.

Harrison, P. N. *The Problem of the Pastoral Epistles.* Oxford: Oxford University Press, 1921. Modern arguments against Pauline authorship stem from this study. Any serious student of the problem must master the linguistic arguments here set out. The discussion is continued, apart from introductions and commentaries, in academic journals: *The Expository Times* 67 (December 1955): 77–81; 70 (December 1958): 91–94 by Bruce M. Metzger; *New Testament Studies* 2 (1956): 250–61 by Harrison; 6 (October 1959): 1–15 by K. Grayston and G. Herdan; *The Evangelical Quarterly* 32 (1960): 151–61 by E. Earle Ellis. The validity of the statistical method is questioned.

COMMENTARIES

Falconer, R. *The Pastoral Epistles: Introduction, Translation and Notes.* Oxford: Clarendon Press, 1937. Learned comment, somewhat impressed by Harrison's linguistic arguments though disagrees about date.

Guthrie, Donald. *The Pastoral Epistles: An Introduction and Commentary.* Tyndale Bible Commentaries. Grand Rapids, Mich.: Wm. B. Eerdmans, 1964. Very helpful in every way. It maintains the golden mean between excessive technicality and a frustrating brevity. The path traced is from the Greek through the King James Version to the ordinary—and serious—reader.

Hendriksen, William. *First and Second Timothy and Titus.* New Testament Commentary series. Grand Rapids, Mich.: Baker Book House, 1957. The author's own translation to introduce his comments. This series has a high reputation.

Jeremias, Joachim. *Die Briefe an Timotheus und Titus,* part (with Hebrews) of vol. 9 of *Das Neue Testament Deutsch.* Göttingen: Vandenhoeck & Ruprecht, 1963. A sane conservatism and devout erudition.

Kelly, J. N. D. *A Commentary on the Pastoral Epistles.* Black's New Testament Commentaries. London: Adam & Charles Black, 1963. This significant work of recent scholarship is based on the Greek and mediated to the Greekless through the author's own translation. Its standpoint is independent; it favors Pauline authorship; and is critical of the "fragment hypothesis."

Lock, W. *A Critical and Exegetical Commentary on the Pastoral Epistles.* Edinburgh: T. & T. Clark, 1924. One of the *International Critical Commentary* series. A useful beginning for those who are ready for detailed comments on the Greek.

Scott, Ernest F. *The Pastoral Epistles.* Moffatt New Testament Commentary. London: Hodder & Stoughton; Naperville, Ill.: Alec R. Allenson, 1936. Written from the standpoint of a more advanced criticism.

Simpson, E. K. *The Pastoral Epistles: The Greek Text with Introduction and Commentary*. Grand Rapids, Mich.: Wm. B. Eerdmans. Robust evangelical exposition, reinforced with a wealth of classical learning.

Spicq, *Les Épîtres Pastorales*. Paris: J. Gabalda et Cie., 1947. A profound and meticulous work which no advanced student should miss.